Beyond Tracking

Beyond Tracking

Multiple Pathways to College, Career, and Civic Participation

JEANNIE OAKES and MARISA SAUNDERS

Editors

HARVARD EDUCATION PRESS

CAMBRIDGE, MASSACHUSETTS

Library of Congress Control Number 2008928883

Paperback ISBN 978-1-934742-04-4
Library Edition ISBN 978-1-934742-05-1

Published by Harvard Education Press,
an imprint of the Harvard Education Publishing Group

Harvard Education Press
8 Story Street
Cambridge, MA 02138

Cover Design: Nancy Goulet/studio;wink

The typefaces used in this book are ITC Stone Serif for text and ITC Stone Sans for display.

Contents

Preface

This edited book is made up of research essays written by a distinguished group of scholars from a wide array of disciplines who examine Multiple Pathways—a revolutionary approach to high school education. Multiple Pathways, as defined here, transforms the structures, pedagogy, and purposes of the comprehensive high school. Perhaps most significantly, it moves beyond tracking, the century-old practice of sorting students into different courses based on the presumption that some high school graduates will go to college and most will either go to work or stay home and raise children. The Multiple Pathways approach recognizes and seeks to prepare all students, including the large numbers who currently drop out of high school, for a new reality in which all young people must prepare for both higher education and careers. The thirteen chapters examine the promise and challenges of this approach from the perspective of social science theory and research.

The impetus for these essays was a request from Anne Stanton, director of the youth program at the James Irvine Foundation. The foundation was initiating projects aimed at dramatically increasing the proportion of young people, ages 14 to 24, who complete high school on time, pursue postsecondary credentials, and leave formal schooling prepared to meet the challenges of work, civic participation, and lifelong learning. The tens of thousands of young people from low-income families and those with limited English proficiency were the targets of greatest concern—individuals who are not expected to graduate high school without additional incentives and support.

Included in Irvine's plan was a major investment in developing and promoting academically challenging career and technical education that would smooth young people's transitions into college and training for high-skilled, high-wage jobs. Irvine shares the view that all high school students must be held to high academic standards and be ready for higher education. However, rather than requiring all students to take a traditional college-preparatory curriculum, Irvine sought an approach grounded in the belief that not all students can or should find their way to postsecondary education and careers in the same way. Irvine asked us to help them understand the intellectual underpinnings of such an approach and to identify both the potential strengths and vulnerabilities that might guide the foundation's initiative and advance the high school reform dialogue.

We come to this project as education researchers and former teachers concerned primarily with schooling inequalities that mirror inequalities in American society, especially Latino and African American students, who have fewer opportunities and experience less success than their white counterparts. We have been colleagues at University of California–Los Angeles's Institute for Democracy Education and Access (IDEA), a research center whose mission is to make high-quality, equitable public schooling and successful college participation routine occurrences in Los Angeles and across urban America. IDEA conducts research and work with policymakers, educators, and communities to use research to promote and support the school achievement, postsecondary choices, and life chances of *all* the state's diverse children. We saw Irvine's intention and Multiple Pathways as well aligned with these goals and were delighted to invite a group of established scholars to join us in this work.

The scholars met at the outset of the project to work toward a common understanding of how Multiple Pathways has proposed to transform high schools, to raise the research questions that need to be answered, and to explore how their distinct disciplines might shed light on these questions. Several months later, after much discussion with us, we all met again, this time in Sacramento, California. We shared our findings with members of the state legislature interested in education reform. Since that meeting, the phrase "Multiple Pathways" has become common vernacular in the state capitol and a matter of substantial discussion and debate. We are extraordinarily pleased to have played a small role in the public deliberation about high school reform in California, and we offer this book as a way to extend it beyond our state borders.

Not surprisingly, this work is the result of the contributions of many. In addition to our gratitude to Anne Stanton, the Irvine Foundation, and the impressive group of chapter authors who participated in this project with us, we are especially appreciative of the support of our IDEA colleagues. Martin Lipton has been a partner in this work from the outset, helping to frame the project initially and providing thoughtful reviews and developmental editing as each essay took shape. Erica Hamilton provided extraordinarily valuable research assistance. As always, Jerchel Anderson, Jessie Castro, Nery Orellana, Carolyn Castelli, and Jared Planas provided the day-to-day assistance that makes our IDEA work possible.

Jeannie Oakes
Marisa Saunders

Multiple Pathways

Promising to Prepare All High School Students for College, Career, and Civic Participation

Jeannie Oakes and Marisa Saunders

In 2004, the San Diego Unified School District shut down Kearny High, a large high school in a low-income, mostly Latino community north of downtown. Seeking to disrupt a persistent pattern of abysmal test scores, high dropout rates, and few graduates going on to college, the district restructured the campus into four small, autonomous magnet schools: School of Science, Connections and Technology; School of International Business; School of Digital Media and Design; and the Stanley E. Foster Construction Technology Academy (CTA). Known collectively as the Kearny High Educational Complex, the four schools now offer "all students a rigorous college preparatory curriculum in a personalized learning environment," as well as the "opportunity to select a theme that matches their interests and allows them to make real world connections."[1]

At one of the schools, the CTA, a diverse student body of 475 ninth-through twelfth-graders (more than one-half Latino and one-fourth English learners) attend classes in the former shop buildings, now strikingly remodeled as open-space classrooms and laboratories. CTA's mission was crafted by an advisory committee of professional labor and management organizations, development corporations, university officials, school district leaders, teachers, and parents. The mission emphasizes college preparation integrated with the hands-on study of architecture, engineering, and construction:

> Construction Tech Academy is designed as a project-based learning environment that will engage and support students in learning while having a

positive effect on the school, its students, and its surrounding community. In this cross-curricular setting, students work together to solve real-life problems that are present in both the local and global arenas. Large project-based themes are created to integrate all subject matter, as well as prepare students for further education or a professional path upon graduation.[2]

Daily routines at CTA look almost nothing like those at the old Kearny High. Replacing the old six-period day are courses combined into 75- to 90-minute blocks, each meeting a few times per week, that permit the flexible use of time for mastering academic subjects and exploring the world of construction, engineering, and architecture. Each day, CTA's academic and vocational teachers at each grade level share common planning time, during which they discuss their students' needs and adjust interdisciplinary assignments and learning supports to meet them. Principal Glenn Hillegas makes home visits when students are struggling. A former vocational educator specializing in the construction trades, Principal Hillegas told the city's newspaper, "The theme is the hook, if you will. What really matters is the small classes and the one-on-one relationships between students and teachers."[3]

Throughout the year, students work in teams, using the latest industry design software and sophisticated computer equipment to complete pre-engineering courses designed by Project Lead the Way, Inc. They also create construction, engineering, and architecture projects for hypothetical real-world clients. As in adult work settings, these complex projects (supported by mentors from the construction industry) require diverse skills and abilities and draw on both academic and technical subjects. Many CTA students become so engaged that they spend their free time before school, at lunch, or after school working on the projects with teachers and mentors. One formerly less-than-eager student, sophomore Tatiana Tudor, told a reporter from San Diego's daily newspaper, "I look forward to school now, and that has not always been the case. . . . The classes are real. They are not as boring as normal classes."[4]

CTA's juniors complete a project in which they redesign a square block of downtown San Diego, as if it had been destroyed in a disaster. The work teams study the neighborhood to determine the most effective land use and design, and then they work from the underground up. The teams consider every aspect of reconstruction from utilities and building code requirements to building design and construction to presenting the project to their clients. CTA teachers grade students' mastery of the state's education standards, and panels of architects, engineers, city building inspectors, contractors, and members of construction trade unions assess the quality of each project.[5]

Despite its theme and engaging career-related projects, however, CTA is not primarily an occupational training program. CTA students also have access to Advanced Placement classes in fifteen subjects and to nearby Mesa College's Fast Track program, where they can enroll in college courses while completing their high school requirements. The school's contextual, hands-on pedagogy and rigorous curriculum prepare students for direct entry into college, apprenticeship programs, a job, or a career, whichever they choose. Graduates have priority enrollment into San Diego State University's College of Construction Management and Engineering with a full scholarship guaranteed. In fact, 81 percent of CTA's 2007 graduating class were accepted to college; 36 percent were accepted to four-year universities. Notably, the 2007 class included 99 percent of the students who were enrolled as ninth graders four years earlier (a small number transferred to other high schools). The students who did not go to college entered apprenticeship programs or joined the military.[6]

THE HIGH SCHOOL REFORM DEBATE

CTA offers a striking contrast to the typical American high school, particularly to those serving low-income students of color. Evidence abounds that high schools simply don't work very well: Witness strikingly high dropout rates, large percentages of graduates unprepared to succeed in college or career, education gaps that jeopardize African American and Latino students' life chances, and widespread student disengagement. This pervasive dysfunction exacts a high price from students and from the nation's social, economic, and civic welfare.

Few disagree that there is a problem. But no consensus exists about the best way to fix it. Policymakers, educators, and researchers argue about whether smaller high schools are better than large ones, whether graduation "exit exams" will increase achievement, whether choice and competition will increase opportunity, and so forth. Policy proposals that consider moving in any of these directions prompt fierce debate. Among the most contentious questions is whether high school students need more rigorous academics or a more relevant occupation-related curriculum. As state legislatures and local school boards weigh strategies for high school reform, two perspectives often emerge:

- Increase rigor! High schools should enroll *all* students in an academic, college-preparatory curriculum. Vocational education is a dumping ground that robs students, particularly poor and minority students, of high-quality schooling.
- Get real! High schools should expand career and technical education and stop "force-feeding" college preparation. Many students don't want go to college; they need courses that motivate them to stay in school and prepare for work.

Such arguments may focus on what is best for the economy and future workforce needs, what is important for an increasingly diverse population, what best meets individual students' needs, and more. Some advocates argue for making college preparation the default for all high school students. They say that only with a rigorous academic curriculum can American students achieve at levels comparable to their peers in other developed nations. They note also that well-paying jobs increasingly require postsecondary education. They maintain that providing college preparation to all students is in the country's best economic interest and that it guarantees that students who are traditionally underrepresented in college, such as African Americans and Latinos, will stand a chance.

On the other side, advocates for career and technical education[7] have countered that a one-size-fits-all academic curriculum is wrongheaded. Most students won't go to college, they argue, and these students need occupationally specific training to enter the skilled workforce after high school. According to their read of current job projections, only a small fraction of skilled jobs, now and in the future, will require a college degree.

We have watched this argument up close in California. In his 2007 State of the State Address, Governor Schwarzenegger said, "I love career tech, love it," and declared his intention to reinvigorate career and technical education in the state with increased funding. The governor's remarks represented a victory for a coalition of vocational education advocates seeking to persuade state policymakers that educational dollars would be best spent on providing high-quality career and technical education to all middle and high school students. The very next morning, the state's college-prep-for-all advocates fired back. The state director of Education Trust West told the *Sacramento Bee*, "rather than creating choices for students, these [career and technical courses] are going to be gatekeepers, they're going to limit their options for success."[8]

The debate between advocates of academic and vocational education regularly reappears in times of economic and social crisis. A hundred years ago, civic leaders and educators disagreed about whether the high school—then in its infancy as a mass institution—should give the nation's increasingly diverse students a traditional academic curriculum or specialized vocational preparation.[9] The solution at the time was to do both, by creating separate academic, general, and vocational curriculum tracks and sorting students into the track that best matched their talents and likely futures. This standard practice emerged as a seemingly sensible response to the proliferation of publicly supported high schools and the growth of the nation's urban industrial economy. It should be no surprise that the debate has appeared again in today's period of dramatic demographic and economic shifts.

A THIRD POSITION

Over the past decade, however, schools like CTA have provided a third position in the debate, one that challenges and shifts this century-old discussion about how to improve high schools.

> High schools can and should prepare all students for *both* college and careers. Programs that contextualize academic learning in the real world of adults will improve learning, reduce the dropout rate, and bring economic benefits.

This new position is being advanced by reform groups and educators under the rubric "Multiple Pathways." Arguing that graduates who go directly to work need solid academic skills and those who go to college will also have careers, Multiple Pathways advocates seek to move beyond what they see as a tired debate between academic and vocational education and the traditional practice of tracking students into different high school courses, depending on whether they are seen as bound for college or work. They assert that the twenty-first century economy will forge new relationships between schooling and work, with most adults changing jobs over the course of their careers. Such transitions will require adults to move between work, job training, and school to learn the knowledge and skills that new jobs require. Some Multiple Pathways advocates also invoke contemporary understandings of learning: that students learn more and better when they can apply academic knowledge and skills to real-world situations and problems. Accordingly, the approach should improve learning for today's already-successful students as well as for those who struggle.

Multiple Pathways has captured the imagination of school reformers, a growing number of policymakers, and major philanthropy. Its appeal is obvious: a new way of thinking about schools that does not pit college preparation against work preparation or stratify students into one or the other. At the same time, Multiple Pathways increases achievement and high school graduation rates.

In the remainder of this chapter, we continue the discussion by offering a working definition of Multiple Pathways and providing a brief account of its emergence as a reform idea. We conclude with a brief summary of the themes woven through the entire collection of essays in this volume.

WHAT ARE MULTIPLE PATHWAYS?

We define Multiple Pathways as high school reform that replaces the ubiquitous comprehensive high school with a portfolio of smaller high schools and programs within high schools ("pathways") that provide both the academic and real-world foundations students need for advanced learning, training, and preparation for responsible civic participation. The various pathways may differ considerably in their curricular emphasis (e.g., their "theme" or career focus), how they organize coursework, how much time students spend on and off campus, their relationships with two- and four-year colleges, and their partnerships with business and industry. Pathways can be made available by many school structures, including career academies, small autonomous schools, magnet programs, small learning communities within large high schools, and occupational training centers.

Despite this considerable diversity among pathways, we conceptualize all Multiple Pathways schools as having four essential components to ensure high standards, program coherence, and personalized learning:

1. A college-preparatory academic core that satisfies the course requirements for entry into a state's flagship public university through project-based learning and other engaging instructional strategies. These strategies intentionally bring real-world context and relevance to the curriculum by emphasizing broad themes, interest areas, and/or career and technical education.
2. A professional or technical core well-grounded in academic and real-world standards.
3. Field-based learning and realistic workplace simulations that deepen students' understanding of academic and technical knowledge through application in authentic situations.

4. Additional support services to meet the particular needs of students and communities, which can include supplemental instruction, counseling, transportation, and so on.[10]

In this conception of Multiple Pathways, students and their families chose from a variety of options, all of which lead students to the same destination: preparation to succeed in college *and* careers, not one or the other. All students graduate with the choice of a full range of postsecondary options. This single destination of the various pathways defies and seeks to change a long-standing high school hierarchy that makes college better than work and makes preparation for work the default for those who aren't expected to succeed in college. Notably, Multiple Pathways are also seen as a powerful way to enact the school's responsibility to prepare students for their civic responsibilities. By engaging actively in the adult world, students can examine, up close, the connections among the workplace, politics, and social life.

CONSTRUCTING MULTIPLE PATHWAYS: WHAT MUST CHANGE?

Constructing these Multiple Pathways demands a radical reworking of the comprehensive high school. Reforms adopted under the name Multiple Pathways will likely replicate the status quo unless they provide for nontraditional structures, integrated curricula, innovative teaching and assessment practices, different placement strategies, and quite different assumptions about what students can accomplish in high school and beyond. These Multiple Pathways also require new and different relationships between high schools and postsecondary institutions, including alternatives to the traditional requirements for admission, as well as meaningful connections between schools and work settings. The CTA, which opened the chapter, includes all these elements, and we describe them briefly here.

Nontraditional Structures

Multiple Pathways change two firmly fixed high school structures: the location and timing of teaching and learning. Likely new sites include small schools in nontraditional facilities, large schools broken up into smaller schools or learning communities on the same campus, community and four-year colleges, and off-campus learning settings. Many Multiple Pathways reject the traditional organization of the curriculum into six or seven instructional periods, with each class providing a different subject taught by a different teacher, opting instead for teaching teams working in more flexible blocks of time.[11]

Integrated Curriculum

A Multiple Pathways curriculum seeks to give all students highly valued knowledge, skills, and attitudes to apply basic information and well-developed thinking habits to the unpredictable problems and circumstances of the working world. This demands a curriculum that integrates "information-rich subject matter content with an experience-rich context of application."[12] When they see the practical applications of mathematics, science, and reading, students are motivated to learn the facts, core principles, and applications of these traditional subjects. Such curriculum defies categorization as either academic or vocational.[13]

Instruction

In one sense, Multiple Pathways pedagogy is fundamentally different from typical academic instruction or traditional career and technical education. But in another sense, it selects the best pedagogies from both traditions, and this hybrid of the two makes the most profound difference. Many schools turn to project-based learning to ensure that instruction emphasizes learning processes and values that sustain life and work skills: cooperation, team problem identification and solving, communication, making decisions, commitment, confidence in abilities, and boldness in developing ideas and approaches. Depth, rigor, and intensity should characterize students' learning activities, as all three count heavily in the real world of careers.

Student Assignment and Choice

In a Multiple Pathways system, students choose pathways based on their interests, and they are not selected or directed based on their past achievement or presumed postsecondary destination. Accordingly, each pathway enrolls heterogeneous groups of students who learn in a shared environment. Practitioners and researchers have confirmed time and again that students of diverse cultural, skill, and academic backgrounds can learn together in academically rich, problem-based learning settings.[14] In addition to preserving students' postsecondary options, this diversity obviates the institutionalized labeling and stigma that vocational education students have suffered, permits all students access to learning-oriented and achievement-valuing peers, ensures that all students receive the instructional benefits that accrue when teachers perceive that able students are present in the classroom, and enhances the learning of all students with a rigorous curriculum.[15]

Assumptions about Students' Capacity

Perhaps most critically, policymakers, educators, and students must believe that, given the right environment, all students can master complex academic and technical concepts. Individual differences cannot translate into differentiated school practices that imply "headedness" for some and "handedness" for others. This does as great a disservice to the "heads" as it does to the "hands." The fundamental premise of Multiple Pathways is that all students can benefit from a balanced, integrated curriculum. The learning of both the "brightest" students and those who struggle most will be enhanced by the multidimensional learning experiences, problem-solving focus, and academics presented in the context of real-world experience.

THE EVOLUTION OF MULTIPLE PATHWAYS

As far as we've been able to determine, Multiple Pathways first appeared in the educational literature as a reform strategy in a 1997 article, "Redefining the Comprehensive High School: The Multiple Pathways Model," published in the *NASSP Bulletin*, the journal of the National Association of Secondary School Principals. The author, Robert J. Monson, superintendent of Independent School District 197 in Mendota Heights, Minnesota, had developed and implemented the concept in the suburban Minneapolis-St. Paul community. Monson believed that the concept could address two key problems of the comprehensive high school: the lack of intellectual depth for most students and the social and racial inequalities associated with tracking.

Although not a perfect match, Monson's Multiple Pathways model bears a clear resemblance to our working definition. Monson proposed an array of high school programs leading to the same outcome: all high school students achieving a common set of rigorous learning standards. The standards he used to anchor the pathways (the Minnesota graduation standards) bridge disciplines and emphasize cognitive competencies (e.g., "conducting research and communicating findings") rather than the acquisition of a body of knowledge. The pathways were to span learning settings (traditional high schools, "evening schools," community colleges, four-year universities, and workplaces) and offer a wide range of pedagogies, including the blending of academic and technical content, an inquiry-based approach, and replicating the schedule and instruction of traditional college courses. Finally, Monson proposed replacing "seat time" with students' demonstration of proficiencies (with an emphasis on performance-based assessment) as the basis for awarding credit.[16]

Multiple Pathways jumped onto the national policy stage in 2003, with the release of several policy reports advocating a "pathways" or "multiple pathways" approach to restructuring high schools. Supported by national foundations, including the Bill & Melinda Gates Foundation, the Wallace-Reader's Digest Foundation, and the Carnegie Corporation of New York, projects by leading policy organizations all explored strategies that would provide a variety of options for ensuring that all students graduate with academic competencies and career preparation. Jobs for the Future, the National Governors Association, the Aspen Institute, and the American Youth Policy Forum (AYPF) conducted many of these projects and actually used the term "Multiple Pathways."

The 2003 report of a joint project of Jobs for the Future and the National Governors Association, *Ready for Tomorrow: Helping All Students Achieve Secondary and Postsecondary Success*, argued that that all high school graduates must meet two sets of standards, one set "calibrated" to the academic requirements for college, and another set incorporating the "new basic skills" needed for productive employment, such as applied problem-solving and communications skills. The report asserted that large, one-size-fits-all high schools are "too impersonal, inflexible, and alienating for young people, especially those who need extra academic and social support to catch up and succeed."[17] It called instead for "wide variations . . . in the structure, pedagogy, and institutional characteristics of learning environments that help students meet the standards."[18]

Jobs for the Future released a second paper in 2003. In "Multiple Pathways and State Policy: Toward Education and Training Beyond High School," Patrick Callan and J. E. Finney added that the array of pathways would require "engaging the full range of education and training programs, regardless of the education provider, . . . [and] collaborative efforts across educational sectors or redesigned structures."[19] Callan and Finney argue that "Multiple pathways do not imply multiple standards—but rather clear standards at various levels and many ways of moving toward the standards."[20]

A third, widely distributed 2003 paper from the AYPF, "Rigor and Relevance: A New Vision for Career and Technical Education," argued more explicitly for the integration of academic and career education. Its recommendations focused on multiple programs of study that provide "students with a pathway to postsecondary education and a career by detailing academic and occupational competencies needed for advancement" and housing these programs in a variety of settings, including "small career-themed schools, career academies located in comprehensive high schools, technical high schools with various career clusters, or early or middle college high schools with a career theme."[21] These basic ideas were also published in book form in 2004.[22]

By 2005, Jobs for the Future and the Aspen Institute had become quite blunt in their expectations of career and technical education in high school reform. Their report, *Remaking Career and Technical Education for the 21st Century: What Role for High School Programs?* asserted that "CTE at the high school level must either change or die."[23] Unless career and technical education becomes an integral part of broader high school reform and "a high-quality high school pathway" infused with academic rigor,[24] it will lose the political and fiscal support, not only of policymakers and practitioners, but also of employers, who increasingly prefer new hires with college-level experience.

The Gates Foundation, the James Irvine Foundation in California, and other philanthropies have also provided considerable financial support for school development projects. The Gates Foundation supported the CTA described earlier, as well as other theme-based small schools in many parts of the country. In its own publications, Gates actively promotes "a portfolio of great high schools" that provide college and career preparation for all, across a variety of educational settings:

> After all, students learn in different ways; their schools should *teach* in different ways. In this new landscape, schools may have different emphases, teaching approaches, or philosophies, but they will all prepare every student for college. In a system with a diverse portfolio of schools, no single school will fit every student. But every student will fit at least one school.[25]

The Carnegie Corporation of New York and the Wallace-Reader's Digest Fund have been major supporters of the policy discussions on reforming career and technical education convened by the AYPF.

In California, the James Irvine Foundation has played a leading philanthropic role in advancing Multiple Pathways. For Irvine, the diversity of California's population of young people makes building multiple pathways a particularly attractive strategy for increasing the number of low-income youth in California who complete high school on time and attain a postsecondary credential by age 25. Notably, however, Irvine sees this approach as appropriate for all students and as bringing considerable advantages even to those who succeed in the current college preparatory curriculum. On its website, Irvine makes its advocacy of Multiple Pathways clear:

> To close the gap in academic achievement, we believe that young people must be offered different ways of getting to the same destination: success in high school, college and careers. We see the need for a "multiple pathways" approach that recognizes the diversity of student interests and abilities, and engages students in academically rigorous work by demonstrating its relevance to the real world. [26]

Accordingly, Irvine has supported several projects seeking to improve instruction and student support services in the state's high schools and community colleges, including some that blend academics with career and technical education for low-income youth.

The challenge of creating and scaling up Multiple Pathways was taken up in 2006 by ConnectEd: The California Center for College and Career. Under the direction of Gary Hoachlander, ConnectEd seeks to identify, study, and advocate for multiple pathways that prepare all students for both college and career. ConnectEd promotes challenging, comprehensive programs of study that connect academics with professional and technical education and are organized around industry or fields that include the biomedical and health sciences, building and environmental design, engineering, law and government, transportation, arts and entertainment, and education and social services. Its current network of fourteen model programs includes schools and programs organized around health careers; construction, engineering, and architecture; and the arts and media.

As this body of work demonstrates, strong national support for Multiple Pathways currently exists. To maintain the momentum for Multiple Pathways, however, additional study and evidence is required to document its promise to meet the learning needs of a diverse student population and demonstrate its responsiveness to society's need for a productive workforce and engaged citizenry.

IS THERE EVIDENCE TO SUPPORT MULTIPLE PATHWAYS?

The thirteen essays in this book seek to inform the discussion with research-based perspectives and tough questions about this emerging third position. Before leaping into a fundamental reinvention of the comprehensive high school, those who are considering adopting Multiple Pathways reform require evidence-based answers to several critical questions:

- Could Multiple Pathways reform actually improve learning, raise high school graduation rates, and enhance college readiness?
- Might it increase educational and economic opportunities for the most vulnerable students: those in impoverished neighborhoods and English learners?
- Will Multiple Pathways prepare young people for effective civic participation?
- Could Multiple Pathways contribute to a healthy economy and address the state's future workforce needs?
- Is the concept well suited to an increasingly diverse population?

Even if the answers to these questions are positive and compelling, we must also understand the feasibility and costs of Multiple Pathways reform. What would it actually take to move beyond a century-old structure of tracking that provides students with differentiated high school curriculum—often either academic or vocational—that leads them explicitly to different and limited postsecondary options? As the example of CTA illustrates, Multiple Pathways requires fundamentally different school structures, curriculum, and teaching; relationships with postsecondary and industry partners; and learning supports for students that integrate the best of both college preparatory academics and career and technical education. It also requires very different views about what high schools can and should do. Accordingly, we also need to know

- What challenges is the adoption and implementation of Multiple Pathways reform likely to face?
- What policies might address these challenges and support and encourage effective Multiple Pathways reform?

To help generate research-based answers to all these questions, we turned to leading scholars in education, psychology, sociology, economics, labor studies, business, demography, and social welfare. Using California as a case example, we asked the scholars to review, interpret, and synthesize scholarly research in their fields that sheds light on whether and how Multiple Pathways might address future educational, social, and economic challenges. We also asked them to consider what technical, political, and cultural considerations might affect the course of such reform. Finally, we asked them to write their responses for a broad audience of policymakers, professionals, and other interested citizens.

Why California? Certainly, the issue of high school reform and the struggle to broaden the postsecondary opportunities of all students is not limited to California. But California provides a relevant and useful example. California is a bellwether state in terms of the social and economic shifts the nation will experience in the next half-century and the educational challenges those shifts will bring. As the demographics of California continue to change (predominantly nonwhite groups as of the 2000 census), the state faces growing challenges to the effectiveness of traditional school practices and to escalating societal divisions. California is also instructive in that Multiple Pathways has been proposed in the state's high school reform discussions. The way Multiple Pathways intersects with, and responds to, the California context can provide useful guidance and forewarning to educators and policymakers throughout the nation.

Looking primarily at California, the researchers examined the intersections of a changing economy, increasing population diversity, widening social and economic inequality, and patterns of school failure in racial and ethnic communities. They explored the links between current structures (structures that maintain a divide between career and technical education and academic education) and inequality. They also analyzed various programs that attempt to provide multiple pathways to high school graduation while preparing for career, college, civic responsibility, and community leadership. Their findings are laid out in the thirteen hopeful and sobering essays that comprise the remaining chapters of this book.

We've clustered these essays into three sections. The essays in the first section address the potential of Multiple Pathways to increase students' academic engagement, learning, and rates of high school graduation and college preparation. Those in the second section consider whether Multiple Pathways can promote a healthy economy and democracy more effectively than traditional high schools. The third section delves more deeply into the technical, cultural, and political obstacles facing Multiple Pathways reform. We should note, however, that each essay speaks to all three of these schooling issues.

PROMISE, CHALLENGE, AND CAUTION: THEMES IN THE EVIDENCE

Together, the essays offer considerable evidence for the potential of Multiple Pathways. The promise of this concept lies both in its capacity to meet the learning needs of a diverse student population and in its responsiveness to society's need for a productive workforce, engaged citizenry, and future leaders. Looking at the thirteen essays, we conclude that evidence for Multiple Pathways appears quite promising. If it is fully implemented, Multiple Pathways promises to improve school achievement, high school graduation rates, and access to higher education; increase the educational and work opportunities for vulnerable students; and prepare California's population of young people for responsible participation in public life. Done right, it could also respond effectively to demographic shifts and address future economic challenges.

That being said, the authors also persuade us that doing Multiple Pathways right is a formidable task. To achieve the benefits of Multiple Pathways, policymakers and educators must confront a number of challenges. These include technical barriers, such as reworking school schedules and providing students with transportation to off-campus learning sites; political resistance to redistributing resources for academic and vocational programs; and cultural obstacles, such as widespread low academic expectations of low-income students of color, to name just a few. Fortunately, though, the essays do not leave us with only a list of possibilities and challenges. They also offer a wealth of policy ideas that could help policymakers and educators create the right conditions for such reform.

These essays also caution us that Multiple Pathways alone cannot solve the many other social and economic problems that disproportionately harm low-income, African American, and Latino youth. Huge increases in childhood poverty, brought about in part by significant shifts in the economy, combine with the lack of social safety net programs to leave many young people without stable housing, health care, or parents with access to well-paying jobs. These conditions place enormous burdens on families and the educational system. Also needed are strong economic and employment policies that focus on the unique labor force problems associated with low-income communities of color, such as spatial and skill barriers to employment, discrimination by employers, and access to good jobs. Ultimately, a Multiple Pathways approach to high school education will work best with a social safety net that includes labor standards, health, housing, and other measures that address the negative effects of residential segregation, income inequality, and concentrated poverty.

MULTIPLE MEANINGS OF MULTIPLE PATHWAYS

Our conception of a Multiple Pathways system of schools, to which the scholars in this book responded, is not the only version of Multiple Pathways on the table in discussions about high school reform. In some places, reforms labeled with the phrase "Multiple Pathways" bear a striking resemblance to traditional tracking practices. The term has also been used to advocate "new and improved" vocational education programs. In other places, Multiple Pathways refer to the alternative school sector that connects various education providers to help over-age, undercredited, and disengaged students get back on a pathway to high school completion and some sort of postsecondary credential. We consider these other versions in some detail in the final chapter of this volume. We focus particularly on the extent to which these versions resist changes that would transform the comprehensive high school, including the practice of tracking, which the version we describe seeks to replace.

This book does not weigh in on all solutions to the problems of the contemporary American high school or resolve the debate about the relative merits of the academic and vocational sides of schooling. We hope, however, that these essays clarify the possibilities and challenges of the strong version of Multiple Pathways we've outlined here. Reading the book should prompt and inform a useful dialogue among scholars, policymakers, and educators committed to higher-quality high schools for all young people.

Multiple Pathways and Student Success

Possibilities and Challenges

The four essays in Part I tackle core problems that limit the educational success of American high school students: large, impersonal schools; a curriculum lacking depth, rigor, and relevance; instruction that does not engage
or motivate; and inequities that provide different opportunities for different
groups of students. These problems are widely seen as the cause of soaring
high school dropout rates and the lack of preparedness of those who do graduate with the academic or technical knowledge and skills required for success
in postsecondary institutions, the workplace, and civil society.

Can Multiple Pathways be part of the solution to these problems? Can
Multiple Pathways actually increase students' academic engagement, improve
learning, raise high school graduation rates, and enhance college and workforce readiness? In brief, the overall answer seems to be yes.

This seems to be the conclusion of a diverse set of scholars who look at
Multiple Pathways' impact on students' educational outcomes: cognition and
literacy scholar Mike Rose; economist David Stern and his coauthor, practi-
tioner Roman Stearns; education philosopher Karen Hunter Quartz and her
coauthor, school designer Elliot Washor; and education psychologist Patricia
Gándara. Adopting a conception of Multiple Pathways that offers both college and career preparation to all students, these scholars explore how this
integration can affect students' learning, motivation in school, and rates of
high school completion and college enrollment. They also examine various
modes for delivering Multiple Pathways education (e.g., theme-based academies including career academies, small schools, small learning communities,

magnet schools, regional occupational programs/centers). Significantly, the essays make clear that these are not neutral structural arrangements: Each adds learning and social value (and sometimes obstacles) to schooling. Gándara's essay also explores the potential benefits of Multiple Pathways for some of the country's most vulnerable students: immigrants and English learners.

Based on their own research, together with extensive reviews of other relevant studies, the authors of these four essays find considerable merit in Multiple Pathways as a way to meet the educational needs of individual students. They attribute this, in large part, to Multiple Pathways' confrontation of the century-old divide between academic and vocational education. They find that, contrary to common perceptions, intellectual rigor and cognitive content are also found in work and in traditional conceptions of career and technical education. The authors also anticipate that these individual gains will have a positive impact on the social and economic well-being of individuals and of society as a whole. (Societal benefits are discussed in Part II.) Here, we preview briefly some of their findings about the potential individual benefits of Multiple Pathways. We also introduce the challenges these authors find to the reform's large-scale implementation.

THE POSSIBILITIES

Multiple Pathways Could Increase Academic Engagement for All Students

David Stern and Roman Stearns emphasize that Multiple Pathways' combination of academics and real-world learning provides students with opportunities to see applications of academic subject matter outside of school; organizes disparate knowledge around a common focus; and fosters relationships between adults and young people in small, personalized learning communities and work-based learning and internships. Each of these elements promotes student engagement. They, along with Karen Hunter Quartz and Elliot Washor, conclude that both college-bound and non-college-bound students are likely to find the Multiple Pathways approach to academics more engaging than either the typical abstract, classroom-bound, college-prep curriculum or the equally abstract lower-level courses aimed at teaching basic skills. Norton Grubb's essay in Part III returns to this important theme.

Multiple Pathways Could Enhance Learning for All Students

The authors find that, when students apply academic subject matter in out-of-school contexts, they deepen their understanding and retention of academic concepts. Mike Rose illustrates how the substantive content of work and the pedagogy of learning complex, work-related tasks can foster the development of other important cognitive abilities, such as acuity in perception and observation; knowledge of tools and their capabilities and limitations; skills in planning and prioritizing tasks; increased ability to solve both routine and nonroutine problems; the development of analytical reasoning skills; increased skills in applying mathematics to support planning, troubleshooting, and problem-solving; use of writing to aid learning and task completion; enhanced communication and interactional ability; and skills in reflecting on one's own actions and modifying them to improve task performance. Many of these competencies, he notes, are similar to the broad skills that experts predict are essential to obtaining secure jobs in the future. Furthermore, these skills are highly prized in those pursuing a college education.

Multiple Pathways Could Increase High School Graduation and College-Preparation Rates for All Students

Quartz and Washor's essay brings to bear the experience of the small schools movement. The authors argue that when schools connect adults and students in relationships that support learning, provide program flexibility to meet students' needs, and organize around a meaningful thematic focus, they increase the students' chances of completing high school and accessing a range of postsecondary options. Stern and Stearns conclude that a well-defined Multiple Pathways sequence of college-preparatory and career and technical courses can prevent struggling students from falling into unproductive course-taking patterns that are closely associated with dropping out of high school. They also find (with some caveats) that connecting academic knowledge and skills to work appears to motivate students to stick with academic courses that prepare them for college. Perhaps most important, the alignment of college preparation with workforce readiness keeps college an option without sacrificing workforce preparation, a benefit also noted by authors in other parts of the book.

Multiple Pathways Could Address the Special Needs of Immigrants and English Learners

Because it integrates real-world contexts and tasks with academic skills, Multiple Pathways can be an effective strategy to increase achievement for English learners. Patricia Gándara explores how students who have not yet fully mastered English can learn and demonstrate their learning by doing, through hands-on, project, and portfolio activities. Such opportunities for success can improve morale and self-concept, thus providing a major incentive to stay in school. Additionally, Gándara notes that Multiple Pathways' off-site learning experiences could make available strong English-use models and opportunities to use emerging English language skills in contextually meaningful ways. English learners benefit from learning in the community, where they have purposeful work and education contacts with people who have knowledge of students' language and culture. Such knowledgeable others can increase students' exposure to career opportunities and encourage students to take advantage of flexible educational timelines.

THE CHALLENGES

Even as these four essays provide compelling arguments for Multiple Pathways' potential impact on student learning, achievement, graduation rates, and college readiness, they also spell out the obstacles and challenges such reform would face. The authors point out that much else needs to change, in schools and out of schools, including large-scale structural changes that Multiple Pathways implementation requires. For example, Stern and Stearns write of the need to bridge the academic-vocational "divide" characterized by disparate program standards, funding streams, and accountability requirements; they point to the difficulty of bringing together teachers with different professional training and certification—all presenting dicey policy problems. Quartz and Washor caution that the relationships between educators and students must change, and schools need to increase academic and social supports. They note that theme-based schools may offer curricular alternatives, but without explicit attention to the collective aims of schooling, these choices can cast education as only a private good. Finally, Multiple Pathways must challenge commonly held conceptions about students' capacity, particularly those from vulnerable groups. The fundamental premise of Multiple Pathways is that the learning of all students—both the "brightest" students and those who struggle most—can be enhanced by an integrated curriculum that includes rigorous academic preparation, technical knowledge, and opportunities to learn from real-world settings, including work.

CHAPTER 1

Blending "Hand Work" and "Brain Work"

Can Multiple Pathways Deepen Learning?

Mike Rose

Mike Rose is professor of education at the University of California–Los Angeles. He is author of The Mind at Work: Valuing the Intelligence of the American Worker, Lives on the Boundary: The Struggles and Achievements of America's Underprepared, Possible Lives: The Promise of Public Education in America, *and* An Open Language: Selected Writing on Literacy Learning and Opportunity.

In this essay, Rose uses the lens of research on cognition and literacy to examine the potential of Multiple Pathways for student learning. He explores the intellectual rigor and cognitive content found in work, in traditional conceptions of career and technical education, and in academic instruction. Rose suggests that a Multiple Pathways approach to high school curriculum might draw on the often-neglected cognitive content of work- and career-based education to develop competencies prized both in college and on the job. Citing examples such as acuity in observation, knowledge of tools, ability to solve both routine and unusual problems, and analytical reasoning, Rose challenges the easy cultural distinctions made between "hand work" and "brain work." He broadens our discussion of intelligence within the frameworks of educational policy and democratic theory.

INTRODUCTION

We are living in a time of vibrant debate about the high school—debate about its purpose and structure, its curriculum, its place in the early twenty-first century's economy and social structure. One of the more compelling themes of this debate has to do with courses and programs classified as "vocational" (to use the old term) or "career and technical" (to use the new). What place should this long-standing feature of the high school have in the modern curriculum? How can such courses and programs be reformed, made more rigorous, and beefed up with or integrated into the academic course of study? How, in fact, should such courses and programs be defined during the process of reform?

The idea of Multiple Pathways responds to these and other questions by challenging the public education system to provide a variety of ways for students to complete high school with a rigorous curriculum that leads to further educational and occupational options after graduation. The focus of this chapter is on recent efforts to reform career and technical education (CTE). I provide an alternative perspective on these efforts, one that I hope will contribute to the Multiple Pathways discussion.

CAREER AND TECHNICAL EDUCATION

Much of the recent policy literature on CTE offers these shared goals and claims:

1. If it is to continue and develop, CTE will have to become more academically rigorous.
2. Such reform would enhance opportunity for CTE students' further education and occupational training.
3. Such reform would better complement current and emerging labor markets.

These goals and claims address long-standing concerns about vocational education and are in line with reforms sparked by the Perkins Act and other legislation from the last two decades. And they are clearly in line with the spirit of Multiple Pathways reforms.

The research literature addressing whether CTE is meeting these goals ranges from meta-analyses of the effects of vocational education to detailed articulations of standards and outcomes to case studies of successful programs. The overall picture is a mixed one. For example, several studies of theme-based schools and career academies have documented some successes in increasing opportunities for further education and employment.[1] And while the comprehensive National Assessment of Vocational Education did demonstrate some benefits to enrolling in CTE courses, it also concluded that little progress has been made toward the goal of using high school CTE to improve academic achievement.[2] I'm struck, though, by several themes and perspectives missing from or thinly treated in this literature, and I think that they might benefit attempts to reform CTE and to create robust Multiple Pathways. In essence, the literature undervalues the intellectual content of work and displays a reluctance to critically engage the academic-vocational distinction itself.

First, a few words on the background to my comments. They emerge from a research project that explored the cognition involved in blue-collar and service work, published as *The Mind at Work*.[3] I had several goals in doing the study: to portray the cognitive content of everyday work, to challenge the easy cultural distinctions we make between "hand work" and "brain work," to broaden our discussion of intelligence, and to consider these issues of work and intelligence within the frameworks of educational policy and democratic theory.

The occupations I studied included waitressing, hairstyling, three construction trades (carpentry, plumbing, electrical), welding, and factory work. I observed people at work, interviewed them, recorded examples of their work for analysis by other competent practitioners and by scholars in cognitive psychology and education, and read social and technical histories of their occupations. In most cases, I was able to study both experts and novices, and, therefore, some of the study took me into high school, community college, and workplace educational and training programs. It is this aspect of the study that is most pertinent to our discussion.

One more prefatory note: The kinds of work I studied would be classified in our current lexicon as "old economy" work, not the kind of work featured in CTE reform or in most of the Multiple Pathways literature. But, if one finds rich cognitive content in old economy work, then new economy work—work that is putatively more cognitively demanding—should display such content as well. Additional research that focuses on new economy work could discern these differences.

AN ALTERNATIVE PERSPECTIVE ON CAREER AND TECHNICAL EDUCATION

A perspective on CTE that can be helpful in addressing the possibilities of Multiple Pathways that integrate academic and career-related curriculum is one that focuses on the cognitive content of work and on the pedagogy of high-quality CTE classes.

Looking at the Cognitive Content of Traditional Academic and Career and Technical Education

The CTE literature tends to focus on infusing traditional academic content in vocational education rather than on the cognitive content of vocational education and the work from which it draws. The effect is to depict CTE as cognitively inferior not only in its practice (which, sadly, it can be) but also in its essence. This depiction inflames long-standing subject area battles between CTE and academic folk (which spells trouble for reform) and reinscribes cultural biases and simplifications about manual versus mental activity, blue-collar work versus white-collar, hand versus brain.

We should applaud attempts to bring a liberal course of study more fully into CTE. But it also would be helpful to turn the epistemological tables and articulate the substantial cognitive potential of the world of work. That is what Dewey and Whitehead did long ago in complicating the distinction between "academic" and "vocational," and it is what experimental schools do today, such as The Met in Providence, Rhode Island, or High Tech High in San Diego, California.

As a starting point, let me list some of the skills and abilities that good CTE can foster:

- Acuity in perception and observation
- Ability to attend and remember
- Knowledge of tools and their capabilities and limitations
- Skill in planning and prioritizing tasks
- Ability to solve both routine and nonroutine problems
- Analytical reasoning skills
- Ability to use and communicate with a variety of symbols, including mathematical symbols
- Skill in applying mathematics to support planning, troubleshooting, and problem solving
- Use of writing to aid learning and task completion
- Ability to use a variety of reading strategies and to select the appropriate strategy for the task at hand
- Enhanced communication and interactional ability, including ability to learn from teachers and students and from coworkers on the job

- Reflection on one's own actions and modifying them to improve task performance and avoid injury or error
- Aesthetic and craft values
- Motivation to learn and work

Many of these CTE competencies are similar or identical to the broad skills that some experts predict are essential to obtain secure jobs in the future.[4]

How does the best CTE help students develop these important skills and abilities that would be integral to Multiple Pathways and that could form a base for further education and employment? My research identified some key features of CTE that seem to foster these goals.

Key Features of Good Career and Technical Education Classrooms and Programs

1. *Many of the tasks students do are authentic, real-world tasks with consequences.* Examples are building a display cabinet on commission; repairing the plumbing in a women's shelter; contributing time to a Habitat for Humanity construction site; mastering various welding tools, processes, and materials for practical repairs and as a medium for artistic expression; learning the chemistry of hair coloring with the goal of applying it under supervision.

2. *These tasks are rich in opportunities to develop knowledge of tools, processes, and materials and to solve problems, make decisions, abstract, discuss what one is doing or has done, reflect on practice, and so on.* The best teachers enhance such cognitive work through the way they present tasks, ask questions, and supervise student activities. I think of two teachers in particular, a plumber and a carpenter, who took a Socratic approach. They asked students what to do next and why and had them think ahead to the consequences of their actions. They would also do things to get students to entertain other perspectives, to see things in a new light. For example, the carpentry teacher occasioned the flash of insight into structure by walking students to other parts of a house frame to give them a different take on the effects of their work.

3. *Traditional academic pursuits (mathematics, reading and writing, science) are embedded in these tasks.* The best teachers point out to their students that they are actually doing math, science, and other subjects. Such connections to academic content and academic classes happen readily in career academies or integrated programs where teachers plan such integration.

For example, in a graphic arts academy that I observed, students study the chemistry, structure, and other qualities of the ink they use in the graphic arts lab, and the teachers refer often to chemical properties and their applications.

4. *When a curriculum is based on authentic tasks, assessment of student performance can also become authentic.* The tasks themselves guide a process of self-assessment or joint assessment by the student and the teacher or supervisor. If the print on an announcement is blurry, a weld is uneven, or a light bulb doesn't go on, it is clear to teacher and student alike that something went wrong. The powerful thing about such an event is that it also provides the occasion for further learning by retracing one's steps, troubleshooting, and reflecting on performance. As research on authentic or performance assessment has established, this approach to assessment enables learners to demonstrate ways in which they construct their own meaning for content and concepts, and solve various real-world problems.[5]

5. *The environments in which students learn are real-world work environments (e.g., a hair salon) or simulate them.* The best of the real-world environments are modified, however, by the presence of supervision and some explicitly pedagogical interaction. So expert professionals determine what tasks the students do and in what order, provide guidance, pose questions, and guide performance. The simulations, or modified environments, range from various kinds of models (e.g., a 12-foot by 12-foot house frame on which students practice electrical wiring) to large classrooms equipped with many of the tools and machines one would find in an actual print, carpentry, or welding shop.

    The physical environments are also symbolic or cultural environments: They are places that have traditions, values, and attitudes toward the work. This dimension of the environment is created on several levels.

    - The way the instructional work space is organized and the objects in it (e.g., the embodiment of tradition in the cabinet full of old woodworking tools, the awl, the spokeshave).
    - The values expressed by the teacher and the mode of practice he or she presents. ("A bridge is only as strong as its weakest weld," a welding instructor tells her community college students. "You're like a surgeon, but you're working on metal. You're taking two separate entities and making them one. So take it to heart.")

- The traditions and experiences that some students bring from families of craftspeople, health care workers, cooks, or hairstylists. (CTE spaces are hospitable to these traditions.)
- The reaction of people who are on the receiving end of the students' work. (I was struck by how moved a student was when he saw a cabinet he had built being used in his school's office.)
- Students' own descriptions and self-initiated efforts. (One boy spoke of the "integrity" of working with wood; another rewired a perfectly functional fixture because he thought his earlier work was "ugly.")

6. *Blended with the cognitive and the technical are craft values, ethical concerns, and aesthetics.* These values and concerns are beneficial both to individual development and to the social good. Ethical and aesthetic concerns can guide performance (and thus achievement) in these settings, and are sometimes hard to separate from more strictly cognitive motivators and outcomes.

7. *Good teachers share some predictable characteristics.* They are knowledgeable practitioners of their occupations, and this knowledge is a source of respect: Students know that their teachers speak from experience. These teachers seem committed to student development, both in terms of occupational skills and in more general cognitive and social domains. Whether they learned it through a teacher education program or from work experience, they have good pedagogical sense. They move around the room, continually checking in on students or being summoned by them. They shift strategically from explaining to demonstrating to asking questions. They give students room to try things out and blunder, but they know when to intervene and guide. They sometimes offer personal and career counseling. They want to develop competent carpenters, welders, and hairstylists, but I think it's fair to say that they hold these more general cognitive and social goals for their students as well.

IMPLICATIONS OF THE ALTERNATIVE PERSPECTIVE ON CAREER AND TECHNICAL EDUCATION

It would be generative to lay a list of the above CTE competencies (e.g., development of ability to attend and remember, skills in planning and prioritizing tasks, problem-solving ability) alongside a typical list of academic competencies and note the points of convergence and difference—and then try to imagine how the two lists could fuse and what conditions could spark a new synthesis.

Identifying the convergences and differences among academic and vocational competencies might bring into focus a conceptual and methodological problem with how scholars and educators typically study the impact of CTE on academic achievement. As the CTE list suggests, important cognitive effects of CTE may not be reflected in measures like academic grade point average. Although studies find that CTE has little effect on educational outcomes, it is possible that particular programs do show significant effects but get washed out in the aggregate. Furthermore, it is commonplace in such studies to distinguish between academic and nonacademic or nonschool kinds of thinking. Again, the CTE competency list suggests that such distinctions are problematic because many of the items listed have high academic value.

Debates within educational psychology and cognitive science address the transfer of training from one domain to another as well as the generic or situated nature of knowledge and cognitive strategies. One element in these debates is particularly relevant to my discussion: Policy discussions tend to define school knowledge or formal knowledge as abstract, generic, and transferable (e.g., that principles learned in chemistry can be applied by a student in a range of domains to a range of problems). In contrast, the informal knowledge acquired in a work setting and knowledge acquired in vocational or applied courses are usually defined as local, specific to the task at hand, and not transferable to a range of problems (e.g., the student who learns how a carburetor is built and how to repair it is not necessarily able to apply the principles about combustion embedded in the task to other domains).

The dichotomy between learning *principles* and learning *specific routines* can be misleading. Teachers often integrate specific skills and principles in the laboratory or auto shop. Further, the learning of specific skills and routines can be integrally related to the learning of principles. Not surprisingly, such integration can depend on how a subject is taught, the context in which it is taught, the materials used, and other factors. Chemistry can be taught in a way that has no transfer or relevance beyond the classroom, and occupational instruction can give rise to rich and powerful knowledge. In future, policy deliberations about CTE thinking and learning must be defined in less dichotomous, more nuanced ways.

There is a second implication of the alternative perspective I offer on CTE. Though the CTE reform literature occasionally refers to the civic, moral, and developmental dimensions of education, the focus is primarily economic:

the economic benefits to both student and society. (A fair amount of the Multiple Pathways literature tends to do the same.) Such focus is not necessarily a bad thing; the economic motive has long driven mass education in the United States. The issue, I believe, is how narrowly or richly "vocation" is defined and whether the student is defined primarily as an economic being. Unfortunately, the economic rationale is so powerful that it typically trumps all other justifications for education and ends up constraining our image of the young people in question. Discussions of CTE should be located in a comprehensive view that includes personal development and intellectual growth, the social contract and civic awareness, the ethical and aesthetic dimension of schooling, as well as the prevailing economic rationale.

BARRIERS TO ACHIEVING THE GOALS OF CAREER AND TECHNICAL EDUCATION

Why do schools continue to exclude the learning potential inherent in work, jobs, and careers from the domain of traditional academic education? There are several reasons, the first two of which are familiar—and daunting—topics in the CTE reform literature.[6]

Tradition and Legislation

In 1917, the original Smith-Hughes Act stipulated that the structure and curriculum of vocational education be separate and different from academic education. More recent legislation, such as the amendments to the Perkins Act in 1990 (Perkins II) and 1998 (Perkins III), have sought to mitigate this definition and separation, with various degrees of success.

Teacher Education and Development

The typical education of either academic or vocational teachers does not prepare them to think across subject matter divides. Perkins-inspired attempts at curriculum integration reveal scant success at blending vocational and academic courses of study, in part because teacher-preparation programs continue to focus on their members becoming subject matter specialists. Even in the more effectively integrated programs I witnessed, the teachers were educated in quite different subject areas; they came at teaching and defined competence in distinct ways. They had different credentialing requirements. They didn't have a history of collaboration. And they resided in physically, and symbolically, separate areas of their campuses. I was struck by the amount of creativity, good will, and tolerance for ambiguity it took to make the programs work.

Defining Career and Technical Education and Its Students

Two further barriers to comprehensive CTE reform are less discussed.

Our discussion of vocation and career leans toward the socially and philosophically narrow, especially where CTE students are concerned. Though there are cultural traditions and educational literatures that define "vocation" and "career" in rich ways, they are found in higher-status professions, such as law, medicine, or management. As we slide down the occupational ladder, our discussion of education for those careers tends toward the functional, task-specific, and philosophically one-dimensional. As one policy analyst I interviewed put it, ideas for vocational education programs tend to "get implemented in the lowest, least imaginative form possible."

The relatively low status of the one-dimensional vocational programs cannot be separated from the perceived characteristics of CTE students themselves. Since the early days of vocational education, VocEd students have typically been characterized as not being on a cognitive par with their academic peers. They are "hand minded," as opposed to the "abstract minded" who take an academic curriculum. This distinction reflects cultural biases that still infect policy discussion today.

Of course, by the time students enroll in high school CTE programs, many are underprepared. Such students tend not to do well in their academic courses, and their performance supports the school's belief that they cannot handle intellectually challenging material. This belief is often reinforced by the students themselves, who may feel that they just don't like school, and don't trust it, either. The challenge for policymakers and teachers alike is to be clearheaded in separating a student's current poor performance or detachment and defensiveness from intellectual possibility.

We must not assume—as many curriculum developers seem to—that poor academic preparation renders students incapable of sustained and serious involvement with core ideas in the academic disciplines and with material of intellectual consequence. Fostering such involvement on a program level by insisting that all students leave high school prepared for the full range of educational and occupational options is one of the laudable features of Multiple Pathways reform. Our schools have typically responded to students' limited educational backgrounds with reductive, trivial academic curricula, or "skills and drills," thereby revealing assumptions about the students' limited cognitive capacity. A Multiple Pathways strategy could demonstrate that a rich, hands-on curriculum provides both career and academic preparation, without dividing students into groups that are thought to be more or less capable.

TOWARD A NEW CONVERSATION ABOUT CAREER AND TECHNICAL EDUCATION AND THE WORKFORCE

The CTE policy literature understandably focuses on the immediate educational circumstances of the CTE student: curriculum, pathways to further education, and occupational opportunities. Similarly, the advocates for an academically oriented, "college-for-all" approach focus on making the traditional curriculum accessible, even to students who are not conventionally prepared for academic success. But I've come to believe that the vocational-academic divide—and thus the efforts to bridge the divide through Multiple Pathways—could become the site of a broadly significant conversation. This conversation would affect CTE and Multiple Pathways programs and extend beyond them to some of the key occupational and educational issues facing us today. It would challenge fundamental beliefs and values that currently make the divide seem far more reasonable than curricular integration.

The first challenge must be to the concept of intelligence itself: its definition, the limits of our standard measures of it, and our lack of appreciation for its manifestation in the everyday. Our notion of intelligence is strongly influenced by the IQ test and traditional verbal and quantitative school tasks. Doing well on such tests and tasks may indicate some dimensions of cognitive competence, but what about all the other ways that intellectual ability reveals itself? There is the plumber making a judgment by the feel of old pipes behind a wall. Or a hairstylist determining a style from a client's imprecise description. Or the technician with an intuitive sense of how to use an instrument to its full capacity. Or the ICU nurse ordering and reordering the flow of tasks emerging in a dynamic, changing environment. A Multiple Pathways agenda could provide opportunity to move beyond traditional measures of intellectual ability through multiple high school curricula/programs that are at once academically rigorous *and* inclusive of the range of aspirations and abilities of a diverse student population.

Related to the issue of defining intelligence is the tangled relationship between beliefs about intelligence and occupational status. We live with a set of cultural assumptions that attribute low intelligence to entire categories of work and to the people who do the work, often poor people, people of color, and immigrants. There is our impoverished sense of what work, any kind of work, requires and an arrogant denial of the intricate human dimension of technology. For all our talk about the new workplace and the need for smart workers, many believe, as does this manager of a Motorola plant overseas, that "we really need to get the human element out of the process."[7] What else but human consciousness makes the process work?

Second, there is the issue of how to accommodate differences among students in aptitude and interest. Though our schools have put some effort into dealing with heterogeneity among students, the schools end up responding to difference in pretty simplistic ways. They develop limited categories for courses and for student placement, partly to achieve administrative efficiency. However, the categories are both cognitively reductive and susceptible to quick rank-ordering.

Given, for example, the distinctions we make between the academic and the vocational, difference quickly devolves to deficiency. With few exceptions, most policy and curricular deliberations about CTE have somewhere within them assumptions of cognitive limitation—and these assumptions shrink our curricular imagination. This is a concern that Multiple Pathways reformers need to keep ever in mind.

A third issue is the long-standing and seemingly self-evident distinctions among levels and kinds of knowledge. Certainly, distinctions can be made; expressions of mind are wide and varied. But there is a tendency, in the school as in the culture at large, to view the knowledge and skill associated with nonprofessional work as rudimentary. It is "technical," or "applied," or "practical," and these words imply kinds of knowledge—and thus levels of thinking—that, though needed, are not as intellectually consequential as pursuits that are conceptual, theoretical, and abstract. These terms are part of the academic-vocational discourse, and like the academic-vocational binary, they neatly segment a more complex cognitive reality, blurring and morphing blue-collar and white. So, for example, when a carpenter builds a staircase or installs French doors, tool use and mathematical abstractions play back and forth in assembly. The use of tools is guided by mathematical knowledge and mathematical abstractions become embodied in the staircase and doors. Similarly, the surgeon's manual dexterity is informed by a web of anatomical and physiological concepts. As any surgeon will tell you, dexterity and concepts would each be useless without the other. From neuroscience to cosmology, advances in theory depend on and are informed by practical advances in technology.

This combining of kinds of knowledge occurs naturally in the best of CTE classrooms, as conceptualizing and application, thinking and doing blend in practice. Furthermore, an integration of pathways is not limited to CTE classrooms (within the comprehensive high school) but can be organized and offered through a range of educational settings that include academies, industry/career majors, magnet schools, small learning communities, and regional opportunity centers, the best of which explicitly consider needs for program coherence, high standards, personalized learning, and accountability.

Finally, overlying the considerable programmatic and economic challenges that usually dominate discussions of CTE, there is a broader domain of concerns that affect important quality-of-life issues through the intersection of schooling and work. These include meaning and identity, tradition and ethics, values, and relationships—all in the context of living in a participatory democracy. When schools do address these important topics, they do so in abstract or trivial ways. At their worst, the issues are conveyed through moralizing lectures.

Yet there are so many moments in the practice of challenging work where values, ethical questions, or connections of self to tradition emerge naturally, with consequences, and ripe for thoughtful consideration. When I visited high school or community college CTE classes, I frequently witnessed students measuring themselves against a model or a craft tradition or their own best work. Sometimes their concerns were about function, but at other times they were bothered by the look of their work. These concerns about craftsmanship were powerfully motivating; typical was a young man carefully repairing a tiny seam in the base of a bookcase that would not be visible once the case was upright. It was also common that such revision of one's work would conflict with the demands of production: doing a job well versus doing it fast. Such conflicts took one quickly to issues of job structure, the tensions of employment, and economics.

The early architects of VocEd wiped many of these concerns from the curriculum, and vocational education has been pretty anemic on topics of meaning and identity, tradition and ethics, values, and relationships. The tragedy here is that young people are at the stage where they're realizing how important work will be in their lives, how it will frame who they are and what they can do in the world. They are desperate to be somebody, to possess agency and competence, to have a grasp on the forces that affect them. This desire creates the conditions for an education with multiple meanings that extends beyond the programmatic and economic to include social issues.

CONCLUSION

It is difficult to teach creatively in the intersection of the academic and the vocational. It involves the delicate negotiation of turf and subject-area status, which sparks teachers' suspicions and self-protection—the touchy personnel dimension of the academic-vocational split. Then there is the bureaucratic dimension: the finessing of work rules, curriculum frameworks, and district guidelines. And there is the crossing of disciplinary boundaries and culturally sanctioned domains of knowledge, something that the typical undergraduate curriculum and teacher education program does not prepare one to do. Thus, even the most willing teacher is hampered by traditional vocabularies and definitions and status dynamics that make it so hard, for example, to articulate—and then to teach—the cognitive and aesthetic dimensions of manual skill.

It *is* difficult. It means developing classroom activities that represent the authentic knowledge and intellectual demands of the workplace and, conversely, bringing academic content to life through occupational tasks and simulations. It means that the house or the automobile could be the core of a rich, integrated curriculum: one that includes social and technical history, science and economics, and hands-on assembly and repair. It means learning about new subjects and making unfamiliar connections: the historian investigating the health care or travel industry, or the machinist engaging the humanities. It means fostering not only basic mathematical skill, but also an appreciation of mathematics, a mathematical sensibility, through the particulars of the print shop, the restaurant, the hospital lab. It also means seeking out the many literate possibilities running through young people's lives—on the street, in church, in romance—and connecting them to the language of the stage, the poem, but the tech manual, too, and the contract, and the Bill of Rights. Of course, such teaching might well mean providing instruction in "basic skills," but in a manner that puts the skill in context, considers its purpose, and pushes toward meaning beyond rote performance.

Teachers who accept this challenge are well rewarded. "It's the most powerful thing," says one teacher, "that I've ever done in education." While these educational reforms can involve all children, I am impressed by the special meaning they have for students who are not on the educational fast track. This kind of teaching is significantly different from that found in established policy documents that describe these young people with the language of practicality and preparation, inflected with a sense of their limitation. There is little sense of promise, of the excitement of cognitive and civic development. What's lacking is a deeper, richer, more involving orientation toward working people and their children, akin to a fundamental political commitment or article of educational faith.

What's required is a belief in the kind of human potential that enables social movements, the extraordinary emergence of agency and strategy where little was thought possible. It is noteworthy, in this regard, that voter registration activist Bob Moses developed his program to teach algebra to children in poor communities from his political organizing experience. In the same way that the civil rights movement assumed that all people are capable of political deliberation and participation, the Algebra Project assumes that everyone—absent brain damage—is capable of understanding the conceptual fundamentals of algebra. "How can a culture be created," write Moses and his colleagues, "in . . . which every child is expected to be as good as possible in his or her mathematical development?"[8]

In the early days of debate over vocational education, compelling voices articulated a belief in the capacity of the common person and connected education to an egalitarian vision of human and cultural development. John Dewey, Jane Addams, and other academics and state-level committee members pressed this view. But this view of mass education was erased from final policy. It needs to be reclaimed, for it is so pertinent now. This reclamation could end up being a defining and potent feature of Multiple Pathways reforms.

Without such bedrock beliefs and commitments, we will never comprehensively revitalize CTE, or bridge the academic-vocational divide, or create a diversity of fresh and engaging courses of study that provide substantial pathways through and beyond high school. We will continue to take good ideas and squander them, dumb them down, trivialize them, for the beliefs about intelligence and the social order that underlie a curriculum are as important as the content of the curriculum itself. It is at this point that democratic principles and educational practice become one, an act of intellectual and civic realization. Thus, those teachers who do work diligently at the breach between the academic and the vocational are engaged in a kind of applied political philosophy. They challenge the culture's assumptions about hand and brain, and the rigid system of educational theory and method that emerged from them, making the schoolhouse more truly democratic by honoring the fundamental intelligence of a broad range of human activity.

CHAPTER 2

Evidence and Challenges

Will Multiple Pathways Improve Students' Outcomes?

David Stern and Roman Stearns

David Stern is an economist and professor of education at the University of California–Berkeley. In addition to his research on the relationship between education and work, Stern has served as vice chair of the faculty committee that sets admissions policy for the University of California, as director of the National Center for Research in Vocational Education, and as principal administrator in the Center for Educational Research and Innovation at the Organization for Economic Cooperation and Development in Paris. Roman Stearns is director for policy analysis and development at ConnectEd: California's Center for College and Career, and he has served as special assistant to the director of admissions at the University of California. In that position, Stearns worked with schools to design academically rigorous career-technical education curricula that meet the college preparatory course requirements for admission to California's public universities.

For this volume, Stern and Stearns review empirical studies of programs blending career and technical education with academic coursework. They conclude that such programs can enhance motivation in school and increase employment and earnings after high school, without reducing high school completion or college enrollment. However, they also warn that Multiple Pathways must overcome both systemic and programmatic challenges, including the complexities of limited time and course scheduling, if it is to make college an option for more high school students. They propose that Multiple Pathways, characterized by choice

and opportunity, would allow for various ways of combining college and
work or alternating between them.

OVERVIEW

Combining college preparation and career-related learning is not a new idea.
Federal legislation in the 1990s encouraged states and localities to "integrate"
academic and vocational education, and such integration continues to have
appeal. Increasingly, reformers are exploring whether a combined academic
and career-technical approach can make college an option for greater numbers of students. This chapter discusses the potential benefits of and barriers
to this combined strategy and suggests strategies for moving forward.

In the first section of this paper, we explain why blending academic coursework with career-technical education (CTE) could make college an option for
more high school students. This integration is one among several possible
kinds of pathways that could serve that purpose. In the second section, we
briefly review research on combining academic coursework with CTE. Getting clear-cut findings has been difficult because most studies have not determined whether apparent effects are due to particular programs or to selection
of particular kinds of students into those programs.

In California, the high school courses required for admission to public
universities are spelled out in a list known as "A through G" (A–G). The A–G
courses must be approved by the University of California (UC). Since 2000,
the UC has been helping high schools understand how to get CTE courses
approved as courses that fulfill the A–G requirement. The third section of this
paper describes some of these approved courses and the process by which UC
approves courses proposed by high schools.

In the fourth section, we explain some of the obstacles to curricular integration posed by the California Education Code, teacher credentialing, and
other regulatory requirements. We will conclude with recommendations for
meeting these challenges, in order to create combinations of courses that
prepare students for college *and* careers.

WHY COMBINE ACADEMIC AND CAREER-
TECHNICAL EDUCATION IN HIGH SCHOOL?

Everyone knows that college graduates on average earn substantially more
money than high school graduates, who in turn make substantially more
than high school dropouts. The professional and managerial jobs that require

bachelor's or advanced degrees also offer nonmonetary benefits, including prestige, comfortable working conditions, and greater autonomy. So it is no wonder that the vast majority of high school students say they aspire to complete a bachelor's or advanced degree, and their parents express similar aspirations for them.

Vocational education, on the other hand, has traditionally been defined as a pathway that does not lead to a bachelor's or advanced degree. The original Smith-Hughes Act of 1917, which provided the first federal grants for vocational education, clearly stipulated that the "purpose of such education shall be to fit for useful employment; that such education shall be of less than college grade." Reauthorizations of the federal law continued to distinguish vocational education from college preparation. The 1998 Perkins Act defined vocational and technical education as "a sequence of courses that provides individuals with the academic and technical knowledge and skills the individuals need to prepare for further education and for careers (other than careers requiring a baccalaureate, master's, or doctoral degree)." The 2006 reauthorization of the Perkins Act finally removed this restriction, opening the possibility for creating more programs that combine CTE with preparation for college.

Because the traditional purpose of vocational education was to prepare students for work and not for college, students aspiring to achieve a bachelor's or advanced degree would logically avoid CTE in high school. Indeed, students who go directly from high school to a four-year college or university tend to take fewer vocational classes in high school.[1] As college-going rates increased during the twentieth century, vocational course-taking rates declined. Some have argued that CTE should be allowed to disappear from high schools altogether, leaving community colleges as the main providers of CTE.

But career-technical educators rightly point out that most high school students still do not go on to complete bachelor's or advanced degrees. Although 80 to 90 percent of high school students say they want to get a bachelor's or advanced degree, only about 30 to 35 percent actually get one. As of March 2004, the Current Population Survey found only 30.2 percent of 25- to 34-year-olds had completed bachelor's or advanced degrees. An additional 8.8 percent had completed associate degrees, while another 19.3 percent had some college but no degree.[2] Given the gradual rate at which the percentage of bachelor's or advanced degree completers has grown over recent decades, it will probably take decades before they become a majority of 25- to 34-year-olds.

To address the enormous gap between college aspirations and actual college completion, three different but overlapping strategies can be distinguished. The first, college for all, is constrained by the capacity of the labor market to absorb such large numbers of degree holders. The second, tracking, is the much-discredited policy of matching students' educational programs (often at an early age) with their purported intelligence or likely destination in broader social and economic landscape. The classic tracking approach is to separate students into college *or* vocational pathways. A third policy strategy, college as an *option* for all (broadly referred to in this chapter as Multiple Pathways), has the potential for capturing the democratic power and rigorous learning of college for all and avoiding the inevitable dysfunctions and abuses of curriculum tracking.

Those arguing for college for all assert that the country needs a lot more college graduates in order to remain competitive in the global economy. The strategy calls for raising academic expectations for all students in high school, so that many more will be prepared to succeed in college and graduate with bachelor's degrees.

Raising academic achievement is indisputably desirable for a number of reasons, including preparation of adults who are more capable of participating in civic life and understanding public issues. However, the economic rationale of college for all is not compelling. A rapid increase in the number of new college graduates will tend to reduce the earnings advantage associated with a college degree. As a result, college will become a less attractive investment, and fewer high school students will choose to attend. This happened in the 1970s, after large numbers of college-educated baby boomers flooded the labor market.[3] A 2006 study found that states in which the supply of college graduates expanded during the 1990s also experienced a reduction in graduates' relative earnings.[4] There is a limit to how many college graduates the market will absorb. The current rate of return to college is high enough to warrant some increase in the number of college graduates. But pushing the bachelor's degree completion rate to 100 percent would not make economic sense. Even 50 percent would be an ambitious 20-year target.

For the next couple of decades at least, it is realistic to expect that no more than half of high school students actually will go on to complete bachelor's or advanced degrees. High schools have to deal with the fact that most students will not complete college, even though the students sincerely aspire to do so.

A second policy strategy is tracking. If college for all is not feasible in the foreseeable future, then high schools can offer one set of courses for students who are academically inclined and a different curriculum for the non-college-bound. The 1917 Smith-Hughes Act was part of the development of separate curricular tracks in U.S. high schools. By various means, students were assigned to different course sequences, the main ones being vocational, academic, and "general."[5]

However, tracking was eventually discredited as unfair and wasteful. It is unfair because, as many studies have shown, students assigned to the noncollege tracks tend to be less affluent, less likely to have parents who attended college, and more likely to belong to racial, ethnic, or linguistic minorities who are traditionally underrepresented in higher education. Tracking also is wasteful because students in noncollege tracks are given less challenging coursework, and therefore do not develop their academic and intellectual capabilities as much as they would if they were challenged and motivated. For these reasons, counselors, administrators, and school boards grew uncomfortable saying they practiced tracking. Explicit forms of tracking became less widespread in the latter decades of the twentieth century, though tracking has persisted in less obvious ways.[6]

In the 1980s, influential representatives of the nation's employers began to point out the inefficiency of tracking. They complained that graduates from high school vocational programs lacked the academic knowledge and thinking skills to participate in the newly emerging economy, where incessant change requires continual learning and problem solving.[7] Employers had been the most politically important backers of vocational education since its inception, so these statements had a decisive effect on the debate in Congress when the federal law authorizing support for vocational education came up for its periodic renewal.

The 1990 amendments to the Carl Perkins Act shifted the direction of vocational education, requiring that the basic federal grant to the states for vocational education be spent only on programs that "integrate academic and vocational education." This idea was subsequently reinforced and elaborated by the 1994 School-to-Work Opportunities Act, though that law expired in 1999 and was not renewed. The 1998 amendments to the Carl Perkins Act again mandated "integration of academics with vocational and technical education programs through a coherent sequence of courses to ensure learning in the core academic, and vocational and technical subjects" (section 135(b)(1)).

A third strategy thus presents itself: college as an *option* for all—or at least for greater numbers of students. While recognizing that most high school students will not complete bachelor's degrees, this strategy aims to avoid both the waste and the unfairness of tracking. Like college for all, this third strategy aims for *all* students to complete a set of academic courses that prepares them to succeed in a four-year college or university. At the same time, high schools would offer a variety of pathways designed to accommodate students' diverse interests and methods of learning. Among these multiple pathways, some would offer a set of challenging CTE courses combined with college-preparatory academic coursework.

A college-as-an-option-for-all strategy enables students to pursue various sequences of schooling and work. Students who take a concentration of high school CTE coursework could go directly to a bachelor's degree program and earn more money "on the side" to support their college participation. Others would enter two-year colleges, postsecondary vocational training, or full-time work—but they all would have completed the academic prerequisites to enter a bachelor's degree program later on, if they so choose. Students' options and choices might be responses to developing aspirations, career opportunities, long-term economic and job market shifts, and more. Meanwhile, those who entered bachelor's programs immediately after high school, but who do not complete their degrees, could turn to alternative options if they gained work-related knowledge and skill in their high school CTE. This strategy therefore allows for the various ways of combining college and work, or alternating between them, that characterize the American system.

IS THERE EVIDENCE THAT COMBINING ACADEMIC AND CAREER-TECHNICAL LEARNING IN HIGH SCHOOL IMPROVES PREPARATION FOR COLLEGE?

Pathways that blend academic and career-technical learning could prepare students for work while avoiding a tracked system that does not prepare students to enter college. To accomplish this, blending CTE with college preparation should mean that students pursue both at the same time, rather than making an irrevocable decision by choosing one or the other.

Overlapping the content of academic and CTE courses can enable students to see applications of academic subject matter outside of school, which may increase students' motivation, understanding, and retention of concepts. This has been part of the rationale for integrating academic and career-technical coursework.[8] However, research to date has not yet produced conclusive evidence about the extent to which blended programs increase college-going and degree completion. A number of correlational studies have produced positive findings, but other explanations confound these findings, as we will explain.

Correlational Studies

Several studies have looked at outcomes for high school students who take a sequence of CTE courses along with a college-preparatory academic curriculum. The first such study, in 1989, discovered a positive interaction between the number of academic courses and the number of vocational courses in predicting post-high school earnings for males who did not attend college, but this study did not measure effects on college attendance.[9] A subsequent study found, four years after high school, that individuals who had completed both an advanced academic and a vocational sequence in high school had the greatest likelihood of being employed in professional, managerial, or skilled jobs—and the greatest likelihood of being enrolled in postsecondary education.[10]

Two studies have analyzed achievement test results. One found that students who combined a college-preparatory academic curriculum with a specific vocational sequence had gains in math, reading, and science test scores during high school that were similar to the gains of students who took only the college-prep curriculum—and both of these groups gained substantially more than other students.[11] A second study (a National Education Longitudinal Study, or NELS) analyzed the same data and found similar results when comparing *average* gains, but looked at more closely, the study showed that the academics-only group had significantly higher gains than students the study's authors called "dual concentrators." Further, these dual concentrators also started at a lower level in grade 8, so they fell further behind the academic-only group during high school.[12]

The latter study also tested whether course-taking patterns were associated with dropping out of high school. Overall, a higher ratio of CTE credits to academic credits was associated with a smaller chance of dropping out. Extrapolating this result to its logical conclusion would imply that replacing all academic courses with CTE courses would minimize the dropout rate. To preclude this implication, further analysis suggests that an optimal balance of CTE and academic courses could be achieved: A ratio of three CTE courses for every four academic courses would minimize the likelihood of dropping out, other things equal.[13] Finally, the finding that dropouts tend to take relatively fewer CTE classes does not, in itself, mean that more CTE courses will prevent dropping out. Because more CTE course-taking generally occurs in grades 11 and 12 than in grades 9 and 10, many dropouts have not stayed in high school long enough to take as many vocational classes as students who stay.

Correlational studies such as these do not provide clear evidence of whether (or why) different kinds of curriculum produce different results because the students who take different kinds of courses do not have comparable characteristics or prior experiences. For instance, students who do not like academic subjects are presumably more likely to drop out of high school and more likely to take CTE classes.[14] Students who combine a strong academic curriculum with an occupational sequence perform better both at school and at work, but these students may start high school already possessing more confidence, self-discipline, or awareness of what it takes to do well in the world. They may have had teachers with more or fewer skills or qualifications, have been in larger or smaller classes, or had other advantages. Since the available data do not include good measures of many individual student characteristics and prior educational opportunities or experiences, correlational studies may be misleading. Despite attempts to finesse these problems and rid the data of bias due to unmeasured differences among students, findings do not inspire much confidence in the possibility of reaching clear conclusions about cause and effect from correlational studies.

Program Evaluations without Random Assignment of Students

Correlational studies provide information about naturally occurring variation in the types of courses students take. Somewhat stronger evidence about the effects of combining academic and vocational coursework in high schools comes from evaluations of programs that include a planned mix of academic coursework and CTE. The largest program of this kind is High Schools That Work (HSTW), a network launched in 1987 to raise academic achievement by blending a rigorous academic curriculum with vocational studies.[15] The network had grown to more than 1,200 high schools in 2006.[16] Since its inception, HSTW has used standardized tests based on the National Assessment of Educational Progress to monitor the achievement of CTE completers, and has shown positive trends based on comparisons of successive cohorts of students. However, these data cannot be used to measure growth of a given group of students over time, or to compare progress of students in HSTW with non-HSTW students.

Another common program of this kind is known as a career academy. Career academies organize a college-preparatory curriculum around a work-related theme such as health, business and finance, arts and communications, information technology, engineering, or law and government.[17] Starting in Philadelphia in 1969, the career academy model has been widely replicated; approximately 2,000 career academies now exist in U.S. high schools. Key features of career academies are:

1. School-within-a-school organization, in which academy students at each grade level take a set of classes together, staying with the same small group of teachers for at least two years
2. Curriculum that includes academic courses meeting college entrance requirements, along with CTE classes, all related to the academy theme
3. Employer partnerships to provide internships and other experiences outside the classroom, related to the academy theme[18]

Because the career model is relatively well defined, and examples have existed now for more than three decades, it has been possible to compare changes over time between career academy students and similar students (not in a career academy) in the same high schools. Between 1985 and 2000, six different researchers or research teams used longitudinal data from different sets of academies to make such comparisons.[19] None of these studies assigned students at random to the academy or nonacademy groups. Most researchers used statistical regression techniques to control for some observed differences between academy and nonacademy students. In some studies the researchers and teachers chose each comparison student individually to match one of the academy students.

All these studies reported academy students performing significantly better than comparison students while in high school. Post-high school differences in further education and employment have been less consistent, but where significant differences have been found, they have favored the academy students. Although these studies statistically controlled for measured differences between academy and nonacademy students, the possibility remains that unobserved differences account for the results. For example, there might be a systematic tendency for career academies to attract more-motivated or better-organized students. In addition, innovative educational programs also may attract more-motivated teachers and administrators.

Program Evaluations Using Random Assignment of Students

The classic method for eliminating bias due to selection or self-selection is for researchers to use a random procedure to assign some subjects to the treatment group and the others to the control group. This procedure ensures that the average difference between the two groups—on both observed and unobserved variables—will be negligible, given a large enough sample. Despite this great advantage, there are well-known drawbacks and limitations to using random assignment in educational field studies. Denying a beneficial treatment to a control group may raise ethical questions. Some important educational variables (e.g., completing high school) cannot be experimentally manipulated. Even when random assignment is feasible and ethical, absence of a placebo means that Hawthorne effects and other biases may influence the result. Nevertheless, a well-designed random-assignment study can eliminate the problem of initial selection bias that plagues much educational research.[20]

In 1993, researchers at MDRC (founded as Manpower Demonstration Research Corporation) began a random-assignment evaluation of career academies at ten sites. The nine remaining academies were in high schools with large proportions of low-income and minority students. Each was the only career academy in its high school. At the start of the MDRC evaluation, the academies recruited more applicants than they could accommodate. Applicants knew they might not be admitted. MDRC randomly assigned about two-thirds of the applicants to the academy; the others became the control group. For more than 10 years since the evaluation began, MDRC has collected student records, surveyed students during each of their high school years, and conducted follow-up surveys one year and four years after high school.

During the high school years, the career academies studied by MDRC produced several positive impacts on students' experience and achievement. Compared to the control group, academy students reported receiving more support from teachers and from other students.[21] They were more likely to combine academic and technical courses, engage in career development activities, and work in jobs connected to school.[22] As of spring of senior year, academies retained a larger fraction of the students whose initial characteristics made them more likely to drop out.[23] Among students at less risk of dropping out, academies increased participation in CTE courses and career development activities without reducing academic course credits.[24]

The first follow-up survey, one year after scheduled graduation, found no significant impacts on students' high school completion, GED acquisition, or participation in postsecondary schooling. It also showed no significant impact on employment or earnings, though students who had been assigned to career academies were working and earning somewhat more than the control group.[25]

MDRC's second follow-up, about four years after scheduled graduation from high school, found large and significant impacts on employment and earnings, and no difference in educational attainment.[26] In the full sample, students assigned to career academies earned higher hourly wages, worked more hours per week, had more months of employment, and earned about 10 percent more per month than the control group. All these differences occurred for both males and females, but they were not statistically significant for females. Impacts on high school completion or postsecondary education were not significantly positive or negative for the sample as a whole or for any subgroup, but the researchers note that both the academy and control groups had high rates of high school completion and postsecondary enrollment compared to national (NELS) data on urban high school students.

In sum, the most recent results available from MDRC indicate that students who *applied* to the career academies had high college-going rates, whether or not they actually *participated* in the academies. There was no statistically significant difference in college-going between academy participants and the control group. However, graduates from the career academies did earn significantly more money than the control group. In other words, the benefit from career academies occurred in the labor market, not in further education, but the labor market gains also did not come at the expense of academy students' further educational attainment.

Apart from the MDRC evaluation of career academies, only one other study has used random assignment to test the effects of combining academic instruction with CTE.[27] This was a more limited intervention than the career academies, which represent a multiyear pathway involving much of a student's high school curriculum. The Stone study focused on individual CTE classes as settings in which to improve students' performance in one academic subject, namely, mathematics. A total of 134 CTE teachers took part in the study: 60 were randomly assigned to the experimental group, and the remaining 74 were the control group. Each CTE teacher in the experiment partnered with a math teacher from the same high school. The treatment consisted of bringing together the CTE teachers in each of five disciplines— agriculture, auto technology, business/marketing, health, and information technology—with their math teacher partners to identify mathematical content embedded in the CTE discipline and develop lesson plans to teach the math in the occupational context. All students in the experimental and control classrooms were given pre- and post-tests in math. After one year, students in the experimental classrooms scored significantly higher on Terra-Nova and Accuplacer math tests, though there was no significant difference in performance on the math portion of WorkKeys, which assesses less advanced skills. These findings demonstrate that it is possible to provide professional development for teachers that lead to improved math achievement by students in CTE classrooms. Such professional development could be part of a strategy to make college an option for more students by combining academic and career-technical instruction.

SATISFYING UNIVERSITY ENTRANCE REQUIREMENTS WITH COURSES THAT COMBINE ACADEMIC AND TECHNICAL CONTENT: THE EXAMPLE OF CALIFORNIA

In California, the 1960 Master Plan for Higher Education directed the University of California (UC) to draw from the top 12.5 percent of high school graduates, and the California State University (CSU) system to draw from the top one-third. To qualify for admissions at either UC or CSU, a student must complete a specific sequence of courses, known as the "A through G" requirements: (a) history/social science; (b) English; (c) mathematics; (d) laboratory science; (e) language other than English; (f) visual and performing arts; and (g) college-preparatory electives. Courses must be completed with a grade of C or better.[28] Currently, about 30 percent of California high school graduates satisfy the A–G course requirements. Making higher education an option for significantly larger numbers of students in California means enabling more students to meet these course requirements, which are similar to those of four-year institutions of higher education in other states.

If the strategy to increase college-going involves combining college-prep academic classes with a CTE sequence, it becomes advantageous to maximize the overlap between the content and time spent learning academic and CTE coursework. This overlap has a pedagogical rationale: A blended program might motivate more students to study academic subjects and might improve their understanding through application to practical contexts.

A second reason is logistical: Students' time is limited. On a typical high school schedule, taking six courses a year for four years, a student would complete 24 year-long courses. The minimum course requirements for UC and CSU eligibility amount to 15 of those 24; the "recommended" sequence for UC includes 18 year-long courses. Gaining competitive advantage for admission to the most competitive UC and CSU campuses may dictate that students take more than the 18 courses. Successful CTE-academic programs should seek to attract a representative proportion of these most college-competitive students. A CTE sequence of one course per year adds another four. That should be possible to accomplish in theory, but in practice the complexities of high school scheduling, along with other requirements like physical education and health, can make this difficult or impossible. However, if one or more of the CTE courses can satisfy a university requirement (or vice versa), the scheduling problem diminishes.

University of California Approval of High School Courses

Unlike other state university systems, UC actively reviews individual course descriptions from each public and private high school in the state to determine whether a course meets faculty guidelines and thus satisfies one of the A–G requirements. Every public and private California high school that is accredited by (or affiliated with) the Western Association of Schools and Colleges maintains a list of UC-approved courses.[29] The list is used in counseling prospective students and in admissions reviews of applicants to UC.

The fundamental purpose of the A–G requirements is to ensure that potential university students are prepared for university-level coursework.

Recognizing that UC is primarily an academic institution, the guidelines for course approval reflect that mission and focus on preparation in academic subject areas, rather than career-technical areas. However, CTE courses can be approved to satisfy A–G requirements. UC recognizes that some high schools have reformed their curricular paths and integrated higher-level academics into their career-technical courses in order to simultaneously prepare students for college and careers. In the past few years UC has accepted an increasing number and broader range of applied academic courses in subject areas including agriculture, business and finance, engineering, media and entertainment, and health and bioscience. According to an October 2007 report by the California Department of Education,[30] more than 5,600 career-technical courses have been approved for A–G credit, representing over 20 percent of all CTE courses offered at California public high schools.

UC approval of larger numbers of CTE courses has been the result, in part, of UC's own A–G Guide Project,[31] which was launched in 2000 to (1) provide high school educators with more and better information about the UC A–G subject area requirements and the course approval process; (2) offer a broad range of tools, resources, and professional development to assist schools in designing courses that meet the A–G criteria; and (3) clarify UC policy and streamline UC procedures for approving courses that meet the requirements.

As a result of this project and other initiatives, high school educators increasingly have integrated academic and CTE content to create courses that are both academically deep and personally relevant to students. Courses that integrate CTE are approved only if they make teaching of the academic concepts central to technical understanding. For example, UC has accepted courses in sports medicine that require biology as a prerequisite, focus substantially on anatomy and physiology, revolve around the understanding of body systems, and use science texts to drive acquisition of scientific knowledge. Similarly titled courses have not been approved if they prioritize first aid and injury prevention and treatment, are organized around body parts (rather than systems), and use technical manuals with limited scientific teaching.

In the visual arts, UC has accepted many design courses (e.g., graphic, architectural, fashion, furniture) as well as some courses in video/film production, digital media, and animation. An acceptable architectural design course, for example, would accentuate the art in architecture. It would emphasize knowledge of architectural styles across cultures and historical periods. A student's work products would grow from understanding the elements of art and principles of design and enable students to replicate ancient and modern structures and express their own ideas through architectural sketches, designs, and models, perhaps using a variety of media. Students also would be expected to critique architectural designs using appropriate vocabulary. In contrast, courses that focus primarily on the technical aspects of architecture, such as building codes, materials, and costs, would not be approved.

UC approval of CTE courses for A–G credit is a hurdle in a strategy that would make college an option for greater numbers of students in California. However, UC approval of larger numbers of CTE courses indicates that the UC is moving in a direction that could ease these concerns. In spring 2008, the UC faculty committee that is responsible for formulating the A–G requirements approved new criteria for the elective (G) requirement that explicitly include CTE courses for the first time.

BARRIERS TO CURRICULAR INTEGRATION AND HOW TO OVERCOME THEM

In the twentieth century, educators, legislators, and public perceptions sharply distinguished academic from vocational education, or college preparation from career preparation. We have postulated that preparing larger numbers of students for college will require Multiple Pathways, including a blend of academic and career-technical coursework. Such a change faces systemic and programmatic challenges.

Systemic Challenges

The separation between academic education and CTE is written into existing law. The California Education Code and the regulations of various educational agencies fund these programs from different sources, maintain distinct facilities, follow different sets of curricular standards, and require different kinds of credentialing procedures for academic and CTE teachers. Until California's Education Code is changed, the state will continue to incur the social and economic consequences of operating dual—and dueling—systems of education.

Let us start with an example. Suppose a high school wanted to combine a physics course with auto mechanics, so that students taking physics would see how theories and formulas are applied in the world outside school, and students taking auto mechanics would understand the underlying physics of automotive technology. An immediate challenge would be finding teachers who possess the knowledge and skills to offer this kind of integrated course. The typical physics teacher has gone from high school to college and back to high school again, learning physics and then teaching it in a primarily abstract and theoretical way without experience in its practical applications. The auto shop teacher typically comes out of private industry with substantial experience under the hood, but little theoretical knowledge of physics.

The teacher credentialing requirements for teachers of core academic subjects differ significantly from those for the majority of career-technical teachers.[32] These differing requirements tend to produce teachers who have expertise to teach either the theoretical underpinnings of a core academic subject (e.g., physics) or the practical applications of it (e.g., auto mechanics), but rarely both.

Instead of collaborating, teachers may feel they have to battle one another in order to preserve their programs, retain their funding, gain prestige, or protect their educational beliefs and philosophies. They may not realize that both their favored disciplines' and their students' success may lie in discarding the existing paradigm and embracing a new way to educate youth that may be more effective.

Current accountability policies, based on tests in academic subjects, put pressure on CTE teachers to beef up the academic content of their courses. This may be an incentive to collaborate with their academic colleagues, but there is no corresponding pressure on teachers of academic subjects to link their courses with CTE. The main priority for high schools now is to address state content standards, meet state targets measured by Academic Performance Index and federal targets defined by Adequate Yearly Progress, and get students to pass the California High School Exit Exam. CTE teachers are getting requests, often demands, to incorporate the academic content standards into their CTE courses in a more significant way.

In 2002 the California legislature passed a law (AB 1412) mandating the California Department of Education to develop distinct CTE standards, which the State Board of Education approved in 2005. These standards are intended to clarify and legitimate what is taught in CTE courses. They give CTE teachers something to stand on. But since they are not included in the state and federal accountability measures that currently drive high schools, the CTE standards are irrelevant from the standpoint of academic teachers. Separate sets of academic and CTE standards reinforce the dual and dueling systems of education.

The systemic separation of academic education and CTE is embodied in procedures for collecting basic data about course offerings. The California Basic Education Data System (CBEDS) requires every public school to submit, each October, a broad range of data items, including the number of students enrolled in CTE, excluding Regional Occupational Centers/Programs.[33] CBEDS does not define CTE, but the presumption is that CTE courses are distinct from courses in academic subjects. Courses such as agricultural biology, engineering, journalism, architectural design, or photography may successfully combine academic and CTE content—and may even be approved by UC for A–G credit—but there is no way to designate such courses as integrated curriculum in CBEDS.

Despite the continuing systemic separation of academic and CTE curriculum, there is some promise of combining them. The new CTE standards include academic foundations, which suggests that schools should intentionally overlap academic and CTE curricula. As cited earlier, a 2007 California Department of Education report lists over 5,600 CTE courses approved to satisfy one of the A–G subject requirements.[34] The same report shows a dramatic increase of the A–G-approved CTE courses from year to year. Through the A–G Guide Project, UC continues to promote curricular integration. Another positive sign is the work of ConnectEd: The California Center for College and Career,[35] backed by the James Irvine Foundation.[36] ConnectEd is a statewide center that promotes the development of comprehensive programs of academic and technical study. Finally, the large and growing number of career academies and pathways in California high schools continues to provide settings in which to offer a planned mix of academic and CTE coursework.

Programmatic Challenges

Overcoming the systemic separation between academic and CTE curriculum will require changes in both policy and practice. Sometimes practices change first, prompting the reexamination of policy. We discuss two programmatic challenges to high schools combining academic and career-technical courses that prepare students for both college and careers.

The first challenge is the traditional high school's master schedule: the typically rigid grid that inflexibly locks in time units (such as a 55-minute class period) for instruction. Because most high school elective courses compete with one another for student enrollment, and priorities are given to "requirements" (e.g., mathematics, English, history, science, physical education), few class periods and little flexibility remain for elective courses (which may include foreign language, art, music, drama, dance, leadership, computer applications, computer programming, or the whole range of CTE options, from auto mechanics and engineering to floral design and video production). If a school limits students to the traditional six-period day, it is difficult to find time for a course sequence that meets college requirements and also includes a CTE sequence.

Some schools have tried to solve this problem by shifting to more creative and flexible schedules (e.g., 4x4 block schedule) that allow students to take up to eight courses per year, thereby significantly increasing the total number of courses they complete before graduation. If more California high schools used these scheduling options, more students would be able to prepare simultaneously for college and career.

A second programmatic challenge to blending academic-CTE course sequences in practice is the long-standing tradition of departmentalization. When high school teachers and courses are departmentalized (e.g., English, business, technology, science), often the curriculum of each course stands alone. Some courses are quite theoretical and abstract; others are more applied and practical. Too often, students are left to their own devices to see any connection between lessons learned in their English and business classes, or physics class and auto shop. Students may have the chance to take both academic and CTE courses, but rarely do teachers of these subjects coordinate the curriculum in a way that promotes connections between theory and practice.

Career academies and other pathway programs attempt to overcome this barrier by grouping a cohort of students and a team of teachers around a particular industry sector. They attempt to connect the career-technical and academic course content in a coordinated program that reaches across departmental boundaries. However, creating and sustaining a team of teachers, providing shared planning time, and scheduling groups of students to take a set of classes together all require substantial commitment on the part of school administrators, counselors, and faculty.

Team teaching offers another solution. Starting with the CTE course and trying to enhance the academic content may be the most natural approach, given the predominance of academic criteria in current accountability standards. An alternative approach, equally promising, would begin with an academic course and seek to build in related career-technical skills through a laboratory, practicum, or field study component. For example:

- A geometry course could use carpentry as a practical activity for students to gain a deeper understanding of geometric principles by solving real problems related to perpendicular and parallel lines and planes, area, volume, angles, and trigonometric functions.
- A psychology course could use a day-care center to examine how development theories related to cognition, language acquisition, learning, morality, and psychosocial and personality development play out among children at different stages of development.

This approach is likely to yield academically rigorous courses that satisfy an A–G subject requirement. However, beginning with an academic course may compromise a portion of the more specialized job-related skills that are customary in CTE.

CONCLUDING THOUGHTS

Blending high school academic and career-technical coursework in a coherent curriculum that prepares students for both college *and* careers is not a new idea.[37] All the specific programmatic options we have described here have been tried before. Yet the idea continues to have logical appeal as one that would make college an option for greater numbers of students, while recognizing that most students still do not complete bachelor's degrees. Several studies have found that students who combine academic coursework with CTE perform better in high school, but there is not yet much evidence about whether this kind of blended curriculum in high school improves the chances of college enrollment or completion. In sum, there are good reasons to try to expand the availability of integrated academic and career-technical curricula in high school, while recognizing the systemic and programmatic barriers—and making serious efforts to evaluate whether these options are producing the desired results.

CHAPTER 3

Meeting the Individual and Collective Aims of Schooling

Can Multiple Pathways as Small Schools Strike a Balance?[1]

Karen Hunter Quartz and Elliot Washor

Karen Hunter Quartz, a philosopher by training, is director of research at Center X at the University of California–Los Angeles and cofounder of the Los Angeles Small Schools Center. Elliot Washor is cofounder and codirector of The Big Picture Company, a nonprofit that creates and supports innovative, personalized schools where students blend classroom learning with real-world community experiences.

Quartz and Washor bring considerable expertise on small schools reform to their consideration of Multiple Pathways. They identify concepts central to the small schools movement—personalization, educational fit, and school theme—and discuss how these also are at the core of Multiple Pathways. They caution all reformers, including small schools and Multiple Pathways advocates that conflating personalization with choice can emphasize the differences among students rather than their commonalities. In this sense, the Multiple Pathways strategy to offer students curricular alternatives carries potential risks for students and society. Even if all the alternatives are designed to have high social, academic, and career value, over time they may replicate current patterns of sorting and segregation. With these risks in mind, Multiple Pathways, like small schools reforms, can emphasize strong and caring school cultures with high expectations for all students, treating all students as members of a collective that is grounded in the common good and the democratic purposes of schooling.

When we try to improve schools, we are trying to improve society. In both pursuits we struggle to accommodate the competing interests and values that lie at the heart of our liberal democratic, capitalist society. In this paper, we analyze the enduring tension between individual freedom and civic virtue relative to the current reform movement to create new small high schools. The small schools movement and the Multiple Pathways agenda are closely related. Both include a range of educational options that tie college-prep high school education to the broader enterprises of work, community, and civic life. We suggest that different small schools represent different pathways, each having its own local approach to rigorous and relevant education. The development of small schools as Multiple Pathways to college, career, and civic participation faces a number of challenges. We map out these challenges using three intersecting essential concepts from the small schools movement—personalization, educational fit, and school theme—that capture the struggle for individual liberty and the common good. We conclude that the Multiple Pathways agenda must proceed with caution and carefully attend to the dual aims of schooling.

FOUNDATIONS

The relationship between individual freedom and civic virtue[2] is both fundamental to our way of life and enormously complex, as evidenced by centuries of scholarship and political debate. At the nation's founding, John Adams warned that real liberty depends on "a positive passion for the public good,"[3] yet as Alexis de Tocqueville observed fifty years later, American individualism is a powerful "habit of the heart."[4] In 1971, John Rawls framed the tension in terms of the priority of the right over the good, mapping out how a theory of justice founded on individual liberty would best produce a just society.[5] Communitarians responded, appealing to Aristotle and arguing for the priority of virtuous communities in defining and shaping individuals. Versions of this foundational debate about the relationship between individuals and the common good rage across many disciplines, including education.

Education scholars grapple with the dual aims of schooling: enabling individual students to flourish while at the same time reproducing a stable and just social order. For instance, Amy Gutmann outlines a democratic ideal of education as conscious social reproduction, focusing on "practices of deliberate instruction by individuals and on the educative influences of institutions designed at least partly for educational purposes."[6] In the struggle to educate free individuals and reproduce a just society, schools have come up with a range of policies and practices. Some provoke little controversy nowadays, such as allowing students to take electives or requiring them to take civics. Others are contested as unjust, such as tracking or one-size-fits-all pedagogy. Bundling policies and practices into reform initiatives, such as the small schools movement, elucidates the struggle between freedom and civic virtue even further.

The current small schools movement has developed into a major national reform effort over the past decade, rooted in the success of small high schools (e.g., Central Park East, Urban Academy, The Met) that developed alternative educational structures and practices to the dominant factory model or "shopping mall" high school. These early small schools, and many that have developed since, are philosophically rooted in progressive education principles (e.g., the Coalition of Essential Schools' Ten Common Principles[7]). Spurred by an enormous influx of funding from the Gates Foundation, the movement has grown to include hundreds of new small high schools across the nation, some of which diverge from the original movement's progressive and participatory roots. At their core, however, most small schools attempt to use their size to personalize learning so each student is known well and supported to succeed.

The small schools movement grapples with the individual/collective tension in a unique way. On one hand, its attempts to make schools smaller and more personalized can foreground differences among students rather than their commonalities. In this sense, the small schools movement is driven by a Multiple Pathways agenda, in which students choose among a variety of small school alternatives to the traditional high school pathway, often integrating college and career preparation in schools organized by specialized themes. On the other hand, small schools use their size to build strong and caring small-school cultures with high expectations for all students, treating all students as members of a collective that shares democratic and social values, such as fairness, respect, and trust.

These two aims often clash. How can schools be both caring, supportive places where students learn to contribute to the common good and also specialized structures where students learn to individuate themselves and later find a place in adult society? In this chapter, we tackle this tough question by unpacking three concepts that lie at the heart of both the small schools movement and the Multiple Pathways agenda: personalization, educational fit, and school theme. Our aim in doing so is to situate small schools and their multiple pathways in the larger culture and history of school reform.

PERSONALIZATION

"A school worth going to makes you feel like you have a name and aren't just a number."[8] What is it about being known well that helps ensure a student's success in school? Here are two more reactions from students:

> There's nothing more important than a teacher believing in students and encouraging them. You don't know if parents are giving a kid this support. For me, what turned things around was when my teacher believed in me—and pushed me. "I know you're smart," she said. "I'm not going to let you fail, I'm not going to take no for an answer." (Juan)[9]

> The ability to choose what I want to do each year has been extremely important. . . . Because the curriculum is so specific to the individual student's personality and goals, it's important for teachers to know students pretty well to help develop learning plans that are acceptable to the students and the school's requirements. (Laura)[10]

What we look for in "personalization" are emotional support and intellectual engagement. The two students express different dimensions of these qualities. Juan's response reflects the emotional benefits of knowing students well, benefits rooted both in our human need to belong and feel valued and in society's norms about success and achievement: Work hard, don't give up, and expect a lot from yourself and those around you. Laura's response speaks to something different: knowing students as learners with unique interests. Laura's teachers and mentors help her find and express personal significance by leading her to ask critical questions: Where do I fit in this world? What is my life's work? What makes me feel passionate, fulfilled, or happy? Laura's teachers and mentors know her well so they can help steer and deepen her learning, not just press her, by name, to work hard.

In small schools, educators strive to develop close relationships with their students to accomplish both aims of personalization. In contrast, the division of labor between counseling and teaching in traditional high schools, along with a number of factors (e.g., high counselor-to-student ratios and class size), act against any form of personalization. In large schools, personal relationships with teachers tend to be happenstance, unconnected to the school's mission, and occur only at the margins of school. Small schools are designed with structures for both emotional support and intellectual engagement. For instance, in many small schools, small groups of students meet regularly with the same advisor. These advisory sessions are consistent with

Nel Noddings's "ethic of care."[11] Oakes and Lipton characterize a caring class-room relationship as a "search for competence":

> The student's search is his own discovery of what he knows and how he knows it. The teacher's search—an act of care and respect—is also discovering what the student knows and how he knows it. The teacher expresses caring by searching for the child's competence.[12]

Searching for competence is shared work in which student and teacher are emotionally and intellectually engaged.

To illustrate the challenge and aims of personalization, we consider the example of William, a recent graduate of MetWest, a small school in Oakland, California, which is part of a national network of Big Picture schools.[13] Students work closely with school advisors and community mentors to personalize rigorous and relevant learning plans that are based on Learning Through Internship (LTI) and travel opportunities, all situated within a community of learners.

> As a ninth grader, William interned at KDOL TV of the Oakland Unified School District, where he was invited to pursue his deep interest in filmmaking. A combination of William's interest and his mentor's real-world need for a creative product resulted in William's writing, directing, photographing, and editing several documentary videos that aired on KDOL.
>
> Later that year, William's mom passed away, and he struggled to stay connected to school. His relationships and his work at MetWest helped keep William engaged and moving forward in spite of his hardships. School staff worked closely with William, his mentor, and his adoptive parents. Together, they developed a learning plan that included the adults, tools, and learning opportunities William needed to continue. Being an independent thinker and doer, William was given more independent work time. In return, he provided detailed analysis and evidence of how he spent it.
>
> William contributed to the community in a manner most beneficial to him. Instead of participating in student government or peer tutoring, William created the first MetWest video. He also taught other students how to build an Aboriginal didgeridoo.
>
> In the tenth grade, and his second LTI, William brought together his interests in cars, arts, and science. He inquired into how different gases affect the quality of the welding process, the mathematics of automobile gears, the effect that auto racing technology has had on street car technology, and the highly technical workings of automotive brake and electrical systems. Over the next three years, William's mentors helped him bring the

shell of a 1950 Volvo race car back to life. During this time he studied aerodynamics, torque, and gearing ratios, and he researched the history of racing in the fuller context of United States history. His mentors directed him to Laney College to enroll in physics and math classes. At MetWest, William's growth was measured over four years with consistent observations by the same adults. Through Big Picture's work with the Board of Admissions of the University of California, MetWest received "A–G course approval" for its work with students in alternative settings, including internships. As a result, William completed his nontraditional personalized learning plan and attends UC Irvine, where he studies engineering.

William's story points to several structures that facilitate emotional support and intellectual engagement, structures that depart radically from the history and culture of traditional high schools. Through internships, students and adults are able to work together on something they both care about. These shared activities allow students to see the connections between interests, work, and the larger world. Another structure for personalization is the role of Big Picture advisors: adults who are prepared for and committed to knowing students well and are guided by a rigorous, individualized learning plan. The advisor-student relationship is artful, with its own aesthetic that helps define the emotional and intellectual value of personalization. Finally, without a structure in place to translate William's nontraditional learning into useful educational capital, personalization would be an unproductive and unkind endeavor, ultimately denying students access to college.

EDUCATIONAL FIT

> Students learn in different ways; their schools should teach in different ways. In this new landscape, schools may have different emphases, teaching approaches, or philosophies, but they will all prepare every student for college. In a system with a diverse portfolio of schools, *every student will fit at least one school* [emphasis added].[14]

This perspective grounds a particular approach to small school reform that we will call "the portfolio agenda"—an agenda that differs in important respects (detailed later) from the original effort to create small schools two decades ago. According to the portfolio agenda, students fit into schools, not the other way around. This view of fit helps explain why reforms like small schools and Multiple Pathways appeal to many people: The prospect for a finer-grained universe of schooling options seems to offer better matches between schools and groups or categories of students (e.g., by interest, "learning style," career). This school-based notion of educational fit suggests the school itself personalizes education. Its focus, theme, organization, or goal reaches out to engage groups of students who already have something in common. The Gates Foundation, for example, prescribes three categories to define these commonalities: traditional, theme-based, and student-centered small schools.[15] Students, they assume, fit into at least one of these categories, but how? For instance, do students fit into student-centered small schools by virtue of being students—learners in the broadest sense—in contrast to traditional college-bound students or arts- or business-focused students? If so, student-centered schools seem to cast a wide net that includes all students, in contrast to more specialized schools that seek to catch particular groups of students defined by their interests or goals. The small schools portfolio agenda is therefore driven by competing notions of educational fit that define how wide the net should be cast and who is accommodated within a particular school or educational pathway. As we argue below, this practice derives from a long history of schooling as a mechanism for social stratification.

For over a century, schools have been used to determine where and how individuals fit into society. We are guided by the meritocratic assumption that schools are well suited to certify which students, because of inborn ability and hard work, will best succeed in particular pursuits, thereby contributing to the common good. As years of research on educational inequality have demonstrated, however, this assumption is deeply flawed.[16] Schools are not suited to sort and stratify students equitably.

If William had had a traditional urban high school experience, he may have dropped out and never made it to college. Does this mean that William fits in MetWest but not a traditional school? MetWest's robust notion of educational fit acknowledges that individual differences interact with the world in complex ways and that "fit" is not something that happens before students walk through the schoolhouse door. MetWest did not so much provide William with a pathway as it allowed a structure through which William and his teachers constructed a pathway, fitting and refitting it to meet his needs in ways that were unique, opportunistic, local, and relational. Today, William is enrolled in a prestigious engineering program, and he will likely enter the workforce with a hefty salary and considerable social status.

Students find their way to certain schools and life pathways for a variety of reasons, which may or may not be related to dispositions, abilities, and goals. As one student put it,

You want the opportunity to make choices, but you also want to be able to change your mind. It's hard when they ask you to sign up for a particular academy when you're just starting out, like in ninth grade. In my case, I chose technology and engineering. But I didn't really know what these subjects were or how long they'd interest me.[17]

Instead of choosing a school or educational program based on a commitment to a particular theme, career, or technical field, many students decide that they fit because their friends are going, or they have a connection to one of the teachers, or the facility is clean, or it seems better than their other options.

Moreover, extensive research on school choice demonstrates that the educational marketplace tends to offer fewer high-quality choices to students whose families are poor.[18] Fitting in a school or educational program becomes more difficult when choices are constrained by available resources. The politics of race and gender further complicate the notions of fit and choice. Cooper's study of African American mothers' educational views, experiences, and choices "reveals that race, class, and gender factors are critical to their school decision-making, in which the mothers perceive traditional public schools as sites of sociopolitical and cultural resistance."[19] Clearly, the process of choosing where to go to school is complex, laden with competing factors situated in long histories and cultural struggles.

Consider the case of career academies. The late 1960s saw a movement to transform vocational tracks into higher-status and more rigorous career academies: small learning communities or schools-within-schools that combined a college-preparatory curriculum with a career theme.[20] Today, career academies are spread across more than 1,500 high schools. The National Career Academy Coalition (NCAC)—"a driving force for collaborative support of career academies worldwide"—is celebrating its tenth anniversary. NCAC has deep ties to business and industry and "has developed career networks or 'strands' through organizations such as the Public Relations Society of America, the American Society for Public Administration and the Association of General Contractors."[21] Career academies represent only one option among theme-based small schools, yet it is a growing and well-researched segment that illustrates the struggle between the individual and collective aims of education.

To elucidate what it means to fit into a career academy, we evoke the long and disturbing history of tracking and social stratification. As John Dewey warned almost a century ago:

Any scheme of vocational education, which takes as its point of departure from the industrial regime that now exists, is likely to assume and perpetuate its divisions and weaknesses, and thus become an instrument in accomplishing the feudal dogma of social predestination.[22]

For decades, the comprehensive high school was the model for meeting communities' common educational needs (all students were educated under a single roof, so to speak) along with meeting individual needs of particular students (the "shopping mall" high school, with its multiple tracks and electives—some designed to provide preparation for college, others with general knowledge, and others with vocational preparation).[23] As Dewey predicted, persistent inequalities in the workforce and schools' adoption of the broad enterprise to prepare adolescents for this workplace infused judgments about who fit into one or another track with race and social class inequalities.

As a report on vocational education from 1969 to 1990 summarizes, "participation in most vocational program areas decreased as graduates' socioeconomic status, academic ability and high school grades increased."[24] College-going follows a similar trend; in 1982, for example, 72 percent of high school graduates with 0–2 vocational education units attended a four-year college versus 12 percent of graduates with 8 or more units.[25] Moreover, despite reform efforts to increase the academic rigor of vocational education, by 1994 only 33 percent of "vocational concentrators" met the New Basics core academic standards, compared with 90 percent of college-preparatory students.[26]

Today, educational discourse rejects overt differentiation associated with tracking (i.e., dividing students by race, purported intelligence, or predicted life outcomes) and career academies have sought to break this pattern. In their study of career academies, Kemple and Rock discuss the legacy of these trends:

> Academies have come under increasing pressure to demonstrate broad appeal and to show positive results. One response has been for the Academies to market the programs more aggressively to students who are likely to succeed in high school and to go on to college. Including a broader mix of students helps to dispel the perception that the programs are only for "low track students," to build school-wide support by showing that an Academy is appropriate for all students, and to promote mutual support among high- and low-achieving students.[27]

Research on career academies suggests that they may represent the most promising strand of vocational education—renewed as the field of career and technical education—although evidence of their success is far from straightforward. As Stern and Stearns explain, "most studies have not been able to determine whether apparent effects are due to particular programs or to selection of particular kinds of students into those programs."[28]

Most small schools also eschew social stratification, but many foreground their different themes as the basis for recruitment, curriculum, and instruction. The core reform question is whether theme-based choices re-create traditional within-school tracking as between- or across-school tracking. We explore this question in the next section by unpacking the concept of a theme. What is the variety of school or educational program themes? What do themes signify about educational fit and personalization, particularly those based on career pathways? Are themes necessary, and how do they function?

SCHOOL THEMES

Choosing a theme or focus is usually one of the first steps in designing a new small school. Ideally, like-minded educators, community members, parents, and students meet to determine the school theme. The purposes of the theme are to unify commitments, develop an institutional identity, aid in recruitment, integrate curriculum, and make learning relevant, among other goals. The variety of themes is staggering. Consider, for example, the themes that have emerged in 86 New York City small schools as part of New Vision's New Century High School Initiative: 37 career themes, 15 "democratic" themes (citizenship, social justice, leadership, and community development), and a handful of "academic" themes (history, Latin, letters). Some are college-prep themed, two are single gender, others target recent immigrants, and several carry more traditional identities, named after communities or people.

In February 2007, New York City eighth graders and their families were invited to a series of New Schools Fairs and received a booklet entitled "Small Schools: Big Choices" from the NYC Department of Education. The introduction states, "As an eighth grade student you are about to make one of the most important decisions of your life—you are about to choose a high school. You are in luck. New York City has more than 300 schools from which you and your family can choose. Each is different. . . . No school is right for everyone."[29] The district booklet outlines the small school choices in short blurbs and counsels students to "Know yourself and your needs" as they make this fateful decision at the age of 12 or 13. As discussed above, students will make these choices based on a whole host of factors that may or may not be related to their purported needs or to the schools' themes.

One way to frame efforts to develop a portfolio of diverse small schools is to argue that all these schools, regardless of theme, are equally good choices because they share a common vision of learning as personalized, inquiry or project based, connected to the world, and college prep. If so, we may not need to worry about how students are distributed across small schools because they will all graduate with the same high level of education and postsecondary options. If they don't, however, how will schools explain failure? Failure may be attributed to a misalignment between the school's theme—and likeminded group of educators—and the student's interests or abilities when fit is thought to be the key to success. As such, educational matchmaking is crucial and themes must function as recruitment mechanisms to enlist groups of students with desired traits, interests, learning styles, and so on. This is a dangerous function because many group distinctions (e.g., vocational education students, who learn best by doing) rest on long legacies of discrimination. As David Tyack warns, "Invidious distinctions produce injustice."[30] One response to this danger is to broaden the scope of themes so they are more inclusive.

Some claim that themes are important primarily because they provide motivational hooks or vehicles for learning. As the principal of the new Manhattan Theater Lab School explains, "My school is a college preparatory school in disguise. Theater is not the end, theater is the vehicle for their learning."[31] Stern et al. explain further: "By linking academic coursework to career themes and workplace experience, academies motivate students to stay in school and attend to their studies—as a number of evaluations have demonstrated."[32] This heightened motivation may be a result of the career theme at work or the integration of real-world and academic learning experiences, but it may also be the more basic sense of belonging engendered by defined social groups. As the classic Robbers Cave experiment by Sherif and colleagues demonstrated, young people develop a strong attachment to groups that require them to cooperate around shared goals. Small school themes may also function to define group membership.[33]

Another function of themes is to promote curricular integration that deepens learning. Ancess and Allen distinguish themes that achieve this function as integral, versus marginal or nominal themes.[34] As the Small Schools Workshop, a reform organization that supports new small school development, explains: "Small schools are schools of focus, that is, depth is valued more than breadth."[35] This progressive education mainstay dominates the small schools movement and is captured in the Coalition of Essential Schools' second common principle, "less is more":

> The school's goals should be simple: that each student master a limited number of essential skills and areas of knowledge. While these skills and areas will, to varying degrees, reflect the traditional academic disciplines, the program's design should be shaped by the intellectual and imaginative powers and competencies that students need rather than necessarily by "subjects" as conventionally defined.[36]

Themes can stimulate and contextualize intellectual and imaginative competencies. Moreover, when the theme is connected to hands-on, experiential learning, it is based on a richer conception of the mind at work, or, as Rose explains: "Not as slots along a simplified cognitive continuum or as a neat high-low distribution, but as a bountiful and layered field, where many processes and domains of knowledge interact."[37] Integrated instruction, offered through career academies and other small schools, contributes to students' intellectual engagement with the world.

Themes, therefore, seek to personalize learning in three ways: They bring together like-minded educators and students; they motivate and support students through defined group membership; and they leverage deep learning and intellectual engagement. Yet, the cross-school tracking concern remains. Themes also function, in Dewey's words, as "an instrument in accomplishing the feudal dogma of social predestination." In their recent analysis of how small school themes have played out in New York City, Ancess and Allen describe themes as codes that are read and accessed differently by different segments of society.

> Math and science themes are code for academically high-performing students, particularly boys. Career (or vocational) themes such as health or business are code for workforce orientation rather than college ambition, and in some cases preparation for entry-level, dead-end jobs for large corporations. Social justice and leadership themes are often associated with poor communities. Arts themes send mixed signals; their academic standards are seen as less demanding, but the arts themes, especially if accompanied by talent screening, confer elite status. Small, nontheme liberal arts schools that offer access to high-stakes knowledge and enrichment signal preparation for competitive colleges and a particular peer group: middle class and upwardly mobile, comprising all races, but Whites in particular.[38]

How can schools avoid the theme-driven social stratification described by Ancess and Allen? As discussed above, many reformers argue that if all small schools are college preparatory, the risks of cross-school tracking will be reduced. This argument depends, however, on how the risks of tracking are framed. When reproducing inequitable patterns within the workforce is framed as the risk, enabling students who might otherwise enter vocational fields straight out of high school to attend a postsecondary institution may result in redistribution within the workforce hierarchy. For example, instead of using his high school vocational experience rebuilding a Volvo to become a mechanic, William gained access to college and became an engineer.

The risks of tracking may also be framed as differential access to the high-status skills and knowledge that enable students to navigate the twenty-first-century workforce. Without these skills, students risk being stuck in one job for life, as the following quote from a career academy student illustrates: "Instead of us just sitting in class and learning about it, they took us out and hands-on and said, 'Well, this is what we do and this is what you will do.'"[39] To ensure that this student's future is not confined to one trade or career, college-preparatory education is held up as the vehicle to provide the essential skills for success in future job markets. Levy and Murnane cite five such essential skills:

1. *Learn on demand.* The ability to construct and apply new knowledge from work activities.
2. *Expert thinking.* The ability to generate solutions that are not rules-based using technical knowledge.
3. *Complex communication.* The ability to adapt communication skills to multiple situations and cultures.
4. *Interdisciplinary design.* The ability to integrate content from multiple disciplines, including both arts and sciences.
5. *Mobility.* The ability to transition across projects, firms, disciplines, and work/learning experiences.[40]

William learned these skills in a variety of contexts at MetWest and in his internships, although few would recognize the scope and sequence of his learning as a traditional college-prep education. For this reason, as detailed earlier, MetWest secured "A–G" approval from the University of California, signifying to colleges and others the rigor of William's work.[41]

In contrast to the risks of school-based tracking related to students' future participation in the workforce, there is an additional risk: that different theme-based small schools will differentially prepare students for civic participation. Providing college preparation for all may be one way to ensure that all students have the intellectual and practical skills to participate in and contribute to civic life. College preparation for all, however, may not be the best way to address the complex endeavor of civic education. Public schools teach students what it means to engage in civic life only when schools themselves are places of civic virtue.[42] As such, they have the opportunity to establish John Adams's "positive passion for the public good" each day, over time, in multiple contexts, based on a variety of relationships.

Small schools pioneer Deborah Meier makes a poignant case for the virtue of trust being at the heart of democratic education, just as it should be in democratic societies. Creating good schools is a matter of building trustworthy communities where students learn how to become citizens in the company of trusted adults.[43] Other democratic virtues, such as justice, courage, and honesty, are likewise learned in schools that are themselves just, courageous, and honest places. Good small schools use their size to attend to these virtues by emotionally supporting and intellectually engaging students in constructing personalized pathways through high school. In this way, good small schools are consciously reproducing a better society by attending to individual liberty and civic virtue through Multiple Pathways and a just and caring school culture. It is this consciousness that guards against cross-school tracking, not college readiness per se. Only when schools carefully attend to the pathways they are setting for students as citizens, workers, friends, and parents can they mitigate the inequities of the past. And only when students have the opportunity and guidance to examine these pathways honestly and critically in their historical, political, and economic contexts can they freely choose among them.[44]

If schools want to prepare all students for democratic participation, the education system must make explicit and enact the values that undergird democracy. For example, William's school, MetWest, is part of a larger network of Big Picture Company Schools—so named to signify that education is situated in a larger context and in the company of people. Big Picture schools educate students to become accomplished, happy, and productive citizens within a very complex world. This big-picture theme translates into an inclusive conception of educational fit; as Jesse, a student at the Big Picture's first school, The Met, explains:

> I have been asked what kind of kid should go to The Met. All kids should go to The Met. The Met is not only for kids who stand up to authority, or for "college bound" kids, or for artists, mechanics, mathematicians, scientists,

writers. It's not only for these kids, it's for all kids. This wide group of students creates the diverse learning environment, which is The Met.[45]

The Met and many other successful small schools are consciously democratic places that fit all students, striving to create in their alternative, well-designed spaces a microcosm of a better world.

CONCLUSION

We argue in this essay that school reform is fundamentally a struggle between the individual and collective aims of schooling. The small schools movement frames education as both a process of individuation and consciously democratic social reproduction. Yet, the movement also emphasizes educational fit and career themes that can work against the collective aims of schooling. For example, the small schools portfolio agenda submits that no school is right for everyone; instead students must find where they fit. School themes orchestrate the educational matchmaking process by communicating the type of student each school is seeking, differentiating by gender, language, academic strengths, career interests, as well as political and ideological commitments. Themes function as motivational tools that inspire group membership and school completion. They also help educators integrate academic and real-world learning and deepen students' knowledge around a common focus. Together, these efforts to differentiate among students and schools pose a threat to the common good of a free, just, and equitable system of public education. The current reform landscape addresses the risks of cross-school tracking by holding college readiness as the common high bar for all small schools. We discuss how the integration of college preparation serves to increase the status of career and technical education and ensure twenty-first-century workforce skills that will give students options. But we question how college readiness functions as a symbol of democratic education. As such, we suggest that small schools must also be places of civic virtue.

The original small schools movement of the 1980s carefully balanced the individual aims of personalization with common democratic hopes. As Michele Fine (2005) argues, however, this movement is under siege:

It breaks my heart to see the small schools movement commodified, ripped from its participatory and radical roots, and used to facilitate union busting, privatization, faith-based public education, and gentrification. To be sure, public education has always been a contested space; educational reforms have always blended elements that were potentially oppressive and subversively liberatory. But educational reforms, of late, have been systematically transformed into political efforts to undermine our most inclusive and democratic institutions in the service of privatization and perpetual inequality. And the small schools movement is no exception. Before "small" becomes the vehicle by which top-down, neoliberal reform dismantles the common good of public education, I say—for so many of us—not in our name.[46]

When New York City teenagers and their families hear that "no school is right for everyone," that they must find their place, and choose wisely, the very foundation of common public education is rattled. New efforts to create Multiple Pathways (whether in small or large schools) would do well to examine how and whether personalization, educational fit, and school themes attend to the common good.

CHAPTER 4

Immigrants and English Learners

Can Multiple Pathways Smooth Their Paths?

Patricia Gándara

Patricia Gándara is professor of education at the University of California–Los Angeles, codirector of the Civil Rights Project/El Proyecto de CRP, and associate director of the University of California Linguistic Minority Research Institute.

In this analytic essay, Gándara asks if a Multiple Pathways approach can open doors to higher educational attainment and higher-paying jobs for immigrants and English learners. For most immigrants and English learners, education as it is currently structured is not a vehicle of upward social mobility. Gándara finds that broad and fundamental reform is required to create schools that could meet these students' needs. She cites research that demonstrates the tenuous position of English learners and immigrants in California, noting that this issue is of growing concern to the country as a whole: Immigrants now account for more than one in 10 residents in the United States,[1] and in 2000–01, English learners represented 10 percent of all public school students in the country.[2] Gándara finds that Multiple Pathways that incorporate both academic and career technical education may be especially relevant to immigrant and English learner students. Especially promising are the potential for meaningful coursework, participation of students in adult work settings, career models, postsecondary options, and opportunities to earn while they learn. Multiple Pathways could make available strong models and opportunities for using emerging English language skills in ecologically meaningful ways. An important challenge to this reform approach is to avoid channeling immigrants and English learners into the least prestigious and remunerative occupations.

The majority of young people in California enter the labor market without college credentials and with little preparation for moving into the workforce. Only one-third of California's students complete a college degree, and the completion rates for students of color, immigrants, and English learners are much lower than for other groups.[3] Although completion rates of some ethnic groups are improving, Latino students—from whom the majority of immigrant students and English learners are drawn—appear to be making little progress toward earning college degrees (see table 4.1). Many recent reform proposals have focused on the need to strengthen the pipeline to college for these students, without discernible positive outcomes.

At the same time, relatively few high school classes focus on vocational preparation, and their quality is extremely uneven.[4] Because of the stigma attached to "low-level" vocational classes and the increasing academic requirements to enter competitive, selective universities, few high achievers in high school enroll in the vocational classes that are offered.[5] Career and technical education (CTE) takes place largely in segregated classes for the non-college-bound. This is notable in light of evidence that the requirements for a good entry-level job with benefits that does not require a degree are essentially the same as the requirements for college.[6]

Neglect of CTE and its current low status have prompted arguments for its reform and expansion, but race and class stratification in U.S. society have complicated these efforts. High-status students continue to gravitate toward college-preparatory classes, and lower-status students are channeled into "general" education or vocational education courses. Moreover, although high-quality vocational courses are often more costly than textbook-based courses, funding has not flowed proportionately to vocational programs.[7]

TABLE 4.1: Percentage of 25- to 29-Year-Olds Who Completed a Bachelor of Arts Degree or Higher, by Ethnicity

Ethnicity	1975	1985	1995	2000	2005
European American	24	24	29	34	34
African American	11	12	15	18	18
Latino	9	11	9	10	11

Source: United States Department of Education, National Center for Education Statistics, *Digest of Education Statistics*, 2001.

Multiple Pathways could merge the disparate tracks of CTE and academic education, thereby benefiting all students while diminishing the preparation and outcome gaps between high-status students and immigrant and English learner students. Although attempts to combine "the head and the hand" in school curricula are not new and have encountered numerous philosophical, political, and financial barriers in the past, it is time to put into action what we have learned over the last couple decades about doing this right, and to avoid what Pastor (in this volume) refers to as "multiple Californias."[8] High dropout rates and increasing concerns about the inability of immigrant students to fill the jobs being vacated by better-educated baby boomers lend urgency to this issue.[9] The governor's California Performance Review commission has recently added its voice to the chorus of those appealing for such an innovation.[10] This chapter explores the potential of a Multiple Pathways strategy for improving the educational outcomes of immigrant and English learner students and preparing them better for career and college opportunities.

A PROFILE OF IMMIGRANT AND ENGLISH LEARNER STUDENTS IN CALIFORNIA

Immigrants and English learners are the students who are most likely to perform at low levels and drop out of school.[11] Approximately 15 percent (or about 1 million) of all school-age children in California are immigrants, and approximately 158,000 are recent immigrants (4 years or less in the country) at the secondary school level.[12] More than one out of four students in the K–12 system is designated as an English learner at any one time.[13] About 40 percent of California's students come from homes in which English is not the primary language spoken. Most immigrants are at some point English learners, but most English learners are not immigrants. Thus, these are two overlapping but not identical populations that may have quite different needs.[14] For example, immigrants, especially those who are undocumented, often have additional struggles of lack of access to social services and unreliable employment. They may not know who to contact to help meet critical family needs or they may be barred from doing so. Their tenuous position in society can lead to high residential mobility and a lack of attachment to school.[15] Not knowing English is simply one among many educational obstacles.

Large majorities of both immigrants and English learners in California are Latino, with lower but not insubstantial numbers of Asians. Latino parents have lower levels of education than virtually all other groups. For example, almost 40 percent of Latino parents have not completed a high school diploma and 11 percent have a bachelor of arts degree (BA) or higher, compared to 4 percent of white parents without a diploma and 39 percent with a BA or higher.[16] Many Latinos are also segregated into communities where they have little contact with mainstream U.S. culture or language, and they attend schools with fewer resources of all kinds than most other students.[17]

The two largest immigrant groups—Asians and Latin Americans—have vast differences in educational background and experiences. Portes and Rumbaut provide data on the percentage of individuals who immigrated to the United States between 1980 and 1990, who are age 25 or older, who completed the equivalent of high school, and who hold college degrees.[18] Seventy-four percent of Asian immigrants completed high school, and 37 percent entered the country with college degrees. For Latin American and Caribbean immigrants (the highest percentage of whom are Mexican), 40 percent had completed high school and only 8 percent held college degrees.

Unlike East Asians, who tend to outperform European American students in school, many Southeast Asian, Latino immigrants, and English learner students tend to perform poorly in school from the very beginning and are often tracked into low-level, remedial classes.[19] Many of these students drop out of school after repeated academic failure and social and educational exclusion,[20] and most have very limited postsecondary educational and occupational options.[21] Many of these immigrant and English learner students will form part of the growing underclass of low-skilled, low-wage workers with little job security and few opportunities for social mobility. From this category of individuals will come most of the chronic unemployment, homelessness, and economic despair in California.[22]

The public schools are, of course, the primary avenue out of this economic dead end, and some immigrant and English learner students manage to use the schools in this way. However, for most students of Southeast Asian and Mexican origin who are immigrants and/or English learners, education as it is currently structured is not a vehicle of upward social mobility, and the schools leave many behind.

WHY ARE SCHOOLS NOT MEETING THE NEEDS OF IMMIGRANTS AND ENGLISH LEARNERS?

In California, English learners perform at significantly lower levels on statewide achievement tests than other students. They fail to pass the high school exit examination at higher rates than any other group except Special Education students. For example, by the eleventh grade, 78 percent of the more than 60,000 California students who were classified as English learners in 2007 scored at "below basic" or "far below basic" in language arts. They did not fare much better in math. Between 76 percent and 86 percent of these eleventh graders scored at below basic or far below basic in algebra 1, algebra 2, and geometry.[23] That is, only about one in five (on average) of these English learners was even at the "basic" academic level in core subjects. In the same year, 64 percent of tenth-grade English learner students failed the English language arts portion of the high school exit exam, and 53 percent failed the math section.[24] Students cannot receive a diploma without passing both of these sections.

There are numerous reasons why English learner students perform so poorly in school, including poorly prepared teachers and inadequate materials, lack of access to core curriculum, inaccurate assessment, segregation into linguistic "ghettos," weak professional development for teachers and staff, and antiquated facilities in which English learners receive a demonstrably weaker education than their English-speaking peers.[25] Students who have had little real access to the curriculum being tested cannot be expected to perform well on the test; such access is limited when students cannot understand the language of instruction, when the instruction is delivered by a teacher with a weak understanding of the subject matter, or when students have not been enrolled in classes where the required information is taught. Of course, this becomes a cycle of poor test performance, followed by assigning students to stultifying remedial classes in which they still do not understand the language of instruction, followed by more failure and often culminating with students dropping out in frustration.

Language Policies

Language policies that push English learners rapidly into mainstream classes, providing little or no linguistic or educational support, can stifle students' academic education. A command of academic English must be explicitly taught; it does not occur naturally. Children learn the language of conversation through their daily activities in the environment (e.g., conversations, play, popular media), but no child automatically knows the language of the classroom.[26] English learner students encounter more obstacles when their teachers cannot communicate with them in their primary language and do not have sophisticated training to teach them.[27]

Aspirations and Expectations

Although upward of 80 percent of all students report that they intend to go to college, These Latino students have lower expectations for postsecondary education than other groups.[28] Many family members of Latino immigrant and English learner youth have had little exposure to the U.S. school system, and they do not understand how to guide children through American schools or the particular benefits that accrue from school success. Latino parents often do not understand the routine of homework, the necessity of studying for tests, and the high premium placed on classroom participation. They may not appreciate the need for or have confidence to perform the parental role of being a "squeaky wheel," including advocating for their children, insisting that they receive services to which their children are entitled, or complaining about a neglectful teacher. By comparison, Brittain found that Chinese immigrant parents often learned a great deal at home in China from friends and relatives who had experience with American schools about how to manage the U.S. system.[29]

Information about College

Latino immigrant parents' lack of exposure to the U.S. K–12 school system often accompanies a lack of awareness of the importance of attending college. They may assume that children from their social class do not go to college and cannot possibly afford it.[30] Many immigrant parents and students, including those with strong aspirations to attend college, do not understand college requirements, in part because counseling is so rationed in low-income schools.[31] With such poor information, academic preparation, and support in weak schools, these students' vague ambitions to go to college never develop into a specific and informed college focus that fulfills their postsecondary aspirations.

Segregation

Segregation of immigrant Latinos and English learners has significant consequences for academic outcomes. The segregation of Latino students has been increasing since it was first measured in 1968, with particularly dramatic increases in California and Nevada. Latinos are also more segregated by poverty than any other group, clustered in poor schools with inadequate resources. Going to school with other children from low-income families also limits these students' access to essential social and cultural capital.[32] For example, they may experience fewer informal, peer-to-peer conversations about which classes meet college requirements, who are the best teachers, when and where to sign up for college nights, and so forth.[33] Similarly, English learners are more likely to attend school with other English learners than they are to attend school with English speakers.[34] This can limit their access to good models of spoken English and opportunities to practice their English among peers. Even where mainstream peers attend the same schools, immigrant students and English learners are not likely to have extensive contact with these students because class assignments and course-taking patterns typically segregate middle-class, college-bound students from their lower-income and lower-aspiring peers. Latina females may feel they do not belong in their schools, and high percentages of Latino males may eschew school norms and culture altogether, creating their own subculture that has little contact with the wider school.[35]

In sum, immigrant and English learner students often have weak academic preparation, in part because of their personal circumstances and community resources and in part because of the schools' inability to meet their needs. They have unmet language development needs and are segregated and isolated in the least stimulating classes in the poorest schools, where they are exposed to few postsecondary options. While many may express aspirations to go to college, they have little knowledge of how to plan for postsecondary schooling or enter the workforce. Some suffer from lack of legal documentation, and many feel uncomfortable in school, as though they "don't belong." Others feel ignored or discriminated against by other students, and most see few models of upward educational or job mobility. In low-income circumstances, where families immigrate to find work, the perceived pressure to be a contributing member of the family can be intense. Moreover, even if schools were able to provide the needed courses and supports for educational success, many of these students would still require more time to accomplish the cultural, linguistic, and academic tasks necessary to allow them to graduate from high school fully prepared for the workforce or for postsecondary education. Broad and fundamental reform is required to create schools that could meet these students' needs. One such reform that is frequently mentioned is more vocationally oriented education that opens doors to higher-paying jobs.

VOCATIONAL EDUCATION: A ROSE BY ANY OTHER NAME?

Vocational education has long been viewed as the alternative to college preparation: a course of study taken by students who intend to enter the labor force without going on to college.[36] Students who take vocational courses have traditionally been seen as lacking the ability or desire to pursue academic work. Overwhelmingly, these classes are filled with low-income, minority, immigrant, and English learner students. Some scholars have argued that the vocational track has little to do with vocational preparation and much to do with reproducing the social order, relegating lower-income students to inferior curricula, and allowing upper-income students to maintain their social and economic advantage through coursework geared toward higher education.[37] Whether or not this is the case, there is little evidence that vocational education actually leads to enhanced job skills or placements.[38]

Recurring critiques of vocational education in the high schools have observed that equipment and training are outdated, programs are underfunded and unarticulated with workforce needs, and students lack the level of motivation required to succeed in school.[39] Given these views, vocational education was reformed in the 1970s and partially reborn as "tech prep," with the goal of high school and community colleges keeping vocational students in school, continuing their education into postsecondary institutions, and gaining marketable vocational skills. The 2 + 2 programs—two years of high school linked to two years of community college—were at the foundation of the tech prep movement, but studies showed that articulation with the workplace was weak, and many students dropped out before the eleventh grade.[40]

THE POTENTIAL OF MULTIPLE PATHWAYS

In 1984, John Goodlad argued that all students should take both vocational (experiential) and academic courses as a part of their high school curriculum, and all should be prepared for the rigors of higher education and the real world of work. He offered data showing that even the most academically inclined secondary school students enjoyed vocational (and art and physical education) classes, where they had the opportunity to do, rather than just write about or talk about, the things they were learning.[41]

Because students enjoy this type of class, Goodlad argued that vocational education could provide the natural opportunity for students from different backgrounds (and supposed interests and motivations) to study together side by side, thereby breaking down the segregation of college-bound students from those less likely to attend college. Goodlad's vision, much derived from Dewey, was an integrated education in which the disciplines could be applied to hands-on experiences in such areas as construction, agriculture, and the arts and in which all students would participate.[42] His vision of a high school for all students that unites head and hand, thinking and doing, addresses the false dichotomy of academic versus vocational education.

A curriculum that incorporates both academic education and CTE may be especially relevant to English learners and immigrant students. The opportunity to learn and demonstrate learning through hands-on, project- and portfolio-type activities has been shown to improve the exam pass rates for English learners.[43] Moreover, cooperative learning strategies and project-based curricula can scaffold instruction for students who have not yet fully mastered English. Extending courses into the community with people who also have knowledge of students' language and culture can constitute additional human capital resources for these students.

HOW COULD A MULTIPLE PATHWAYS APPROACH ADDRESS SOME NEEDS OF IMMIGRANT AND ENGLISH LEARNER YOUTH?

Grubb outlines eight more-or-less successful ways that educators have tried to integrate vocational and academic approaches.[44] They range from reforms requiring few organizational changes to radical school reorganization. Reforms requiring the least institutional change simply incorporate more academic content into vocational courses, involve more academic teachers in the vocational program, or make academic courses more vocationally relevant. For academies, magnet schools, and occupational clusters or career paths within schools, however, whole or partial school reorganization is required, along with new curricula. Although more difficult and costly in terms of both time and resources, the larger structural changes are more likely to change outcomes for students.[45]

Multiple Pathways approaches can make use of various sites, both on and off the school campus, to "deliver" the curriculum and engage English learner students with opportunities they do not now receive. At the school site the curriculum can integrate a rigorous (college-preparatory) curriculum with real-world vocational experiences and experiential classroom pedagogies. Off-site opportunities can include public spaces (e.g., community colleges, museums and libraries, community arts groups) and workplace settings and relationships (e.g., businesses, internships, paid employment, mentoring).

Curriculum that integrates college-preparatory and vocational studies has the potential to benefit immigrant students and English learners in at least six ways:

1. *Offer vocationally meaningful coursework.* Immigrant and EL students must be able to succeed in areas that are not wholly dependent on their English language skills or their store of cultural capital. Students who are

still learning English in high school are typically placed into non-college-preparatory or weak courses. Most take intensive English and remedial classes that often do not provide credit toward graduation requirements. Students may be "mainstreamed" into classes where they cannot understand the English or are unfamiliar with the cultural content of the lessons. Sometimes they are simply given a shortened day if no reasonable classes are available for them.[46] In any case, these students have few opportunities to feel competent in school. The frustration of feeling behind and peripheral to the conversations and activities in the classroom can lead to low morale and alienation.

The opportunity to take classes in which they can demonstrate competence by doing can be critically important to morale and self-concept. Moreover, if students earn course credit for these classes, they can also feel that they are moving successfully toward high school completion—a major incentive to stay in school.

2. *Increase immigrant parents' involvement with the school and with their children's learning.* Many of these parents have skills that can be shared with students and support their learning. Parents' and other community members' "funds of knowledge" can help support teaching of rigorous curriculum in real-world contexts, thus honoring the valuable knowledge of people who are often viewed as lacking important skills. Examples include dressmakers, who use mathematics to design and cut clothing, and construction workers, who have a sophisticated command of geometry, building design, proportionality, and related skills. A truly integrated curriculum can allow parents and community members to provide "laboratories" for using math, science, and other skills that students are learning in regular classrooms. Parent involvement of this sort generates tremendous good will and helps overcome the chronic problem of getting parents to come to the school and participate in their children's education.[47]

3. *Make classrooms places where all students want to participate.* Cognitive science has established that students learn better when they are allowed to do as well as observe; social science has shown that students enjoy classes in which they can actively engage in real-world tasks.[48] Rigorous academic study that includes opportunities to apply knowledge could be attractive to students who aspire to attend college as well as those who, for the moment, do not plan on college. The result could be to break down the barriers between the "smart" kids and the immigrants and English learners. Thus, immigrant and English learner students could

interact routinely with college-bound students and be exposed to the social capital they have in abundance. Importantly, immigrant and English learner students bring cultural capital of their own, and the "capital sharing" can go both ways. This could be a fundamental strategy to break down segregation and tracking of students.

4. *Introduce a full range of career models.* Many immigrant students and English learners lack a breadth of educational models in their daily lives. Many low-income students living in rural or inner-city settings see few occupational opportunities and know few people who hold interesting jobs. Low-income students from immigrant and non-English-speaking backgrounds typically see their vocational options from an "either/or" perspective; that is, getting a job at McDonald's or going to college. For these students, few intermediate options exist because they know little about the full range of jobs for students who go to college and for those who don't. With such limited vistas, it is not surprising that many students quit school or do not take it very seriously. It is not clear to many of these students just how high school is related to good jobs, to college, or to anything in their future. A Multiple Pathways curriculum would allow students whose communities or personal contacts do not include a wide range of careers to connect subject-matter learning and vocational opportunities and to interact with people who hold jobs that are different from any they have encountered.

5. *Make known the demands and structures of community college.* The great majority of immigrant and English learner students who go to college will go to community college. Preparation and familiarity could make attending a community college more attractive and more successful. The tech prep 2 + 2 model has been disappointing because high schools and community colleges have seldom found good ways to work together.[49] However, there are other models, including the very successful middle college pioneered at La Guardia Community College, in which students complete their last two years of high school through the community college and emerge with work skills.[50]

6. *Offer opportunities to study the arts and humanities.* With increasing course requirements, students often feel compelled to take one more science or math course to be competitive for college, and many schools now offer a bare minimum of arts and humanities courses. The Goodlad data cited earlier, as well as numerous studies and reports, have pointed to the importance of the arts (including music and dance) in the curriculum.[51] Arts courses hold many students in school when little else appeals to

them; the arts provide a place for creative engagement and personal and social growth. The arts are not necessarily dependent on language skill or mainstream cultural knowledge, and can be an avenue for expression of the cultural knowledge that immigrant and English learner students bring with them to school.

Off-site, real-world learning opportunities, because they change the context for learning, have the potential to dramatically change the way students learn and are taught. The potential benefits of this strategy include:

7. *Give students a chance to earn while they learn.* Working too many hours while in school is detrimental to academic achievement,[52] and some students can be distracted from school by the lure of earning money.[53] Working moderate amounts of time can actually reduce the chances of students dropping out for work.[54] Further, students have many fewer job opportunities in some geographic areas than in other areas. For example, black and brown students in Los Angeles have fewer opportunities for working moderate amounts of time in large part because there are fewer jobs where they live. Paid internships and other paid work could support education and training and could reduce the competition between work and school and provide an incentive to stay in school (if, as Ong and Terriquez note, transportation is provided).

8. *Provide contexts for students to use and develop their emerging English language skills in ecologically meaningful ways.* It is difficult to learn English well when there are few people with whom to practice regularly. This is a particular problem in places like California, where English learners tend to be segregated into schools with high percentages of other English learners and into communities that offer few opportunities to hear English. Exposure to strong English models in the workplace/learning space could provide many more opportunities to develop English language skills. Moreover, internships and job placement could be structured to include opportunities for students to use their bilingual skills.

9. *Increase the comfort level of students who are older than their grade cohort.* Immigrant and English learner students who are either held back or require more time to complete their studies may be inclined to drop out of school. Some schools are experimenting with five- and six-year high school programs for English learners and immigrant students who require more time to catch up with native-born students. However, being

over-age for grade level has traditionally been a strong predictor of dropping out,[55] in part because students feel awkward, but also because their friends tend to be out of school and they have few relationships at the school to anchor them. The option of taking classes at a community college or in a work setting can reduce the stigma of being older than one's high school peers.

10. *Allow for flexible schedules.* Students who are classified as English learners in the secondary schools almost always need extra time to build their English skills and to complete the requirements for graduation and post-secondary preparation. Schools, however, have great difficulty reorganizing their schedules while conforming to the standard 8 a.m.–3 p.m. school day and the 180-day school year. By allowing students to complete some of their coursework in off-site settings, schools may be able to find more schooling time for these students without incurring drastically increased costs or requiring massive reorganization of the traditional school day and calendar.

11. *Provide greater exposure to career opportunities and the future job market.* Schooling opportunities within the job market, especially if they are jobs that will be available to them with advanced study, motivate students to stay in school. Studies appear to bear out this positive effect of internship and apprenticeship programs.[56]

12. *Expand the number of adults in students' lives to guide, nurture, teach, and monitor students' progress.* Most public high schools do not have enough qualified adults to guide and monitor students. In California, the typical counselor-to-student ratio is almost 850:1.[57] Teachers routinely teach 120–150 students daily. To provide the guidance that low-income, ethnic-minority students especially need but seldom receive, an extensive network of extracurricular college-preparation programs has grown up around the country. But even these programs serve only a small fraction of the students who need them. When students move into the community for nontraditional learning opportunities, they connect more easily with informal mentors and counselors at those sites. Increased social networks and mentors are a particular advantage of the apprenticeship/internship model.

POTENTIAL CHALLENGES TO THE MULTIPLE PATHWAYS APPROACH

The challenges discussed below deal with larger cultural shifts—issues that restructuring alone would have difficulty influencing. Grubb distinguishes between "weak" and "strong" versions of Multiple Pathways.[58] While a weak version would restructure high schools to include multiple theme-based pathways, it would not adequately respond to the many critiques of high schools or to issues of motivation and engagement. A strong version, which views restructuring as necessary but not sufficient, would focus on the attitudes of students, parents, and teachers about preparation for life after high school and preparing all students for college and career. This could generate even more powerful reforms related to the quality of instruction, equity, tracking, and providing extra assistance—reforms that are critical to improving the outcomes for immigrant and English learners.[59]

Parents of traditional college-bound students (e.g., more affluent, white, native English speakers, multigenerational college-goers) exert considerable influence in schools to maintain their children's academic advantages. Parents use their social capital to influence their children's school experience, including the teachers and programs their children are assigned to.[60] Such parents have greater access to special programs, such as gifted education, and they often eschew any courses that do not adhere to traditional content or format.[61] Many parents may not think of English learners and immigrant students as college-bound, and they may be suspicious if their own (high social capital) children are placed in an inclusive Multiple Pathways program, in which curriculum and classmates depart from traditional schooling norms. These parents may respond by preventing Multiple Pathways programs from starting, possibly by working to undermine the inclusive intent of the programs or by boycotting them.

Similarly, some parents of immigrant students and English learners might worry that their children are being relegated to an inferior curriculum. Many students who have been partially educated outside the United States have very traditional expectations of school and might excel in a traditional curriculum (if it were offered to them in a language they could understand). Immigrant parents sometimes even resent bilingual placements, seeing them as "less than" the curriculum that other students receive and worrying that their children will be shortchanged both in academic content and opportunities to learn English. Schools generally do a poor job of explaining programs to parents of English learners and immigrants, and schools will be especially challenged to explain Multiple Pathways clearly and compellingly.

Schools must also avoid the status and value hierarchies of academic and vocational options. Just as academic courses vary in the rigor and value of their content, so do vocational courses. Integrating the two will require considerable skill. If options are not equal, students who are self- or school-identified (often, years earlier) as likely college-goers will gravitate to the more coveted courses. Other students, including immigrant and English learner students, might not be as adept at selecting classes, setting up self-limiting course choices and academic tracking.

A Multiple Pathways curriculum will require a new kind of teacher, one who has strong workplace skills as well as academic background, who has the pedagogical knowledge to teach students who do not speak English well, and who may have little familiarity with the cultural content of the course. Such teachers must relate well to these students and speak their native language(s) sufficiently to guide them, especially where learning technical and academic language is required. Currently, teachers who meet traditional qualifications are in short supply, especially at the secondary level. Teacher preparation and professional development for a Multiple Pathways curriculum would require major retooling of preparation and professional development programs. For example, we know that most vocational education teachers (88%) hold BA degrees or higher, but much of their experience has been in the world of work, while few regular education teachers have work experience outside of education.[62] Moreover, for both types of teachers, there remains a significant shortage of bilingual and culturally diverse personnel.

A Multiple Pathways curriculum must not give English learner students less time for explicit and intensive instruction in academic English.[63] These students require guided writing assignments with personalized feedback, along with other chances to practice academic English through structured assignments. The curriculum would need to be carefully designed to take into account the specific needs of English learners and immigrants.

To the extent that internships and other off-site learning opportunities exist, students will face the added hurdle of finding transportation.[64] Policies must anticipate and correct unfair distribution of off-site opportunities between English learner and immigrant students on one hand and more socially capitalized, affluent, and stronger English-speaking students on the other.

As students spend more time at off-campus sites, schools could lose (or eagerly give up) control of students' learning environment. Because English learner and immigrant students may not be as familiar with how things work in nonschool settings, they will require both monitoring and coaching for these new experiences. For example, many Latino students in a college-prep program were uncomfortable talking with adults they did not know, and so failed to return phone calls from their community-based mentors. They needed extensive coaching on how to communicate with adults in business environments.[65] It is notable that the Verbum Dei School (profiled by Ong and Terriquez in this volume) provides two-week orientations for students before sending them out to internship placements.[66] Finally, immigrant and English learner high school students can feel so much pressure to earn money that new workplace opportunities can help encourage some to leave school. Off-site and work-experience environments need to maintain a constant focus on the rewards for being well prepared when one enters the workplace.

CONCLUSION

While fully acknowledging that there are many difficulties in attempting to construct a Multiple Pathways approach to educating English learner and immigrant students, on balance it appears that there would be more benefits than liabilities with such an approach. High schools are not working well for these students. A new approach is clearly in order. If students can be engaged in meaningful activity, learn about workforce opportunities, and prepare for postsecondary education and a college degree, we could make school more appealing to more students who are traditionally marginalized. In addition, we could probably produce a more balanced and useful education for all students. If well implemented, a Multiple Pathways approach would demonstrate that, given the opportunity, immigrant students and English learners can succeed in K–12 schools, postsecondary institutions, and the workplace.

Multiple Pathways and Societal Benefit

Possibilities and Challenges

The four essays in Part II of this volume continue our discussion of the potential benefits of Multiple Pathways and the likely challenges in realizing those benefits as reformers seek to transform the comprehensive high school. However, these essays expand the discussion of the educational benefits to students to consider the potential impact of Multiple Pathways reform on society as a whole. Labor economist Manuel Pastor, urban economist Michael Stoll, urban policy scholar Paul Ong, sociologist Veronica Terriquez, and education researchers John Rogers, Joseph Kahne, and Ellen Middaugh all contemplate the economic and societal consequences of bridging the academic-vocational divide and giving all students both college and career preparation.

Using California as a case study, the authors examine the possibilities and challenges of Multiple Pathways in light of the intersections among the changing economy, increasing demographic diversity, widening social and economic inequality, and patterns of school failure across racial and ethnic communities. As Manuel Pastor notes, for example, increasing fragmentation across economic and social lines and the factors that contribute to these divides threaten both the economy and the political stability of the state. Within the next half-century, other states may learn from California's experience.

Within this imposing context for education reform, the authors of these four essays address a set of critical questions: Might Multiple Pathways increase economic opportunities for an increasingly diverse population of high school students, including those who live in impoverished neighborhoods? Could Multiple Pathways address future workforce needs and contribute to a healthy economy? Can Multiple Pathways' emphasis on career-related themes also prepare young people for effective civic participation?

The authors are cautiously optimistic. Although schooling alone cannot be expected to resolve the nation's economic and political dilemmas, Multiple Pathways may be more efficacious than traditional high school education. Increasingly, good jobs require a good education. The failure to complete high school—prepared for a range of postsecondary opportunities—including college and workforce readiness, is ever more likely to lead to a life of underachievement in the labor market. Academic success affects not only jobs, income, and lifestyle but also the overall health of our economic and political systems. Increasing the rates of high school completion and college preparation will result in a better-trained and -educated workforce and in adults who are better prepared to participate in civic life.

The four essays in this part also discuss the challenges to a Multiple Pathways approach. As summarized by Manuel Pastor, "even such a hopeful and appropriate educational plan must be nested in a broader approach that pays attention to improving economic growth, creating career pathways, and ensuring social guarantees that will ease transitions, retraining, and other adjustments in the years ahead. . . . This will require a new level of social cohesion and political will, not just in California but in the nation."[1]

THE POSSIBILITIES

Multiple Pathways could prepare the skilled and nimble workforce that the future requires. Together, the four essays in Part II find that Multiple Pathways' integration of academic and technical curricula and its use of multiple modes and settings for learning can accomplish three important goals relevant to the quality of the future workforce. It can prepare more students for college, meeting future needs for additional college-educated workers. It can teach the "soft skills" (e.g., problem solving, the ability to work in groups and communicate with others) that jobs at all levels increasingly require. Finally, because all students are prepared to be good students as well as good workers, Multiple Pathways can prepare young people to move nimbly between work, on-the-job training, and higher education (community college or four-year) as the changing economy and shifts in job requirements make retooling necessary.

Multiple Pathways could link young people with meaningful, well-paying jobs. Manuel Pastor's, Michael Stoll's, and Paul Ong and Veronica Terriquez's essays all suggest that exposure to the real world of adults provided by Multiple Pathways enables informed career choices. Compared to traditional high schools, the Multiple Pathways approach gives students access to sites of meaningful work and to social networks that link students to career knowledge. Students learn about the existence of certain jobs (and varied opportunities within careers); they learn where the jobs are located; they meet people who can refer and recommend them; and they can imagine themselves at the workplace. Echoing the findings of Stern and Stearns' essay in Part I, the authors in Part II find that when students take a coherent sequence of career and technical courses, along with college-preparatory academics, they fare better in the labor market than students who do not. This is a particularly robust finding for young people from working-class or minority backgrounds. They also find that Multiple Pathways programs help students prepare for the increasingly common "learn while you earn" combination of employment and further education—a conclusion that other essays in this volume also make. Often this combination makes college possible for students from low-income families.

Multiple Pathways could promote a healthy economy in the context of changing demographics. As Manuel Pastor observes, the current educational system cannot ensure a thriving economy built on meaningful, well-paying jobs for its workforce, given its failure to educate the fastest-growing groups, such as Latinos and immigrants. Widening social chasms (a result of current practices) is likely to make the state less competitive, load economic and social burdens on the "most productive" residents, and damage economic growth. To the extent that Multiple Pathways can improve minority students' educational success at a number of points (e.g., public K–12, transitions to postsecondary school, and lifelong education) it will have a significant, positive economic impact.

Multiple Pathways could promote civic learning. Schools seek to teach young people the skills and commitments to participate and exercise leadership in electoral politics, public institutions, and civic organizations, as well as to understand the purpose and function of government. As John Rogers, Joseph Kahne, and Ellen Middaugh explain, Multiple Pathways are especially well suited to prepare young people for their roles as members of a democratic society by engaging them in civic learning that includes the facts, skills, and values required for community participation and leadership. Their participation in the world of adults, as well as in classrooms, allows young people to observe collective problem solving and leadership firsthand. It can also create contexts for students to study the relationship between democracy and the economy and to extend the civic lessons they learn at school into the workplace.

THE CHALLENGES

Educational policy alone, including Multiple Pathways, cannot fully address the educational, social, and economic constraints on students vulnerable to the effects of residential segregation, income inequality, and concentrated poverty. Even the best schooling policies cannot succeed without other strong economic and public policies that focus on the unique labor force problems associated with low-income communities of color. As the authors of these essays warn, the risk of furthering divisions through tracking or limiting opportunities for some can be obviated if this broader picture is kept in mind.

CHAPTER 5

United or Divided

Can Multiple Pathways Bring Together Multiple Communities?[1]

Manuel Pastor

Manuel Pastor is professor of geography and American studies and ethnicity at the University of Southern California, and director of the Program for Environmental and Regional Equity at the university's Center for Sustainable Cities. Pastor is a labor economist whose research has focused on environmental justice, regional inclusion, and the economic and social conditions facing low-income urban communities in the United States and abroad. His most recent book (coauthored with Chris Benner and Laura Leete) is Staircases or Treadmills: Labor Market Intermediaries and Economic Opportunity in a Changing Economy.

In this essay, Pastor examines education reforms for their potential to increase economic opportunity. Using California as a nationally relevant case study, Pastor cites demographic research and other analyses that demonstrate how Multiple Pathways can mitigate the inequitable effects associated with an increasingly divergent population, economic tracking, and geographic isolation. Economic projections show that the fastest-growing occupations will require the skills that a Multiple Pathways approach to schooling is well suited to deliver: an integrated curriculum, real-world experience, internships, and so forth. Multiple Pathways could prepare students to move nimbly between work, on-the-job training, and higher education (two-year or four-year) as job requirements shift and retooling is necessary. Pastor cautions that while Multiple Pathways reformers must bear in mind the state's labor market needs, realistic

*preparation for the workforce requires supporting policies that address
the state's residential segregation, income inequality, and concentrated
poverty. Similarly, Multiple Pathways must be formulated in the context of
a social safety net that includes labor standards, health, and housing. The
risks of a Multiple Pathways approach, such as tracking, limited opportunities for some, and racial divisions, can be obviated if this broader picture
is kept in mind.*

Los Angeles Mayor Antonio Villaraigosa has called high school dropout rates
in L.A. County "the civil rights issue of our time."[2] Those who are dropping
out, particularly in California's urban communities, are predominantly poor
and largely African American and Latino, and their failure to complete and
go beyond high school is likely to lead to a life of underachievement in the
labor market. Concern for retention and advancement has extended beyond
the usual educational and civil rights circles to many others who recognize
that the future of the state's economy depends on the capabilities and skills
of today's youth.

As educators, civic leaders, and policymakers grapple with issues of student retention and advancement, a variety of innovative ideas have emerged.
Among these is the Multiple Pathways approach, which simultaneously prepares students for participation in the labor market and for advanced education. Multiple Pathways reform is both an educational strategy and an
outcome goal. The strategy refers to how K–12 education is conducted, and
the goal is for all students to graduate high school with multiple career and
higher education options, as well as the ability to switch between these paths.
This combination seems to have great promise: It could engage students
with more practice-based learning, keep options open as their career tastes
change, and create permanent capacities for smoothly moving between the
labor market and, say, the community college system to better prepare individuals for the lifelong learning processes that are expected to be a key part
of tomorrow's employment opportunities.

However, some parents, educators, and policymakers are concerned about
Multiple Pathways becoming another form of tracking, a system that has
placed students, especially immigrants and youth of color, into poor-quality
classes that limit their educational prospects. Some who have fought for more
college-preparation courses in their schools might see Multiple Pathways as a
step backward, from a strategy that emphasizes college for all to one that typ-

ically limits some students to vocational training for low- and medium-wage occupations. For this reason, some worry that Multiple Pathways could exacerbate the trend to multiple communities, with one group of young people steered to the lower reaches of the labor market while another group receives the academic preparation needed to excel in a globalized economy.

Is a Multiple Pathways strategy a recipe for worsening distributional trends or a realistic remedy in a changing economy? Other authors have dealt with the educational aspects and theory that inform this new approach, using California as a case study. This chapter seeks to provide a broader context for answering the question of how Multiple Pathways interacts with the larger disease plaguing the state: social, economic, and political fragmentation.

There are, in fact, multiple Californias: The state is increasingly divided by class, race, and residential location. It is the first major state to become "majority minority," meaning that no ethnic group comprises more than half the state population, and demographic projections suggest further change ahead. These population shifts have been accompanied by a changing economy, one which relies on high-tech and high-skill employment on one hand and low-skill and sometimes undocumented labor on the other. The Economic Policy Institute reports that California is among the worst ten states in terms of economic disparity by income class.[3] The state's geographic landscape reflects the disparity: Even as researchers proudly reported that racial and class segregation had declined in the nation as a whole during the 1990s, they noted that it was on the rise in California.[4] In sum, California is demographically diverging, economically tracking, and geographically separating.

Multiple Pathways reform may be part of a remedy to this problem. It is a strategy that accommodates labor market needs and provides potential benefits to students, workers, and the economy as a whole. It recognizes the different learning styles of different students while keeping the dream of college alive for all. And it implicitly acknowledges the growing diversity of our population by allowing students to choose a career trajectory and to change over time. A true Multiple Pathways strategy is not simply an education intervention that can be inserted into any extant education system and social context; it will also require policies that address other major challenges in California and elsewhere, including immigration pressures, declining labor standards, and slowing economic growth. In short, it requires a policy package that recognizes the intersections between changing demography and rising economic inequity.

This chapter seeks to make the case for cohesion between policy reform and broad, multifaceted social concerns. I begin by noting the deepening fault lines in California along the dimensions of income, race, and nativity. This fragmentation and the reasons behind it threaten the economy and the future. I stress education, particularly the growing returns for those who pursue advanced education and the positive impact of a better-trained and better-educated workforce. Multiple Pathways can be a part of response to workforce needs, but only in the context of adequate social safety nets that include labor standards, health, and housing. The risks of a Multiple Pathways strategy (e.g., tracking, limited opportunities for some, and further divisions) can be obviated if we keep this broader picture in mind. And while the application is to California, the lessons may be useful elsewhere, particularly since recent studies project that other states will experience the demographic and economic conditions of California.

MULTIPLE CALIFORNIAS

Although California's diversity is arguably one of its greatest strengths, the divisions along the lines of race, class, and location have also created a fractured population and landscape, a conglomeration of multiple Californias rather than a unified state.

Demographically Diverging

California had become a majority-minority state by the time of the 2000 Census: White residents were 47 percent of the population; Latinos, just under one-third; Asian/Pacific Americans, 11 percent; African Americans, 7 percent; and the remainder consisting of Native Americans and those marking (non-Latino) mixed race. The change was rapid. In 1970, whites made up more than three-fourths of the state population; Latinos, 12 percent; African Americans, about 7 percent; and Asian/Pacific Americans, 3 percent.[5]

It is projected that by 2030, Asian/Pacific Americans will comprise 13 percent and the African American share will be unchanged. Trading places will be the white and Latino populations: White populations will decline to just under 30 percent while the latter will comprise a near-majority at 47 percent. Furthermore, in some respects, the future is now. According to the 2000 census, two-thirds of Californians over 40 are white, and two-thirds of those below the age of 18 are children of color. This is California's generation gap: the demographic divergence between those voting and paying taxes and those who are the state's future.[6]

Research has suggested that where such generation gaps are large, equitable investment suffers. Pastor and Reed, for example, calculate a specific measure of "demographic divergence," or the difference between the share of whites in the population who are 65 years or older and the number of whites under the age of 18.[7] They then assess the cross-state relationship between this measure and per-capita capital/infrastructure outlays by the state.[8] They find that the larger the difference between the ethnic composition of the old and the young, the more likely it is that states will have a substantially higher share of outlays at the local level as opposed to the state level. The localization of spending may reflect a desire to husband resources close to home, but it also suggests a "circling the wagons" mindset and clearly works against using state resources to address imbalances in basic community assets and local educational systems.

Older, whiter, and wealthier voters do not always see their fate as tied to that of younger, minority, and poorer residents and are therefore unwilling to tax themselves for that future.[9] Public opinion data also provide some support of the age-ethnicity axis: In a poll conducted to assess the public's view of infrastructure spending, the Public Policy Institute of California found that 62 percent of people ages 18–34 said that low-income and minority schools should get more money for facilities, while 54 percent of those age 35–54 and 49 percent of those 55 years and older thought so.[10]

Economically Tracking

California once prided itself on broad opportunities for economic advancement and personal transformation. The state now possesses deep economic cleavages and restrictions for certain populations. Between 1980–82 and 2001–03, the real income of the bottom one-fifth of California families grew 11.4 percent, while income for the top 5 percent of Californians grew by 73.3 percent.[11] The rise in inequality was a national phenomenon, but California's rich saw their incomes rise about six and a half times faster than the bottom 20 percent, while the national elite saw their incomes rise four and a half times faster.[12] Thus, by the 2001–03 period, for example, California had become the sixth most unequal state in the country when comparing the top one-fifth of households to the bottom one-fifth of households, the tenth most unequal when comparing the top one-fifth to the middle one-fifth, and the eighth most unequal when comparing the income of the top 5 percent to the bottom 20 percent.[13]

To calculate changes in income at various decile points in the income distribution during a more recent time frame, we used the Current Population Survey (CPS). Income was inflation-adjusted to reflect 2004 dollars.[14] I broke the data into three periods: 1988–90, a boom period; 1998–2000,

FIGURE 5.1: Household Income Changes (at Various Breaks in the Distribution) in California, from Business Cycle Peak to Peak and 2002–2004

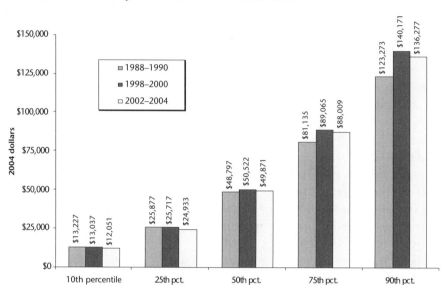

another boom period for the state economy; and 2002–04, the most recent similar-length period and one that reflects the tail end of the state recession and the beginnings of a tepid recovery. Figure 5.1 reveals the pattern: Income for those at the tenth decile actually declined steadily, income at the twenty-fifth rose slightly from boom to boom but fell again, and income at the median stagnated. Although those at the seventy-fifth and ninetieth percentiles saw declines in the last recession, they were much better off over the whole period.

The pattern of inequality is not disconnected from the new demography detailed in figure 5.1. Poverty in California differs dramatically by race. To look at this, consider the experience of individuals living below 150 percent of the federally defined poverty level. In 2004, the official poverty rate for a family of four with two children was $19,157, and the 150 percent level was $28,736, which is much closer to what most analysts would consider struggling in California's high-cost housing markets.[15] By that measure, nearly 40 percent of Latinos lived below the poverty rate in the 1999–2004 period, with the figure for African Americans being 30 percent; for Asian Americans, 18 percent; and 15 percent for whites.[16]

An alternative view of the distribution divide can be seen in figure 5.2. This figure reflects the ethnic composition of households by income deciles in California for the period 2002–04. Note that the white (Anglo) share of households steadily rises in the higher deciles, peaking at 71 percent of households in the top decile; African Americans have a very high representation in the lowest decile; the Asian American community is bifurcated, with significant representation at the lowest and highest deciles; and Latino households peak in the second, third, and fourth deciles. The latter pattern reflects the fact that Latinos are often disproportionately working poor.[17]

Household income differences are driven in part by different outcomes in the labor market. Reed and Cheng found that in 2000, the median hourly wage for white men in California was $20.83 per hour, substantially higher than the $16.96 hourly wage of Latino men and the $15.41 hourly wage of African American men.[18] White women made $17.03 per hour, while Latina and African American women earned $13.40 and $14.57, respectively. Despite affirmative action and other policies meant to increase equality, the researchers found no evidence of a substantial change in the wage gap

FIGURE 5.2: Ethnic Composition of Households by Household Income Deciles in California, 2002–2004

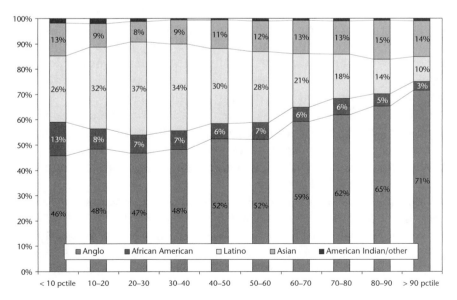

between whites and U.S.-born Latinos and African Americans between the years of 1979 and 2000.

I explore the reasons for these wage gaps in more detail below, utilizing a brief regression analysis to point out the factors that lie behind wage differentials. As it turns out, discrimination in labor markets still plays a role, but an important underlying factor is the difference in education and the increasing returns from learning in today's economy. For this reason, efforts to address the unequal educational system could have long-lasting impacts on social inequality in general.

Geographically Isolating

As the social and economic differences widen, California's geography is transforming into an economic and ethnic patchwork, with groups migrating and clustering along race and class lines. Although the state is multiethnic and multicultural as a whole, economic segregation is rampant. Even as minorities are moving into parts of the state that had seen low populations of such groups in the past, there remain distinct pockets of racial homogeneity.

One type of geographic separation, concentrated poverty, is defined as the proportion of all poor people citywide who live in neighborhoods where more than 40 percent of families have incomes below the poverty threshold. A recent study from the Brookings Institution found that the number of people living in high-poverty neighborhoods in the United States had actually declined by 24 percent in the 1990s—except in California, where the population in high-poverty neighborhoods had increased by 87 percent.[19] Of the U.S. metropolitan areas with the largest increases in concentrated poverty, seven of the fifteen were located in California. A more recent Brookings study, *Katrina's Window: Confronting Concentrated Poverty Across America*, found that Fresno, California, was the metro area with the highest rate of concentrated poverty in the entire country, beating out even New Orleans, the supposed focus of the study. Three additional California cities also ranked in the top twenty cities with the highest rates of concentrated poverty: Long Beach, Los Angeles, and San Diego.[20]

What about middle-income households? Another Brookings study found that the proportion of middle-income families and neighborhoods in metro areas across the country is shrinking, but that this trend is especially evident in California. Between 1970 and 2000, the Los Angeles, San Francisco, and Oakland metro areas each saw their middle-income populations drop, while their very low-income and very high-income populations grew.[21] And of the hundred largest metro areas in the United States in 2000, Los Angeles's share of middle-income neighborhoods was the smallest (28.3%). As a whole, fewer than one-third of neighborhoods in California are middle income.[22]

Other studies have examined the geographic migration patterns of various racial groups in California. While whites, Latinos, African Americans, and Asian Americans are all increasingly migrating to the interior areas of California, the population of whites in California's large metro areas is dropping as the population of Asian Americans and Latinos rises.[23] Even when Latinos and Asian Americans suburbanize, they often spread out to immediately adjoining inner-ring suburbs with older infrastructure and fewer economic opportunities.[24]

One research team examined racial segregation in Los Angeles County using a measure that charts the likelihood of having neighbors of a different ethnicity. White isolation from African Americans has remained steady over the last twenty years, and white isolation from Latinos and Asian Americans has increased.[25] California as a whole shows similar isolation. Based on analyses of data from the U.S. Census Bureau's Housing and Household Economic Statistics Division, nearly three-fourths of California's metro areas saw a rise in white segregation, while more than three-fourths of the rest of the nation's metro areas saw a decline in such segregation.[26]

Politically Dividing

Voting results in California also reflect racial, economic, geographic, and age divides. A record number of nonwhite Californians voted in the 2004 election, but nonwhite voters account for a smaller percentage of voters than they represent in the general population. Latinos were 34 percent of the state population but 18 percent of the voters in 2004. Asian Americans, with 7 percent of the voters, were 12 percent of the population.[27] Part of the reason for the disparity is that California's nonwhite groups are generally younger than the white population. Furthermore, many of the state's Latinos and Asian Americans are noncitizens and cannot vote. This means that political voice does not necessarily reflect the numbers affected by electoral decisions.

There are also large differences between the political preferences of each racial group. In the 2004 presidential election, whites were nearly evenly split between votes for George Bush and John Kerry, whereas nonwhite voters strongly favored Kerry, with 66 percent of Latinos, 83 percent of African Americans, and 64 percent of Asian Americans voting for him.[28] There are also significant geographic dissimilarities in California's voting patterns. In San Francisco and Los Angeles, for example, the majority of voters chose

Kerry (63% and 69%, respectively), compared to only around 40 percent of voters in the inland regions.[29]

These racial and geographic gaps are especially significant because they align with different attitudes of California's Republican and Democratic voters on the issues of government poverty programs, immigration, and other state economic conditions.[30]

In short, our demographic divergence has been matched by increasing inequality, increasing segregation, and increasingly polarized political perspectives. The Multiple Pathways approach to education makes great sense, but any large-scale change in the education system will require public and political support that reaches across long-standing and growing demographic boundaries. The social challenges presented by our state's fragmentation cannot be remedied by any particular educational innovation, no matter how novel or well conceived. Rather, our current complex set of problems will require an equally complex mix of solutions and coalitions.

FRAGMENTATION AND THE FUTURE

Increasing public and political support for large-scale change is constrained by current understandings (formal and informal) of economic theory. Concerns about inequality are generally seen as the province of well-meaning liberals: Worried about fairness, they suggest ways the government can ameliorate the pain and injustice. Yet, increasingly, economic vitality is invoked to make the case for addressing inequality and fragmentation. Deep social chasms can make the state less competitive, load economic and social burdens on the "most productive" residents, and damage growth, particularly at a regional level.

Traditional economic theory generally offers growth as the fairest and most efficient way to address inequality. In this view, the focus should be on growth per se, and eventually benefits will trickle down to those at the bottom of the labor market and income distribution. But new research is suggesting that inequality itself matters: It can result in underinvestment in basic education (a point alluded to in our discussion of demographic divergence), and the resulting social tensions can damage consensus on tough economic decisions and erode the social capital that can tie a region together.[31] Many statistical studies now find support for the connection between equity and growth.[32] Economists from the Federal Reserve recently looked at growth factors for midsize regions, including such measures as a region's workforce skill level, the role of small businesses, quality of life variables, and the costs associated with a declining industrial base. They also included measures of ethnic diversity and minority business ownership, racial inclusion, and income inequality. They found that a skilled workforce, high levels of racial inclusion, and income equality correlate strongly and positively with economic growth.[33]

The bottom line is that doing good and doing well can go hand in hand. Investments and commitments needed to overcome the fragmentation wrought by residential segregation, income inequality, and concentrated poverty can positively effect per-capita income growth. Why then has the state been drifting apart rather than growing together?

Why Did We Fragment?

There are many reasons for California's social and economic fragmentation; here I focus on the intersection of income differentials in the state with ethnicity and nativity. Certainly immigration has increased the state's diversity. While the rest of the country has seen the immigrant share of its population grow from 4.7 percent to 8.1 percent (1960–2000), California's share tripled from 8.5 percent to 25.9 percent (see figure 5.3). It is no surprise that the cur-

FIGURE 5.3: Immigrants as a Share of the Population, California and the Rest of the United States, 1960–2000

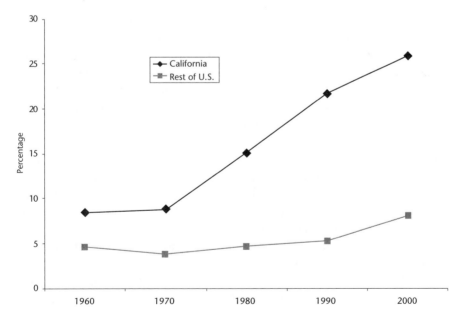

FIGURE 5.4: Educational Attainment for Work Force by Ethnicity and Immigration in California, 2000–2005

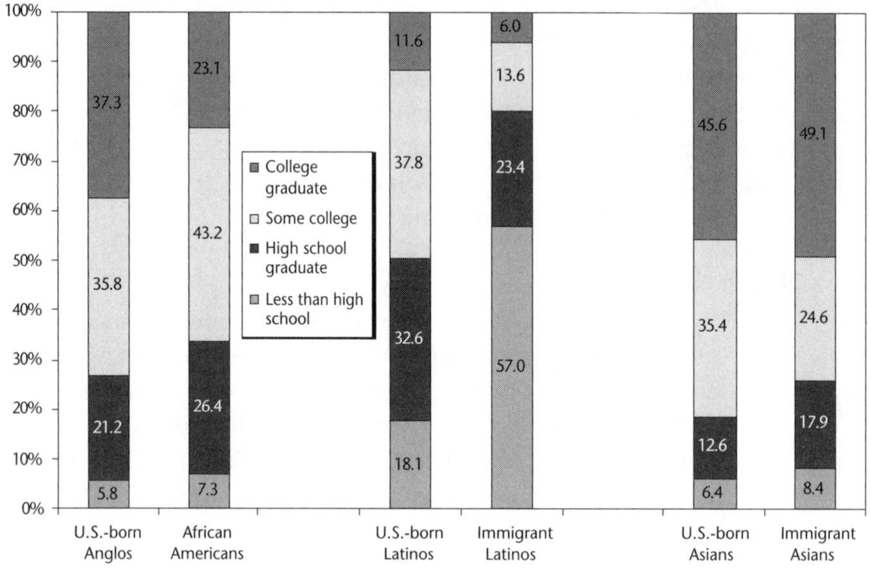

rent national debate about immigration and its consequences seems like an echo of the debates heard in California in the 1980s and 1990s.[34]

The rise in the state's immigrant population is often linked to both the general level of inequality and the high rates of poverty in the state. Many new immigrants, particularly those from Latin America, are poor and poorly educated. Figure 5.4 shows the educational attainment of those in the labor force. Fifty-seven percent of Latino immigrants lack a high school degree, and there are significant differences in college-degree attainment between whites and Asian Americans on one hand and African Americans and Latinos on the other. Even beyond the education difference, there is a "wage penalty" for being a recent migrant, partly because of documentation issues, partly because of an initial unfamiliarity with U.S. labor markets, and partly because of the job steering associated with ethnic-specific social networks.[35]

Some argue that influxes of low-skill immigrants have pushed down the wages of other low-skill workers, but other economists have found almost no effect of large influxes of immigrants on the wages of other low-skill workers.[36] Some studies even find a correlation (though not causality) between cities with fast economic growth and a large presence of immigrants.[37] The reasons for the muted effects are complex and probably due to the fact that immigrant labor can complement rather than substitute for established low-wage workers. Certain industries remain in a locale if low-wage labor comes to them, rather than leaving for places that have an abundant supply. Retaining these industries generates ancillary employment and wages for those who were there before.

What is in less dispute is that the rewards for work have shifted in ways that increasingly value education (with some attributing the higher returns for education to increased global competition and others to technological change). The real hourly wages of workers at various education levels between 1973 and 2003 for the United States as a whole dropped by 14 percent for those with less than high school education, while the wages of college grads rose 19 percent, and those with advanced degrees earned 24 percent more per hour. Changes in wages from 1990 to 2003 were less drastic but followed the same patterns. The drop in real wages for jobs requiring less than high school education was 0.5 percent, while jobs requiring college education and advanced degrees saw 16.5 percent and 14.6 percent wage increases, respectively.[38]

This holds true in California. In table 5.1, I report on the results for a regression in which I test for the effects of various factors on hourly wages for workers in California; the data comes from the CPS, utilized for many of the other charts here.[39] The variables reported are quite traditional in wage equations, including measures of the worker's educational achievement, work experience, ethnicity, marriage status, and gender, and certain characteristics of the job (whether it is unionized, in a large firm, full-time, or year-round). The innovation here is to pool for two time periods (1989–1995 and 1999–2005) to see if the reported coefficients on educational achievement have increased over time.

Indeed, the returns to education seem to have risen. With the base case being an individual without a high school degree, the premium for a high school degree, some college, and a college degree have all increased. This is a remarkable increase in the importance of education in a short ten-year period; moreover, the negative effect of being Latino in the labor market has declined, suggesting that some of this discrimination has shifted into education differences.[40]

With regard to migrant status, unfortunately, the CPS did not start collecting nativity data on the labor force until 1994, and so we redid the regressions above comparing 1994–96 to 2003–05. While we do not report the details

TABLE 5.1: Regression Results on Hourly Wage for Two Time Periods in California

	1989–1995		1999–2005	
	Coefficient	Sig.	Coefficient	Sig.
High school grad	0.177	***	0.214	***
Some college education	0.270	***	0.344	***
College graduate	0.522	***	0.6111	***
Work experience	0.024	***	0.025	***
Square of work experience	0.000	***	0.000	***
African American	−0.060	**	−0.085	***
Latino	−0.183	***	−0.018	***
Asian	−0.133	***	−0.089	***
Married	0.084	***	0.057	***
Female	−0.129	***	−0.082	***
Employed in large firm	0.091	***	0.074	***
Union member	0.297	***	0.224	***
Full-time, year-round	0.167	***	0.130	***
Adjusted R-squared	0.394	—	0.320	—
Number of observations	4011	—	4935	—

*** means significant at the .01 level; ** means significant at the .05 level.

here, two results are of interest. First, the negative coefficient for Asian Americans in the wage regression above becomes insignificant, thereby suggesting that discrimination against that group is mostly against migrants. Second and more important to our point here, the returns to education increase, even during this shorter time period. Moreover, the attempt to control for immigrant status actually yields a bigger increase in the returns for having a high school degree and some college (the increase in the premium for having a college degree is the same).[41]

These results suggest that Multiple Pathways—in which students are encouraged to finish high school, think about career trajectories that will require some post-high school training, and think about college—may be particularly important for native workers, who can benefit from shifting from their current employment to higher-skill employment as an increasingly immigrant labor force serves as complementary labor. The generally increasing importance of various forms of education suggests that the approach of Multiple Pathways, which tends to keep options open, may be particularly suited to addressing underlying inequalities.

Multiple Pathways to What?

The social fragmentation discussed above manifests along racial, geographic, educational, immigration, and economic lines (to name just a few). Further, there is reason to believe that each of these aspects has at least correlational, and likely causal, effects on one another—effects that are complex, reflexive, and iterative. We might conclude, then, that as a general rule, addressing any one aspect of fragmentation (such as education or poverty) without focused consideration of the others simply multiplies the difficulty of change. Indeed, many failures of education reform can be attributed to narrow school-based interventions that ignore or exacerbate other dimensions of fragmentation.

A Multiple Pathways approach to education requires learning contexts, both within and outside schools, that address all aspects of social fragmentation. Neglecting some, or in some cases one, will seriously diminish the efficacy of the approach. However, the Multiple Pathways approach as envisioned in this volume seeks to create learning environments that neither reflect nor reproduce today's fragmentation.

Of course, schools' "effectiveness" in preparing students for the real world hinges on conditions in that world. Will there be a match between education goals, career preparation, and the job market? Projections show that while the fastest-growing occupations often require some education beyond high school, those with the largest growth will actually require few hard skills (although they will require the sort of soft skills that can be garnered from various modes of delivering a Multiple Pathways approach, such as job placement, an integrated curriculum, real-world experiences, and internships). For example, the California Employment Development Department indicates that of the top ten jobs for numerical growth (2002–12), six require no more than short-term on-the-job training, one requires moderate-length job training, one an associate degree, one a bachelor's degree, and one a bachelor's plus experience.[42]

This is not simply an anomaly at the top. Table 5.2 offers the numbers for all future occupations in the state.[43] The table includes job growth (the net increase in the number of jobs) as well as job openings, a calculation that takes into account separations (that is, retirements and other departures) and thus provides a better idea of where job searchers will be looking for new employment as they enter the labor market. Over half of the projected new jobs will require only short-term or moderate training or postsecondary vocational education. In this sense, Multiple Pathways that prepare students for both work and postsecondary education could allow them to move nimbly between work, on-the-job training, and higher education (community college or four-year) as job requirements shift and retooling is necessary.

Moreover, Multiple Pathways may be especially important because the need for "ready-to-work" skills seems to be escalating, even for occupations that formerly required only short-term training. Murnane and Levy argue that skill requirements are increasing even for entry-level jobs, and they suggest that the "new basic skills" include a strong reading ability; mastery of basic math and problem solving: and the ability to work in groups, communicate with others, give presentations, and perform basic computer tasks.[44]

TABLE 5.2: Occupational Projections for the State of California, 2002–2012, by Educational Requirements

Wage Levels		Educational Requirements
Mean	Median	
$10.60	$10.29	Short-term OJT
$18.36	$17.42	Moderate-term OJT
$21.79	$22.64	Long-term OJT
$24.47	$23.40	Work experience
$18.29	$17.74	Postsecondary VocEd
$28.35	$32.87	Associate degree
$31.27	$28.63	Bachelor's degree
$47.71	$48.33	Bachelor's degree + experience
$28.33	$30.70	Master's degree
$58.79	$62.26	Professional degree
$36.09	$33.63	Doctoral degree

*Wages are in 2005 dollars; OJT = on-the-job training.

A Multiple Pathways approach focuses on these skills for both college-goers and non-college-goers.

Even though the skill needs may be higher, the wages are not. Table 5.2 shows that jobs requiring only short-term training have wages that leave employees well below the poverty threshold for a family of four. Jobs requiring moderate or vocational training—the sort of work that Multiple Pathways students might fill—have wages that allow the employee to creep just above the 150 percent poverty threshold line. Thus, education alone cannot address the marginal poverty that many workers face: We need labor standards as well.

What about the skill composition of future employment? Table 5.3 suggests that about 27 percent of the new jobs will require a bachelor's degree or higher, a figure that is not far away from the 29 percent figure of all those in the labor force with such a degree for the 2000–05 period. But while this presents the general impression that there is a near match between job needs and jobseeker skills, there are significant differences in college completion by ethnic group: about 46 percent for U.S.-born Asian Americans and 37 percent

TABLE 5.3: Occupational Projections for the State of California, 2002–2012, by Educational Requirements

Job Growth	Job Openings	Educational Requirements
33.3%	41.4%	Short-term OJT
15.9%	15.7%	Moderate-term OJT
8.6%	7.7%	Long-term OJT
5.7%	5.5%	Work experience
3.6%	3.4%	Postsecondary VocEd
5.2%	4.0%	Associate degree
17.6%	14.1%	Bachelor's degree
5.6%	4.6%	Bachelor's degree + experience
2.7%	2.2%	Master's degree
1.2%	0.9%	Professional degree
0.6%	0.5%	Doctoral degree

OJT = on-the-job training.

for U.S.-born whites, but just 23 percent for African Americans, 12 percent for U.S.-born Latinos, and 6 percent for immigrant Latinos. This suggests the possibility of a permanent and widening racial gap in the labor force.

Over the longer run, education requirements may rise and make the distribution worse. Murnane and Levy's more recent work indicates that the labor market will increasingly bifurcate: Computers may replace moderate- and less-skilled workers, but they complement the work and enhance the productivity of high-skilled employees, thus raising the demand and wages for workers at the top. Meanwhile, moderate- and less-skilled workers, who in previous decades had been able to secure a place in the middle class, will face smaller paychecks or spottier employment in the growing low-wage, low-skill service sector.[45]

David Neumark of the Public Policy Institute of California has stressed that the projections of education requirements may be incorrect, partly because employers may have educational attainment preferences that exceed the requirements stated in job descriptions.[46] Other research from the Public Policy Institute of California recognizes the shifting industrial mix, noting that over 40 percent of workers in the fast-growing service industries have a college degree, but only 28 percent in the shrinking manufacturing industry have a college degree. Projections show that employment demand for workers with a college degree will be 39 percent in 2025, but college graduates in 2000 comprised only 30 percent of the workforce population.[47]

The analysis raises two issues. First, given the uneven distribution of educational attainment, the likelihood that racial disparities in incomes will rise is even more pronounced under Neumark's scenario. Second, the difference between the short-term projections of the state and Neumark's more optimistic medium-term projections suggests transition problems between the immediate future, when low-skill jobs dominate, and a more distant future, when the industrial shakeout raises educational requirements. That longer-term projection underscores the importance of a Multiple Pathways approach in order for workers to go from one path to another over time.

PUTTING IT TOGETHER

Although the Multiple Pathways approach may have a good fit with current and projected economic circumstances, we must recognize that this approach will be swimming upstream in a river of inequality. While a Multiple Pathways approach can begin to address the broader challenge of both economic and social equity, we also require a broad vision and commitment that takes into account three fundamental facts.

First, any new approach to educating California's youth and workers must be accompanied by strategies that address the state's growing population, changing demographics, and shifting labor market. Californians must not assume that education, or Multiple Pathways, is the silver bullet, that it will erase income differentials and teach us to avoid discrimination and segregation.

Second, a Multiple Pathways strategy must be in sync with the true nature of the economy, neither an idealistic version in which everyone attends college followed by high-paying careers nor a supposedly unalterable one that accepts race, class, and gender segregation of the labor market. When all California children learn about and have the support to reach the fullest range of employment possibilities, then all Californians benefit.

Third, we must embrace the diversity of the labor force. The California labor market of the future needs an array of workers with a variety of skills. Multiple Pathways in education must mean permeable categories and paths, not stereotypes or boxes. Unlike tracking, Multiple Pathways must offer all students education and skills that can be used to achieve a variety of career goals. It is not about overemphasizing differences but about tailoring education to both the talents and challenges of California's students and workers, and to the needs of the labor market itself.

What is the broader policy mix that will need to accompany Multiple Pathways if we wish to move the needle on inequality? As the editors of the *Economist* suggested when discussing rising income inequality in the United States: "Inequality is not inherently wrong—as long as three conditions are met: first, society as a whole is getting richer; second, there is a safety net for the very poor; and third, everybody, regardless of class, race, creed or sex, has an opportunity to climb up through the system."[48] Increased prosperity, protections for the poor, and equity in opportunity and mobility: What is the combination of strategies that can achieve these objectives in California?

Economic growth is key, and Californians know this. A 2004 survey of California residents found that the economy topped the list of most important issues for the state in the future.[49] In fact 24 percent of respondents felt that the most important issue facing the state in the next twenty years is the economy, jobs, and unemployment, and this concern was even higher among Latinos (33%), African Americans (33%) and Asian Americans (32%) compared to whites (18%). It is little wonder that respondents of color were more focused on this: Rapid economic growth tends to shrink differentials, partly because employers begin to hire those they may not have in the past. Indeed, the only brief progress in arresting the long-term negative distributional trends depicted above occurred in the late 1990s, when the economy was buoyant.[50]

Whether the racial and economic rifts between Californians widen or are mended depends in part on the quality of the state's mid- and long-term economic strategy and a corresponding educational strategy. Of course, improving our workforce skills can be a part of this, but there will also be important choices ahead with regard to supporting particular industrial clusters (e.g., biotechnology or the logistics industry) through a combination of subsidies and infrastructure. Multiple Pathways can play a role in this growth: Delivery systems (i.e., career academies, magnet programs, integrated curricula) can focus on providing the skills required for particular industrial clusters. Resolving planning complexities that protect our environment but slow business investment may also be important. I avoid any discussion of particular choices because the simple point is that those concerned about equity need to develop a much clearer position on how growth will be promoted and not just redistributed.

At the same time, pro-growth sectors, including business leaders, need to be challenged on just how far we let people fall. This essentially means labor standards in California: measures that range from minimum wage laws to health insurance guarantees to efforts to encourage unions. Many cities across the state have begun to adopt living-wage ordinances, but while these are higher than the current minimum wage, they often apply only to a small sector of the local workforce. The governor and the state legislature have agreed on future increases in the state minimum wage, and both seem interested in expanding provision of health insurance. One approach is to attach health insurance to jobs, but recent efforts to do so have been under concerted attack by business groups.

However, driving the economy forward and protecting the bottom does not get at a key issue: pathways to the middle class. This requires an emphasis on mobility and training, particularly for those already in the labor force. The current discussion about education, including Multiple Pathways, tends to focus on those still in school. This effort to rescue the long-term future, in the absence of attention to incumbent worker training, could sacrifice a whole generation of current workers, who are, moreover, often the parents of the students that the new educational strategies hope to help.

Critically important for the advancement of working people is the community college system: It primes the less-prepared students for university and provides a plethora of practical training activities for jobseekers and incumbent employees. This is an especially important entry point for California's immigrant population, whether they have high school degrees, are seeking advanced job skills, or lack a college degree and need convenient access to higher education resources. Yet a recent study found that California's community colleges ranked forty-fifth out of forty-nine states in terms of revenues spent per student. It also found that the last thirty years have seen increases in real per-student revenue of nearly 25 percent for the University of California, while the community colleges saw only a 4 percent increase in real per-student revenue.[51]

Education is not just K–12, the university, and the community college system. Adult education and basic job training are also critical. English skills for adults are especially important because they can boost wages for full-time workers by more than 15 percent, even controlling for education, immigrant status, and other factors that usually affect wage outcomes.[52] Training also needs to be geared to those who are already working, that is, to the working poor; this leads to an array of mundane matters like the timing of classes, the desirability of on-site training, and the need to couple vocational English training with worker education about basic labor rights.[53] My simple point is this: If Multiple Pathways also provide a path for lifelong learning, lifelong learning possibilities need to be in place.

Today, California's demography, geography, and economy can be characterized by its famous ground-shaking earthquakes, which create multiple Californias rather than a unified state. California's "social earthquake" is caused by dramatic demographic shifts and by migration patterns that are occurring along racial and economic lines, with increased isolation of the poor being one result. And the increasing economic inequality warns us of violent aftershocks to come, aftershocks that could rip apart California's population and crumble its economy.

The Multiple Pathways approach appropriately recognizes the growing premium placed on college education and the likelihood that that premium will continue to increase. It seeks to prepare all students for college, and thus allows them to enter college later, should they decide to work full-time at first. But even such a hopeful and appropriate educational plan must be nested in a broader approach that pays attention to improving economic growth, creating career pathways, and ensuring social guarantees that will ease transitions, retraining, and other adjustments in the years ahead. This will require a new level of social cohesion and political will, not just in California but in the nation.

CHAPTER 6

Can Multiple Pathways Link Vulnerable Groups to Changing Labor Markets?

Michael A. Stoll

Michael A. Stoll is professor of public policy in the School of Public Affairs and associate director of the Center for the Study of Urban Poverty at the University of California–Los Angeles. Stoll's publications examine the labor market difficulties of less-skilled workers and in particular the role that racial residential segregation, job location patterns, job skill demands, employer discrimination, job competition, transportation, and job information play in limiting employment opportunities.

Stoll's essay explores the potential of Multiple Pathways for addressing the workforce and educational needs of youth who are most at risk for leaving school without a high school degree, specifically, racial minorities living in areas with heavily disadvantaged schools and those who complete high school but do not complete a college education. Through a synthesis of the research, Stoll finds that significant economic and social transformations have changed the economic opportunities of and rewards from work for those with limited education, especially young people living in poor, urban, and minority communities. Stoll examines the high school completion and college-going rates of particular disadvantaged groups, documents the labor market "cost" of leaving school before completing a high school degree, and the costs for some groups even after achieving a high school degree. Stoll then examines the changing skill requirements of jobs in the economy, the reasons for these changes, and how they have influenced employer hiring behavior

*in the labor market. He concludes that Multiple Pathways' integration
of requisite knowledge and skills in the current economy with relevant
and rigorous academic instruction is likely to be effective in linking
underserved and disaffected youth to a labor market in which jobs may or
may not require a baccalaureate degree.*

INTRODUCTION

Over the past two decades, significant economic and social transformations
have changed the economic opportunities of and rewards from work for
those with limited education. In particular, good jobs that require only a
basic education are disappearing from poor, urban, and minority communities. Increasingly, young people in these communities are having a hard time
finding work and forming strong labor market attachments, thus raising the
"cost" of a limited education. Labor market trends indicate that new employment opportunities require "advanced generic skills" that apply in a wide
range of real-world jobs. To meet this need, high schools must teach new
skills in new ways for new jobs.

The Multiple Pathways approach is one way to address this challenge.
Incorporating hands-on, skills-based education alongside college preparation, Multiple Pathways prepares students for entry into a changing labor
market and for a college-level education. This chapter explores the potential
effectiveness of blurring the distinction between preparation for college and
preparation for the labor market. The approach is likely to benefit the entire
workforce, especially racial minorities in areas with heavily disadvantaged
schools.

Schools have not responded to the changes in the types, locations, and
skills of today's good jobs. This failure disproportionately harms black and
Latino youth, whose decisions to leave school early or not pursue college after they graduate is increasingly costly. Because a Multiple Pathways
approach integrates knowledge of the requisite skills in the current economy
with relevant and rigorous academic instruction, it is more likely than traditional school approaches to engage students and to link underserved and
disaffected youth to a labor market in which jobs may or may not require a
baccalaureate degree.

Of course Multiple Pathways is but one schools-based approach among
others that can improve the economic fortunes of these groups. As this chapter makes clear, the array of challenges facing less-educated black and Latino
youth in poor, urban, and minority communities (e.g., spatial and skill bar-

riers to employment, persistent discrimination) require a variety of policy approaches, including those over which schools have little direct control. These include expansionary monetary policy and broad-based antidiscrimination efforts.

To address this larger context in relationship to schools, the chapter examines the high school completion and college-going rates of particular disadvantaged groups and then documents the labor market economic cost of leaving school before completing a high school degree, and the costs for some groups even after achieving a high school degree. This cost has increased in terms of declining wages over the past twenty years. Then I examine the changing skill requirements of jobs, the reasons for these changes, and how they have influenced employers' hiring behavior. Next, we explore different educational approaches that could address the changes in the labor market as well as opportunities for youth who do not follow traditional trajectories through college, jobs, and careers. I also look at traditional vocational education approaches and some German models that seem to be more successful than the U.S models in linking youth with good jobs. Career academies are one of the most widely used approaches to integrating academic and career-based learning. Of the extant high school models, career academies may best meet the goals of a Multiple Pathways approach to high school reform.

THE CHANGING COST OF LIMITED EDUCATIONAL ATTAINMENT

As College-Going Increases, Gaps Remain

Education has played a key role in social mobility in the United States, and for many marginalized and immigrant groups, it has been an institution for social advancement. Over the past few decades, though, the importance of education appears to have accelerated in the labor market. Technology and work specialization have increased the need for skills and credentials. Moreover, the earnings of those with a college degree have risen relative to those with only a high school degree.

College attainment has grown rapidly over the past twenty to thirty years. This is partly due to the increased "payoff" that investment in college brings. Education is a good investment when it brings higher future earnings—earnings that overshadow the current costs of going to school (e.g., tuition, books) and the lost earnings from being in school instead of earning income.

Between 1980 and 2000, rates of high school completion and college attainment rose for most racial and ethnic groups, including disadvantaged blacks and Latinos. For example, black men earned college degrees at a rate

3 percent higher in 2000 than in 1980, and their rate of leaving high school without a diploma fell dramatically over that period.[1] The percentage of black women who earned a college degree or more rose from 60 to 66 percent over this period, and the percentage of those who did not earn a high school degree fell by 15.5 percentage points between 1980 and 1990. However, over that same time period, college attainment rose much faster for more advantaged groups, such as whites. As a result, the large college attainment gap, between blacks and Latinos on one hand and whites on the other, did not change.[2]

The increase in college attendance for blacks and Latinos is attributable to a number of factors, including modest improvement of primary and secondary schools, affirmative action in college, and increasing academic preparedness.[3] But growing political opposition and legal challenges to affirmative action programs in higher education, rising college costs, and federal rollbacks in government-sponsored financial aid will surely limit blacks' and Latinos' college-going in the near future and likely put the brakes on closing the college education gap with whites. Furthermore, intense competition from well-represented groups (wealthy, whites, Asians) for increasingly scarce seats in colleges continues to raise the bar for college admissions; as a result, underrepresented groups can make gains in attainment and yet fall further behind in college participation.

Changing Economic Costs of Low Educational Attainment

The good news of the decline in the percentage of high school dropouts from disadvantaged racial groups between the 1970s and 1990s is tempered by the changing economic misfortunes of those with a high school degree or less. From the early 1900s through the 1960s, the real earnings of less-educated male workers grew markedly,[4] bolstered by increased productivity, relative shortages of less-educated workers, expanding unionization, and federal minimum wage legislation. As a result, a high school degree or less education had little negative consequences on economic well-being. This began to shift in the 1970s.

In the 1970s and 1980s, especially after the oil embargo and recession of 1973, less-educated men earned less in absolute terms, as well as relative to the earnings of more educated (i.e., college-educated) workers. These declines accelerated during the 1980s, especially for young males with a high school degree or less.[5] Furthermore, young, less-skilled black men's outcomes fell relative to those of less-skilled whites.[6] This pattern reversed trends from about the 1940s, when a decade-by-decade convergence of black-white earnings was observed.[7]

Many explanations have been offered for this reversal in the economic fortunes of less-educated men: slackening employer demand for less-educated workers as the skill requirements of jobs increased; falling unionization rates; and declining levels in the real value of the minimum wage.[8]

Other factors specific to black men have probably contributed as well, including weakened enforcement of antidiscrimination policies and restricted affirmative action programs.[9] Changes in the industrial/manufacturing sectors and declines in the economic vitality of central cities have undoubtedly played a role also.[10]

This period of deterioration of earnings and employment for men with less education occurred at the same time that American cities were transforming from centers of goods production to centers of the new service economy. In 1950, about one in three metropolitan residents worked in manufacturing, mostly in central city plants. By 1990, only about one in five worked in manufacturing, with most employed in suburban plants.[11] Jobs in central cities were increasingly replaced with service jobs that, on average, required more skills and educational credentials.[12]

In the 1980s, William Julius Wilson's landmark study of the connection between race and concentrated poverty proposed that this transformation helped marginalize less-skilled black men in the labor market.[13] More recent studies support Wilson's analysis.[14] Not only did cities lose better-paying manufacturing jobs, but they also lost low-skilled jobs, generally. Advances in communication and transportation allowed firms to move to cheaper suburban land, and job loss in central cities became a central economic tendency. Increasingly, black and Latino poor became geographically distant from labor market opportunities, contributing to their declining employment and earnings.[15]

Important social transformations accompanied these economic transformations. Between 1970 and 1990, the number of poor people living in high-poverty areas nearly doubled. Much of this growth occurred in predominantly black and Latino neighborhoods, the vast majority of which are located in inner cities. Moreover, much of the increased poverty occurred not because poor peopled moved there, but because poverty spread to more and more neighborhoods.[16] Thus, the declining fortunes of less-educated workers, coupled with changes in the economic structure of cities, influenced the growing social isolation and concentration of the poor.

Wilson noted that social isolation disconnected the poor from prosocial institutions, such as functional schools and active churches, and distanced them from strong middle-class role models—all of which contributed to negative "concentration effects." [17] Concurrently, middle-class children left inner-city schools as parents relocated to suburbs, as did jobs and other assets. This left the poor isolated, disadvantaged, and concentrated in ways not seen before.

These changes continue to result in the dismal labor force participation rate and employment rates of inner-city youth and prime-age adults (those aged 25–55), especially men with limited education. Over this period (1980–1990), black males aged 16–24 with a high school education or less experienced a drop in labor force participation from 81 percent to 71 percent. Similarly, over the same period, black males between ages 25 and 34 with a high school diploma or less exhibited a drop in labor force attachment from 91 percent to 82 percent.[18] Thus, the labor market attachment of even prime-age black men fell dramatically during this period. The imminent consequences of these trends include lower employment and income, as well as the related economic and social ills that may result, such as declining income support for families.

Attachment to the labor market declined over this period for all prime-age men, and especially for those without a high school degree. While the labor force participation rate for prime-age white men without a high school degree declined by 14 percentage points, the drop for black men was 23 percentage points. Though less sharp, these same patterns occurred for those with only a high school degree.

More startling is the decline in employment of less-educated prime-age men since the late 1980s, especially the decline for black men without a high school degree: Their decline was 20 percentage points from 1990 to 2000, while the decline for white men without a high school degree was 12 percentage points. In 2000, only about 45 percent of prime-age less-educated black men were working, while nearly 73 percent of similar white men were working. These figures are even worse for young people aged 16–24. By 2000, only 29 percent of all young black men without a high school degree were working, while the equivalent figure for whites was 63 percent.

Thus, over the past three decades, significant economic and social transformations have changed the economic opportunities of and the rewards from work for those with limited education, especially those living in poor communities. Increased investments in schooling could have attenuated these harmful labor market trends by providing skills and credentials to access the broader metropolitan labor market.

SKILL CHANGES AND EMPLOYER REQUIREMENTS IN LABOR MARKETS

Increased job skill requirements are partly responsible for the worsening economic position of less-educated workers, especially skills associated with the increasing computerization of the workplace.[19] But such computerization could lead to both down-skilling and up-skilling of work, depending on how the technology is used and introduced at the workplace, and for what management reasons.[20] For example, down-skilling might occur if computers were substituted for certain skilled clerks and only basic data input was required. Up-skilling could result from increased demand for software programmers, network administrators and consultants, and computer designers. Although much of the research suggests that computerization could result in both of these outcomes, on average, up-skilling appears to have a greater effect on skill requirements.[21]

Computerization of work is but a subset of the growing information technology economy and its effects on less-educated workers. By information technology we mean "the infrastructure and knowledge that is necessary to market information readily available."[22] In 1984, about one-fourth of all U.S. workers used a computer at work.[23] By 2000, this fraction had risen to over two-thirds.[24] Information technology occupations and skills are now integrated into the economy, most notably in the financial and health industries.[25]

The skill requirements of jobs that require use of computers change rapidly. Thus, workers who have few computer skills are at a distinct disadvantage unless they receive continuing education at community colleges or other such institutions.[26] Given the unequal access to computers by race in this country, the skill barriers to employment by less-educated minorities are likely to be compounded. Indeed, it is estimated that roughly half of Asians and whites have computer access at home, compared to about one-fourth of Latinos and blacks, with even less access in the central city than elsewhere and for the less educated. Moreover, there is evidence that these gaps widened during the 1990s.[27] Community technology centers (CTCs) are growing rapidly. CTCs provide computing and Internet access and training in mostly minority, underserved communities and are sponsored and financed by a wide range of actors, including the federal government, nonprofits, and foundations. Along with increased computer access at inner-city schools, CTCs are contributing to closing some dimensions of the digital divide, but more could be done, as Manuel Pastor argues in chapter 5.

Employer Hiring Behavior in Labor Markets

Before considering educational approaches that might improve the effectiveness of school-to-work linkages, especially for disadvantaged minority youth, it is useful to provide some context by reviewing some general facts about employer hiring behavior.

The following generalizations can be made about employer hiring behavior in entry-level labor markets:[28]

- Virtually all employers seek basic work readiness in prospective employees, while many seek additional hard and soft skills, even in low-wage markets;
- Since most skills are not directly observable at the time of hiring, employers generally seek applicants with certain credentials that signal employability and skill and tend to avoid those with certain stigmas, such as ex-offenders;
- Employers vary in the amounts of resources they can apply to hiring and compensation decisions, as well as in their information and expertise on these matters;
- Recruiting and screening choices (as well as compensation, promotion, and retention decisions) are often made informally, and can reflect varying degrees of employer prejudices, perceptions, and experiences;
- Employer access to a reliable and steady pool of applicants is also affected by its physical proximity to various neighborhoods and groups, its employee networks, and the tightness of the local and national labor markets.

The basic work-readiness that virtually all employers seek involves personal qualities such as honesty and reliability, an inclination to arrive at work on time every day, a positive attitude toward work, and the like. Avoiding problems associated with high absenteeism and poor work performance, such as drug abuse or physical/mental health difficulties, is often viewed as critical.[29]

Levy and Murnane note in their influential book, Teaching the New Basic Skills,[30] additional skills needed to function in the new economy and earn a middle-class income:

- Hard skills: basic mathematics, problem-solving and reading abilities of at least high school levels;
- Soft skills: working in groups and making effective oral and written presentations;
- Using computers to do simple tasks.

Beyond these, even low-wage jobs require basic cognitive skills, such as reading and writing; arithmetic skills, such as making change; rudimentary use of a computer, and similar skills. Soft skills frequently include interacting with customers or coworkers. Employers use credentials such as high school diplomas, previous work experience, and references to indicate applicants' qualities and skills that employers cannot observe directly. Skill tests are rare. Many employers infer job candidates' basic skills from applicants' educational attainment, the quality of writing on the application, and the interview, though these judgments are known to be unreliable.

Small and medium-size employers, where many young people apply for work, often lack human resources departments or the time, staff, or financial resources for formal recruitment and screening techniques, so they often make their selections informally (e.g., with help-wanted signs, referrals from their current employees). They may rely on simple written applications, interviews, or credentials to signal the desired employee skills and qualities.

Accordingly, the personal experiences of employees and perceptions about them will be more important to smaller establishments, and the potential for discriminatory judgments will be greater.[31] Discrimination might arise out of the employers' own biases, the perceived biases of their customers and/or employees,[32] or simply their lack of information about individual qualities and attributes among their applicants and therefore a reliance on group characteristics.

Employers seem most reluctant to hire young and less-educated black men, whom they often perceive to be threatening, either generally or on the basis of perceived criminality.[33] In contrast, immigrants are frequently perceived as being reliable and having good work attitudes and are therefore preferred, particularly in jobs where cognitive skill or language demands are minimal. Indeed, some employers use ethnic "niches" to obtain workers who are recommended by current employees and therefore deemed trustworthy.

Many employers, including smaller ones, have access to a steady stream of desirable applicants by virtue of geographic location; similarly, they can simply avoid applicants whom they do not want to consider.[34] However, all else being equal, smaller firms are much less likely to hire minorities, especially blacks, and are more likely to engage in statistical discrimination against mostly black men on the basis of perceived criminality.[35]

Employers' ability to generate sufficient applicants through largely informal sources also depends on the tightness of local and national labor markets. During the late 1990s, when unemployment sank to thirty-year lows, job vacancies climbed. Because traditional sources could not meet demand, employers seemed relatively open to hiring from groups they might otherwise have avoided.[36]

Black and Latino youth who leave school early are at greater disadvantage than similar white youth because they live in inner-city areas. There is evidence that jobs and industries that require more skill are located more centrally than less-skill-intensive industries, thus further constraining the employment possibilities of these youth.[37] To the extent that this pertains, jobs in central cities may have higher skill requirements than those in the suburbs, even though central cities may account for a smaller fraction of the metropolitan areas' jobs as a result of decentralization.[38]

Kasarda shows that skill requirements of jobs are rising beyond the skill attainment of workers in these areas. From 1970 to 1990 in most large metropolitan areas, the percentage of jobs in the central city that require a college degree is much higher than the share of residents with a college degree.[39] Moreover, he documents that the percentage of jobs in the central city that require a college degree increased dramatically from 1970 to 1990, and rose much faster than central city residents' attainment of a college degree over this period.

The problem is of particular importance to the employment and earnings of Latino workers, especially those of Mexican descent. Mexican Americans represent the majority of Latino workers and are one of the most economically disadvantaged groups in the United States. Mexican Americans have also accumulated less human capital than most racial and ethnic groups in the United States, though much of this is accounted for by recent Mexican immigrants who arrive with very limited education. The educational/human capital disadvantage of workers of Mexican descent is the principal reason why they earn less than other U.S. workers.[40] Thus, the problem of rising skill requirements of jobs is likely to hit the Latino community particularly hard if educational attainment levels do not rise.

Implications of These Trends for Educational Reform

These trends imply that schools must prepare students to be adaptable within a changing labor market that increasingly relies on problem-solving skills.

Competence in basic skills as well as training and knowledge in advanced specific skills are both necessary; furthermore, to accomplish these goals, schools must teach advanced generic skills in applied settings. A Multiple Pathways approach to education can arguably integrate applied knowledge and a college-preparatory education, providing the school (and intellectual) structure is responsive to the evolving labor markets. In particular, the active learning in applied settings that Multiple Pathways engenders can complement institutional and structural possibilities for continued on-the-job training. Multiple Pathways also facilitates movement through two-year and four-year institutions over the course of a career and movement from one career to another.

HIGH SCHOOL REFORM

One traditional pathway to the labor market has been through vocational education programs. For some high school students, the vocational emphasis on hands-on learning and career preparation supports school persistence and graduation rates. And, as Mike Rose argues in this volume, vocational education can engage students in many authentic, real-world tasks that provide the context for problem solving, decision making, and abstracting.[41] Some vocational programs have succeeded in connecting disadvantaged students to jobs. Successful programs have had close ties to employers; as a result, on-the-job training and job search assistance were based on relevant and up-to-date information from employers.[42]

Traditional vocational education programs, however, are at best an incomplete model for addressing the central challenge of educating the workforce of the twenty-first century. Many vocational programs, for example, are viewed as poverty programs, not training programs, and employers have been skeptical of the skills and productivity of program graduates. As such, these programs are seen as irrelevant to meeting labor needs.[43] Others in this volume critique vocational programs on a variety of dimensions, pointing to tracking and stigmatizing students, lacking relevant skills training, disconnecting academic learning from work, and other problems.

Apprenticeships

Youth apprenticeship programs have the potential to increase the skills and employability of youth. The framework for youth apprenticeship programs is found in the 1990 Perkins Vocational Education Act and, more specifically, in Clinton's School-to-Work Opportunities Act of 1994. The latter act proposed to build partnerships of employers, educators, and others to design school-to-work systems at the local level that can prepare young people for successful careers. The program was jointly administered by the Department of Education and Labor.[44]

One model frequently cited for an apprenticeship system comes from Germany. German students begin exploring occupations when they are in the seventh grade. At this point many are tracked toward either a university or an academic-technical program, primarily based on assessments of competencies. By age 16, the academic-technical group begins spending as many as four days a week at a worksite learning such skills as bookkeeping, electrical engineering, or auto mechanics. In exchange for on-the-job training, students receive stipends averaging $400 a month and take interim and final exams supervised by their employers. More than half of the apprentices remain with the firm where they are trained, and a larger share spend their careers in the same occupation.[45]

Inspired by Germany's "dual system," which places more than 60 percent of 16-year-olds in apprenticeships, youth apprenticeship projects have sprung up in some twenty states since the 1990s. Students complete a Certificate of Initial Mastery in basic skills such as reading and math, and then at age 16 pursue either a traditional college-prep track or a "technical and professional" track, which is expected to include substantial time on the job in the form of youth apprenticeships.

To date, U.S. youth apprenticeships require a three- to four-year commitment to a trade and an employer, spanning the last year or two of high school and the following two years. The amount of hours spent at the paid job might rise from twenty per week in year 1 to full-time in year 4. In the classroom, teachers and employers teach reading, math, and other courses using workplace applications. In addition, one or more technical courses are tailored to a specific trade, usually chosen by students from a menu of trades. At the conclusion of the program, students graduate with a high school diploma, significant work experience, credits toward a two-year associate's degree, and some kind of certificate of trade mastery.[46]

However, there are potential problems with such apprenticeship programs. First, apprenticeship programs may discourage youth from pursuing a four-year college degree. In the best of circumstances, youth apprenticeship programs would include credits toward completing the requirements to enter a two-year associate's degree program. Because many associate's credits are not transferable for a four-year bachelor of arts degree, and work experience is rarely accepted by colleges for degree credit, a youth apprenticeship graduate would have difficulty obtaining a bachelor's degree. And despite assurances that the work-based learning track will not restrict students' options, occupationally specific courses often crowd out courses required for college, such as foreign languages.[47]

Concerns about tracking are compounded because the programs are mostly located in public, urban high schools where minority students are disproportionately represented.[48] These students will make up nearly 50 percent of the entering workforce by the year 2010.[49] Research has established the differential distribution of students to high-, middle-, and low-ability groups or academic tracks versus vocational tracks.[50] Ethnicity, race, and socioeconomic status affect track placement, with an overrepresentation of low-income and minority students in vocational education programs.

Thus, the susceptibility of work-based learning and apprenticeship programs to tracking may reproduce racial hierarchies. Given the already low rate of college enrollment by minority public high school students, youth apprenticeship programs may be a further disincentive for minority youth to enter college and gain high-tech or professional skills, without sufficiently increasing their contact with employers or skill sets.

Career Academies

More promising than apprenticeships are career academies. Career academies are schools within schools that link students with peers, teachers, and community partners, including employers, to foster skill development and academic success. This is accomplished, as Stern and Stearns note, through small learning communities, a college-preparatory curriculum with a career theme, and partnerships with local employers.[51]

Here, the key questions are whether career academies retain students who would otherwise leave school early and whether the programs improve the career options of those who graduate. Although there is positive evidence on the first question, there is very little if any evidence on the latter. Future research should address whether and how career academies improve career options, especially for those who do not go on to college.

Several studies in California have found that career academy students perform better than similar students in the same high school. Other studies demonstrate that academy students have better attendance, earn more credits, obtain higher grades, and were more likely to graduate than a comparison group.[52]

Moreover, annual data collected from state-funded academies in California continue to show improvement after students enter an academy and while they are in it.[53] High school dropout rates in academies average about 7 or 8 percent over three years—about half the rate in the general population of California students—despite the fact that state-funded academies are required to recruit a majority of students who are economically or educationally disadvantaged.

Still, there are several reasons to believe that these apparent benefits of career academies may not be causal or generalized. Tracking issues might emerge in unexpected forms. For example, career academies could recruit students with relatively high levels of motivation. Similarly, a single academy in a larger high school that houses multiple academies could attract relatively innovative and enthusiastic teachers. Likewise, students in the most advanced classes might gravitate to some career academies, while other students might select or be counseled to other academies. All this creates a hierarchical ordering among the several academies in the high school. As in traditional forms of tracking, the potential danger is that students in the less prestigious academies would be systematically harmed because teachers would expect less of them.[54] These potential problems are not insurmountable if schools monitor enrollment trends and prevent such results.

More specifically, some worry that career academies target students who do not plan to go to college, tracking them into classes and work experience that direct them toward immediate entry into the labor market. And like the criticism of apprenticeship programs, there is concern that college-bound students substitute career and technical classes and work experience for academic classes and experiences that would qualify them for college. However, there is little direct evidence on these issues.

Overall, evidence indicates that career academies are a promising reform. Maxwell and Rubin found that high school students who had attended career academies were just as likely as academic-track students to be enrolled in four-year colleges.[55] They also found that students in career academies obtained significantly better grades, and this was not the result of easier grading standards within the academies. The higher grades of academy students appear to be the main reason for their higher rate of college attendance compared to nonacademy students.[56]

Finally, Maxwell found that academy graduates were more likely to come from high schools with large proportions of low-income minority students, were less likely to need remedial coursework at the university, and were more likely to receive their bachelor's degrees, compared to other graduates from the same district.[57] These findings suggest that academies help disadvantaged students finish both high school and college. Just as important, these findings also imply that the improvement in high school graduation rates was not accomplished by lowering academic standards in the career academies.

PROMISING PRACTICES TO STRENGTHEN CAREER ACADEMIES

Career academies can be useful structures for implementing a Multiple Pathways strategy if they pay careful attention to creating options for continuous learning, preparing students for careers in changing labor markets, and pursuing strong employer links that ensure relevant and timely skill training and post-high school employment assistance.

Stronger Employer Links

Career academies with strong employer involvement are likely to be strengthened through access to current information on work standards, skill requirements, and state-of-the-art technologies. The links could also provide employers with incentives to hire graduates. Employers involved in academies might reduce their search and training costs because of greater access to an appropriately trained labor supply.[58] Career academies with strong employer links may also help to mitigate the discrimination against hiring minority youth, as previously discussed. This would be especially welcome in the current climate of weak antidiscrimination enforcement. To the extent that employers come to see graduates of career academies as credible and important to their business needs, they may be more willing to hire them irrespective of their race. This view is consistent with the idea that "certification" limits discrimination against stigmatized groups.[59] Targeting minority employers to work with career academies with large numbers of minority graduates is likely to be particularly effective since they are much more likely than other employers to hire minority youth.[60]

Hence, stronger employer links are likely to lead to greater placement and employment rates, wages, and retention for graduates of academies with greater employer involvement. At the same time, these employers are likely to benefit through increased productivity, increased profits through lower search and training costs, and greater retention of employees.

Relevant and Timely Skills Training

Relevant and timely skills training seems essential if career academies are to prepare students for rapidly changing job requirements. By following established skills standards for particular occupations, academies can work with employers in occupations that have standardized the skill sets required for particular jobs. For example, the National Skills Standards Board defines these standards as "performance specifications that identify the knowledge, skills and abilities an individual needs to succeed in the workplace."[61] These standards can help employers, trainers, and educational institutes to determine the exact skill requirements of jobs and guide career academies as they develop curricula. This alignment of training and certification (e.g., high school diplomas) provides employers certainty about the bundle of skills that potential graduates possess and gives the graduate a marketable credential.

The literature indicates that combining "hard" skills training (e.g., familiarity with the job-specific skills) with "soft" skills (e.g., teaching, workplace, and professional codes; teamwork) during training and education produces the greatest positive effect on employability and job retention.[62] Presumably, this combined training and timing before placement creates a synergy between greater learning skills and greater confidence and ability once on the job.[63]

Postgraduate/Employment Preparedness

Finally, to accommodate changes in the workplace and to maintain students' job fitness and retention, students need to be equipped to learn new skills quickly and continuously after program graduation. As Pastor argues, a Multiple Pathways approach could create opportunities to move seamlessly, responsively, and flexibly between the labor market and educational institutions to better prepare individuals for the life-long learning processes that career trajectories and labor markets increasingly require.[64] Community colleges might play a key role in this regard.

Recent research indicates that postemployment programs, such as on-the-job training or formal apprenticeship programs in which employers provide continued job skill instruction, can be particularly effective, especially when developed in conjunction with employers who are sensitive to specific workplace dynamics.[65] Postemployment supports could extend beyond skills training and issues that confront workers, such as child care, transportation, and conflict management. Mentors, who in fact could be graduates of career academies, are a good source to tap to fill these needs.

CONCLUSION

This chapter has sought to identify some important policies that could improve the career options of racial minorities and others who have traditionally not gone on to college. Such groups are far more likely to attend urban schools that currently do not prepare students with job skills needed for success in the changing modern economy. Calls to improve school resources, teacher quality, school and class size, accountability, and so forth do not necessarily accompany the structural changes in which all high school students will graduate from college or meet employer needs for a relevantly skilled workforce. To enhance career options for all, we must continue efforts to increase college-going rates, and we must address the education of those who do not go to college for postsecondary degrees. Highly promising are programs that allow schools to integrate work experience with many of the traditional hallmarks of a college-preparatory academic curriculum.

Over the past decades, significant economic and social transformations have changed the opportunities for and rewards from work for those with limited education, especially for young people living in poor, urban, and minority communities. The disappearance of good jobs paying good wages and only requiring a basic education has raised the economic cost of a limited education. Many of these jobs have been replaced by those that require more advanced skills, which can change rapidly with changes in technology.

The Multiple Pathways approach, especially one that uses career academies as an educational option, can engage students and keep them in school by providing concrete links between schooling and career options. Academies can prepare students for multiple trajectories and changes in skills in the changing labor market, partly through an experiential learning curriculum that allows for reflection and problem solving in the classroom. Moreover, if designed appropriately, career academies can provide incentives and the institutional structure for students to move seamlessly in and out of training and school over a career lifetime. Partnerships with local community colleges are particularly promising in this regard. And yet, tracking in any educational program that combines some form of work-based learning with general education remains a concern. Students of color are most vulnerable to being tracked into lower-quality classes that do not meet enrollment requirements for state universities. These concerns can be allayed if career academies are fundamentally committed to preparing all students for college. In the programs referenced in this chapter, all students must take courses that are required for entry into all state universities.

Of course, Multiple Pathways or any single educational structure or reform cannot address the full range of limited career options and economic success for all students. Also needed is a deliberate, expansionary monetary policy that helps create strong economic and employment conditions. While it is much easier for less-educated minority workers to get jobs during economic growth periods than during economic busts, uninterrupted growth is unlikely, and even periods of rapid growth do not guarantee that strong employment will follow. Further, economic growth alone cannot overcome the persistent joblessness and poverty that characterize many low-income minority communities.

As a result, additional policies and programs must be pursued, especially those that link less-educated minorities to jobs for which they qualify and that increase their competitiveness in local labor markets. To accomplish this, we need targeted public policies that focus on the unique problems of these communities, such as spatial and skill barriers to employment, persistent discrimination by employers, and access to good jobs. Thus, policies that reduce the spatial divide of work, that increase the rewards of work (e.g., implementing living-wage policies and promoting unionization), and that lessen discriminatory practices of employers are likely to be particularly effective. Moreover, these interventions are likely to be that much more effective when the economy is strong and labor markets tight.

CHAPTER 7

Can Multiple Pathways Offset Inequalities in the Urban Spatial Structure?

Paul Ong and Veronica Terriquez[1]

Economist Paul Ong is professor of urban planning, social welfare, and Asian American studies at the University of California–Los Angeles. He has conducted extensive research on the labor market status of minorities and immigrants, displaced workers, welfare-to-work issues, and transportation access. Veronica Terriquez is a PhD candidate in sociology at the University of California–Los Angeles. Her research focuses on school and urban spatial inequalities, parent involvement, and community organizing.

Ong and Terriquez examine how the urban spatial structure can affect high school students' access to workforce environments in which they can observe, learn, and eventually participate. They explore the potential of Multiple Pathways to provide all students with access to positive work-based educational programs and experiences. They show that, although high school youth employment has been commonplace for decades, students from disadvantaged backgrounds are less likely than white or affluent students to benefit from these work experiences. Moreover, despite the intentions of school-based vocational and employment programs, these programs have not necessarily provided positive education or career outcomes for young people from working-class or minority backgrounds. In their review of the research, Ong and Terriquez conclude that effective programs confront challenges created by the urban spatial structure, including challenges to residents of

low-income communities of color, who typically lack sufficient access to
nearby jobs. The authors conclude that Multiple Pathways that provide
work-experience education can assist in breaking this cycle.

INTRODUCTION: FRAMEWORK

The public educational system is deeply embedded in the urban spatial structure due to the link between residential segregation and school segregation.[2] Differences in school outcomes are produced by greater educational needs and challenges in low-income and minority neighborhoods, combined with insufficient or inadequately distributed resources necessary for student learning. The larger socioeconomic and political disparities in the urban spatial structure further hinder schools and students in low-income communities of color. As a result, marginalized parents and neighborhoods have fewer resources to support and complement public schools.

The Multiple Pathways initiative can be seen as an intervention to offset the inequalities embedded in, and generated by, the urban spatial structure. For the purpose of this chapter, the urban spatial structure is based on three key and interacting components: relative locations, networks, and institutions.

- First, we consider the relative locations of people, economic activities and institutions. In particular, we are interested in the spatial configuration of students, employment opportunities, and high schools.
- The second component comprises the physical and nonphysical networks that link people, economic activities, and institutions, including the transportation and communication systems capable of overcoming geographic separation.
- The third component consists of the activities and actions of institutions (e.g., neighborhoods and schools) that can influence the levels and types of goods and services available to members and influence outcomes for members of these institutions. For example, high schools, as public institutions, have the potential to determine students' access to different types of employment opportunities and career pathways through their partnerships with private and public sectors.

Based on the literature and our findings, we believe that complementary real-world career-training education, and rigorous academic curricula, developed with a full understanding of each community's urban spatial structure, can open the "Multiple Pathways" students need for informed and unrestricted career choices and college opportunity. Students respond favorably to the prospect of real-world, hands-on experiences that are integrated into their schooling.

In a 2006 poll conducted for the Irvine Foundation, 91 percent of low-achieving ninth and tenth graders said they would be more motivated to work hard if they attended schools that offered more opportunities to acquire skills and knowledge relevant to future careers.[3] Many high school students have paying jobs, but work can offer more than just money. Part-time employment can be a valuable learning experience when it is a part of a systematic curriculum that enhances skills while teaching how the labor market functions. Schools can provide "added value" to students' work by helping students reflect on their employment experiences, including interactions with employers, supervisors, coworkers, customers, and clients.

Experiential learning through employment can be an integral part of career-training education as long as it does not preclude opportunities to obtain a college-preparatory education. Tracking students into vocational, nonacademic education programs limits the educational attainment of working-class students and students of color. We do not favor work-experience programs as a substitute for access to college-preparatory training, preferring what David Rattray (in this volume) refers to as a hybrid approach built on complementary elements of career and academic learning.[4] Work-experience programs should place students in worksites that expose them to promising careers in growing or stable industries. Developing specific plans to implement such reform are beyond the scope of this paper. Rather, we provide background on high school youth employment and the urban spatial structure that can inform those who develop work-based elements of Multiple Pathways programs.

Attention to the urban spatial structure is useful for understanding the socioeconomic and political inequalities that influence the connection between career and education. For example, racial and class segregation in the housing market, along with unequal economic development across neighborhoods, can limit employment opportunities by imposing formidable job search and commuting costs on those least able to bear those costs. Combined spatial and transportation mismatches hold particular disadvantages for high school students who are geographically isolated from employment opportunities and who have fewer transportation resources than adults. Furthermore, even though many school reform efforts promote school-business (or school-employment) partnerships, students may not realize the full value of such relationships because of inequalities or imbalances within the spatial structure. Since institutions play an important role in reinforcing or attenuating spatial and transportation mismatches, high schools, which are the primary public institutions that serve inner-city youth, can provide "Multiple Pathways" for overcoming the inequalities embedded in the urban spatial structure.

The rest of the chapter is organized into four sections. The first section provides information on patterns of youth employment, on academic and career outcomes related to youth employment and school vocational programs, and on the link between the urban spatial structure and employment opportunities.

The second section offers a case study of Los Angeles County. We use micro-level data from the decennial census to examine employment patterns of high school students and identify inequalities, including those attributable to the urban spatial structure. We find that high school employment rates vary significantly by race, socioeconomic status, spatial-economic inequalities, and access to transportation. Schools have a unique opportunity to address some of the unequal urban spatial structures that disadvantage many urban youth.

The third section focuses on three career training programs in the Los Angeles Unified School District (LAUSD): career academies, work-experience course offerings, and regional and occupational centers and programs (ROCP).

The chapter concludes with recommendations, including some based on two examples of successful practices that have overcome spatial mismatches to reveal the world of work to students. The first example is based on a college-preparatory parochial school that offers students an extensive, well-developed work-experience program that provides transportation to job sites. The second example is an occupational center that uses video conferencing to link its students to a corporate partner, thus facilitating valuable interaction with industry representatives.

YOUTH EMPLOYMENT, STUDENT OUTCOMES, AND THE URBAN SPATIAL STRUCTURE

This section of the chapter draws on readily available statistics and existing literature to provide summary information on youth employment trends, student outcomes linked to employment and school vocational programs, and the influence of the urban spatial structure on employment opportunities. These synopses can inform efforts that seek to design career-training education that is consistent with Multiple Pathways to college and career.

Over the last several decades, a significant proportion of high school-aged youth has participated in the labor market. Data from the Current Population Survey, compiled by the U.S. Bureau of Labor Statistics, indicate that over the long run, approximately three in ten 16- to 17-year-olds have worked during the school year. Figure 7.1 depicts the employment-to-population ratio for those 16 and 17 years old from 1948 to 2006, regardless of school enrollment status. Those enrolled in school work substantially less than those who are not in school.[5] The data in the graph are reported quarterly; figures for the winter quarter (January, February, and March) provide insights into employment during the school year, while higher figures for the summer quarter (July, August, September) show employment during the summer vacation. Data indicate that employment rates exhibit pronounced short-term swings, ranging from an all-time low during the school year of 22 percent in 1965, to an all-time high of 35 percent in 1979. Since fluctuations are tied to the business cycle, it is important to note that youth are more vulnerable to changing economic conditions than older workers with greater skills and experience. Changes in public attitudes and social norms regarding high school student employment may also affect trends.

Differences in employment rates across demographic and economic groups suggest unequal access to the labor market. Although current employment levels are similar for males and females, they differ significantly by race. For example, statistics for June 2006 show that among high school students over the age of 15, 28 percent of whites are employed, while only 13 percent of blacks and 15 percent of Latinos hold jobs. Asian high school students work least, with employment rates of 10 percent.[6] Other disparities also exist. A report by the U.S. Department of Labor indicates that youth from higher-income and from two-parent families are significantly more likely to work than those from low-income or single-parent families.[7] Native-born students hold jobs at higher rates than the foreign-born, but among those employed, foreign-born youth generally report working more hours than the native-born.

High school students' employment has mixed benefits for their academic performance and subsequent labor-market outcomes. Although some studies show negative effects on educational achievement,[8] other studies show that light to moderate work may have no negative effects.[9] In some instances, moderate work commitments are positively correlated with postsecondary

FIGURE 7.1: Employed to Population Ratio, 16- to 17-year-olds

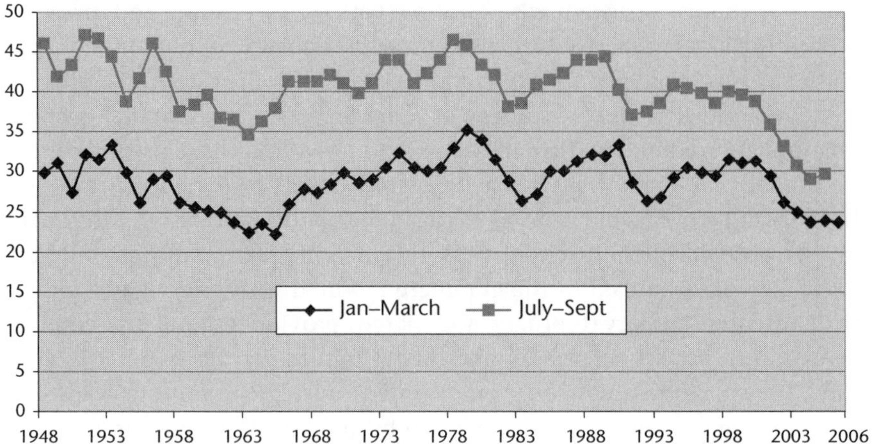

Data Source: Current Population Survey 1948–2006

educational attainment.[10] Working moderate hours during high school can lead to positive labor outcomes several years after high school graduation, including greater earnings[11] and a higher occupational status, particularly for those who do not complete one or more years of college.[12]

While moderate employment during high school may lead to positive outcomes for youth, school-based vocational and employment programs often limit educational attainment. This is partially the result of tracking practices that have guided traditionally non-college-going youth into these school-based vocational and employment programs. Tracking students into a series of vocational, nonacademic courses can negatively affect educational attainment, especially for students of color and others from disadvantaged groups, who are more likely than economically and racially privileged students to be unfairly denied access to rigorous academic coursework.[13]

Despite sometimes limiting college access for less privileged students, vocational programs can occasionally lead to positive educational or career outcomes. For example, Linnehan finds that African American students who participated in a high school work-based mentoring program for over half a year generally improved their grade point averages and school attendance rates, after controlling for previous performance and attendance.[14] In some instances, vocational training may even improve labor market outcomes immediately after high school for at-risk youth, as evidenced by a study of California's regional occupational programs.[15] School-based programs can connect academic instruction and the world of work.[16] Moreover, research suggests such contextualized learning promotes the development of critical thinking, self-regulated learning, problem solving, and other skills.[17] Although past research points to the benefits of school-based vocational and employment programs, future work-experience programs should not track low-income students and students of color in courses that do not prepare them for postsecondary education.

School programs that aim to prepare students for labor force participation must overcome the spatial inequalities that limit that goal. An extensive literature documents the unequal urban spatial structure and how it is both a product of, and contributor to, socioeconomic inequalities. For example, racial discrimination, limited housing opportunities, and unequal firm investments have caused an overconcentration and segregation of minorities in the inner city. "White flight" to the suburbs and the lack of affordable housing in the newer sections of metropolitan areas have reinforced patterns of segregation. At the same time, "capital flight," the migration of companies and investors to the suburbs, created a job shortage in the inner city. These trends separated employment opportunities from disadvantaged minorities and low-income populations who lived in the declining urban core.[18] As a result, a significant proportion of jobs that remain in downtown areas near the central city today require skills that many inner-city residents do not have.[19] The impact of this spatial mismatch can be seen in how it affects the job search. Application rates from blacks and Latinos living in predominantly minority neighborhoods are inversely related to distance to potential employment sites.[20] The lack of employment opportunity because of spatial mismatch can have profound consequences on a local community, and in the worst case, may lead to the development of an underclass neighborhood.[21]

The spatial mismatch alone does not explain how the urban structure limits employment opportunities for disadvantaged populations. The increased geographic distance between residential and employment spaces also affects white and affluent neighborhoods because this phenomenon is a fundamental feature of modern metropolises. Long commutes exist not only from the inner city to the suburbs; suburb-to-suburb commutes also have become longer. Access to effective networks that overcome these spatial mismatches varies across racial and socioeconomic groups.[22] For example, many low-income individuals depend on public transit, a poor substitute for the automobile.[23] Such transportation mismatch negatively affects labor-market outcomes.[24]

Spatial mismatches can be mitigated by effective transportation, and conversely, poor transportation can contribute to a spatial mismatch. The nexus of this spatial-transportation mismatch is reinforced by other spatially based phenomena. For example, employee recruitment is not as prevalent in minority communities as in more affluent or white communities because of the perceived quality of the workforce.[25] Additionally, social networks for employee referrals are weak for disadvantaged populations and communities.[26] Consequently, those residing in disadvantaged communities have less information about potential jobs.

Although most studies on the impact of the urban spatial structure focus on adult employment trends, some research has looked at the effects of spatial and transportation mismatches on high school youth employment patterns. For example, O'Regan and Quigley find that youth in low-income and racially segregated minority neighborhoods are less likely to be employed than otherwise comparable young people living in less segregated neighborhoods.[27] They argue that neighborhood segregation isolates young people from adults with access to informal networks useful for employment. Raphael notes that residential distance from nearby jobs may explain at least a fifth of the racial inequality in youth employment rates at the neighborhood level, but may account for up to half of the overall employment gap between black and white male youth.[28] Transportation mismatches may also contribute to racial inequalities in youth employment. For example, Ihlanfeldt and Sjoquist find that white youth average shorter commute times than black youth, and that commute times correlate with employment rates.[29] Although physical distance between residential locations and employment sites contributes to unequal patterns of youth employment, race continues to play an important and independent role in determining unequal opportunities.[30] The extent to which spatial and transportation mismatches contribute to unequal youth employment opportunities needs further exploration, particularly as these mismatches interact with each other and with race.

EMPLOYMENT PATTERNS OF HIGH SCHOOL STUDENTS IN LOS ANGELES

Employment patterns of high school students in Los Angeles County are examined here. This analysis uses individual-level data from the decennial census and does not examine data on school programs. In many ways, census data show that employment patterns of high school students in this region are similar to the national patterns described previously. Our findings show that a significant percentage of high school students have some work experience. Not surprisingly, the vast majority of the teens work in entry-level jobs that require very few skills and pay essentially minimum hourly wage. Considerable inequality manifests itself across demographic and class lines; teens who are non-Hispanic whites from more well-to-do families demonstrate higher employment rates. The analysis also finds that the urban spatial structure contributes to the systematic racial inequality in determining employment outcomes. Finally, transportation barriers contribute to employment inequalities. In a sprawling metropolitan area such as Los Angeles, those with access to a car are more likely to work. And among those who work, those with access to a car are less burdened by travel time.

For our analysis, we use the Public Use Microdata Samples (PUMS) from the decennial census to examine high school student employment patterns.[31] Our sample is restricted to youth in Los Angeles County between the ages of 16 and 18 who are enrolled in high school and not in the military. Employment status is determined from two variables. The first variable is based on whether the person was employed during the week prior to the census. The second is based on employment in the prior year (e.g., in 1999 for the 2000 census) or any time up to the time of the census (based on occupation of current or any previous job). This information is used to construct three employment indicators: (1) currently employed ("current week"), (2) employed either currently or any time last year ("one plus year"), and (3) employed any time. Each measure provides a different time span in determining work experience.[32]

Figure 7.2 presents the employment rates for youth in Los Angeles County between the ages of 16 and 18 who are enrolled in high school and not in the military calculated from the 1980, 1990, and 2000 censuses. The statistics for the first two time periods are fairly similar, with slightly more than one-fifth of students working during the week before the census. The least restrictive employment measurement (employed anytime) indicates that approximately two-fifths of students had some work experience. Interestingly, all three employment rates are lower for 2000 than for the previous two decades. The reasons for this drop are unknown, but changes in the business cycle appear to be a strong explanation since temporal differences in the percentages of "ever worked" are less than differences in the percentages that report working the "current week" and "one plus current week" of the census. Changes may also be due to shifts in social norms and values that discourage working while in high school.

FIGURE 7.2: High School Employment Rates in Los Angeles

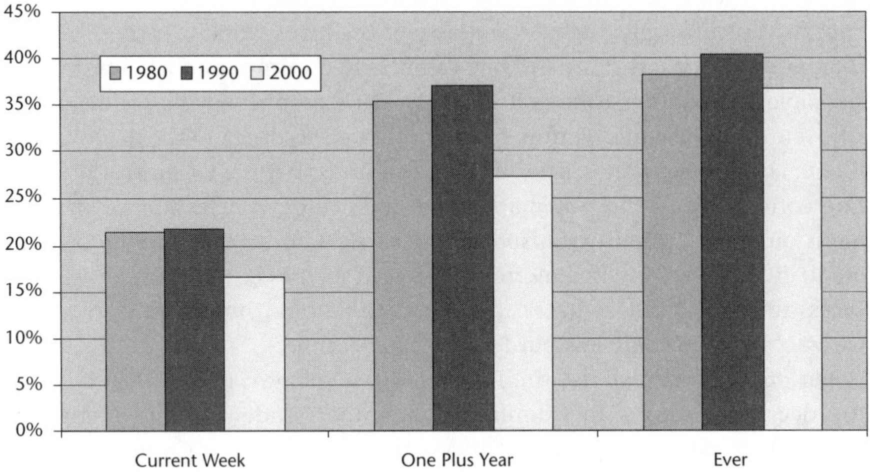

Data from the 2000 census provide information on the types of jobs held by high school students. Among those who "currently" work, most were in entry-level, low-paying occupations requiring few skills: 22 percent in food-service jobs, 31 percent in retailing jobs, and 17 percent in clerical positions. Nearly half (49%) worked after school hours (as indicated by leaving for their jobs after 2 p.m.), and over one-fourth (27%) worked before school hours (leaving for their jobs before 8 a.m.). Those working during the middle of the day may have been doing so during the weekend, but there is no information measuring employment by days of the week.

Employment rates vary considerably by race/ethnicity and class.[33] Figure 7.3 summarizes the patterns for 2000 employment in the week prior to the census. Economic status is calculated as a multiple of the federal poverty line (FPL), which has two advantages: It determines relative hardship and adjusts for family size. However, because it is not geographically adjusted for regional differences, it may underestimate the economic hardship in urban areas with a high cost of living. Four categories are used: (1) high school students in families living below the FPL; (2) those living at or above the FPL but below three times the FPL; (3) those living at or above three times the FPL but below five times; (4) and those living at or above five times the FPL.

The data clearly show that high school students who are non-Hispanic (NH) white and from more affluent families have the highest employment rates. The employment rate for NH whites is nearly two times larger than the rates for blacks and for Asians.

Though not shown in figure 7.3, an even larger racial gap exists when using the broadest measurement of employment (worked either last week or last year or both). Whereas 37 percent of NH whites reported working, only 25 percent of Latinos, 22 percent of blacks, and 21 percent of Asians worked. Figure 7.3 also shows a substantial gap by economic status (relative to the FPL). Approximately one-fifth of those from the middle and upper classes (those from families with incomes that were at least three times the FPL) reported employment the week prior to the census, but just over one-tenth of those from poor families (those living below the FPL) reported employment. Similar disparities exist for the broadest measurement of employment (worked either last week or last year or both).

One-third (34%) of those from the most affluent (at least five times the FPL) had some work experience, but only 18 percent of those from poor families did.

We determined that communities with higher economic status have higher employment rates among high school students. We examine two fac-

FIGURE 7.3: High School Employment Rates by Socioeconomic Status, April 2000

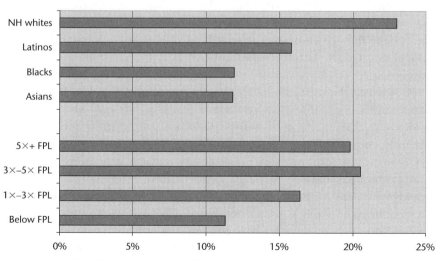

Key: NH whites = non-Hispanic whites; FPL = federal poverty level.

tors related to the urban spatial structure: the economic status of communities and access to transportation. The PUMS identifies subareas within Los Angeles County that contain at least 100,000 individuals, which are known as Public Use Microdata Areas (PUMAs). These units comprise cities or census places. Because of its large population, Los Angeles City is divided into 67 PUMAs. Employment rates across PUMAs vary substantially. For employment in the week before the 2000 census, the estimate rates range from 7 percent to 36 percent, with a standard deviation of 6 percent. The geographic differences correlate with the economic status of PUMAs, which we define relative to the FPL. More specifically, we use the average multiple of FPL for the high school students in our sample. The correlation between PUMA-level high school student employment rates and the PUMA-level average multiple of FPL is .59, with a p < .0001.

The same pattern can be seen in figure 7.4, which tabulates employment rates for individual students by the economic status of their PUMA. Poor PUMAs are those where the average is less than twice the FPL, and affluent PUMAs are those where the average is over three times the FPL. Each of these categories contains about one-fourth of the sample, and the rest falls into a middle group containing about half of the sample. The results show that high school students in affluent areas were nearly twice as likely to work as those in poor areas.

Various conditions can account for the systematic spatial inequality. Concentrations of individuals with higher odds of being employed (those from more affluent families) are likely to have more options for transportation, to live close to jobs, or both; the converse is true for poor families. This compositional effect demonstrates how fundamental socioeconomic inequality is manifested geographically. Results can also be explained by an inverse correlation between the socioeconomic status of communities and geographic job access. Another possible interpretation is that students may be stigmatized by where they live (a form of statistical discrimination), thus harming their perceived employability.

Of course, in Southern California, access to a car is a strong proxy for "transportation," and such access appears to have a significant impact on employment. The bottom part of figure 7.4 presents statistics by the number of vehicles available within a household. High school students in households with one or no vehicles have the lowest employment rates,[34] whereas over one-fifth of teens in households with three or more vehicles report employment. PUMS data also demonstrate the importance of the car among

FIGURE 7.4: High School Employment Rate, Spatial and Transportation

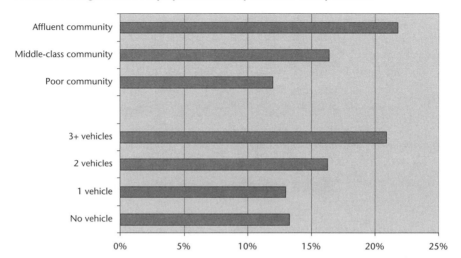

employed students. Three-fourths (74%) commute to work in a private pas-
senger vehicle, and nearly half of the employed drove alone (45%). PUMS
data also show a significant difference in travel time among employed high
school students. Those using a car to get to work reported an average commute time of 16 minutes, compared to 23 minutes for all others.

The urban spatial structure determines opportunities for high school students to obtain employment, regardless of their class and racial backgrounds
and whether or not their families own more than one vehicle. The above
bivariate influences of individual, family, community, and transportation
characteristics hold in a multivariate analysis, which isolate the effects of
each variable. Figure 7.5 summarizes the adjusted results for the key variables on employment probability in terms of odds ratios, all other things
being equal. For race, the excluded category is NH whites, and the findings
show that minority high school students are considerably less likely to work.
Interestingly, Asian high school students have the lowest odds ratio of being
employed relative to NH white high school students. This pattern may be
explained both by differences in employment opportunities and culturally
based norms not favoring youth employment. Access to a car also produces
its own independent effect. The estimate measures the impact of having
more than one vehicle in the household compared to having only one or

FIGURE 7.5: Adjusted Odds Ratios

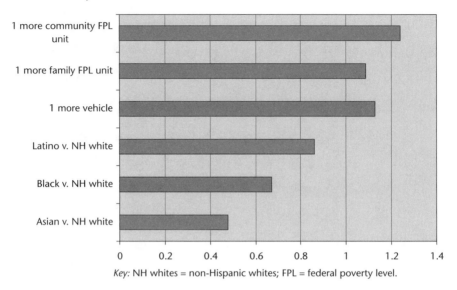

Key: NH whites = non-Hispanic whites; FPL = federal poverty level.

no vehicles. The analysis shows that an additional vehicle in the household also increases the odds of being employed by one-eighth. In other words, car ownership is important in expanding employment opportunities within the urban spatial structure. Although increasing either the economic status of the family or the community (as measured by a change in one FPL unit) positively affects the likelihood of employment, the effect of community characteristics is far greater. In other words, a teenager's location of residence significantly influences how likely the teen is to work.

CAREER-TRAINING PROGRAMS IN THE LOS ANGELES UNIFIED SCHOOL DISTRICT

This section examines career-preparatory programs targeting high school students in the LAUSD, the second largest school system in the United States. The district serves over 727,000 students in K–12, which is more than 11 percent of all students in the state of California. LAUSD's career-training education programs target students with varying educational trajectories, including those who may go to college and those at risk of dropping out.[35] We focus on three programs: career academies, work-experience education, and

ROCPs. To the extent possible, we examine how these programs are embedded within and influenced by the urban spatial structure.

LAUSD seeks to provide much of its career-training education through career academies. LAUSD defines a career academy as a small school within a larger high school that offers an integrated college-preparatory curriculum with a career focus.[36] LAUSD operates over 60 comprehensive high schools serving, at minimum, grades 9–12, of which two-thirds offer some form of a career academy.[37] Career academies typically contain a team of teachers who work with the same group of students enrolled in the academy. LAUSD high schools may offer from one to five career academies. In total, there were 82 separate career academies during the 2005–06 school year. Career focuses include teacher training, media and performing arts, technology and information technology, police and public safety, business and trade, travel and tourism, culinary arts, and health careers. The most popular types of career academies focus on media and performing arts, and teacher training; both types of career academies are offered at 14 schools. Other common types of academies include business and trade (9 schools), technology and information technology (8 schools), and police and public safety (7 schools).[38]

The mean population in schools with career academies is 3,508 students, which is approximately double the mean population of schools without career academies. Given that black and Latino students are overrepresented in LAUSD's largest schools, career academies serve higher proportions of these two groups than the district average. Indeed, career academies are being used as a method to break up large comprehensive LAUSD high schools into smaller learning communities.

Because of their potential to link students to internships that complement their classroom learning, we explored how LAUSD high schools with career academies compare to those without career academies, and whether they are better situated within the urban spatial structure to take advantage of nearby jobs. We used geographic information system (GIS) software and a combination of business and public-sector data from 2000 (the most recently available) to estimate the number of private and public sector jobs located in the census tracts that have their center within a 1.5-mile radius of each high school. Although the analysis does not distinguish between the numbers of entry-level jobs appropriate for high school students and all other jobs, variations in the total number of jobs in census tracts can be used to capture rough variations in entry-level positions. We estimate that on average, both high schools with and without career academies averaged between 6,000 and 7,000 nearby jobs, indicating that career academies do not have a loca-

FIGURE 7.6: Los Angeles Unified School District

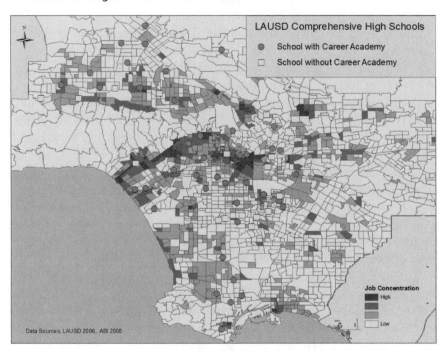

tional advantage compared to other schools. The map in figure 7.6 shows job concentrations in Los Angeles County by census tract and by LAUSD high schools with and without career academies.

On average, access to nearby jobs does not differ between career academies and high schools without them; however, we note a drastic variation among schools that do have career academies. For example, Hollywood High School houses the Culinary Arts, New Media, and Teacher Academies, and is located near an estimated 27,500 jobs within a 1.5-mile radius. Meanwhile, Verdugo Hills High School houses the New Media Academy and is located near a much smaller estimate of 1,700 jobs. High schools located near lower concentrations of jobs may face challenges placing students in internships because local job competition may be higher and students may have to commute longer distances to find jobs. School location near job-rich areas can be an advantage, but this depends on two things: whether jobs are entry level or appropriate for high school students, and whether a school makes an effort to connect students to local jobs. Further analysis can ascertain whether a career academy is located near a high concentration of jobs in the industry for which it aims to prepare students.[39]

Career academies, a separate career-training education program offered at LAUSD high schools, can also connect students to work-experience education.[40] Work-experience courses place students at a worksite during the school day while providing classroom credit. LAUSD policy dictates that teacher coordinators of work-experience courses monitor student worksite performance through regular contact with the students' supervisors. The teacher coordinator is also responsible for implementing curriculum that develops skills, activities, and habits useful for obtaining a job and succeeding in the workplace. The curriculum includes resumes and applications, job interviews, workplace expectations, career options, employee rights, and budgeting. Ideally, this curriculum can assist students in securing and maintaining employment, enhance their on-the-job learning, and reveal career pathways. Required to achieve these goals are available worksites in growing or stable industries with career ladders.

Although approximately one-fourth of high school students work, enrollment in work-experience education courses is very low in LAUSD, with less than 1 percent of students participating in such courses in the 2004–05 school year.[41] Moreover, in spite of very low overall enrollments in work experience, we found notable variations in enrollment across schools. Interestingly, we found that schools that did not offer work-experience courses averaged more jobs within a 1.5-mile radius, and those with relatively high enrollment in work-experience education averaged the lowest number of jobs. We also found a negative relationship between the number of students enrolled in work-experience courses and the black and Latino composition of the schools, after accounting for differences in school socioeconomic status (as measured by the percentage of free- and reduced-lunch recipients).[42] Data do not provide conclusive evidence that black and Latino students have less access to work-experience courses in LAUSD when compared to white students, yet it is possible that patterns of enrollment in work-experience courses reflect and reproduce the relatively lower employment rates experienced by black and Latino youth.

ROCPs comprise an important third component of LAUSD's career education training programs. Established in 1967, ROCP is a statewide program that provides high school students and adults with entry-level career and technical training. ROCPs generally partner with businesses that offer worksite experience and hands-on training. In the 2004–05 school year, 375,462 high school students enrolled in ROCP courses statewide, comprising 70 percent of the program's enrollment.[43] ROCP high school enrollment numbers were equivalent to approximately 20 percent of the entire public high school population in California.

LAUSD operates eleven Regional Occupational and Skills Centers, each with its own facility. Although run independently from the comprehensive high schools, the district also manages regional occupational programs on many individual school campuses. Regional occupational program courses provide vocational skills and some academic training, but courses do not always count for high school credit. The LAUSD school board has the primary responsibility for holding ROCPs accountable, and the California Department of Education serves in an advisory role. Since the state does not require ROCPs to report detailed enrollment and outcome data, we could not provide an analysis of LAUSD's ROCP system.

We do know, however, that ROCPs often serve high school students who are most at risk of dropping out and those who have already left the high school system. Programs therefore enroll youth who transition into the workforce as full-time employees at younger ages than those who enroll in college. A longitudinal study conducted by the University of California–Riverside School Improvement Research Group found that high school students enrolled in ROCP courses improved their grades and attendance and were more likely to enroll in postsecondary education compared to a control group.[44] The study also found that students preferred ROCP classes over regular high school courses because they felt that career-training courses were more relevant for preparing them for their adult life. The authors concluded that ROCP can be an effective intervention for lower-achieving, at-risk students, significantly improving their employment prospects. However, the study's sample size was limited. ROCPs merit future study because they may help prepare the non-college-bound for the workforce. Moreover, they are more likely to serve segments of the population most at risk of unemployment. Increasing the data reporting requirements and public availability of data can allow researchers to assess the extent to which ROCPs prepare young people for the workforce.

CONCLUDING REMARKS

We have shown that a significant proportion of high school students currently work. The existing literature indicates that real work experience at a reasonable level is not harmful to academic performance, and in some cases may be beneficial. However, labor market participation varies among different groups of high school students. As our findings from Los Angeles County show, high school students who reside in more affluent communities and/or come from white and higher-socioeconomic-status family backgrounds are more likely to work than students residing in low-income communities or those from minority and lower-income family backgrounds. Spatial mismatches, coupled with transportation mismatches within the urban spatial structure, contribute to unequal employment rates.

High schools and their affiliated programs, like ROCPs, are key components of the urban spatial structure in the lives of teenagers. Schools, specifically those located in low-income segregated communities, have the potential to help young people overcome the socioeconomic inequalities present in their environment by increasing access to employment opportunities. Furthermore, schools can make employment even more valuable through an experiential learning curriculum that allows for reflection and problem solving in the classroom. We believe that reforming career-training education by incorporating real-world work experience should be seriously considered in developing Multiple Pathways, but numerous challenges arising from the urban spatial structure must be addressed. Here are two examples of educational programs for high school students that address some of those barriers. We should note that our examples, Verbum Dei High School's work-experience program and the Friedman Occupational Center's use of video conferencing, are not based on a systematic review of all possible programs. These programs were brought to our attention through the media and informal networks.

Verbum Dei High School, a boys' parochial school located in a low-income neighborhood in south Los Angeles, serves approximately 340 students. The school's work-experience program offers a potential model for connecting students to meaningful work experiences in white-collar occupations. All students, predominantly Latino and African American boys from modest socioeconomic backgrounds, are placed in a work-study program and are required to work one full day a week, generally performing entry-level clerical and administrative duties. Verbum Dei hires staff to identify worksites and coordinate communication between the school, the employer, and the student. The school's curriculum includes basic employment skills. Each year the school's incoming students receive a two-week orientation that aims to develop basic skills necessary for functioning properly at a worksite. Once the students are placed at an employment site, the school provides a structured curriculum that enables students to evaluate their worksite activities systematically and reflect on lessons learned.

Verbum Dei is located in a neighborhood with relatively few nearby jobs, but it overcomes the spatial and transportation mismatch by providing daily transportation to and from school and the worksite. The school contracts a bus that drives 35–40 students each day to an area with high job density: downtown Los Angeles. The school also owns seven smaller vans that drive students to worksites throughout the county. The money students earn is used to pay for their school tuition and to cover the costs of operating the work-experience program, including transportation costs.

It is important to note that while Verbum Dei provides work experience for its students, it also offers all students the academic coursework necessary for admission into the University of California and California State University systems. Work experience, therefore, complements preparation for college and is not a substitute for academically rigorous coursework. The school claims to send over 95 percent of its graduates on to higher education.[45] In fact, we estimate that Verbum Dei graduates enroll in California's public colleges and universities at much higher rates than the overall enrollment rate for students who attend California public high schools.[46] Although Verbum Dei's combined work-experience and college-preparatory program occurs in a private school setting, many aspects of the program can be adopted in public schools.

The animation program at the Friedman Occupational Center offers a second example of how school programs can overcome challenges presented by the urban spatial structure in order to expose students to the world of work. Located on the southern edge of downtown Los Angeles, the Friedman Occupational Center provides basic training for those interested in a career in the animation field. The program offers a model for using advanced telecommunications to connect high school students to corporations. An increasing practice in the private sector, telecommuting, allows employees to work from home (or other off-site locations) and connect to branches and satellite operations through computer and Internet technology. While very few telecommuting jobs are appropriate for high school students, Friedman has used the technology to enhance interaction between high school students and corporate mentors. Through a video-conferencing link with a major animation studio, Friedman links students to professional animators, who share information about careers in the industry and review and critique student projects. The animation studio is located nearly 14 miles away via some heavily congested corridors. Telecommunication is not a substitute for on-site work experience, but it can be a useful strategy for overcoming spatial and transportation mismatches.

The Friedman Occupational Center, like other occupational centers in Los Angeles Unified, allows concurrent enrollment so students can receive high school credit earned on Saturdays and between school sessions. Such an option may allow students to obtain the academic courses required for admission into a four-year college at their regular school while accessing additional career-related courses through the occupational center.

In implementing strategies to overcome the barriers embedded in the urban spatial structure, high schools and their affiliated programs should explicitly aim to address the racial and economic inequality in employment opportunities for disadvantaged high school students. As documented in this chapter, minority and low-income teenagers are less likely to work, and this disparity is reproduced within the current educational system. In reforming career-training education, a major challenge will be to ensure that everyone has fair access to job opportunities that provide exposure to potential careers. Schools can do very little to alter the inequalities embedded in local communities and economies, but districts and schools can allocate resources to equalize opportunities. Placing high school students at worksites can be one strategy for addressing racial and economic inequality in employment opportunities. Schools should aim to place students in growing or stable industries that can provide promising future careers rather than in dead-end occupations. Such exposure to the labor market must go hand in hand with access to college-preparatory courses, so that students can graduate with the training and information to pursue a variety of postsecondary education and career paths.

CHAPTER 8

Multiple Pathways and the Future of Democracy

John Rogers, Joseph Kahne, and Ellen Middaugh

*In this essay, Rogers, Kahne, and Middaugh suggest that a Multiple
Pathways approach must consider the civic role of schooling. John Rogers
is professor of education and codirector of the Institute for Democracy,
Education and Access at the University of California–Los Angeles. His
research centers on the democratization of knowledge and power as a
means for creating socially just conditions in urban schools and urban
communities. Joseph Kahne is the Abbie Valley Professor of Education
at Mills College and director of the Civics Engagement Research Group.
He is currently conducting a study of the civic/democratic commitments,
capacities, and activities of high school students throughout California.
Ellen Middaugh is a doctoral student in human development at the
Graduate School of Education at the University of California–Berkeley and
a research associate at Mills College in the Institute for Civic Leadership.*

    *The authors begin by comparing historical arguments for vocational
education with the contemporary case for Multiple Pathways reform. They
find that prevailing formulations of Multiple Pathways are more attentive
to equity than earlier arguments for vocational education; however, as
Multiple Pathways strategies develop, they must emphasize key elements
of democratic education. These elements include helping students gain
procedural knowledge about the formal workings of government and
substantive knowledge about critical policy issues; a normative vision of
democracy, including economic democracy and the democratic workplace;
and the skill, understanding, and commitment to participate effectively
in the workplace. Employing this Deweyan framework, Rogers, Kahne,*

and Middaugh argue that framing a Multiple Pathways approach around democratic purposes holds great potential for revitalizing education and civic life.

* * *

The kindred question of industrial education is fraught with consequences for the future of democracy. *Its right development will do more to make public education truly democratic than any other one agency now under consideration. Its wrong treatment will as surely accentuate all undemocratic tendencies in our present situation, by fostering and strengthening class divisions in school and out.*

—*John Dewey[1]*

Educators and policymakers interested in providing Multiple Pathways through high school can learn much from John Dewey's contribution to the public debate on vocational education between 1913 and 1917. Dewey focused on education's civic role, on preparing students for public deliberation, communal problem solving, and joint action to advance the common good. He argued that, in formulating the relationship between so-called vocational and academic education, the primary consideration must be the democratic goals of schooling. In other words, vocational and academic are not competing emphases, nor should either stand alone; rather, they are two goals that together serve greater social, economic, and democratic ends. He reasoned that civic education should not be neglected as reformers reshaped the traditional curriculum. Dewey held that vocational education offered new and powerful opportunities to advance democracy. His presumption was that the "right" vocational education would support the development of students into adults who press for democracy in the workplace, the political sphere, and in broader social relations.

This essay looks to Dewey's scholarship on democratic vocational education as a model of how to advance civic skills and commitments. Dewey pointed to the importance of treating work in the broader political economy as a subject for study. He called for students to examine opportunities for workers to use their intelligence and make decisions in the workplace. Dewey wanted students to use the methods of social science inquiry to explore the cause and effect of economic and social problems as well as how these problems can be addressed. Such engaged study, he reasoned, would provide young people with the knowledge, skills, and commitments necessary to participate effectively in an industrial democracy.

This essay explores how the Multiple Pathways approach might incorporate Dewey's democratic aims for education. We begin by comparing historical arguments for vocational education with the contemporary case for Multiple Pathways. We find that prevailing formulations of Multiple Pathways are more attentive to equity than earlier arguments for vocational education. Nonetheless, contemporary advocates of Multiple Pathways do not attend sufficiently to the civic role of schooling. We next examine the growing public concern for low and uneven levels of youth civic engagement. We review the current state of civic education and find that public schools must aggressively promote civic education to ensure that students will develop essential civic skills. We then turn to Dewey's writing on vocational education to identify how he introduced and reconceptualized vocational education in light of civic purposes. This analysis points to a Deweyan framework for a democratic vocational education that promotes "industrial intelligence" for an "industrial democracy."[2] We then consider what lessons this framework holds for career and civics education. In conclusion, we discuss the possibilities and challenges of reshaping Multiple Pathways in light of democratic purposes.

HISTORICAL AND CONTEMPORARY DEBATES ON VOCATIONAL EDUCATION

Dewey's contemporaries built the case for vocational education on narrow economic grounds. Early-twentieth-century reformers reasoned that the traditional school curriculum was not preparing large segments of America's youth for adult roles in a global economy. The influential Commission on National Aid to Vocational Education warned that "the rising demand for a better product" in both domestic and foreign markets necessitated that American labor be "as efficient and as trained as the labor of the countries with which we must compete."[3] The Commission noted a fundamental mismatch between the labor market demands for skilled artisans and factory workers and the academic programs of traditional high schools that were "largely planned for the few who prepare for college."[4] Posing "learning by doing" as a strategy for reengaging students, the Commission asserted that vocational education could "attract and hold" the nine out of ten urban students who dropped out of school before graduating.[5] In this way, vocational education would introduce "the aim of utility to take its place in dignity by the side of culture, and to connect education with life by making it purposeful and useful."[6]

There are striking parallels and important differences between the vocational education debate Dewey entered in 1913 and the discussion of Multiple Pathways today. Advocates of Multiple Pathways[7] point to the demands of the global economy as evidence that high schools must incorporate career and technical education.[8] "The globalization of business and industry," argues Hans Meeder of the Association for Career and Technical Education, means that "competitor nations are surging forward" in producing more highly educated workers.[9] American school systems thus must provide students with the "core skills" that can be applied in "a wide and rapidly changing variety of work settings."[10] Yet, large numbers of students do not develop such skills in high schools organized by a traditional academic curriculum. In many schools, particularly those serving large numbers of students of color and students from low-income families, students become disengaged from the traditional curriculum, and many drop out of school.[11] The advocates of Multiple Pathways assert that integrating career and technical training into the high school can engage students by promoting more active learning and giving students a sense of how their learning is tied to future goals.[12]

While current advocates of Multiple Pathways echo some of the early-twentieth-century arguments, they consciously seek to distance themselves from two key themes of the earlier vocational education reformers. First, advocates of Multiple Pathways reject the view that high school students must choose between a pathway leading directly to work and one leading to college. "The past division between preparation for college and preparation for work," argues Betsy Brand, "has become a false dichotomy."[13] Brand holds that all work has become knowledge work requiring "higher literacy, numeracy, and technical skills" and hence postsecondary education.[14] Second, and related, advocates of Multiple Pathways posit a different understanding than the early vocational education advocates of what it means for young people to be included in the new economy. Whereas the early advocates for vocational education believed that students with "different tastes and abilities" should follow different pathways into highly differentiated adult roles,[15] the Multiple Pathways advocates[16] assert that all students should become highly trained knowledge workers. In this way, students could follow Multiple Pathways toward a common goal of college and career training. Table 8.1 summarizes the differences between traditional vocational education and Multiple Pathways and compares both to a Deweyan approach.

TABLE 8.1: Conceptions of Education

	Traditional Approach to Vocational Education	Multiple Pathways Approach	Deweyan Approach
Vocational education and academic curriculum	Dual curriculum: One track for students on pathways to college, one track for students on direct path to work.	Integrated curriculum: Students study college-prep curricula *and* participate in internships.	Unitary curriculum: Students study the workplace and the broader political economy. Students develop academic, vocational, and civic skills.
School-based activities	Routinized skill training in vocational track; humanistic studies in academic track.	Academic lessons applied within context of career themes and worksite internships.	Project-based learning that promotes inquiry in and about the workplace.
Purpose of education	Schools should prepare some for manual work and some for decision making and professional work.	Schools should prepare all for college and careers in the knowledge-based economy.	Schools should prepare all to be active citizens and change agents in workplace and society.

SILENCE ON THE DEMOCRATIC PURPOSE OF SCHOOLING

The advocates for Multiple Pathways are largely silent about the democratic purposes of schooling. This is not to say that they reject Dewey's egalitarian commitments. Advocates of Multiple Pathways recognize that the new global economy creates winners and losers based on access to formal education and career training. Their hope is that new educational structures can expand the pool of winners by ensuring that all young people have the human capital necessary for highly skilled and well-paid jobs.

Nonetheless, with the exception of a couple of fleeting references to preparing young people for citizenship, the advocates of Multiple Pathways pay no attention to education's democratic purposes.[17] This inattention suggests that a Multiple Pathways approach might give short shrift to civic education at a time when declining and unequal patterns of civic participation pose a serious threat to multiracial democracy. Such concerns are heightened by the fact that so much of the rhetoric of career and technical education focuses on the private, rather than public, returns to education.

Further, by not attending to democracy, advocates of Multiple Pathways are left with narrow, instrumental goals for integrating academic and career curricula. Building human capital calls for curriculum aimed at developing generic skills (of numeracy, literacy, technology). It does not aim to develop a critical understanding of how social consequences are shaped by the ways that workers deploy these skills in the context of the workplace. For example, lessons in car mechanics that are used to teach principles of physics can also generate critical and political discussions related to alternative fuels and emission standards or consideration of the roles of the auto industry and the United Auto Workers in shaping the working conditions under which cars are manufactured. In other words, the goal of skill development, as it is currently constructed, does not envision young people as change agents in the workplace and in the broader public realm. In contrast, Dewey's consideration of democratic ends provides a powerful framework for thinking about how and why key elements of merged vocational and academic education are also relevant to civic education and participation.

THE NEED TO ATTEND TO CIVIC EDUCATION

Over the last decade, policymakers and scholars in political science and education have renewed attention to the need for youth to understand the government's purpose and function and to develop the skills and commitments to participate robustly in electoral politics, public institutions, civic organizations, and (where necessary) protest activities.[18] This examination of the "civic mission" of schools reflects concerns with the health of American democracy.[19] Reports and scholarly books and articles have described a "crisis" in youth civic engagement.[20] This crisis is characterized by declining youth interest, knowledge, and participation in formal politics. It is also evidenced in disparate patterns of youth civic engagement across lines of class and race.

The results of a recent study of California high school seniors offer a sobering case in point. In 2005, we surveyed 2,366 graduating seniors who had completed the state-required twelfth-grade U.S. government course. We wanted a clearer sense of student civic capacities and commitments as they reach voting age.[21] The respondents came from public schools selected to represent student race and ethnicity, geographic region, and school achievement level. We found that a high percentage of the students reported that they intended to vote, but a much smaller percentage said they were informed enough to vote. Their confidence declined further when they were asked about their knowledge of specific issues: Iraq, the economy, taxes, education, health care, and the like.[22]

A large number of the high school seniors had difficulty with questions assessing civic content knowledge. Half the students did not know the function of the Supreme Court, one-third of them could not identify one of their U.S. senators when given a list from which to choose, and almost half could not choose which of the two major political parties is more conservative. Most high school seniors did not recognize a political role for themselves beyond voting. Fewer than half agreed with the statement: "Being actively involved in state and local issues is my responsibility." This lack of interest may be related to their lack of experience with political action. Fewer than one in ten students reported that they had worked to change a policy or law in their community, state, or nation during high school, and only one in three said that they had worked to change a policy or rule at their school.[23]

The limited civic capacity and commitment found in California high school seniors reflect national trends. Voting rates for citizens under age 25 are particularly low relative to the larger U.S. population and relative to youth in other countries. There is also evidence that many young people are not prepared for informed and effective civic engagement. For example, college graduates in 1989 did about as well as high school graduates 50 years earlier on 12 survey items that have been used to assess student knowledge of politics since the 1940s.[24] In addition, on the most recent National Assessment of Educational Progress in civics, only one-fourth of high school students were judged to be proficient and 5 percent scored at the advanced level. One-third of all students did not demonstrate a "basic" level of understanding.[25] In U.S. history, 30 percent of high school students scored below basic.[26]

When scholars speak of the crisis in youth civic engagement, they have in mind both the level and distribution of civic capacity and commitment. Young people from low-income families and young people of color do not participate at the same levels as their more affluent and white peers. Cohen and Dawson show that African Americans who live in areas with high concentrations of poverty are significantly less likely than African Americans who live in areas with low or moderate levels of poverty to belong to civic groups and to have contact with political officials.[27] A path-breaking study by Verba et al. on civic equality found that lower family income predicted lower levels of voting, campaign work, contact with officials, and political protest.[28] This underrepresentation in the political process violates the principle of equal representation and skews decision making in favor of the more affluent. As the American Political Science Association Task Force on Inequality and American Democracy reported,

The privileged participate more than others and are increasingly well organized to press their demands on government. Public officials, in turn, are
much more responsive to the privileged than to average citizens and the
least affluent. Citizens with low or moderate incomes speak with a whisper
that is lost on the ears of inattentive government, while the advantaged roar
with the clarity and consistency that policymakers readily heed.[29]

In the face of these critical concerns about the future of American democracy, a new body of research documents the positive impact of robust programs in civic education.[30] This research demonstrates that civic education
opportunities can promote civic outcomes. William Galston identifies an
array of strategies that gain power when used in concert.[31] These include
instruction in the history and principles of American democracy, classroom
discussion of current events that make a direct and tangible difference in
young people's lives, community service, participation in civic organizations
that address meaningful issues, and participation in public forums and democratic governance in school and in the larger community.[32] These strategies appear to make a significant difference in civic outcomes for low-income
urban students.[33]

The survey of California high school seniors described above offers a more
detailed picture of how particular civic learning opportunities can promote
civic development. In classes where students frequently talked about current
events, 61 percent reported they were interested in politics compared to only
32 percent in classes with no discussion of current events. Further, when
their government classes emphasized why it is important to be informed and
to get involved in political issues, 52 percent of students agreed that they
should be actively involved in state and local issues. In classes where "getting
involved" was not emphasized, 35 percent agreed.[34]

Participation in activities inside and outside the classroom also made a difference in civic outcomes. Thirty-six percent of students who frequently took
part in role-plays or simulations that modeled democratic processes reported
being involved in politics; whereas only 13 percent of the students who had
not had these classroom opportunities were involved. Similarly, 54 percent
of students who worked on projects with peers from different backgrounds
agreed that being involved in state and local issues was their responsibility compared to 29 percent of the students who did not have this opportunity. Further, students who reported having a chance to voice their opinions
about school policies outside of class were more committed to political participation than those who said they had few such opportunities.[35]

Unfortunately, these promising practices in civic education do not occur often enough. When asked whether they had experienced the sort of instruction described above—instruction that supported the development of committed, informed, and effective citizens—the most common answer from California's high school seniors was "a little."[36] A recent study found that 90 percent of U.S. students said they most commonly spent time reading textbooks and doing worksheets.[37] These findings also speak to the enormous pressure on public schools to focus their instructional time narrowly on subject matter for which students and educators will be held responsible in state and federal accountability systems.

Counter pressures make it all the more important for schools to infuse the civic mission across the curriculum. While some aspects of a school's curriculum, such as the high school government course, clearly have the potential to support both educative civic activities and teaching the facts of government, it is also clear that educating for democracy should not rely on a one-semester course taken during the senior year. Rather, opportunities to educate for democracy should exist throughout the high school curriculum and they should build on each other. A schoolwide commitment (which is to say, a community-wide commitment) is therefore necessary.

Linking a Democratic Vision to a Multiple Pathways Approach

What would such a commitment mean in schools that embrace a Multiple Pathways approach? There certainly are challenges to integrating civic learning opportunities across classroom and internship sites that are organized around career themes, but no more so than integration into traditional models of vocational or academic education. As with the traditional models, if career-related internships, for example, are seen as distinct from civic activities, both students and their teacher/mentors will find little enthusiasm or time for such "integration." Moreover, there is some reason to worry that once students pursue different pathways through high school, some pathways will offer more civic opportunities than others. For example, high school seniors in the California survey who did not expect to take part in any form of postsecondary education reported significantly fewer of the opportunities that foster civic commitment and capacities than those with postsecondary plans.[38]

We also found that students taking "regular" college-preparatory (CP) U.S. government courses reported fewer civic learning opportunities than did students in the Advanced Placement (AP) U.S. government courses. For example, 80 percent of students in the AP sample agreed that they had participated in simulations, compared to 51 percent of CP students. Similarly, 80 percent of students in the AP sample agreed that in their classes, students are encouraged to make up their own minds about political or social issues and to discuss issues about which students have different opinions compared to 57 percent of CP students. Care is clearly needed to ensure that those taking part in career-based courses are not subject to similar disadvantages.

The Multiple Pathways approach potentially creates contexts for students to study the relationship between democracy and the economy and to extend civic lessons into the workplace. Unfortunately, neither the civic education literature nor the scholarship in career and technical education speak to how or even why this should be done. To explore this "how" and "why," we return to Dewey.

DEWEY AND DEMOCRATIC VOCATIONAL EDUCATION

Between 1913 and 1917, Dewey joined the public debate over how vocational education programs should be structured and governed. Ideologically diverse groups agreed on the importance of expanding vocational education. As Kantor describes, support came from "businessmen, corporate apologists, . . . efficiency-oriented educators, . . . labor leaders, liberal reformers, and radical intellectuals" who wanted schools to meet the demands of the new industrial economy.[39] Like other spheres of reform during the Progressive era, this coalition was rife with disagreement over the specifics of policy proposals. Labor believed that vocational education should be integrated into the existing public education system; business and manufacturing groups advocated separate autonomous sites for industrial education.[40] The question "should . . . vocational education [be] under 'unit' or 'dual' control" framed the broader policy dialogue and served as Dewey's point of entry into the debate.[41]

Dewey believed the vocational education debate was more than a narrow dispute over administrative structure and control.[42] He envisioned schools as a "projection . . . of the type of society we would like to realize," and he thought that all educational decisions were choices about what sort of democracy should be created.[43] Decisions about vocational education were choices about the future of economic democracy.

> The movement for vocational education conceals within itself two mighty and opposing forces, one which would utilize the public schools primarily to turn out more efficient laborers in the present economic régime, with cer-

tain incidental advantages to themselves, the other which would utilize all the resources of public education to equip individuals to control their own future economic careers, and thus help on such a reorganization of industry as will change it from a feudalistic to a democratic order.[44]

Not surprisingly, Dewey found himself at odds with manufacturing interests and advocates for "dual" control. A prime adversary was David Snedden, the Massachusetts Commissioner of Education, whose 1906 report helped create broad-based momentum for expanding vocational education in the public school system.[45] Snedden argued that those who wanted to use education to democratize factories were "romantic impracticalists."[46] He reasoned that the purpose of vocational education is to create "greater productive capacity."[47] The critical question for Snedden was how this goal could be met most efficiently. He held that separate sites for vocational education could best prepare young people for the "pursuit of an occupation" because these settings could mirror the reality of factory life.[48] In such sites, "shop standards not school standards must prevail."[49] Students would be prepared for highly differentiated adult roles in line with "right standards of efficiency in the economic world."[50]

Noting that the differences between himself and Snedden were "profoundly political and social," Dewey rejected the idea that education's role is to prepare young people for particular trades.[51] "I object to the identification of vocation with such trades as can be learned before the age of, say, eighteen or twenty; and to the identification of education with acquisition of specialized skill in the management of machines."[52] One problem with such trade training was that it neglected the constant change in both machines and the broader workplace that characterized the new industrial economy.[53] In addition, it skewed teaching and learning toward low-level skills. Too narrow a focus on one job or role encouraged educators to emphasize "skill or technical method at the expense of meaning."[54]

Dewey was concerned that Snedden's model of vocational education reproduced class inequalities.

> I am utterly opposed to giving the power of social predestination, by means of narrow trade-training, to any group of fallible men no matter how well-intentioned they may be.[55]

He worried that, in separating cultural and vocational education, Snedden accepted the prevailing separation of mental and manual labor in the workplace. This distinction presumed that social efficiency demanded a hierarchical division of labor in which "a few do the planning and ordering, the others follow directions and are deliberately confined to narrow and prescribed channels of endeavor."[56] Dewey held that such "feudal" relationships were both inefficient and immoral; they wasted untapped talent and undercut meaningful social interaction and development. Wishing to challenge the "industrial regime that now exists," Dewey posed vocational education as an instrument for social change.[57]

> The kind of vocational education in which I am interested is not one which will "adapt" workers to the existing industrial régime; I am not sufficiently in love with the régime for that. It seems to me that the business of all who would not be educational timeservers is to resist every move in this direction, and to strive for a kind of vocational education which will first alter the existing industrial system, and ultimately transform it.[58]

It is noteworthy that Dewey's "desired transformation" points toward a society in which work and economic relations are interwoven with social democracy. He envisioned

> a society in which every person shall be occupied in something which makes the lives of others better worth living, and which accordingly makes the ties which bind persons together more perceptible—which breaks down the barriers of distance between them. It denotes a state of affairs in which the interest of each in his work is uncoerced and intelligent.[59]

This normative vision recasts "vocation" in democratic terms. Vocations are open and accessible to all. Through vocations, workers participate in knowledge work that builds community and is socially productive.

Dewey believed that "genuinely vocational education" prefigures the intellectual and social relations of such work and provides future workers with "industrial intelligence": the knowledge and skills needed to press for industrial democracy.[60] One facet of industrial intelligence lies in the ability to locate one's work within "its historical, economic and social bearings."[61] Dewey stressed the dehumanizing nature of specialized work separated from the larger purpose of the activity. While conceding that efficiency may dictate a certain amount of specialization in the workplace, he wanted workers to understand the origins and purpose of what they were doing. Such understanding, Dewey asserted, enables workers to become more than "appendages to the machines they operate."[62] It provides the insights necessary to develop (rather than merely follow) work plans. Dewey also imagined "the study of economics, civics, and politics" enabling future workers to recognize the problems with prevailing economic arrangements as well as strategies for social reform.[63] In part, he wanted students to study progressive era social issues, such as "child labor . . . and the sanitary conditions under which multitudes of men and women now labor." Dewey also wanted future workers to develop a deeper (and critical) analysis of power and inequality. He called for workers to study the "methods employed in a struggle for economic supremacy . . . [and] the connections between industrial and political control."[64] In short, workers must understand how economic interests influence political processes, and they must understand how political decisions influence both work conditions and the relationships among different sectors of industry.

For Dewey, industrial intelligence manifested itself in skills and dispositions as well as in understanding a body of knowledge. His primary concern was forging a more empowered role for workers. In order for future workers to become an "integral part of a self-managing society," they need to be able to consider, create, and carry out plans of action.[65] This requires "intelligent initiative, ingenuity, and executive capacity."[66] Dewey associated these attributes with the application of the scientific method in social settings, including the ability to identify problems, formulate hypotheses, conduct observations, analyze data, and formulate strategies for change.[67] Dewey also looked beyond such capacities to the "intellectual and emotional traits" that express a commitment to inquiry and democracy. He expected workers with industrial intelligence to insist "upon widespread opportunity, free exchange of ideas and experiences, and extensive realization of the purposes which hold men together."[68]

Dewey recognized that developing industrial intelligence required new approaches to teaching and learning. "As new subject-matter is needed, so are new methods."[69] Neither the "scholastic method of acquiring, expounding, and interpreting literary materials," nor the strategy of "habituation" through repetition and drill could foster the understandings of the political economy or the creativity and initiative associated with industrial intelligence.[70] In part, Dewey called for revitalizing humanistic methods so that, rather than "taking flight to the past," students would be encouraged to "discover the humanism contained in our existing social life."[71] This meant studying academic disciplines as tools of inquiry that could help students understand the "defects of present industrial aims and methods . . . [as well as the] means by which these evils are to be done away with."[72]

In addition, Dewey called for "laboratory methods" that applied the experimental approach to the study of "ordinary industrial activities."[73] The factory floor offered an ideal site for observation and experiment. "[I]n schools, association with machines and industrial processes may be had under conditions where the chief conscious concern of the students is insight."[74] Thus, Dewey hoped that all students would have opportunities to consider and experiment with different ways to organize work processes and the relations between workers. In this way, youth initiated as students of the workplace would be prepared to transform these sites when they became workers themselves.

DEWEYAN INSIGHTS FOR EDUCATION ABOUT WORK AND CIVIC LIFE

What insights can we draw from Dewey's almost century-old contribution to the debate on vocational education? Certainly, advocates of Multiple Pathways in this collection have unmistakably rejected the "social predestination" that Dewey ascribes to Snedden. Yet, Dewey's critique of "trade-training" provides several important warnings for today's educators considering whether or how to link academic and career education.[75] First, his worry that future technology threatens to make obsolete any specialized skills suggests that educators should avoid focusing the curriculum narrowly around work as it is presently constituted. There is simply no guarantee that narrow vocational skills learned today (e.g., repair of today's automobiles) will be marketable in the workplace of tomorrow. Second, his criticism that trade training tends to emphasize the production of goods at the expense of learning points to the need for career education that attends systematically to the production of student learning. That is, care must be taken to ensure that students are placed in the workplace for the sake of their intellectual and social development rather than to advance the interests of any business.

Dewey's third warning is not to neglect a democratic vision of vocation as socially useful work that builds community. This redefinition of "vocation" also holds lessons for Multiple Pathways, and linking to a broader civic imperative offers schools a principle for selecting and shaping career themes.[76] For example, schools might opportunistically partner with and draw from community workplaces, businesses, governments, social services, and industries to construct themes that address shared public concerns. This understanding of "vocation" is similar to Harry Boyte and Nancy Kari's use of the term "public work."[77] They envision citizens involved in a number of practical activities geared toward "building the commons," such as creating schools, supporting volunteer fire departments, and maintaining public parks.[78] Dewey used "vocation" more broadly to refer to any shared enterprise that serves the interests of society. This might mean promoting career themes tied to human services, such as health care. It could mean framing themes, such as building or construction, in relationship to the broader public interest that new structures would serve. Educators, students, and community members would need to grapple with what Dewey's principle means in practice (and such discussions would represent rich opportunities for civic learning).

Further, Dewey's understanding of democratic vocational education represents a powerful framework for teaching and learning. This framework envisions students using the experimental method to study workplaces and other social settings. For example, students could gather and analyze data on how workers use math across different worksites or on how workers in these different settings are compensated. Dewey's framework also calls for students to study the broader relationship between the government and the economy. Students might examine and debate proposals regarding the minimum wage, living wage, or paid family leave. They might examine access to medical care. They might also discuss the role that organized labor and corporations play in the legislative process. The goal of such curriculum is to enable young people to appropriate the skills and disposition of inquiry as well as to promote a broad understanding of how current economic structures and processes came into being and how they might be changed. This approach resonates with some current scholars of career and technical education who call for "liberal," "democratic," or "critical" vocational education.[79]

By attending to social and economic issues, Dewey extends civic education beyond the formal political institutions of American democracy. He notes that "political democracy is not the whole of democracy. On the contrary, experience has proved that it cannot stand in isolation."[80] Schools' common practice of separating courses in "government" and "economics" highlights such a separation of the political from the whole. In contrast, the Deweyan approach frames issues of class inequality and poverty in relationship to fundamental concerns with equality and political participation. It also makes explicit that economic conditions are not natural and inevitable but the result of particular public policy choices.

This broad vision of civics education suggests that students should study democratic practices within a variety of institutions: political, social, and economic. For example, it is common to place students as interns in government agencies or community-based organizations for "service learning" projects that enable youth to learn and generate new questions about substantive issues and to learn how the political process works. Students might equally benefit from internships that allow them to study firsthand how unions or businesses include workers in decision making and governance. In this view, the key consideration should not be whether the internship site is public or private, but rather whether the student will have a meaningful opportunity to study the exercise of voice and collective decision making.

Dewey's vision of democratic industrial education for industrial democracy calls for students to identify both the causes of and solutions to economic inequality. Significantly, this concern with social change might hold particular resonance for low-income youth, who currently are the group least engaged in formal politics. That is, a curriculum that highlights strategies for addressing economic inequality may engage youth who have felt the mainstream curriculum does not attend to problems that directly affect their daily lives.[81] Dewey's vision also highlights the importance of preparing students to be efficacious citizens with the knowledge, skills, and commitments needed to work for fundamental changes in the political economy. This entails providing them with the tools to understand social problems, the vision of a possible democratic future, and the ability and commitment to take action for change.

MULTIPLE PATHWAYS AND THE FUTURE OF DEMOCRACY

Framing the Multiple Pathways approach around democratic purposes holds great potential for revitalizing education and civic life. We would expect students who experience democratic education through Multiple Pathways to develop knowledge and skills along three lines. First, they would acquire procedural knowledge about the formal workings of government and substantive knowledge about critical policy issues, particularly those tied to economic inequality. Second, they would forge a normative vision of democracy, economic democracy, and the democratic workplace. Third, they would develop the skill, understanding, and commitment needed to participate effectively in the workplace, in formal political institutions, and in campaigns to effect social change.

Although our hope rests in educational reform that broadly interprets vocations in light of their civic purposes, the historical record leaves us doubtful about the future of democracy in vocational education. Throughout the last century, economic instrumentality has been the overarching rationale for vocational and career education.[82] Moreover, in large measure, these purposes have been defined by business and elite interests.[83] It is likely that any new effort to promote democratic vocational education will face pressure to differentiate opportunities across pathways, reprioritize academic or vocational curriculum over civic curriculum, and reproduce the values, understandings, and practices of the prevailing political economy.

As in Dewey's era, it is possible that other constituencies might be brought to bear to counter the status quo. For example, organized labor and grassroots community groups might participate alongside professional educators and representatives from business groups in developing and guiding the implementation of new policies. There are many examples from across the country of groups representing the interests of working people joining in educational reform. In many of these cases, the reform efforts highlight the democratic ends of schooling.[84] Clearly, any serious effort to infuse democracy into the Multiple Pathways approach will require robust democratic action.

Adopting and Implementing Multiple Pathways
Possibilities and Challenges

Previous chapters have looked at the potential for Multiple Pathways to become a coherent strategy for integrating key elements of schooling, including learning and motivation; the economic, social, and educational needs of a diverse population; and explicit attention to preparing future generations for active civic participation. In the five chapters that comprise Part III, we examine the process of implementation and adoption—and, of course, the possibilities and challenges this process presents.

THE POSSIBILITIES

As authors of earlier chapters have noted, Multiple Pathways reform lends itself to a number of "delivery" structures, such as theme-based academies, career academies, small schools, small learning communities, magnet schools, regional occupational programs and centers, and majors or clusters within a large comprehensive high school. Collectively, the essays in this volume propose varied and promising delivery structures, each with a distinct emphasis or theme, but all preparing students for both college and employment. In this section, for example, David Rattray looks at successful transitions to small, thematic, rigorous, contextualized learning environments from comprehensive high schools, and points to central issues associated with these transitions and arrangements. Norton Grubb considers the potential of Multiple Pathways structured as theme-based academies, career academies, majors or clusters within comprehensive high schools, and small themed high schools.

Multiple Pathways also provides increased opportunity to forge new and more constructive relationships between K–12 systems and postsecondary institutions. Andrea Venezia argues that collaboration between postsecondary institutions and K–12 systems could narrow the gap that currently exists between college aspirations and college attainment. Innovative programs, such as dual enrollment, could provide smooth, coherent, and more equitable transitions for students. Furthermore, increased collaboration between the two systems would provide students with clearer signals that they belong on a high-value postsecondary trajectory.

THE CHALLENGES

Implementing Multiple Pathways presents structural, political, and normative challenges that must be addressed in concert.[1] Accompanying the challenges associated with any attempt to reform or restructure the high school are a host of obstacles that must be anticipated at every stage of the reform. Moreover, because Multiple Pathways reform proposes fundamental changes to core beliefs and practices, it will be particularly challenging. We briefly describe these challenges below.

Structural Change: Necessary but Not Sufficient

Restructuring the high school through theme-based approaches can respond to many of the historical and recent critiques of the high school (e.g., students' lack of motivation or engagement). Restructuring alone, however, cannot address the current disjunction between the academic character of the standard curriculum and the essentially vocational orientation of most students, including college-bound students who understand college narrowly as professional preparation. According to Norton Grubb, Multiple Pathways must be thought of as more than restructuring within high schools. Creating opportunity for all students to graduate from high school prepared for postsecondary education, work, or both requires a new way of thinking about the delivery of education, including student-teacher relationships and increased collaboration between K–12 and postsecondary institutions. In addition, reform requires changing the attitudes of teachers, students, and the public about preparation for life after high school. Multiple Pathways' implementation through restructuring alone would not reform these current limitations.

Politics and Turf: K–16 Collaboration Demands State-Level and Systemwide Reform

Multiple Pathways requires increased collaboration between K–12 institutions and postsecondary institutions to develop coherent and unambiguous admission policies and expectations, as well as inventive programs that allow for more flexible and smoother transitions between systems. Andrea Venezia writes that accommodating innovative and deep structural changes in high schools as proposed through Multiple Pathways will require collaboration to determine how and what courses count for university admission and how career-based education applies to college eligibility and admission. (David Stern and Roman Stearns also addressed the topic in chapter 2.) Without increased collaboration, Multiple Pathways reform runs the risk of promoting new forms of segregation and tracking for those who believe attending a postsecondary institution is a realistic goal. Collaboration will require state-level support as well as reform at the K–12 and postsecondary level.

Values and Beliefs: Resistance to Changing the Status Quo

At the core of Multiple Pathways reform is the belief that all students, given the right environment, can master complex academic and technical concepts. Effective delivery of Multiple Pathways, therefore, requires explicit rejection of long-standing systems of sorting students and providing them with different curricula based on their expected postsecondary trajectories. All the authors in this volume address this topic, but the essays in Part III examine possible sources of this resistance, including socioeconomically advantaged parents, educators, and postsecondary institutions. Samuel Lucas points out, for example, that socioeconomically advantaged parents seek to secure and preserve academic advantages for their children and may resist reform. These advantages are tangible and measurable, but they are also "relational"; that is, parents may be as concerned that their children's opportunities are qualitatively superior to other children's as they are concerned about the actual opportunities themselves. As such, universalizing access may not reduce educational inequality, given that qualitative differences could serve to effectively maintain inequality. Multiple Pathways reformers will require steadfast attention to the many pressures that advantaged groups can present to hinder the reform's full intention. Significantly, how Multiple Pathways is received and delivered will ultimately depend on how a diverse population perceives the strategy.

Throughout this volume, contributing authors have identified the challenges that will accompany Multiple Pathways reform and proposed policy that could effectively address many of these concerns. In the concluding chapter of this volume, Jeannie Oakes and Marisa Saunders revisit many of these challenges and provide a critical appreciation for the historical processes that created the educational landscape Multiple Pathways seeks to alter. Indeed, what is entailed in reforming a century-old divide between academic and vocational education and the practice of sorting students into one track or the other? Oakes and Saunders argue that Multiple Pathways, unlike other conceptions of the term and efforts to retool career and technical education, has the potential to affect school policy and students' educational opportunities by addressing both sides of the long-standing academic and vocational divide.

CHAPTER 9

Making It Real

Implementing Multiple Pathways[1]

David Rattray

In this essay, David Rattray brings his experience as vice president of education and workforce development for the Los Angeles Area Chamber of Commerce and president of UNITE-LA—the school-to-career partnership of Los Angeles—to examine thematic learning environments as a potential structure to deliver Multiple Pathways. Based in part on his work with the Los Angeles Unified School District, Rattray identifies the potential for theme-based small learning communities to move schools beyond antiquated school practices, policies, and perceptions.

Rattray argues that teaching academic content in theme-based learning environments can best serve the individual and meet the needs of a changing economy. However, changing from a comprehensive high school to a thematic, rigorous, contextualized learning environment is challenging. Using examples of transitions he has experienced in the Los Angeles Unified School District, Rattray proposes key elements for reform. These include the capacity to develop broad themes, new courses, schedules that accommodate the new courses, transitions and articulation through high school to postsecondary institutions, effective counseling and advisories, student choice, space, and work-based learning opportunities.

Americans are accustomed to thinking about their public schools in terms of vocational or academic education. Vocational education—more recently, career and technical education (CTE)—emphasizes preparing high school students for direct entry into the workforce. Academic education emphasizes the traditional coursework that four-year colleges require. Ideas and debates about reforming education follow the same split: On one hand, people argue for CTE that is better funded, more relevant to students, and more responsive to job and market needs. Meanwhile, people clamor for academic education that has higher learning standards, better pedagogy, and is more inclusive of diverse and traditionally underserved groups of students. With rare exceptions, more historical than recent, few reformers or policymakers have not challenged this fundamental separation of CTE and traditional academic education.

This chapter is based largely on my experience as a business community partner and education reformer seeking to help schools.[2] My work has brought me to schools that are rejecting the traditional division between CTE and academic education. Instead, these schools pursue curricula that combine the core advantages of real-world experiences with rigorous, college-qualifying intellectual work, and they accomplish this hybrid approach in novel school structures that embody the most powerful and synergistic elements of learning and teaching.

More specifically, I report on schools that are discovering the advantages and challenges of establishing theme-based small learning communities (SLCs), or small schools that are guided by a Multiple Pathways (MP) approach to high school reform that prepares all students for postsecondary education and rewarding careers.[3] SLCs adhere to principles that foster the flexibility, relationships, and individual attention that a MP approach requires. Technically, the expression "small schools" refers to the size of the student body (or to small groupings within large schools); these schools still require conscious and determined efforts to attain the characteristics of SLCs. Although not all small schools are theme based, the emphasis here is on the potential of themes to contextualize learning and to drive effective schoolwide reform. Because the most successful instantiations of the MP schools that I have seen are organized around themes (which are more or less broadly construed), themes appear to be important catalysts for deriving the greatest educational and social benefits.

Many have commented on the global changes and challenges to America's prosperity and security that the twenty-first century is bringing.[4] Prior educational-policy responses (discussed briefly below) have embraced the notion that CTE has a crucial role to play if the next generation of Americans is to be able to meet these global changes and challenges. However, even though some of these programs were well conceived, they have preserved the distinction between job preparation and postsecondary education.

- Regional and occupational centers and programs (ROCPs) originated in 1967 to provide exemplary career education, career development, and workforce preparation designed to provide business and industry with a pool of highly trained, productive individuals who would drive economic development in California. Today, 74 ROCPs serve more than 520,000 California high school students and adults annually. More than 3,000 ROCP CTE courses selected to meet current and future labor market demands are offered tuition-free in fields such as information technology, agriculture, business, culinary arts, health care, construction, and auto technology.[5]
- The Carl D. Perkins Career and Technical Education Improvement Act of 2006 (originally authorized in 1984) provides federal funds to vocational education programs designed to help individuals gain the technical skills needed to succeed in a skills-based economy and to prepare students for the careers of their choice. Recently, the focus has shifted to emphasize career and technical courses intended to be academically rigorous and up to date with the needs of business and industry.
- The partnership academy model, structured as a school-within-a-school for tenth- to twelfth-grade students, originated with the Philadelphia Academies in the late 1960s. Adopted in California in the early 1980s, there are currently 290 such programs funded throughout the state. The academy model focuses on career themes that are coordinated with academic classes; an interests-based selection process for ninth graders; a team of teachers who plan and implement the program; a close, family-like atmosphere; a viable business partnership; and a variety of motivational activities linked with the private sector meant to encourage academic and occupational preparation (e.g., mentor and internship programs, enhanced curricula, classroom speakers, field trips).
- During the late twentieth century, reforms under the school-to-work umbrella influenced federal funding initiatives, school design and operations, classroom teacher and counselor training, student testing, and the articulation between secondary and postsecondary education.

Several high school reform models in the 1990s included rigorous, career-themed academies, SLCs, small schools, and more personalized environments, and they have achieved some promising results.[6] Some were aligned with career themes, and some themes were vehicles to engage young people in learning (rather than to provide specific vocational preparation). On the negative side, these career-themed academies often became a subtle version of tracking, and they reinforced the old dichotomy of work or academics, with traditionally underserved groups and poor students directed toward terminal high school "job readiness." Moreover, although the school-to-work reforms of the 1990s (later called school-to-career) enhanced the achievement of some targeted groups of students, they did not move the educational system any closer to helping all students succeed. In fact, current high school graduation rates, college retention rates, and joblessness among 18- to 25-year-olds indicate increasingly dire prospects, especially for low-income, urban youth.[7]

Gradually, these early successes and limitations have yielded to whole school reform represented by theme-based small schools and SLCs. Increasingly, schools are attempting to reorganize career-oriented and academic courses into hybrid curricula under the umbrella of single themes. The goal is for students to master a rigorous academic curriculum as well as new versions of the skills that were the hallmark of stand-alone vocational courses—all accomplished in exciting, real-world, thematic contexts. These reforms are grounded in the growing body of research demonstrating the connections among learning, social relationships, and engagement in authentic tasks.[8]

Small, thematic high schools might be seen as a structural component—a setting—for a range of pedagogical, curricular, relational, funding, and other reforms that will address many of the social and economic challenges presented by the shifting global economy as well as prevailing injustice whereby some students are prepared for successful lives and many are not. Each path that a high school student selects in a thematic high school includes mastery of all the academic subjects combined with the abilities to apply that knowledge, to complete university and community college eligibility requirements, and to learn work-related skills.

Traditional academic tracking places students in either a high-achieving (typically academic) or lower-achieving (often vocational) track—the former designed to prepare students for postsecondary education and the latter for careers. In a theme-based SLC, concrete and practical relevance merges with the traditional academic curriculum. All students engage in the full range of learning activities that are concrete and practical, abstract and academic. Such environments allow effective use of resources and student scaffolding (e.g., caring relationships, tutoring) to create a synergy of hands-on, real-world relevance with traditional academic knowledge that the culture values.

SLCs create an environment in which working hard, working together, making and correcting mistakes, and achieving common goals all become normal and expected avenues for everyone to learn.

Despite the promise suggested by earlier reform efforts, however, converting a comprehensive multitrack high school into a thematic, rigorous, contextualized learning environment is extraordinarily challenging. In what follows, I explore several key issues related to launching theme-based SLCs, including the selection of themes, instructional design, unleashing the power of student choice, employing effective "advisories," and necessary facilities and equipment.

THE CHALLENGE OF SHIFTING THE POLICY DISCUSSION

In a recent opinion survey, 81 percent of disaffected high school students said that opportunities for real-world learning (e.g., internships, service learning) would engage them in high school.[9] However, neither relevance nor the opinions of disaffected students are much considered when allocating resources or determining course offerings. More often, these decisions follow debate and negotiations by adults whose self interest or limited vision leads them to maintain the standard uses of categorical funds and traditional thinking that separates preparation for jobs from preparation for college. One of the primary challenges faced by design teams charged with transforming high schools is navigating the habits of thought, rhetoric, and politics of special interest groups or advocates for separate high school programs.

Vocational Education Advocates

Advocates of vocational education and CTE argue for separate courses and programs for students who are not going to college. They cite data showing the low numbers of students who enroll in four-year universities and the low numbers who complete a four-year degree and therefore do not need the knowledge or disposition to succeed in college. This self-fulfilling argument mistakes the results of current policy (underpreparation for and low participation in college) with the need for those courses. Extensive education research makes clear that the most policy-relevant data for improving schools are students' opportunities to learn while in school rather than "outcomes," which simply reflect those opportunities or their lack. In the context of available and limited opportunities, vulnerable students are asked to decide (or have decided for them) between nearly irreversible life trajectories: to take courses that prepare them well for jobs and college or to take courses that prepare them for neither. These decisions typically ignore the realities of today's workplaces—and even of entry-level jobs—which limit the success of employees who lack some level of postsecondary education.

For many years, educational reforms that embody MP principles (e.g., heterogeneous grouping, off-site learning opportunities, "hands-on" and project-based learning) have triggered negative, defensive responses. Indeed, one element of reform is dealing with administrators and teachers who resist programs that fall outside their own experience or who feel insecure about relinquishing their autonomy, comfort level, familiarity with courses and programs, or job security. Many, though certainly not all, have been steeped in educational tradition that favors early identification of college- or work-bound students (often influenced by race, ethnicity, socioeconomic status, and other factors).

A variety of unproductive accommodations have resulted, including restricting funding to a single use (categorical programs), defining course content narrowly, limiting course access, and often reinforcement of tracking. These negative consequences can be predicted even when they are not intended. For example, a primary goal of academies is to raise the achievement level of at-risk students. Meeting this goal, in turn, influences policymakers' perceptions of the academies' success. Because the consequences for the program and for the adults with a stake in its success are considerable, there is an incentive to recruit students who are most likely to succeed and to discourage those with fewer prospects for success. Although there is no statutory rule in California preventing any student from enrolling in themed academies, many opportunities for student selectivity remain.

Another example of the structural limits to reform is a tendency of vocational programs to restrict federal Perkins funds to narrowly defined career pathways (e.g., automotive technology, horticulture, photography) in order to comply with federally required course sequencing. The result is to create the impression that career academies or CTE pathways are only for non-college-bound students and that they cannot or should not help students prepare for four-year, degree-granting institutions. These and other practices make it difficult to creatively integrate CTE and academic courses into a theme-based SLC that blurs the distinction between college and career preparation.

College-Preparatory Advocates

Ideas about schooling that influence educators also influence many parents. This frame of mind contributes to schooling stratification, in which different tracks are necessary and must lead to different career destinations. Where such "top" tracks exist, students not in those tracks have severely limited access to college and high-paying careers. Furthermore, track assignments correspond closely with students' race, family income, or standardized test scores that serve as a proxy for ability.

Until very recently, the college-preparation course sequences, such as California's A–G requirements, were the exclusive province of students who were on this "top" or college track. These courses typically emphasize lecture-based instruction, memorization, and cultural familiarity, which are helped along by middle-class, English-speaking parents who themselves have college experience. Most schools continue to find the need for context-based, applied learning opportunities. In fact, attempts to infuse these modes of instruction into rigorous academic courses are often associated with a dilution of intellectual challenge that is antithetical to college preparation. So advocates for underrepresented groups of students, noting the traditional CTE/college-prep separation along racial and economic lines, argue that integrating CTE and college prep reflects a "soft bigotry of low expectations."[10]

A New Advocacy: Integration for High Achievement for All Students

Increasingly, education reformers, taking heed of global macro-economic trends, argue for combining high-quality CTE and college preparation in rigorous, option-rich pathways for all students. This perspective makes possible strategic alliances among CTE advocates eager to preserve career-relevant high school experiences and college-prep advocates who are protective of rigorous academic curricula.

This new policy discussion is increasingly important, given that educational institutions cannot possibly predict short- and mid-term economic and occupational trends and nimbly adjust their courses and programs to meet immediate job market challenges and opportunities with great specificity. The best safeguard is to offer contextualized learning that reflects broad, long-term trends affecting multiple economic sectors. This can't be done by following traditional conceptions of training workers; instead, we must think about educating productive citizens. The foundation of such an education is cultivating a love of learning and reading, writing, critical thinking, applying knowledge and skills, and the confidence to work and learn both collegially and independently—all these being attributes and skills required to succeed in an expanding global economy.[11]

The potential for integrating academic and vocational curricula is extensive. As table 9.1 demonstrates, many traditional academic disciplines or subjects map onto multiple CTE areas of study.

TABLE 9.1: High School Courses That Could Be Integrated

Academic Area	Career-Technical Area
Geometry	Carpentry, architecture
Basic mathematics, algebra	Accounting, engineering
Chemistry	Food or nutritional science, biotechnology, forensics
Biology	Agricultural sciences, health professions, biotechnology, forensics
Anatomy, physiology	Health care, sports medicine
Physics	Engineering, robotics, electronics, technology, auto mechanics
Visual arts	Graphic design, architectural design, animation, video production
Foreign languages	Health care, child care, social services
Economics	Marketing, business, finance
Psychology, sociology	Marketing, business, human resources, child care

Source: Table adapted with permission from unpublished paper by Roman Stearns.[12]

Some traditional schools have effectively integrated academic content knowledge with career-technical skills. However, an initial reform challenge is to marshal specific examples that allow policymakers and educators to imagine what MP could actually be like. That being said, policymakers and educators also need to understand the obstacles schools face as they design multiple, integrated high school pathways.

IMPLEMENTING RIGOROUS AND RELEVANT PATHWAYS

High schools that have made headway with creating theme-based SLCs have proceeded in different ways according to local conditions and opportunities. Each school brings together unique and powerful combinations of student interests, corporate partnerships, faculty expertise, and so forth. Not surprisingly, each school selects different themes. To illustrate, table 9.2 displays SLCs on the campuses of several large high schools with which I've worked.[13]

TABLE 9.2: Academy and Small Learning Community Themes at Selected High Schools

High School	Themes of the Academy or Small Learning Community
Agnew	Global Environmental Science; Global Safety and Science; International Trade; Maritime Agriculture Tourism Cuisine and Hospitality; Technology and Health Science
Barkley	New Technology High School
Calhoun	Transportation Careers Academy; Acquiring Bilingual Leaders in Education (ABLE) Academy; Entertainment and Media Academy; Naturalist Academy; School for Social Justice; Global Learning and Observation to Benefit the Environment (GLOBE) Academy; Environmental Health and Awareness Academy; Home Engineering Academy; Zoo Magnet
Dallas	Achievement, Opportunity and Scholarship; Discovery School; Innovation School; Renaissance School; Arts and Sciences
Dawes	New Technology High School; School of Social Justice; Academic Leadership; Business and Tourism
Fairbanks	School for Environmental Studies; School for Social Justice; School for Performing and Visual Arts; New Technology High School
Hamlin	Business and Technology; Health Career; Public Service; Humanities; and Fine Arts and Performing Arts
Hendricks	Teacher Prep Academy; Academy of Business and Communication; Creative Arts and Expression; New Technology High School; Global Outlook through Academic Learning
Morton	School of Arts and Entertainment; School of Business, Technology and Finance; School of Fashion and Design; School of Public Service and Social Justice; School of Travel, Tourism and Culinary Arts; School of Construction and Industrial Technology
Tompkins	Activist for Educational Empowerment; Business and Finance; International School; Multimedia, Performing Arts and Design Technology; Visual Arts and Humanities

In the rest of this chapter, I explore eight implementation issues that deserve reformers' careful attention:

- Developing capacity for themes
- Broad versus narrow themes
- Introducing and scheduling new courses

- Transitions and articulation through high school to postsecondary
- Counseling and advisories
- Choice
- Space
- Work-based learning

Each issue is further developed by examples of high school SLCs that are struggling against the academic-vocational divide. These examples illuminate both the potential and the challenges in creating multiple, rigorous and relevant, themed pathways that prepare all high school students for a postsecondary education and career.

Developing Capacity for Themes

The Morton High School Learning Complex has several SLCs, including the School of Arts and Entertainment; School of Business, Technology and Finance; School of Fashion and Design; School of Public Service and Social Justice; and the School of Travel, Tourism and Culinary Arts. A key to sustaining theme-based SLCs, guided by the MP approach is to establish each theme's relevance to real-life work, careers, and postsecondary study. Relevance is measured in two ways: Of course, students must see their curriculum as relevant, but so must parents and other community stakeholders, including colleges. Credibility among corporate partners and local businesses is crucial for maximizing off-site learning, encouraging expert and material support, and garnering political assets when, inevitably, the programs are challenged.

Morton's School of Arts and Entertainment encourages students to explore several art forms, including drawing, sculpting, dance, theater, and graphic design, and the campus is proud of its new performance theater that enables students to present their work as professionals. In the eleventh and twelfth grades, students in this SLC also participate in internships at local entertainment companies. However, in addition to developing their artistic skills, all students must complete a series of courses that meet entrance requirements for the state's four-year colleges while they perform 50 hours of service learning and create a plan for their postsecondary education.

Rigorous arts courses prepare students for a career and for advanced postsecondary study. Each student-created postsecondary plan is reviewed by teachers and other staff in ways that encourage students to think about how high school will support both their career goals and academic focus. Student internships are supervised by the workplace employee host—an important adult mentor from outside the school. This ongoing supervision and attention signals the high expectations the SLC has for the students' education beyond high school.

Morton's School of Business, Technology and Finance prepares students for roles as citizens, consumers, and corporate managers. The curriculum emphasizes economics, business, and technology to enhance students' core education and develop skills for making wise economic and career decisions. Three thematic pathways are built on a platform of college-prep courses:

- Business courses include sales, e-commerce, and business applications for computer graphics and multimedia presentations.
- Finance courses include accounting, finance, and business management.
- Technology courses include introduction to computers, web design, digital computer science, information technology management, and computer programming.

Capacity is enhanced by keeping instructional options broad and expanding the course content and selection to include business, finance, and productive citizenship. Instead of limiting students to learning skills within narrowly defined careers, administrators and staff emphasize the broad application of knowledge in business, technology, and finance to a wide variety of careers (e.g., health, education, entertainment).

In Morton's School of Public Service and Social Justice, students prepare for careers in urban planning, health care, law, social services, or education, where they can apply their acquired skills in civic leadership as social justice advocates. Building on four-year college-prep courses, students develop job skills and the academic background to continue their education in college majors that focus on careers in public service (e.g., workers compensation analyst, librarian, probation officer) and social justice (e.g., environmental advocate, urban planner, social marketer, public policy researcher). This theme draws on the educational and civic interests and support of many community members.

Part of Morton's success at keeping capacity high is due to administrators', teachers', and stakeholders' use of program evaluation as a springboard to broaden, focus, or reinvent their themes. This is particularly useful, given that some Morton SLCs have faced significant challenges to their theme-based pathways as these replace tracking.

For example, Morton School of Fashion and Design struck some people as being a good choice for students who are not academically inclined. Also, educators worried that this high-value field might seem more suited to young women than to all students. As such, the design team has worked hard to incorporate courses required for admission to four-year colleges. Teachers of fashion design-related courses explicitly relate mathematics, language arts, or chemistry to their applications in industry careers. The concepts of design are revealed in products such as cars, home furnishings, video games, and design software in addition to the more traditional clothing or jewelry. This broader application of core design principles has the potential to attract the partnership and interest of community members who might otherwise think that the theme is not relevant to their own careers or businesses. This more inclusive conception also appeals equally to young women and men.

Similarly, Morton's School of Travel, Tourism and Culinary Arts struggles against perceptions that careers in hospitality, tourism, and the culinary arts are careers that don't require college, that lead to low-status occupations, and that are suited for students without college futures (without academic interests or skills). In fact, this theme is not represented by the teenager at the take-out counter or the maid cleaning a hotel room.[14] This industry segment is the largest employer in the world, offering a wide array of high-wage jobs for individuals with postsecondary degrees and specialized professional training. It includes food service management; international hotel and resort development and operations; crossover careers with health service providers, such as nutritionists; and other high-wage opportunities. The initial challenge is to convince school communities that rigorous foundational coursework in mathematics, history, science, and other college-prep courses can lead to credentials (diplomas and degrees) for career success rather than low-status, low-wage employment. By integrating industry-related courses with academic courses (e.g., chemistry and food or nutritional science), students prepare for immediate career options after high school graduation as well as higher education.

This SLC at Morton will benefit from developing corporate partnerships with industry leaders who are also deeply interested in preparing students at the secondary and postsecondary level for jobs in the industry. For example, the National Restaurant Association's ProStart and ProMgmt Programs have course curricula that high schools typically teach as discrete, skill-based electives; these could be more closely aligned with academic courses. The California Restaurant Association has over 22,000 members who recognize the ProStart Certificate in hiring decisions for a wide range of industry jobs.

Morton's School of Construction and Industrial Technology risks being associated with the old vocational education or "electives" paradigm: woodshop, auto mechanics, and typing. Although students may initially be attracted to learning "a skill," it falls to teachers and counselors to see the relationship between these courses and academic subjects that can expand their career and life options. Although carpenters, electricians, and other tradespeople are in high demand and are well compensated, other related and fulfilling options students should know about are engineering, architecture, general contracting, owner-entrepreneurship, and so forth. The career and knowledge relationships are complex and available at every turn (for those who look for them): An electricians needs to know algebra as well as an engineer does, and a carpenter's understanding of geometry must be as deep as an architect's. Physics, history, and English projects can incorporate information and elements from the study of engineering. The SLC team is still in the process of aligning CTE courses in specific trades with academic courses that provide opportunities to integrate project-based learning.

SLC themes are not static. The team leading Morton's School of Construction and Industrial Technology is considering whether to broaden its theme to include advanced manufacturing, biotechnology, or engineering and manufacturing. Another consideration is to incorporate a highly successful and popular pre-engineering curriculum, Project Lead the Way,[15] which calls for articulation with local community college and university programs.

Broad Themes versus Narrow Themes

As seen above, a focus on broad concepts and competencies within SLCs is important for sustaining and increasing the school's capacity to accomplish its goals. There are many other educational reasons for construing themes broadly and not narrowly.

Schools tend to select themes based on teachers' interests, long-standing and established themes, adult perceptions of students' interests, and perceived job market opportunities. One of the most reliable ways to ensure that the themes connect with students is to involve many stakeholders, including students, in developing theme choices. Absent this broad-based involvement in theme selection (along with other aspects of school governance), themes can be limited to the narrow vision of a "founding" committee or the proprietary control of a few teachers. For example, one or two instructors who teach elective courses have been known to establish a narrow, job-specific career academy that does little to integrate the theme with subject-area courses. In other cases, vocational specialists with backgrounds in education or industry have focused exclusively on the job-specific skill requirements. Although some students may obtain marketable skills that lead to high-wage jobs immediately after high school (e.g., in courses that lead to certification as an auto technician, CISCO-certified programmer, or Apple software specialist), their advancement in the field can have a low "ceiling." The benefits of specific career preparation can be offset without the critical skills necessary to solve problems and interpret information,[16] and without the belief that postsecondary education and training is possible.

Many employers say they want an employee with a good attitude, basic literacy and numeracy skills, and an ability and willingness to learn. These broad attributes position the employee for job flexibility and advancement, providing the agility to shift as the market does. Employment opportunities change so fast that educational bureaucracies as well as businesses will always be challenged to keep the workforce equipped with competencies demanded by a changing and competitive marketplace. Broad themes, rather than narrowly constructed ones, are most likely to prepare for long-term employment and lifelong learning.

The Global Outlook through Academic Learning SLC at Fillmore High School is an example of a broad-based theme. The school is focused around learning and leading in a democratic society that supports diversity and promotes democratic values and multilingualism in a globally diverse environment. Its coursework appears designed for students who are interested in careers that require at minimum a baccalaureate degree. The program seeks to equip students to be enlightened leaders in public or private enterprises in a changing global economy. Teachers use problem-based learning and interdisciplinary teaching strategies.

The Global Outlook SLC signals a strong CTE environment, in which students' project-based work is reviewed and evaluated by employers and industry professionals, in addition to their classroom teachers. It exemplifies the virtues of effective CTE instruction, even if students do not experience this strategy as an element of a distinctly CTE course. The program integrates academic coursework with applied, real-world problems and authentic assessment. Through authentic assessments, students perform real-world tasks that demonstrate meaningful application of essential knowledge and skills. Students must engage in worthwhile problems that generate important questions. Like professionals in the field, whether carpenters, historians, surveyors, or health professionals, they must employ empirical information with their own creative intellectual abilities. This style of teaching is a big shift for many who are used to lecture-based classrooms and who are most comfortable with a narrow curriculum and traditional assessments.

Introducing and Scheduling New Courses

In many respects the "master schedule" in a traditional comprehensive high school reflects the school's philosophy and educational values. Trying to change that schedule without simultaneously clarifying and changing the underlying educational values in the school and in the community simply invites frustration. Furthermore, designing the schedule is typically a complex, top-down, and mysterious exercise. The schedule has to maximize a number of key variables that include access to academic and elective courses, balanced teaching loads, space allocations, and budget requirements.

The SLC committee at Hamlin High School struggled to revise a master schedule that designated all the CTE courses as electives, a practice signaling that CTE classes did not stress core academic competencies and that academic courses offered little that was practical or interesting. A common strategy for theme-based SLCs is to use block scheduling, which, among other benefits, lengthens some class periods. (Traditional high schools may offer six or seven 50-minute periods, whereas block schedule classes may go to 90 minutes or more.) The longer classes allow for interdisciplinary teaching and project-based learning, and they increase the likelihood of teacher-student contact. One way that schools might make use of block schedules is to partner a teacher who has traditionally taught CTE courses with an academic teacher in order to bring valuable contextualized learning opportunities to an existing academic course, and vice versa.

The team's task at Hamlin High School was complicated because not all teachers thought the changes to the schedule were necessary. Some Hamlin teachers (especially those with specific vocational credentials and mastery) were reluctant to embrace a schedule that prioritized courses that contextualize academics in themes. The proposed schedule formalized new educational norms and values, and teachers who could not abide by them learned that their teaching positions or resources were in jeopardy if they could not adapt. As the SLC committee moved to align CTE electives with SLC themes in the master schedule, they had difficulty finding teachers on staff to teach the classes. To get beyond this impasse, some new theme-based CTE courses are not added until a veteran CTE teacher decides to leave.

Transitions and Articulation

Students differ in their academic preparedness, their overall maturity, their readiness for making career-oriented decisions; and their capacity to benefit from off-campus experiences. Theme-based SLCs have many ways to accommodate students' differences and preferences and still not fall into the trap of sorting students into college-or-work tracks. Key to being responsive and caring for each student is to create the structures and environment that allow maximum interaction with and knowledge about the students. Two such structures are "freshman houses," and strong middle school–high school connections that increase and inform decision making. A third approach is articulation with community colleges.

A freshman house clusters students for their academic courses, including remedial or support classes, none of which has a career focus. The emphasis is on giving students the structural supports of an SLC while preparing them for informed and mature participation in a theme-based environment. Both Fillmore and Agnew High Schools have freshman houses in which the goal is to help incoming eighth graders gain a solid footing in core academic subjects and give them time to make an informed decision about the SLCs, academies, or other programs available on campus. Researchers studying the Talent Development model created at the Johns Hopkins University believe this first year helps smooth the transition for middle school students to the challenges of the high school environment.[17] Many teachers I've spoken with believe such programs help transitioning students avoid the early failure in English and algebra that has a lasting impact on a student's progression to required upper-level courses.

Several schools, including Calhoun, Hamlin, and the New Tech School, have used the second approach, combining ninth-grade SLC choices with extensive outreach to middle schools and parents of incoming high school students. They've found, however, that the first contacts with prospective students and their families can be very challenging. For example, when first asked to commit on paper to a particular theme-based SLC, many eighth-grade students simply refuse to complete their interest form. Adults must engage students in the decision-making process without making selections for them. It is difficult, yet these schools have had enough success to suggest that outreach to middle schools can engage students and their parents in thinking productively about student pathways. Other cities, such as San Diego, Minneapolis, and Sacramento, have developed robust engagement opportunities for incoming freshmen and their parents, even though these activities are new for school administrators and teachers, who are often hard-pressed for time and resources.

Another powerful articulation option is to offer theme-based or career-based educational opportunities to older high school students through dual enrollment programs. This articulation requires agreements that support mobility and facilitate a seamless transfer of academic credit between the high school and community college. Some dual enrollment programs are formal, such as the tech prep program, which specifies a sequence of courses at the high school and community college. Others are less formal arrangements in which students can earn college credit by taking challenging college-level courses while still in high school. Here too, however, the danger of tracking is ever present. The design and implementation of articulated programs can be exemplary or slide back to the old paradigm of vocational education tracking.

Counseling and Advisories

The constellation of guidance, college, and career counseling professionals on high school campuses represents an essential and increasingly rare resource for millions of youth. For example, with average counselor-to-student ratios of 1:506 in California,[18] it is extremely difficult to make appropriate course assignments. These ratios contribute to a system wherein adults make decisions for students with very little input from students or parents, thereby making it especially hard to move away from the traditional adult-determined tracking system.

Theme-based SLCs that integrate CTE courses and contextualized learning strategies require a blending of counseling resources that are traditionally separate (i.e., career, academic, and college counseling). Formal advisory structures are one way to provide some counseling services in situations where specifically credentialed counselors are simply not available for career (or any sort of individualized) counseling. Some schools have an advisory class period 2–5 days per week for 20–40 minutes a day to provide some personalized counseling attention.[19] These advisories vary in design but generally aim to connect an advisor, a student, and a student peer group. Some schools recruit administrators, counselors, and teachers to be advisors in order to achieve a ratio of 18–25 students per advisor. Some research suggests that sustained relationships with adult advisors maximizes college, career, and life counseling in a way that empowers students and parents to make education and career choices at a developmental pace that is appropriate for each student.[20] The challenge, of course, is to ensure that advisories provide high doses of college, personal, and career supports.

Although Hamlin High School is still in the early stages of implementing advisories, its progress is interesting to follow. Some Hamlin administrators and teachers want to emphasize college preparation or academic tutoring in the advisories. Through such programs as AVID, Cornell Note Taking, and Sustained Silent Reading, they hope to align advisory practices with schoolwide instructional goals and strategies. Others want to include career advising and resources, using portfolios to demonstrate students' learning through hands-on-experience. Because the advisory curriculum is not mandatory, much depends on the adults leading the advisory period to make the exploration of choices compelling. Ongoing scaffolding and professional development for teachers is problematic because of constrained resources.

Choice

Student choice of themes and SLCs is a key MP principle. Not only are students more likely to be engaged in a program they have chosen, but also in a type of market dynamic, student selection over time should cause themes to be eliminated or to evolve if they do not attract or retain students. Many educators in the schools I've observed see student choice as the best counterbalance to traditional tracking. Calhoun and Dallas High Schools provide examples of the challenges that choice plans can create.

The legacy of the struggle between vocational education and college-preparatory advocates continues to challenge Calhoun's reforms, even though program administrators and teachers across the campus are committed to making changes. For example, there is a tendency by the SLC team to promote and describe the Home Engineering Academy as having strong vocational goals, even though (unlike its vocational education predecessors) the students must complete core classes that meet the A–G requirements. In subtle messaging, the Home Engineering Academy's recruitment tends to focus on academic underachievers. Students identified with potential for high achievement are directed by teachers, counselors, and parents to what is perceived to be the more challenging coursework offered in other SLCs at Calhoun High School, such as the Zoo Magnet or the School of Social Justice. This tracking effect is partly driven by the criteria of the California Partnership Academy, which provides funding for the Home Engineering program. Funding requirements for the California Partnership Academy dictate that a significant portion of participating students meet thresholds that qualify them as "at risk." The SLC team struggled to eliminate both the subtle messaging and overt practices that reinforce the sorting of students by perceived ability, while supporting the concept that emphasizing the contextualized learning inherent in specific SLC themes to disadvantaged or underperforming students increases their engagement in learning they find relevant.

Calhoun's struggle reveals the complexity of mitigating adults' preconceptions about students' academic preparedness or willingness to work hard.

Calhoun hopes that the high value the school places on student choice will prevail against administrators', teachers', and parents' inclinations to prese-lect students and create situations where students and parents feel forced in the direction of a specific field, career pathway, or job.

Placing choice over other school assignment criteria has its problems that can cause some people to look back fondly at adult-determined assignments and the traditional master schedule. For example, balancing enrollment among SLCs offered at the same campus can be difficult. Perhaps more trou-bling, Calhoun SLCs were unable to balance students' gender, race, English-language proficiency, special education, prior academic achievement, and other factors across the SLCs.

The Calhoun SLC teams have learned that the degree to which such bal-ance is possible depends on the attitudes and tolerance level of all commu-nity stakeholders, and the capacity of school and other leadership to cre-ate an environment in which choices are good for individuals as well as the community. Calhoun has adopted a long-term policy goal to avoid the cur-rent gaps among students enrolled in the magnet program (which is driven by both the balancing of represented campus ethnicities and preselection by highly motivated and informed parents) and the rest of the school's student population. Calhoun administrators hope that the gap will become small enough to eliminate the magnet's current distinction of being the place for high-potential students, and will become just one option among a set of equally interesting and challenging academic learning communities on campus.

When the stakeholders at Dallas High School created and developed their small schools (Achievement, Opportunity and Scholarship; Discovery School; Innovation School; Renaissance School; and Arts and Sciences), not only did they consider balance in course offerings, they agreed on tolerance ranges for all key demographics, including race, gender, prior achievement, and special education. Students rank their SLC preferences by first, second, or third choice, giving the faculty the flexibility to balance student enroll-ments while still following a principle of student choices. The school would design outreach and attempt to recruit prospective students from groups that consistently avoid certain SLCs (e.g., female students not enrolling in repre-sentative numbers in technology).

Space

Space and proximity are crucial factors for supporting or negating the cohe-sive relationships among students, among teachers, and among programs.

Traditionally, schools isolated their vocational classrooms in one section or building on the campus, making integration of students, teachers, and curricula difficult or impossible. The biases favoring college-prep over vocational programs became matters of public and special identification. When design committees attempt to reinvent a comprehensive high school as theme-based SLCs with aligned CTE courses, many will face the powerful physical constraints of schools.

Hamlin High School's traditional vocational education shops are located in one area of the campus. A design firm recommended that these vocational shops and the science building serve as a hub that allows the SLC to be separate from, yet have easy access to, the large CTE classrooms. Hamlin High School's traditional magnet has been located in a separate area of the campus, thus reinforcing the elite, college-going status of its space. Many theme-based SLCs may see their first challenge as having enough space, but soon they will face important ecological and relational factors created by the particular distribution of that space on the campus and in the community.

Work-Based Learning

Real-world experiences and strong business-school interactions greatly enhance school programs with broad career themes, helping students develop positive perceptions about the relevance of schooling.[21] Work-based learning experiences

- hone specific job skills as a stepping-stone to employment after graduation;
- provide students with mentors who help clarify career aspirations and reinforce the relationship between coursework and the workplace;
- scaffold schools with business and civic partners who help schools contextualize curriculum and sustain project-based learning.

Work-based learning can bring practical efficiencies to SLCs. Traditional (and effective) vocational education programs need learning environments that recreate state-of-the-art workplaces. However, this can require equipment that is costly to maintain and quickly becomes obsolete. The ebb and flow and broad inadequacy of education funding cannot keep pace with the latest technological innovations. Work-based learning programs that include internships, job shadowing, paid work experiences, and cooperative education provide students with relevant experiences that schools cannot afford on their own.

CONCLUSION

This chapter reports on school teams that have combined the best of college preparation, theme-based SLCs, and CTE. These schools have not succeeded entirely, and some are just beginning their work, but their hybrid approaches suggest rich benefits for students, faculties, and communities.

These school reforms contextualize academics in real-life work, jobs, and careers. They spark interest in school. Their SLCs promise to create multiple pathways within integrated, themed learning environments, where students learn to use knowledge effectively and are started toward lifelong learning.

In a "flat world,"[22] the best long-term strategy for every individual is to cultivate the knowledge, skills, and abilities to stay ahead of changes in a job market driven by global, economic, and corporate realities. The goal of a high school education is to prepare students to continually evaluate and reassess their own knowledge and skills and actively seek appropriate learning opportunities that prepare them for a lifetime of personal and financial success. The examples cited here illustrate the potential of the MP strategy to effectively provide students with the blend of academics and contextualized instructional strategies. They also demonstrate that SLCs can provide the structure for sustaining this strategy.

CHAPTER 10

Challenging the Deep Structure of High School

Weak and Strong Versions of Multiple Pathways

W. Norton Grubb

No single reform can counter all the critiques to which American high schools have been subjected for more than three-quarters of a century. Economist W. Norton Grubb provides an in-depth analysis of the problems facing high schools and discusses how a Multiple Pathways approach to reform provides a clear alternative. Grubb is David Gardner Professor in Higher Education and the faculty coordinator of the Principal Leadership Institute at the University of California–Berkeley. His most recent book is The Education Gospel: The Economic Power of Schooling *(with Marvin Lazerson).*

Grubb argues that a "weak" version of Multiple Pathways—one that focuses almost exclusively on restructuring large comprehensive high schools into small, theme-based schools—can respond to many of the historical and recent critiques of the high school, including problems of motivation and engagement. However, several failings of the high school would not necessarily be reformed by this weak version. Grubb argues that a "strong" version would be far more useful—one that views restructuring as necessary but not sufficient. Strong reform requires substantial changes in the quality of instruction, a focus on equity, strategies to avoid "retracking," and innovative ways to help students who are behind. Integral to such strong reform are changes in the attitudes of teachers, students, and the public, generally about preparation for life after high school. This focus on the future might help students understand that a short-term focus and a narrow understanding of learning (e.g., thinking of school as important only for the grades and credits it creates and the vocational advantages it provides) can only undermine their own learning.

The high school seems perpetually in crisis.[1] The constant clamor for high school reform should remind us of Cuban's warning about "reforming again, again, and again": that American schooling goes through wave after wave of change because earlier reforms have been incomplete, or have targeted the wrong problem, or have failed to transform classrooms, or reflect irreconcilable value conflicts.[2]

In the case of high schools, complaints arose as early as the 1930s about the curricular and pedagogical limitations imposed by college admission requirements. Later in the decade, the Roosevelt Commission complained about the weakness of vocational tracks and the dreariness of academic tracks, leading to the first suggestions for integrating academic and occupational education. Complaints in the early 1950s that Life Adjustment Education had dumbed down the high school brought recommendations to focus the curriculum on academic basics. James Bryant Conant's 1960 critique that high schools segregated adolescents with their peers, creating the conditions for "social dynamite," was followed by a surge of reports in the 1970s with much the same criticism.[3] Proposals to get students into the "real world" were offered as a way to temper the influence of the adolescent subculture, a position picked up again in the School-to-Work Opportunities Act of 1994, which provided funding for apprenticeships and work placements. The turn of the twenty-first century brought another burst of critical reports on the high school, with more than a dozen in 2004 alone and more coming out all the time.[4]

Despite these calls for reform, very little about the high school has changed. Innovations during the 1930s (e.g., theme-based curricula and internships) died with the coming of World War II, and appeals to integrate academic and vocational education were ignored until the 1990s. Complaints about low-quality courses in the 1950s eliminated some egregious examples of Life Adjustment Education, but the low-quality general track persisted. The critiques of the 1960s and 1970s about the lack of relevance to the outside world did trigger some internships and work placements, but these remained marginal. The School-to-Work Opportunities Act foundered on the tenden-

cies of high schools to buy more of the same (e.g., more conventional counseling) rather than introducing internships or other substantive changes.[5]

So, after nearly a century of calls for reform, the high school today is
much as it was in the late nineteenth century: dominated by conventional
academic subjects, structured by Carnegie units devised in 1906, focused on
preparation for college, largely insulated from real-world experiences, and as
boring to most students as it was in the 1890s.[6] Of course there have been
changes: The occupational purposes of high schools have become much more
dominant;[7] the distractions of youth culture have expanded; and racial/eth-
nic and class diversity has increased enormously from the early years of the
twentieth century. But from an educational standpoint everything seems
much as it was then, an "industrial-era institution" preparing students for a
twenty-first-century world.

Given the stability of the high school, no one reform idea is likely to
reshape the high school once and for all. But the vision of Multiple Pathways—each pathway having a distinct emphasis or theme, but all preparing students for both college and employment—holds enormous promise.
First, however, it's useful to clarify what forms Multiple Pathways can take.[8]
Perhaps the most familiar form is an "academy," often but not necessarily a
career-oriented academy, that combines several teachers in a school-within-
a-school. Students usually stay with the same teachers for two or three years
("looping"), thus enhancing the stability of teacher-student contacts. An
academy usually includes a math teacher, an English teacher, a teacher in the
subject that gives the academy its distinct theme, and a fourth teacher who
might be a science or social studies teacher. Ideally, the teachers collaborate
in designing the curriculum, so that it is better integrated than in the conventional high school.

In a second form of restructuring, sometimes referred to as majors or clusters,[9] students take most courses from conventional subject-matter teachers,
but also take one or two periods a day in the subject that gives the major its
distinction. The amount of time devoted to courses in the major can vary
from trivial to substantial. Compared to academies, majors may provide
fewer opportunities for teachers to collaborate, since most teaching is done
by conventional academic instructors.

A third form includes entire schools with particular themes or emphases,
something that has occurred in large cities (e.g., New York's Aviation High,
Chicago's Agricultural High) and now in magnet schools and small, themed
high schools. Every teacher and student in a health-oriented high school or

a technology high school is engaged in some area of the larger focus, and all teachers can modify their curricula to fit the theme.

These reforms alter the structure of high schools, but often they change little else. I will refer to them as weak forms of or approaches to Multiple Pathways, and they are sufficient for many purposes, as I clarify later in this chapter. However, restructuring does not guarantee other desirable changes, especially related to teaching and learning. Under "Remaining Challenges: 'Strong' Versions of Multiple Pathways," therefore, I present a strong version of Multiple Pathways that goes beyond restructuring by explicitly incorporating multiple goals for all students. These goals include preparation to enter college, and preparation for certain forms of employment, and preparation for students to think about their futures. Unlike weak versions, these strong versions of Multiple Pathways squarely address problems related to the quality of instruction, equity, the potential for retracking, or the difficulties of helping students who are behind. These issues are critical to reforming American high schools and escaping the endless rounds of complaining about high schools.

RESPONDING TO THE RECURRING CRITIQUES OF THE HIGH SCHOOL

In the many historical and contemporary critiques[10] of the high school, several themes emerge:

1. *Relationships between teachers and students are lousy.* Most high schools are so large that teachers cannot know students well. Students feel anonymous, uncared for, and often treated with disrespect. In particular, the ethnographic literature about African American and Latino students reveals the depth of this problem. Creating smaller high schools or schools-within-schools has been the main response. However, neither evidence nor a robust theory of change supports small size, and some early and enthusiastic supporters are more circumspect about small schools per se.

    Some restructuring approaches to Multiple Pathways—particularly academies with looping, and small, themed schools—can address the scale and anonymity of conventional high schools. If teachers see fewer students each day and come to know them better, then perhaps the mistreatment of students would also be reduced. However, while reducing school size (restructuring) may be necessary, it is not sufficient to improve personal relationships, particularly racial/ethnic dimensions of those relationships. Reforms also must anticipate the need for long-term staff development and the challenges of developing high schools as moral communities.[11]

2. *High schools are places of captivity, stressing order and containment over exploration and learning.*[12] Proposed solutions have included greater flexibility in scheduling (e.g., Breaking Ranks I and II, a pair of national reports on high school reform from the National Association of Secondary School Principals that recommend "the look and feel of college"[13]), but aside from double periods and a few experiments with college-like schedules (e.g., classes meeting on alternate days), this doesn't seem to have gone very far. An alternative solution is simply to truncate high school and get students into college earlier through dual enrollment programs, often with community colleges. But this is an effort to substitute institutions of greater freedom for the high school, not a reform of high school itself.

In several ways, however, Multiple Pathways might reduce the sense of high school as prison. Such approaches often include block periods and schedules more like college. Project-based learning and internships, work placements, and service learning break up the tedium of a highly constrained day. The choice of a pathway, of out-of-school placements, of projects, and of schedules might help develop student-constructed programs rather than curricula prescribed by college entrance requirements.

3. *High school dropout rates are atrociously high.* Despite the debate over measuring dropout rates, no one denies that the rate is too high, affecting 20–30 percent of all students and much higher proportions of Latino and black students. Common proposals to prevent dropping out include academic interventions (many of them small-scale, fragmented, and poorly planned), better personal relations (again), smaller schools (again), alternative curricula (again), improved instructional methods, some structural changes like ninth-grade Success Academies (examined later in the chapter), and various support services. Widespread adoption of specific "brand-name" reforms such as AVID (Advancement via Individual Determination) and First Things First has also been proposed. Overall, however, dropout rates haven't improved since the 1950s. State exit exams may make things worse as high schools adopt scripted instruction, teach to the tests, and strip the curriculum to the barest essentials.[14]

Multiple Pathways have potential advantages in combating the high dropout rate. As discussed, improved personal relationships can reduce estrangement; if students can choose themes related to their interests, they might be more engaged. The quasi-experimental evaluations of academies have confirmed increases in engagement and reductions in dropout.[15] However, the one random-assignment study found increased motivation and engagement[16] but not higher graduation rates.[17] It seems unlikely, then, that Multiple Pathways are complete solutions to the dropout problem, though they are at least steps in the right direction.

4. *High schools crowd adolescents with other adolescents, and the result is "social dynamite."* Conant's old phrase describe the fears that concentrating teenagers with one another can only lead to trouble, including too much sex, drugs, and rock and roll (or rap).[18] Reform proposals from the 1970s and later stress the lack of adults in the lives of high school students; for example, High Schools of the Millennium calls for "immersion in the adult world."[19] Evidence about the effects of peers, for good but sometimes for ill, is also part of this argument. The solutions have been to place students with adults, in internships, or in service learning, community projects, or mentoring relationships.[20]

The advantage of theme-based pathways is that many themes lead "naturally" to out-of-school work placements or real-world experiences. For example, Ryken has documented the benefits for students in a biotechnology academy of work placements in a biotech firm, where students work alongside adult coworkers as peers.[21] At the same time, it is important to remember how difficult it can be to establish worthy out-of-school placements,[22] and the failure of the School-to-Work Opportunities Act of 1994—with its trifling sums of money and five-year deadline, producing more of the same, including ineffective counseling—should remain a lesson.

5. *The high school diploma and high school assessments create the wrong incentives.* The high school diploma is awarded essentially for seat time, not for mastery of any competencies. Bishop notes that the system rewards the quantity of education but not its quality.[23] The solution of the American Diploma Project is to create assessments anchored to the "real world," based on "the knowledge and skills colleges and employers actually expect" (as if they all expect the same thing). Similarly, Tucker has proposed three "gateways," otherwise known as exams, creating statewide standards for admission to subsequent education.[24] Tough Choices or Tough Times has proposed two exams, one at the end of tenth grade and a second, at the level of Advanced Placement (AP) courses or the international baccalaureate program, to allow students access to selec-

tive colleges.[25] These reforms are more preoccupied with creating assessments than with improving the capacities of schools to meet these standards, and they reinforce the conventional academic high school rather than reforming it.[26] Overall, then, these are poor ways to enhance motivation, engagement, and completion.

The potential of Multiple Pathways with explicit themes is that they might lead to alternative assessments. Many such programs have adopted portfolios, and project-based approaches assess students through their projects. Some schools have adopted senior projects,[27] which then drive efforts to develop the students' capacities to carry out these projects. So certain approaches to theme-based pathways sidestep the problems inherent in assessment-driven reforms.

RESPONDING TO ISSUES OF STUDENT MOTIVATION AND ENGAGEMENT

Perhaps the dominant critique of the high school is that it is boring and irrelevant. The conventional college-prep curriculum, an amalgam of college entrance requirements, has been critiqued for lacking any focus or coherence; others note that it is irrelevant for many who won't or don't want to go to competitive colleges. A related problem is the disjunction between the academic character of the standard curriculum and the essentially vocational orientation of most students, including college-bound students who understand college as professional preparation.[28] A similar charge is that, when high school is only a mechanism for getting into college, nothing of intrinsic importance takes place; as Paul Goodman said four decades ago: "If there is nothing worthwhile, it is hard to do anything at all."[29]

A report of the National Academy of Sciences has clarified the conditions that enhance motivation.[30] In every case Multiple Pathways provide substantial advantages in creating the conditions for motivation and engagement:

6. *Students are more likely to be motivated in programs that allow for close adult-student relationships.* Most programs with themes follow this precept by creating smaller learning communities, and many themed high schools are relatively small. The *combination* of themes and small size makes it sensible to develop group work, work teams, and projects involving students collectively. Furthermore, programs with internships give students opportunities to make connections to fellow workers and supervisors as well as teachers. The national school-to-work evaluation found that practices such as small class sizes and weekly seminars helped build rela-

tionships among teachers, students, and worksite personnel, creating a "family-like atmosphere,"[31] and that students valued the programs' one-to-one connections.[32]

7. *Students' engagement increases in environments where they have some autonomy in selecting tasks and methods, and in which they can construct meaning, engage in sense-making on their own, and play an active role in learning.* Following this precept, Multiple Pathways replace a monolithic curriculum with students' choices: first, the choice among theme-based schools or schools-within-a-school; then among projects, including senior or "capstone" projects; and among internships, where students can match their interests to placements. If a theme is broadly vocational, workshops provide opportunities for more active forms of learning, often described (somewhat facilely) as "hands-on" learning:[33] the process of showing and doing; the development of visual, manual, and interpersonal skills, and of higher-order skills like communications and problem solving; opportunities for one-on-one instruction, as teachers help individuals or small groups in the workshop or lab; and opportunities for feedback from errors.

8. *Motivation and engagement are enhanced in well-structured educational environments with clear purposes.* Programs following well-developed themes can be carefully structured and clear in their purposes because they are linked both to future employment opportunities and to subsequent educational enrollment. In addition, high schools with clusters and theme-based high schools often dispense with the proliferation of electives and extracurricular activities characteristic of the "shopping mall high school."[34] Thus these reforms can improve the coherence of the high school, where courses are unrelated to one another and the curriculum is unrelated to future goals aside from college entrance.

9. *Motivation is enhanced in settings with a challenging curriculum, high expectations, and a strong emphasis on achievement.* Theme-based programs, and particularly efforts to integrate academic and vocational education in some broadly occupational area, have often replaced watered-down "academic" offerings offered to "non-college-bound" students. For example, the Talent Development High School model and the Southern Regional Education Board "Schools That Work" reforms replace the general track with more demanding integrated programs. Carefully structured workshops also are designed to enhance learning and can be integrated with classroom instruction involving applications. Internships

provide other settings that support learning, especially if they are integrated with school-based learning through "connecting activities."[35] The students in Ryken's academies learned complementary competencies in school and work settings: Work taught the procedures in biotechnology production, while school components taught the underlying theories.[36] Many forms of nonschool learning can emerge from internships, including the so-called soft skills—punctuality, discipline, persistence, responsibility—that are necessary for life outside high schools.

10. *Motivation and engagement are enhanced when students have multiple paths to competence.* In contrast to the monolithic college-prep curriculum, which allows only one path to success measured by grades and SAT scores, theme-based pathways can provide multiple avenues for success, including artistic success, success in making and fixing things, and success in developing competencies related to employment. Internships provide opportunities to master additional skills. Out-of-school placements as avenues to mastery provide antidotes to Goodman's criticism, since carefully constructed internships provide opportunities for youth to do meaningful work.

11. *Helping students develop education and career pathways can enhance their understanding of school and their motivation.* Students are unlikely to be highly engaged in schoolwork if they do not understand its relevance to future goals.[37] Occupational themes can help students envision careers, develop direct information about careers, and understand related educational requirements. Crain et al. and Pedraza et al. reported that school-to-work programs provided a clear work-related identity for participants.[38] Similarly, Ryken found that biotechnology students began to understand the biotechnology industry with some sophistication, with different understandings developed in high school, in work placements, and in the college component.[39]

Mechanisms to help students choose an appropriate pathway in ninth and tenth grades also connect high school opportunities more clearly to professional goals. For example, in one school offering six majors, students first complete a nine-week "exploratory" in each of six majors, choose two for a second and more intensive exploratory, and then choose a major from those two, thereby providing two choice nodes with serious (but still reversible) consequences.[40] This use of short introductory courses is a powerful advance over conventional approaches to guidance and counseling.

In many ways, then, pathways based on themes can improve student motivation and engagement. However, there are important caveats; if the points above are taken up in weak versions of Multiple Pathways, then the results might be little better than those provided by traditional high schools. So, the following conditions need to be carefully structured in programs that are themselves nurtured in a strong environment. The programs need to appeal to a wide range of student competencies and provide opportunities to expand those competencies. They should integrate content across courses, projects, internships, and other activities. Internships and work-based learning are valuable, but they are especially fragile: Carefully structured opportunities have more positive effects than the work students find on their own,[41] but low-quality placements can do just the opposite. [42] Nothing comes free: The most engaging and educative pathways also require the most careful development.

In contrast, the conventional high school violates nearly every one of these precepts for motivation and engagement. It provides few close adult-student relationships; it provides no autonomy whatsoever in choosing programs of study; and most courses are taught in routine ways with few opportunities for student choices of projects or activities. The purposes of most high school programs are unclear, especially given the academic nature of coursework contrasted with students' understanding that high schools are essentially vocational. There's little in the conventional high school to help students plan for their future life's work. I conclude, then, that Multiple Pathways based on thematic approaches are in every way superior to the conventional high school in enhancing motivation and engagement.

REMAINING CHALLENGES: "STRONG" VERSIONS OF MULTIPLE PATHWAYS

Although restructuring high schools through Multiple Pathways responds to many critiques, such changes are in some ways necessary but not sufficient. Quite apart from the difficulties of implementation,[43] restructuring alone cannot resolve some issues plaguing high schools, including problems related to instructional quality, equity, student orientation toward the future, and overly instrumental and vocationalist conceptions of learning. The "strong" version of Multiple Pathways would include changed attitudes about preparation for life after high school and about preparing all students for college and for other opportunities beyond high school, whether that involves immediate employment, military service, or the combination of employment and further education that has become so common.[44] With this addition, Multiple Pathways could generate even more powerful reforms.

Student Learning and the Quality of Instruction

Restructuring does not enhance learning unless there is specific attention to improving instruction. Improved motivation, attendance, and course completion may not be accompanied by improved test scores or other measures of learning.[45] School restructuring guided by the Talent Development model, career academies, and Puente have enhanced measures of motivation and engagement but not test scores.[46] Conversely, First Things First has increased standardized tests scores as well as student attendance and graduation;[47] First Things First tries to both reshape instruction, through intense staff development and enriched language and math curricula, and create greater support for students though small learning communities and Family Advocates. If students are to be prepared for college as well as alternatives, then the quality of learning must be enhanced, both in the sense that higher grades and test scores are necessary for college entrance, and in the sense that avoiding years of remedial or basic skills instruction in postsecondary education requires mastery in high school.

If, however, Multiple Pathways are ways of giving all students multiple options after high school, then enhancing learning is central to this goal. Accordingly, any restructuring should incorporate balanced approaches. Such changes would also respond to the persistent critiques from students (except perhaps those in upper tracks) about the dominance of conventional drill-oriented teaching. In addition, the National Research Council's *Engaging Schools* explicitly notes the motivational power of more constructivist instructional practices, precisely those that are rarely found in conventional behaviorist teaching.[48] Similarly, many recent reports call for greater use of problem- and project-based learning and contextualized instruction. To be sure, reforming instruction requires explicit attention, long-term professional development,[49] and concerted leadership.[50] But a strong version of Multiple Pathways might be able to improve instruction where most reforms have failed even to try.

The Problem of Tracking and the Equity of High Schools

Another persistent critique of the high school is that it engages in too much tracking and sorting—both the traditional vocational-or-academic tracking and the proliferation of honors, AP, general, college-prep, and other labels that signify course content and expectations that strongly predict college attendance, dropping out, and other consequences.[51] As one antidote to tracking, some reports have argued that the college-prep curriculum should become the default. However, the notion that all students should be prepared for college is usually followed by the "discovery" that not all students want the college-prep curriculum, and then by proposals to recreate different versions of vocational education. This kind of swing between unitary academic approaches versus adopting some vocational programs never imagines what an intermediate solution might be: a "both-and" solution drawing on both academic and vocational traditions, like the many efforts to integrate academic and broadly occupational education.

The debate about tracking has strongly influenced discussions about what themes or foci might be appropriate for pathways. Many proponents of academies and majors have used broadly occupational themes: health high schools and academies, IT programs, agriculture academies or high schools, an automotive tech academy in Philadelphia, Aviation High in New York, hospitality pathways, and travel and tourism academies created by American Express. Because these themes risk re-creating vocational tracking, some advocates of theme-based approaches have shunned occupational themes. A recent review of "themes that serve schools well" mentioned a number of nonoccupational themes.[52] Unfortunately, the discussion of nonoccupational themes versus occupational themes replicates the old divide between academic and vocational education, and from a Deweyan perspective it is important to avoid this either-or perspective.[53] One approach to building a strong version of Multiple Pathways would be to allow occupational and nonoccupational themes, so that themes would never be associated with exclusively vocational goals; this approach would also create broader choices for students. A second would be to avoid occupational themes likely to re-create tracking. For example, health academies focusing on a range of medical occupations, including physicians, should attract students with a variety of ambitions, but a health academy designed to prepare dental technicians re-creates tracking. A business academy encompassing the range of business occupations might not foster tracking, but a hospitality academy is likely to prepare students for low-paid positions in hotels and restaurants. A strong version of Multiple Pathways prepares students for college and careers, and therefore, even occupational pathways do not foreclose any options.

A different equity problem is that some students enter high school behind the academic standards set for ninth grade. If students fail to complete ninth-grade coursework, they are highly likely to drop out[54]; such students are disproportionately working class, black, Latino, and immigrant. It serves no purpose to restructure the high school if there is no help for those behind grade-level norms. One successful approach, in the Talent Development High School, has been to develop a ninth -grade Success Academy, teaching literacy with enriched, content-based materials instead of decontextualized drills. In other cases, one can see high schools developing ninth -grade learning communities, or advisories, where students are in smaller and more supportive environments and can learn basic skills in the context of other coursework. Often, schools recognize that students who are seriously behind have other problems with their families, health or mental health issues, or drugs or alcohol, and then try to include noneducational support services.[55]

Currently, schools appear to be taking one of two polar approaches to working with students who are behind, as well various approaches in between.[56] At one extreme are efforts, like Talent Development, that have developed "enriched" approaches to core subjects like English and math: Students engage in reading for meaning as well as mastering basic skills (decoding, fluency, building vocabulary), and schools create multiple avenues for learning to think mathematically as well as explicitly teaching math procedures. The opposite, impoverished approach is to increase the time students spend on language drills (including scripted and semiscripted curricula like SRA Reach and Open Court) and repetition of math drills that do nothing to develop students' understanding of mathematical concepts. Because "more of the same" requires more time, these students are also taken out of classes in social studies, sciences, and languages, thereby creating a curriculum that has been stripped to the basics. The impoverished approach has almost no chance of helping students over the long run because the skills it teaches are intrinsically useless; both skills-oriented pedagogical approaches and the narrowing curriculum violate every one of the maxims for enhanced motivation presented earlier in the chapter. In addition, with "basics" dominating the curriculum, schools pay little attention to other subjects necessary for college admission. In strong versions of Multiple Pathways, it's crucial to avoid interventions for ninth-grade students that are impoverished and self-defeating.

Orientation toward Future Alternatives

After 1900, as high schools became increasingly vocational in their goals, future-oriented decision making became important because students made choices with serious long-term consequences.[57] Broadly speaking, high schools have never done a good job of counseling students for careers or college. Multiple Pathways would add greater pressures to the already low capacity of school counseling because students' informed choices would become even more critical. One response is to distribute guidance and counseling functions broadly among counselors, occupational and academic instructors, and counseling workshops, and to include internship supervisors and coworkers in appropriate counseling support. Several promising approaches redesign the roles of counselors.[58] First Things First has developed a Family Advocate System in which all teachers, administrators, and qualified staff advise a small group (typically 12–17 students) regarding their paths through high school and on to adult life. The Puente program has an expanded conception of counselors that includes contact with academic teachers, parent meetings, supervising trips to colleges, and recruiting and interacting with mentors. The National School Counselor Training Initiative envisions moving counselors away from one-on-one advising to more central roles, such as collaborating with teachers to influence systemwide changes.

Student Attitudes toward Learning

For about a century, and certainly since A Nation at Risk,[59] the dominant narrative about schooling has been what I call the Education Gospel: the faith that orienting schooling around preparation for occupations will resolve many social and individual problems, ranging from economic growth and competitiveness to individual mobility to greater equity.[60] The Education Gospel has boosted educational expansion and reform, but it has several negative consequences as well. One is that students (and many others) come to see schooling in increasingly instrumental terms, valuable for the credentials that provide access to rewarding occupations. Indeed, when John Goodlad questioned students in the late 1970s, the greatest number (31%) responded that the purpose of high school was vocational, with smaller proportions recognizing personal development (25.6%), intellectual development (27.3%), and social activity (15.9%).[61] These attitudes have surely been reinforced since then, especially with competition for college-going, and they have influenced the views of postsecondary students, especially in community colleges and comprehensive state institutions.[62]

Unfortunately, highly instrumental and vocational views of schooling may undermine learning. As Cox describes this process, students with narrowly instrumental views come to focus on grades, credits earned, and degrees completed rather than on learning.[63] They make detailed calculations of the costs and benefits of schoolwork, rejecting all extra work that might not affect credits or grades; insofar as possible, they try to earn credits with minimal reading, minimal homework, and minimal revisions of papers. With such attitudes, students tend to undermine their own learning in many subtle ways. Consistent with this evidence, my work with National Educational Longitudinal Survey of the Class of 1988 (NELS88) data reveals that students with a more vocational orientation toward high school—more concerned with the economic advantages from completing high school and going to college—are more likely to want to continue their schooling but have lower test scores, presumably as they engage with coursework in more superficial ways.[64] Paradoxically, the Education Gospel stressing the value of education ends up undermining learning.

But if the strong version of Multiple Pathways can place enough emphasis on the long-run goals of high school, rather than short-run credits and credentials, then it might be possible for instructors, individually or (ideally) collectively, to resocialize students: to convince them that learning is more than fact acquisition, and that the development of knowledge should not be viewed in such narrow and instrumental ways. Like the improvement of instruction, this would require teachers to rethink their own teaching and its relationship to students' futures.

The Governance of American Schools

Many changes envisioned in this essay are difficult in a conventionally structured high school. In the dominant Weberian or top-down model that emerged from administrative progressivism, the principal directs the school in a relatively autocratic fashion. Teachers have a great deal of autonomy in their classrooms but participate very little in schoolwide decisions; most are represented by industrial-style unions concerned more about pay and working conditions than about instruction. Pedagogical approaches are dominated by information-transfer and disciplinary requirements, with little concern for students' depth of understanding. High school exit exams, state accountability exams, and AP tests reinforce this approach to instruction. Staff development is relatively unimportant, and usually takes the form of episodic presentations by outsiders (e.g., in Friday afternoon one-shot events).

The alternative has variously been described as a school with internal accountability,[65] or one with distributed leadership,[66] or what Rowan (1990) calls "organic management."[67] The division between administrators and teachers is blurred, teachers participate in a wide range of decision making, and leadership is distributed over all participants in the school. The improvement of instruction is a collective responsibility that takes place with the help of classroom observations, the analysis of students' work, and sustained professional development[68]; teachers' concerns are represented by professional unions rather than industrial unions. Disciplinary boundaries are less important and nonstandard assessments (e.g., portfolios, demonstrations, senior projects, or capstone projects) become more important.

Developing Multiple Pathways is almost surely more difficult in traditional high schools than in high schools with internal accountability. Decisions about which pathways to offer require collective decisions; in high schools where teachers are assigned to academies or majors (rather than volunteering), they teach in conventional ways and the possibilities for collaboration are weakened. Consistency of pedagogical approaches, which is highly desirable if students are taking classes linked to one another, is impossible without collective decisions.

One challenge in implementing Multiple Pathways, then, is shifting from a conventional top-down organization to one that is more "organic" and participatory. In such schools teachers need to be open to more collaboration and participation, so change in teacher preparation may be necessary. In addition, the principal's leadership is critical,[69] though there has been no special attention to preparing high school principals for these roles. One potential solution, aside from reforming principal preparation programs,[70] is to give each pathway its own leadership, creating a team of principals for a high school. The practice of multiple principals has many advantages over the conventional principal-assistant principal structure,[71] and Multiple Pathways with multiple principals may provide a solution to the impossibility of the high school principal's job.

In sum, a strong approach to Multiple Pathways, preparing all students for college and careers and for informed decisions about future options, must not only restructure high schools but also focus on the quality of instruction, tracking, students' attitudes toward learning, and their orientation toward the future. In addition, real reform of the high school will require fundamental changes in governance in addition to Multiple Pathways. Any of these elements can be the initial "wedge" that begins the process of reform, though this initial change must be context specific. For example, some communities, students, and schools might be captivated by an employment focus or a career-technical education approach to pathways, and others by nonvocational themes; some will be captivated by prospects for more hands-on and project-based approaches to teaching; still others will be moved principally by an equity argument emphasizing the heterogeneity of pathways. The key will be whether the compelling arguments and practices can be marshaled to develop these broader approaches rather than continuing to critique the nineteenth-century high school without making any real reforms.

CHAPTER 11

Between High School and College
Can Multiple Pathways Bridge the Divide?

Andrea Venezia

Andrea Venezia, a higher education scholar and coauthor of Minding the Gap: Why Integrating High School with College Makes Sense and How to Do It, *is a senior policy associate for WestEd's Regional Educational Laboratory West, located in San Francisco.*

Venezia argues that the relationship between K–12 and postsecondary institutions is a crucial locus of effective school reform. She describes the importance of collaboration between postsecondary education institutions and K–12 schools for the success of Multiple Pathways, particularly as schools prepare underserved students for postsecondary and career success. Venezia also cautions about two challenges for collaboration. First, postsecondary admissions policies lack coherence, and they do not accommodate innovative, structural changes in high schools. Second, high school students need strong, unambiguous signals about postsecondary preparation if they are to develop and maintain a belief that postsecondary education is a realistic goal. Highlighting sample programs from California and other states, Venezia describes the importance of statewide and systemwide changes, as well as local and regional partnerships, in order to address the complexity and the large scale of needed reforms.

* * *

Real preparation for college is something much more important and vital than the accumulation of 15 prescribed units.[1]

—W. M. Aikin

Recent studies, including Stanford University's Bridge Project, find that secondary and postsecondary systems fail to work in unison.[2] Policies and practices are often so disconnected that they send students conflicting messages about such issues as course expectations. Moreover, course titles and other commonly-used proxies for college readiness are inadequate indicators of preparation.[3]

While these conclusions are useful for the field, they are not new. Over 60 years ago investigators in the so-called Eight-Year Study (undertaken by the Commission on the Relation of School and College of The Progressive Education Association) argued, "The relationship is an unhappy one. Colleges criticize the schools saying that students come to college unprepared for their work, that they are deficient in even the most rudimentary academic skills, that their habits of work are careless and superficial, and that they lack seriousness and clarity of purpose." In an effort to increase the percentage of students who attend and succeed in the state's community colleges and its baccalaureate-granting universities, especially those who are underserved, secondary and postsecondary systems continue to work to figure out their roles vis-à-vis each other and to connect their systems.

This chapter explores how postsecondary education might forge a more constructive relationship with high schools, and vice versa, as high schools develop and implement Multiple Pathways. As a school reform, Multiple Pathways integrates academics and applied skills in ways that motivate students to remain in school and engage in the learning process. Collaboration between postsecondary and secondary education is essential for Multiple Pathways to become equitable, relevant, and coherent trajectories that lead to college and career success. The complexity and scale of such reform demands both state-level or systemwide changes and local or regional partnerships.

This exploration rests on the following views: (1) Neither high schools nor postsecondary institutions are happy with the quality or effectiveness of the coherence (or lack of it) between the two systems; (2) most high school students aspire to some form of postsecondary education, but far fewer obtain a college degree or advanced certificate, and the gap between college aspirations and attainment is greatest for students of color and low-income students; (3) the aspiration-attainment gap partly results from curricula that do not engage all students—more specifically, this refers to the traditional "academic" curricula that remains for many the only legitimate way to prepare students for college[4]; and (4) educational reforms, including those seeking "college readiness for all," must address the impact of student disengagement on the disconnect between the aspirations and attainment of students of color and low-income students. Multiple Pathways reform has the potential to give students more engaging curricula and equitable college chances.

MULTIPLE PATHWAYS TO CLOSE THE ASPIRATIONS-ATTAINMENT GAP

State and national data show that almost all high school students want to attend college after high school, and the majority of high school graduates do matriculate directly to postsecondary education after college. Over 90 percent of high school seniors in the United States plan to attend college (two-year and four-year colleges), and approximately 70 percent of high school graduates actually do go to college within two years of graduating, to either two-year or four-year institutions.[5] The large gap between those who aspire to attend postsecondary education and those who actually attend is partly explained by whether students receive early and adequate information about postsecondary expectations, academic preparation for college, financial aid, and other related issues. A school's capacity to marshal resources and to provide a wide range of opportunities likely causes gaps in outcomes. Rogers et al. found that many of the state's high schools provide insufficient college-preparatory classes, too few qualified teachers to teach those classes, and too few counselors to guide students along the path to college.[6]

"Pipeline" data, showing rates of high school graduation, postsecondary entrance, and college success, identify large inequalities in terms of who persists at each educational level. For example, out of every 100 ninth graders in California, 70 graduate from high school, 37 enroll immediately in college, 25 are still enrolled sophomore year, and 19 graduate within 150 percent time (six years).[7] For Chicanos, for every 100 elementary school students, 46 graduate from high school; 26 enroll in college (17 in community college, 9 in four-year institutions; 1 student transfers from community college to a four-year institution); 8 graduate with a bachelor's degree; 2 earn a graduate or professional degree; and 2 earn a doctoral degree.[8] Studies identify similar trends for African Americans.[9] These data demonstrate that too many students do not make it to high school graduation, and fewer still graduate from college. Connecting the systems has become a focus of states across the country, given both the individual and societal demands for some form of postsecondary education and for greater educational equity.[10] For example, Achieve, an organization that helps states develop policies geared toward connecting K–12 and postsecondary education, is a coalition of thirty-three states including California.

A "college-readiness-for-all" movement is pushing schools to educate all students to "college readiness levels."[11] "Readiness," in this case, means that all students are prepared, academically, for some form of postsecondary education, such as additional coursework necessary for the workforce, a certificate program, a transfer program, or a four-year degree program. One rationale behind the college-readiness-for-all movement is that this charge is necessary if students from underserved groups are to raise their rates of college and other postsecondary participation. College readiness for all is different from a college-for-all strategy. The former accepts that not all students will attend a postsecondary education institution, but that all students must have high-level, high-quality courses—academic and nonacademic. This is consistent with a Multiple Pathways approach that includes career and technical education (CTE) and provides rigorous, engaging, curricular opportunities.

However, many questions about Multiple Pathways remain: Can large-scale curricular change of this kind occur without replicating the social, economic, and race-based course tracking that pervades the state's and the country's schools? What kinds of coursework can engage all students enough to keep them in school and provide them with rigorous academic opportunities? Can a Multiple Pathways strategy that incorporates CTE actually prepare all students for career and college? What combination of local expertise, state and local policy, resources, and capacity make wide-scale implementation possible? Moreover, Multiple Pathways reforms face two significant challenges related to students' transitions between schools implementing Multiple Pathways and postsecondary institutions: (1) new postsecondary admissions policies to accommodate innovative, structural changes in high schools and (2) policies to inform students that they have realistic opportunities to gain college admission or prepare for other postsecondary education.

It will be particularly important to increase schools' and the public's knowledge of how CTE fits into complex formulas for college eligibility and admission. In California, the University of California (UC) and the California State University (CSU) systems include some CTE courses that students can take to satisfy admissions requirements (the A–G course sequence). Also, the California Community Colleges (CCC)—the institutions with the greatest connection to workforce preparation—send scant information to high school students about CTE courses as preparation for the CCC.

Here I suggest two contributions that California's postsecondary systems can make to a Multiple Pathways reform: (1) Send strong, detailed, unambiguous signals about academic preparation for postsecondary education; and (2) continue to construct eligibility and admissions policies that accommodate integrated and applied high school curricula in all academic areas, especially core courses.

SEND STRONG, DETAILED, UNAMBIGUOUS SIGNALS ABOUT SCHOOLS' POSTSECONDARY EXPECTATIONS

Higher education has a long history of influencing reforms in K–12. The most selective postsecondary institutions and systems tend to drive debates and reform, even though approximately 80 percent of all students attend institutions that are not highly selective, such as colleges within the CSU system.[12] For example, Princeton was the first institution to adopt usage of the SAT, followed by other Ivy League schools. Today, most four-year institutions, including many broad-access institutions, use the SAT to determine college eligibility. In California, the Master Plan for Education communicates the mission of the three postsecondary tiers, and the UC's and CSU's A–G requirements are central to college pathway discussions, even for schools "outside" these public educations systems.

The California Education Code stipulates how CTE courses can meet high school graduation requirements.[13] Similarly, the UC and CSU course approval process includes possibilities for CTE courses to be part of the A–G requirements, although the opportunities are few. A recent report from the UC states, "it is manageable for a student to meet the three sets of requirements (high school graduation, CTE recommendations, UC/CSU eligibility) while completing the minimum number of units for high school graduation (22 units/220 credits)."[14] This assumes that students' high schools offer the appropriate courses at times that are feasible for students, and assumes that block schedules, teacher preparation, professional development, and many structural issues are addressed. The same report found, though, that students might follow a CTE-recommended path and a high school graduation path but not be eligible for UC/CSU because they did not take enough UC/CSU-required courses in English, mathematics, general electives, laboratory science, visual and performing arts, or foreign languages.[15]

In 2006, there were 4,021 CTE courses across all California schools that met the A–G requirements.[16] When the courses are broken down by A–G subject area (table 11.1), discrepancies are apparent. Few CTE courses are approved to meet UC/CSU A–G requirements in history/social science, English, mathematics, and foreign languages, especially as compared with the number

TABLE 11.1: Number of California CTE Courses That Met A–G Requirements, 2005–2006

A–G Subject Area	Number of CTE Courses That Met A–G Requirements
A History/social science	21
B English	19
C Mathematics	5
D Laboratory science	684
E Foreign languages	2
F Visual and performing arts	2,107
G College-preparatory electives	1,183

of laboratory science, visual and performing arts, and college-preparatory electives.[17] More courses are being added each year. In 2006, the number increased to 4,705.

With over three-fourths of these courses satisfying either the visual and performing arts or college-preparatory electives requirement, students at comprehensive high schools would have difficulty meeting CTE recommendations and UC/CSU eligibility requirements. Recently, UC has been accepting more applied academic courses in agriculture, engineering, media and entertainment, and other subjects. Certain kinds of restructured high schools (e.g., career academies, theme-based small learning communities) allow students to meet CTE requirements as well as the requirements of baccalaureate-granting institutions.

Alongside the structural challenge of providing appropriate course opportunities for a Multiple Pathways approach, schools must contend with the knowledge of and meaning of postsecondary expectations. Stanford's Bridge Project demonstrated that written policies and legislation do not ensure that students understand, personally and practically, specific educational requirements for admission to and success in postsecondary education. Despite the apparent clarity of the A–G requirements, students often know little about college-readiness requirements. In a regional study for Stanford University's Bridge Project, researchers analyzed the college knowledge of high school students in the greater metropolitan Sacramento area with regard to admission and placement policies at the nearby UC–Davis and CSU–Sacramento. The following summarizes the main findings:

As far as knowledge of curricular requirements is concerned . . . students knew more about Sac State's requirements than UC Davis' . . . students in honors courses displayed more specific knowledge than students in college preparatory courses. Furthermore, students in the high-performing schools were the most knowledgeable about UC Davis' requirements, while students in the low-performing schools were the most knowledgeable of CSU Sacramento's requirements. . . . Students generally had a poor understanding of the English and math placement exams at the two universities. Less than 30 percent of students knew about Sac State's placement exams and less than 20 percent of students knew about UC Davis's exams.[18]

Only 2 percent of the greater Sacramento metropolitan area ninth graders surveyed for the Bridge Project had knowledge of the A–G requirements; that was the smallest percentage of students who knew such postsecondary curricular requirements of any of the six studied states (one region per state). Project researchers had assumed that, since the UC's requirements are very public, a greater proportion of students would know the information. Bridge Project data also showed that the current system creates barriers and is confusing to students—particularly to traditionally underserved students:

The current fractured systems send students, their parents, and K–12 educators conflicting and vague messages about what students need to know and be able to do to enter and succeed in college. . . . [H]igh school assessments often stress different knowledge and skills than do college entrance and placement requirements. Similarly, the coursework between high school and college is not connected.[19]

In addition, schools give much more information about college preparation to students who take traditional academic courses than to students who take more applied courses or integrated curricula. Bridge Project researchers examined differences in college knowledge and policy information between students in college-preparatory tracks compared with students in honors tracks.[20] The differences were stark and consistent: Honors students knew more than students in college-preparatory courses and were exposed to a more useful college knowledge environment, including more informed and engaged teachers and counselors.[21] It is safe to assume that, had the project included students in CTE tracks, the differences would have been more apparent. One straightforward response, though not a solution, to this problem would be for students, parents, counselors, and community-based advocates to enter completed courses and current schedule into a computer program and receive information about which courses they need to take—academic and integrated—to be UC or CSU eligible or to be prepared for success at the CCCs. Indeed, the UC offers the Transcript and Evaluation Service, which attempts to accomplish just this. However, few districts in the state use it, and it is in the pilot stage in other districts.

Although four-year university requirements currently drive course taking and test preparation for high school students who are viewed as college bound, most postsecondary institutions are far less involved in reforms that influence student achievement more generally. For example, higher education had little involvement in the recent work to define K–12 curriculum standards and assessments that are performed in every state. As a result, students can meet high school graduation requirements without meeting college entrance requirements; for example, most high school exit-level tests are geared toward the eighth to tenth grades. Importantly, students who take "general" education courses or follow a career-focused trajectory are not the only ones to be ill prepared for CCC, UC, or CSU success; many students who follow a traditionally academic "pathway" (taking courses identified as college preparatory), are similarly disadvantaged because of poor information, inadequate coursework, and poor planning.

Given that students in California have postsecondary opportunities in addition to the UC or CSU systems, these findings resonate. For example, the CCCs send virtually no signals about postsecondary readiness. This is primarily due to their open enrollment policies to welcome anyone who can benefit from instruction. Yet, the CCCs have established standards for college-level, credit-bearing coursework and for transfer-level courses. As such, the CCCs should engage with the K–12 system to ensure that all students are aware of these standards. In addition, CCCs and K–12 systems need to establish how the state's new CTE standards and frameworks could be used to signal the knowledge and skills that success in community college requires. The current need for remediation of CCC students suggests that college-readiness standards could be very useful. A key issue for the CCCs is to make sure standards do not exclude or dissuade students from attending.

CONTINUE TO DEVELOP ELIGIBILITY AND ADMISSIONS POLICIES TO RECOGNIZE APPLIED AND INTEGRATED CURRICULUM AS COLLEGE PREPARATION

Some research suggests that Multiple Pathways, implemented with rigor and aligned with postsecondary expectations, can prepare students for college. The Eight-Year Study of the 1930s (cited at the beginning of the chapter) compared 1,475 matched pairs of high school students. One member of each pair completed high school in an experimental high school and the other in a traditional high school, and the postsecondary trajectories were compared. Two guiding principles drove curriculum and instruction in the experimental high schools. The first principle was aligned to a theory of learning, namely, that students develop by doing things that have meaning to them. This principle might be contrasted with the traditional view that school is a process of acquiring certain skills and of mastering prescribed subject matter. The second principle embodied schools' moral purpose: High schools must lead students to understand, to appreciate, and to live the kind of life embodied in society's highest ethical, just, and egalitarian aspirations. In an effort to enact those principles, teachers worked together to connect subject areas and to make the learning relevant for students' lives. The experimental schools developed agreements with postsecondary institutions that freed them from subject and credit prescription and, in most cases, from entrance requirements. Hundreds of young men and women entered college from the thirty (experimental) schools without having completed the traditional course sequences. The students succeeded in postsecondary education. For example, these students earned slightly higher GPAs in college (while specializing in the same fields as the comparison group), received slightly more academic honors, were more often judged to have a higher degree of intellectual curiosity and drive, participated in class more frequently, and demonstrated resourcefulness more often.[22] Key facets of Multiple Pathways include a similar integration of curricula and use of hands-on work to make rigorous academic content meaningful, thus making the Eight-Year Study particularly relevant.

Stern and Stearns' summary of research on career academies (in this volume) makes clear that an integrated, hands-on approach to teaching and learning is at least as powerful in promoting learning as the traditional high school curriculum. They conclude that, although blending academic with career-technical curriculum may motivate more students to learn academic concepts and skills required for college, the evidence that this kind of integrated curriculum actually promotes academic achievement is not conclusive.[23] Most studies have not been able to determine whether apparent effects are due to particular programs or to selection of particular kinds of students into those programs. Stern and Stearns, for example, cite Manpower Demonstration Research Corporation's most recent evaluation of career academies, which found positive results in the labor market but no impact on educational attainment.[24]

Several recent reports have analyzed the relationship between (a) the academic knowledge and skills required for postsecondary education and (b) the applied knowledge and skills needed for well-paying, flexible careers after high school. Most have found that, at a minimum, the two bodies of knowledge and skills intersect significantly. For example, the Southern Regional Education Board (SREB), the American Diploma Project (ADP), and ACT (founded as American College Testing) recommend, based on their own studies, that all high school students complete the same core subject areas, regardless of whether they intend to go directly to college or to work. [25] A sample core might be four years of English; four years of mathematics, including algebra I, algebra II, geometry, and a course past algebra II; three years of science; and three years of social studies. According to ACT, "whether planning to enter college or workforce training programs after graduation, high school students need to be educated to a comparable level of readiness in reading and mathematics." ACT researchers reached that conclusion after identifying the knowledge and skills students needed in reading and mathematics to be ready for entry-level jobs that do not require a four-year degree, jobs that pay enough to support a family and offer career advancement. The researchers compared students' test scores measuring workforce readiness with scores that measure college readiness and determined that, "[a]lthough the contexts within which these expectations are taught and assessed may differ, the level of expectation for all students must be the same."[26]

There is some disagreement about the need for high-level knowledge and skills for workforce preparation after high school. The Educational Testing Service (ETS) published a report refuting studies that found that the knowledge and skills needed for college and work are the same, and it also highlighted the need for fundamental reform of the high school education of those students seeking jobs requiring less than a college degree. [27] That report concluded, "This analysis does not find support for the proposition that those not going to college need to be qualified to enter college credit courses in order to enter the workforce. It does, however, find a strong case for advancing the academic skills of a high proportion of those high school graduates if they are to compete successfully for the higher-paying jobs available to those without a college degree, and advance in such jobs."[28] The report's author supports this position with the following findings:

- Employers (aside from those who rely a great deal on teenage employees) do not want to hire high school graduates until they are in their twenties, regardless of how well they did in high school;

- The top reasons employers cited for rejecting applicants for hourly production jobs were "inadequate employability skills" or "soft skills"—not skills that are typically taught in high school or college;
- Advances in technology serve to "up-skill" and "de-skill" jobs, and no one has figured out the impact of changing jobs' skill level on the overall job market;
- Half of the skills for the Bureau of Labor Statistics' projected job openings are learned through on-the-job training (as opposed to classroom learning).[29]

Part of the disagreement between the SREB, Achieve, and ACT reports and the ETS report is likely due to the distinct definitions of "workforce readiness" used by the authors (e.g., readiness for well-paying, flexible jobs versus readiness for basic entry into the labor market) and to overall uncertainty about the future of workforce needs. There is consensus, though, that high school students need higher levels of academic skills. The Multiple Pathways approach would include more rigorous academics within the context of applied career paths. In addition, Multiple Pathways would address two of the concerns from the ETS report: the provision of on-the-job training and teaching "soft skills" through applied academic learning activities.

Finally, the Workforce Strategy Center highlights the following major disconnects between high school preparation, postsecondary education, and CTE, all of which speak to the potential of a Multiple Pathways approach:

- High school and postsecondary curricula stress different knowledge and skills, and few high school students are exposed to postsecondary education and to careers in "knowledge fields."
- Adult basic skills programs and remedial education programs in postsecondary institutions do not adequately prepare students to succeed in postsecondary technical programs.
- The traditional seat-time model for awarding credit, in addition to inflexible academic calendars, makes it difficult for institutions to respond flexibly to the academic needs and schedules of working adults and their employers.
- Funding based on enrollment makes it difficult to sustain technical programs that are high cost.
- Postsecondary occupational degree programs often lack ways to build relationships with employers.
- Few institutions have the capacity to track the labor market and continuing education for their students; those data could provide information

about improving education at those institutions.[30]

Together, these reports suggest the potential of integrated and applied emphasis of Multiple Pathways curriculum to provide both college preparation and readiness for well-paying, flexible jobs. However, postsecondary institutions must go beyond their traditional constructions of academic preparation (and their proxies such as tests and course units). In addition, high schools must go beyond the traditional "vocational" course and ensure that applied courses meet accepted academic standards of rigor. This likely involves team teaching and preservice or professional development opportunities for teachers.

SOME STEPS IN THE RIGHT DIRECTION

Some promising models have been attempted or are in place for postsecondary education participation in the design and implementation of Multiple Pathways reforms. The Oregon University System's (OUS) Proficiency-Based Admission Standards System (PASS) developed standards for taking university-level courses and aligned those expectations with the state's K–12 standards and assessments. The CSU's Early Assessment Program (EAP) combines three high school-level reforms: early assessment, teacher professional development, and curricular change to inform eleventh and twelfth graders about the knowledge, skills, and dispositions required for taking college-level courses successfully. Two national projects—the ADP and Standards for Success (S4S)—developed sets of knowledge and skills standards that postsecondary education systems and institutions have for entering students.[31] All four models contain components that could be useful for California's postsecondary segments as they consider a role for themselves in the current high school reform efforts in the state. These models are explored further later in the chapter.

Oregon's Proficiency-Based Admission Standards System[32]

Oregon's story of reform provides useful information despite its phase-out as of 2008, and some contributions will remain embedded in the system. Oregon's state system of seven universities instituted PASS: a partnership between higher education and K–12 to implement curricular reform that holds all students to high standards and employs useful assessments. Starting in the mid-1990s, the OUS sought to influence the content and direction of high school reforms by specifying the knowledge and skills necessary for university success in English, mathematics, science, social science, second languages, and visual and performing arts, while shifting the focus of the admission process from the courses taken to the knowledge and skills mastered. The PASS requires incoming OUS students to demonstrate that their knowledge and skills meet the PASS standards. It never reached scale across the state, though the lessons learned are useful.

As they developed the PASS, the university system also (1) aligned its standards for postsecondary preparation and success with the K–12 system's standards and assessments; (2) conducted research on the impact of the alignment and reported back to K–12 on what works, what could be improved, and how students are performing; and (3) advocated for its reforms by embedding their alignment in policy and publicly endorsing the K–12 system's efforts to improve students' performance. As a result, the PASS university-preparation standards are now linked to Oregon's tenth-grade benchmark standards and assessment; students who meet or exceed the tenth-grade performance standards also meet some PASS standards in mathematics, reading, writing, and science.

Historically, PASS responded to Oregon's K–12 reforms. In 1991 (and amended in 1995), the state legislature mandated Certificates of Initial and Advanced Mastery (CIM and CAM, respectively). Both were conceived to move away from simply counting seat time and toward proficiency-based teaching and learning. The Oregon Department of Education oversees the CIM and CAM.[33] The CIM, awarded at the tenth-grade level, is designed to convey student mastery of high school standards; it is not required for graduation. To earn a CIM, students had to demonstrate proficiency on the state assessment and on work samples (e.g., writing samples) for the tenth grade. Over time, the CIM evolved from a proficiency-based set of requirements (e.g., examples of student work) to a more traditional assessment approach (e.g., multiple-choice tests). This evolution occurred for a variety of reasons, including policy overload and the ease and cost of a traditional approach. This is a diversion from the original intent of offering more "authentic" or "holistic" approaches to assessment in particular.

The CAM was intended to indicate student mastery of twelfth-grade standards. CAM standards were divided into foundation skills and advanced applications, both of which required the same standards of performance of all students; the objective was to help students develop the skills they need for the career and academic challenges of post-high school life. However, CAM's design and implementation were controversial, and as a result, it was not fully implemented across the state. One of the most significant early struggles was whether CAM should indicate proficiency in academic or vocational areas, or a combination of the two. In addition, members of the university system did not perceive either the CIM or CAM as sufficiently focused on preparing students for college. Portions of the CAM that will remain are the development of student individualized plans that will build on students' aptitudes, interests, and goals.

The OUS initiated PASS in 1993 to ensure that the CIM and the CAM would accommodate higher education's needs and to ensure that Oregon's students would be ready to succeed at OUS institutions. The campuses wanted a greater number of well-prepared students and had two main concerns: that the low academic level of the CIM would mean that more students would need remediation, and that the CAM would focus on preparation for careers rather than college.

After adopting the PASS proficiency standards, OUS developed more detailed descriptions of the knowledge and skills needed to prepare for and succeed in college. Teams of faculty members from over 60 high schools, community colleges, and all the four-year campuses continued to refine these proficiencies over the next six years. The university system provided extensive professional development to PASS teachers (K–12 teachers who completed PASS training seminars) to help them learn, for example, how to judge proficiencies.[34]

The alignment between the CIM, CAM, and PASS was substantial and, once the CIM and CAM disappear, the content alignment will remain. That work was conducted by partnerships between OUS and Oregon Department of Education. Currently, about one-third of the proficiencies identified by PASS are embedded in the CIM. In addition, the rules for the collection of evidence of student work for the CAM are the same as those for PASS.

OUS researchers have reported that students who met or exceeded PASS standards earn a higher freshman GPA than their peers who did not meet the PASS proficiency standards. Eighty-two percent of students who met or exceeded the PASS standards returned for the second year of college compared to 78 percent of those who did not meet or exceed PASS standards. In addition, they found that performance on the tenth-grade CIM assessments did as well at predicting freshman-year GPA as the SAT. Because of its established validity as an indicator of college readiness, PASS is now a recommended component for admission to OUS institutions. The inclusion of assessments of standards-aligned proficiencies in the university admissions process is an important first step toward understanding how Multiple Pathways curricula can prepare students for success in postsecondary education and career.

Following Oregon's example, California's postsecondary institutions could work with K–12 to develop "pathways proficiencies" that include CTE. Students who meet those proficiencies would be eligible for admission, placement into college-level work, and financial aid assistance. Institutions could demonstrate the importance of the pathways by endorsing seals of merit on high school diplomas, creating financial aid opportunities for students who complete a rigorous pathway, or other types of tangible rewards. Whether the completion of the pathways would make students eligible for UC or CSU is a decision that would remain with those systems. By keeping standards high, Multiple Pathways could prepare students for numerous fields of university study. A potential obstacle to Multiple Pathways, however, is the difficulty of garnering resources (e.g., teachers, facilities, partnerships) to achieve and maintain those standards across classrooms and schools. Significantly, these are challenges that California's school programs currently face, including efforts to make college-preparatory courses (A–G courses) the default curriculum for high school students. Core questions are whether the UC and CSU can overcome academia's historical aversion to applied curricula and participate in developing Multiple Pathways that are consistent with their standards, and whether the development of large-scale Multiple Pathways could be rigorous enough to prepare students for success in the CCC, CSU, and UC systems.

California State University's Early Assessment Program[35]

The CSU worked extensively with California's K–12 school system to overcome bureaucratic, procedural, and political problems and to develop test items that will indicate to students whether or not they are ready for college-level work. The CSU's EAP is a collaborative effort between the CSU, the California State Board of Education, and the California Department of Education. The EAP was established to provide high school students with information to measure their readiness for college-level mathematics and English in their junior year and to help them improve their skills during senior year. The EAP's goal is to ensure that California high school graduates who enter the CSU are prepared to succeed in college-level courses. The impetus for the program was the high need for remediation within the CSU: Approximately 50 percent of the system's first-time freshmen require remedial education in English, mathematics, or both.

All the students admitted to CSU institutions have completed a college-preparatory curriculum and earned a "C" or higher GPA in high school (students with averages higher than "B" qualify for the CSU regardless of ACT or SAT scores; students with less than a "C" average are not eligible for regular admission). Thus, it was clear that those proxies (grades and ACT or SAT scores) were not adequate indicators of college readiness and that greater curricular and assessment integration between high school and CSU were needed.

To date, this collaborative work has focused on traditional academic courses. Representatives from the K–12 and CSU sectors augmented the K–12 California Standards Tests (CSTs) with mathematics and English items that measure college-ready knowledge and skills. In mathematics, the items assess whether students have a deep enough knowledge of algebra and geometry. Similarly, the English proficiency standards are aligned with the CST standards in English language arts but focus more attention on students' reading and writing skills than does the CST. K–12 and postsecondary educators developed a twelfth-grade Expository Reading and Writing Course that high schools may pilot and adopt. The course is aligned with California's content standards; it is geared toward preparing students for college-level English; and it focuses on analytical, expository, and argumentative reading and writing. CSU took other steps to augment the CSTs. These included curricular change, teacher professional development, and teacher preservice education—all focused on the knowledge and skills students need to succeed in college-level courses.

CTE was not addressed, and this omission points to the need for state-level discussions about the role of CTE in preparing students for the CSU (and the UC). EAP evaluations would be a useful focus for these discussions. If the EAP does increase college readiness through early assessment, aligned high school coursework, and teacher professional development, could a parallel system— one that includes consideration of CTE for four-year institutions, the CCCs, or both—work as well?[36] Some issues to focus on include whether early signals could dissuade students from preparing for and attending the CSU (or other higher education system), and whether there are appropriate supports and curricula for students after they receive the results of the EAP.

The American Diploma Project[37]

The ADP is a partnership between Achieve, Inc.; The Education Trust; and the Thomas B. Fordham Foundation. Its objective is to "restore the value of the American high school diploma by describing in specific terms the English and mathematics that graduates must have mastered by the time they leave high school if they expect to succeed in postsecondary education or in high-performance, high-growth jobs."[38] The ADP is based on the premise that college and workforce knowledge and skills are the same. To develop the benchmarks, ADP staff worked with K–12, postsecondary, and business leaders in Indiana, Kentucky, Massachusetts, Nevada, and Texas to identify the knowledge and skills in English and mathematics that are needed for the world of work[39] and postsecondary education.[40] The benchmarks are the core knowledge and skills that postsecondary education and well-paying, flexible jobs require.

Since the development of the benchmarks,[41] Achieve has been working with states to build on current K–12 standards-based reforms and "sensibly ratchet up the rigor of standards, assessments, and course-taking requirements over time" to create "a coherent system of requirements for earning a high school diploma that signifies college and workplace readiness." The ADP advises states to require all students to take and pass specific courses, rather than a certain number of years of a subject, and to establish a way to ensure that the course content is taught and learned. To do so, it suggests using end-of-course exams or creating systems that allow students to progress at their own pace while reaching the same standards. It also advocates varied pedagogical approaches to help all students learn the same core knowledge and skills.

Standards for Success

S4S was a project sponsored by the Association of American Universities (AAU) and the Pew Charitable Trusts and led by the Center for Educational Policy Research at the University of Oregon with assistance from the Stanford Institute for Higher Education Research. S4S was initiated by presidents of AAU institutions who were concerned about the impact of current high school reforms on student readiness for college. They were worried that the reforms would create incentives for teachers to stray from analytical thinking and writing—areas that are crucial for academic readiness for college. They also wished to develop their own set of knowledge and skills that could influence high school reforms. S4S identified and developed the knowledge and skills needed for success in entry-level university courses; known as Knowledge and Skills for University Success (KSUS). The KSUS are a "blueprint of the cognitive skills, habits of mind, dispositions toward learning, key principles and concepts of the disciplines, important skills, and key content knowledge students need to have mastered" for success in highly selective institutions.[42] As such, the KSUS are not representative of the knowledge and skills required in broad-access institutions (neither two-year nor four-year) or of workforce expectations. Nevertheless, S4S offers important lessons about the content of university expectations and about the development of standards (from both analytical and procedural perspectives).

Over 400 faculty members from twenty AAU institutions participated in meetings to develop the standards. Participants' input was analyzed, as were course outlines, assignments, tests, projects, and student work from entry-level courses at the twenty institutions. The course-level materials were all used to make sure that faculty members' stated expectations were consistent with what actually went on in their courses.[43]

Such efforts could be used or replicated to define the CTE knowledge and skills required in postsecondary education; such work must involve the community colleges, in addition to the CSU and the UC. California's postsecondary systems should send clear signals to all of California's high school students about whether or not their high school courses of study will prepare them for postsecondary expectations in all three segments (i.e., CSU, UC, and CCC). This means that students should have clear, consistent information about any gaps in expectations between, for example, CTE pathways, general education coursework, college-preparatory tracks, and honors curricula and the expectations the UC, the CSU, and the CCC have for their first-year students to take credit-level courses. Such gaps can have serious ramifications in terms of postsecondary eligibility, admission, placement, persistence, completion, time to degree, and cost.

ESTABLISHING SIGNALS THAT ACCOMMODATE AND ENCOURAGE MULTIPLE PATHWAYS

The PASS, the EAP, the ADP, and S4S do little to close the traditional divide between academic and CTE curricula, and they did not include hands-on, career-specific training and assessment. As these programs continue, their creators might examine long-standing recommendations for K–12 and post-secondary interests to work together to narrow the academic-CTE gap.[44] The CCCs could play a significant role because of their dual mission of providing postsecondary CTE and serving as a "transfer route" into four-year institutions. The CCC could make public its readiness standards (starting with the de facto high-stakes standards represented in placement exams) and ensure that these CTE standards are linked to industry expectations. This is difficult, given the large number of program areas, but the CCCs could start with a few areas. However, all three of California postsecondary segments must participate. The UC and CSU systems need to assure both their own faculties and the broader community that integrated academic and CTE courses meet A–G requirements, particularly in fields where underrepresented groups of students have least access and participation (e.g., mathematics, engineering). It would be ideal, given the problems associated with A–G requirements as a proxy, for the UC and CSU to provide more detailed information about expectations.

The three higher education levels could also improve advising and placement practices. Bridge Project researchers found that academic advising and placement services are often completely separate from the "academic enterprise" of the institution. Faculty members often reported being suspicious of the reliability and validity of advising procedures and placement instruments, and consequently, they often devised their own placement processes for their classes.[45] These multiple criteria for standards and testing add to students' current preparation burdens. And, if the situation is disconnected and confusing for students going from an academic course of study in high school into college, it is likely worse for students who take a CTE curricular path.

Finally, reformers would do well to revisit this admonition of the Eight-Year Study:

> Without intending to do so, the colleges have handicapped schools in their attempt at fundamental reconstruction. . . . The static, frozen pattern of subjects and credits would disappear and secondary education would move ahead with other dynamic forces toward the achievement of greater democracy.[46]

Multiple Pathways holds promise to invigorate high school curricula. But this can only happen if K–12 and postsecondary systems (community colleges, the CSU, and the UC) work together. Most important, the development and implementation of Multiple Pathways must avoid further stratification that replicates past and current vocational-versus-academic divides, and it must provide the appropriate level of academic challenge when implemented on a large scale. Only then can Multiple Pathways help close the gap between college aspirations and college attainment.

CHAPTER 12

Constructing Equal Pathways in an Effectively Maintained Inequality Society

Samuel R. Lucas

Samuel R. Lucas, professor of sociology at the University of California–Berkeley and author of Tracking Inequality: Stratification and Mobility in American High Schools, *conducts research on the links between race, social class, and equitable and effective schooling. Breaking these links is a central challenge to school reform.*

Using his innovative theory of stratification and inequality— effectively maintained inequality (EMI)—as an interpretive lens, Lucas explores ways in which reformers might construct Multiple Pathways proposals to maximize their success. Given the usefulness of EMI theory to evaluate an egalitarian reform's content, framing, and implementation strategy, Lucas considers how proposals for Multiple Pathways to college and career may fare in reducing educational inequality. He cautions that simply universalizing access to college and career preparation may not reduce inequality, given the many and inexorable pressures that advantaged groups can present to thwart the reform's full intention. Comparing the costs and benefits of "confrontational" and "stealth" approaches to Multiple Pathways, Lucas cautions that the ultimate success of the reform in actually deepening students' knowledge and preparing them for college and career will depend on how the strategy is received by powerful interests bent on preserving their own children's educational advantages.

Reform is difficult. Progressive, egalitarian reform is more difficult still. Egalitarian reform faces opposition from powerful interests that compound the complexity of crafting any workable reform in a complex social world. If these interests cannot prevent the adoption of egalitarian reform, they are likely to continue the fight afterward to prevent the reform from succeeding.

Egalitarian reforms are vulnerable to such interests on substantive, rhetorical, and procedural grounds. A reform proposal must be both coherent and disciplined by an awareness of the context in which it must work. After all, it is the content of the policy that will determine whether it will improve, stagnate, or worsen the lot of the disadvantaged. But even when an egalitarian reform is workable, the good-faith efforts by some are often undermined by significant and powerful others who seek its failure. Many factors make neutralizing such opposition to egalitarian reforms challenging, including differences in wealth, access to media, and institutionalized power. To diminish the effectiveness of such opposition, reformers must pay careful attention to the rhetoric they use to describe the reform as well as the implementation strategy they select, as these may matter as much as the substance of the reform.

In this essay I explore this challenging reform context and consider how reformers might construct Multiple Pathways proposals in ways that maximize their potential for success. I begin with a brief overview of Multiple Pathways as an egalitarian reform. Then I offer a general theory of inequality that describes the predicament egalitarian reformers face and that may be useful to those seeking to reduce inequality. Next, using this theory as an interpretive lens, I suggest how the theory may be used to evaluate the content, framing, and implementation strategy for an egalitarian reform. Finally, I use the theoretical framework to consider specifically how proposals for Multiple Pathways to college and career may fare in terms of reducing or failing to reduce educational inequality.

MULTIPLE PATHWAYS: A PROPOSAL FOR EGALITARIAN SCHOOL REFORM

Multiple Pathways reform, as conceptualized in this volume, proposes a new form of high school education so that graduates will be competitive for college admissions or advanced training while also being able to enter the paid labor force directly. The central premise is that, with the creation of multiple high school curricula or programs, each of which includes both academically rigorous, satisfying college-preparatory requirements and challenging professional and technical knowledge grounded in industry standards, more students will graduate from high school prepared for a full range of postsecondary opportunities. Unlike classic high school tracking, the Multiple Pathways approach has the egalitarian goal of keeping postsecondary options open to all students, even as they pursue differentiated curricula. To accomplish this aim, courses must be designed so as to convey practical skills of immediate value while providing the knowledge and the critical thinking skills that have been regarded as necessary bases for college entry and college-level success. No doubt, this is a tall order, but it is not impossible, as other chapters in this volume have illustrated.

EFFECTIVELY MAINTAINED INEQUALITY

Nowhere is the opportunity for reform to transform lives more obvious than in the area of education. That education has long been a public obligation greatly hinders the ability of public officials to abdicate responsibility for attending to it. That education is charged with nurturing vulnerable youth into vigorous adulthood makes it more difficult for opponents of reform to blame the innocent for their plight. Moreover, education marks a passage nearly every adult has trod. As a consequence, reforms seeking to improve the lot of children may resonate even in the hearts of those who are not directly involved. These special qualities of education also help reformers clarify what counts as successful policy and justify the expenditures needed to do the job.

However, educational reform has its disadvantageous aspects as well. For example, parents, key actors in education, tend to act to protect their own children regardless of the consequences for others. So, although many parents might be comfortable relinquishing some of their own advantages, they may recoil from being equally egalitarian with respect to education. Doing so might consign their children to an adulthood stripped of the advantages the parents might otherwise bestow.[1]

In fact, despite considerable advantages, education has not been a site of egalitarianism. In what follows, I explain effectively maintained inequality (EMI), a theory that provides a lens for understanding and responding to the common failure of egalitarian education reforms. Later I will use it to assess the prospects of Multiple Pathways more specifically.

Tenets of Effectively Maintained Inequality

EMI asserts that socioeconomically advantaged actors secure for themselves and their children advantages wherever possible.[2] Such advantages can be quantitative or qualitative. If it is possible to have more or less of something desirable (a quantitative difference), those with advantaged backgrounds will obtain more. If it is possible to have better or worse quality of something (a qualitative difference), those with advantaged backgrounds will obtain better quality. These differences produce different chances for obtaining other advantages; to the extent that those with advantaged backgrounds are able to obtain more quantity or better quality with respect to one set of goods, they will also be effectively positioned for obtaining more or better goods in other domains.

So it may be that as long as something is not obtained by everyone (e.g., high school completion throughout the first half of the twentieth century in the United States), socioeconomically advantaged people use their advantages to secure it for their children. Once they have it, they can secure other goods more easily, such as better jobs. However, once something is obtained by nearly everyone (high school completion today), advantaged people use their advantages to obtain higher-quality versions of it for their children (e.g., studying more prestigious curricula, graduating from better high schools), thereby becoming well positioned to obtain more and better other goods (e.g., higher education, better jobs). This is one sense in which the term "effective" applies to the theory; inequality, no matter how small, may be effective in helping the advantaged secure other things, which in turn maintains inequality.

It is quite possible that advantaged actors use different strategies depending on how widely available a particular good is. Perhaps it is only when something becomes nearly universal that quality differences become important. On the other hand, it is also possible that qualitative differences are important even when something is not widely available; in that case, the advantaged will use their socioeconomic advantages to secure more and better of whatever goods or outcomes they seek.

Assessing Effectively Maintained Inequality

As stated so far, the theory may appear to be a tautology or merely obvious: The advantaged obtain advantage. However, the advantages obtained cut across the spheres of economic, social, and political life, and advantages in one sphere might convey advantages elsewhere, even when nothing in principle requires it. For example, there is nothing that requires that children whose parents have more money be given the best educational opportunities. In the same vein, there is no necessary reason that people with better jobs must receive better health care. Rather, these and other associations flow from the way societies are arranged. Thus, EMI is not a tautology; it is a diagnosis of a particular predicament observed in some societies—and perhaps not observed in others.

As for the obviousness of the theory, it is well known that those with higher incomes, more education, and better jobs obtain other advantages as well. Children whose parents have more years of schooling do tend to obtain better jobs.[3] People with higher incomes do have lower death rates.[4] These and other conclusions from research have been important for establishing the broad outlines of the social hierarchy.

However, EMI is different, offering a specific pattern of predictions. EMI argues that to understand inequality we need assess not only whether some people obtain more goods, but also whether a person is likely to obtain qualitatively better goods on the basis of socioeconomic status. So, for example, among students who are similar on many factors relevant to their high school success but who differ in socioeconomic status, we can predict which ones will be enrolled in advanced placement (AP) or honors English, regular English, or no English, and those who drop out of school altogether—outcomes that carry with them very different advantages and future opportunities. Every student who completes an English class and goes on to graduate will have more education than those who drop out, but the type of English class will determine the quality of the education that graduates obtain.

To assess whether EMI provides an accurate description, we must obtain data on real people and analyze that data using appropriate statistics. Using our statistical results, we may then devise a predicted outcome for two people who are similar in many relevant ways but who occupy different rungs of the socioeconomic ladder. Then, if we find that our prediction of the English course in which they would be placed differs—with the person with the higher socioeconomic status placed in a higher-level course—we have found evidence of EMI. However, if our prediction is that they would be placed in the same course level, then we have not found evidence of EMI in the data about high school course-taking. Thus, it is possible to find a general (statistically significant) association between socioeconomic status and an outcome (in this case, the curriculum pursued in high school) and still reject the theory of EMI. Consequently, EMI is a sharper, more precise theory than has typically been studied.

Distinguishing quantitative (more or less) and qualitative (better or worse) is useful because the distinction exists in the real world and has identifiable implications for efforts to reduce both the level and impact of inequality. EMI helps us understand that simply universalizing access to a good, such as high school graduation, may do nothing to reduce inequality because advantaged actors will seek out whatever qualitative differences exist within the universalized good (e.g., classes at different levels) and secure their access to that better-quality good. And, if access to better quality confers advantage (e.g., access to college), the qualitative differences will serve to effectively maintain inequality.

Selected Intellectual Forebears of Effectively Maintained Inequality

Other proposed theories exist. Raftery and Hout propose maximally maintained inequality (MMI), whose tenets directly concern forces driving educational expansion.[5] Under MMI, socioeconomic inequality at a particular level (e.g., high school graduation, college entry) declines only when all advantaged persons exceed that level. Afterward, socioeconomic inequality at that level is the maximum amount possible given that advantaged members of society have been satisfied. MMI and EMI disagree in that MMI expects social conflict will be low around levels of education that all advantaged persons obtain; in contrast, EMI anticipates continuing social conflict even at such levels of education.

MMI applies to education, whereas EMI provides a general theory of societal inequality. Although MMI was crafted to explain educational inequality specifically, and has some evidence to support it, when EMI and MMI have been directly compared, findings have supported EMI over MMI.[6]

In contrast, EMI has some affinity with queuing theories of earnings inequality.[7] Queuing theories assert that earnings inequality works through ordering processes. People are placed in order based on employers' preferences and are then allocated to jobs based on their place in line. Actual productivity differences between individuals, however large or small, are not key. What matters is their place in line.

EMI and queuing theories both suggest the importance of thresholds whose impact may far exceed the slight difference they represent. As such, both EMI and queuing theories imply that reducing the gap between individuals on some factor such as measured achievement may have little impact on their differential prospects for attaining goods to which the factor of interest appears causally related (e.g., access to college). Consequently, one way to interpret EMI is as a generalization of queuing theories of earnings.

The point of these observations is not to analyze multiple theories of inequality. Instead, the aim is more modest: to acknowledge that other theories may also have important implications for egalitarian reform. Still, the combination of the generality and the specificity of EMI, reflected in the sharpness of its predictions, suggest there may be value to focused consideration of its implications.

QUESTIONS THAT EFFECTIVELY MAINTAINED INEQUALITY POSES TO REFORM INITIATIVES

Any useful theory helps us understand complex phenomena by setting boundaries on our attention and sharpening our focus. EMI focuses our observations on two sets of key actors in social inequality: the advantaged and the disadvantaged. EMI defines the advantaged as those who possess or control resources outside the particular arena we are seeking to understand, such as schooling. In schooling, for example, the advantaged are students with wealthy parents (wealth is a resource outside the schooling arena). Note that EMI does not consider high-achieving students as advantaged, even though high achievement is a resource within and relevant to schooling. Rather, advantaged and disadvantaged children are identified by their parents' socioeconomic and demographic characteristics.

EMI is silent concerning the existence and reaction of other possibly important actors, such as (in the case of education) teachers, principals, other school personnel, and political actors in the environment (e.g., business elites and political elites). EMI is a theory of the way in which contenders for some good who have access to differential resources may be better positioned to obtain the good owing to their access to differential resources. By highlighting this aspect of the process through which goods are allocated, EMI does not deny a role for other actors, but it does emphasize the resources that those seeking to obtain some good are able to use.

Useful theories raise questions that point researchers toward fruitful analytic directions.[8] These theories also raise questions for actors. These are questions that would-be reformers might try to answer (if only provisionally) before crafting particular proposals. In the case of schooling, EMI focuses reformers' attention on the likely different reactions of advantaged and disadvantaged actors. Their different reactions will make a difference in whether the reform will be adopted and, if it is, whether it will exacerbate or ameliorate inequality. The astute reformer will try to answer questions that EMI raises about how the two groups are likely to behave and use those answers to guide their approach to reform.

How Will Various Actors Feel about the Reform?

Perhaps the most important question the theory raises is, how will each class of actors react attitudinally? Will the advantaged or the disadvantaged feel hostile, indifferent, or supportive toward the proposed reform? Will the proposed reform resonate with the principles by which the advantaged or the disadvantaged actually live their lives, try to live their lives, or would like to live their lives? Or will the reform clang in dissonance against any or all of these real, attempted, or desired existences?

Attitudes of various groups cannot be assumed because they reflect in part the rhetoric underlying the reform, as well as the material aspects of the reform. If the material aspects were all that mattered, it would be easy to predict the constellation of forces and alliances that would line up on either side, and advantaged and disadvantaged people would never work against their material interests.

However, even a cursory glance at political developments suggests that matters are more complex.[9] People often act in accord with their interests as they understand them, and their understanding can be shaped by the rhetoric around the reform. Sometimes attitudes reflect a misunderstanding of or even an apparent disregard for the material implications of a proposal. Although attitudes are not completely malleable, and reformers may change others' attitudes through their efforts, reformers must attend to the attitudes a proposed reform may generate among the advantaged and disadvantaged in order to craft rhetoric that may resonate, or at least not clash, with existing attitudes.

EMI leads us to expect the attitudes of the advantaged and disadvantaged toward egalitarian reform to differ, at least initially. As a concrete example, Wells and Serna found that the logic of detracking reform did not resonate with advantaged parents' understanding of how schools should be.[10] It is plausible that their negative attitude stemmed, at least in part, from the threat perceived by the term "detracking" that provocatively promised to end a practice perceived to be in the best interests of the children of the advantaged.

If the attitudes of the advantaged and disadvantaged do not differ initially, the would-be reformer must attend to the developing attitudes throughout the process. No call for manipulation, it is simply a call to remain aware of the way in which attitudes are unfolding as the reform is conveyed. Lose on this terrain, and little egalitarian reform will be possible.

What Resources Might Various Actors Deploy to Secure Advantage?

The second question reformers must ask is, what resources might various groups deploy to secure advantage? With respect to both advantaged and disadvantaged actors, one will want to learn what resources they might use to undermine the proposed reform.

The set of possible resources available to the advantaged is virtually infinite and, therefore, hard to inventory. To the extent reformers fail to consider resources to which the advantaged have access, however, they will make an incomplete assessment of how effectively the advantaged may resist a reform, should the advantaged choose to do so. Thus, reformers should go beyond the one or two most easily recognized resources (e.g., financial assets, social connections) and seek to assess as many major broad classes as possible and cover perhaps the first dozen or so potentially important, distinctive resources the advantaged may employ.

Evidence from detracking reform, for example, suggests that advantaged parents have resources in the form of connections with influential practitioners that can affect the course of reform. Datnow's ethnographic study of detracking, for example, suggests that an old guard of (mostly male) teachers wanting to retain the existing system allied with parents to undermine detracking by invoking existing resources of power and privilege. Their hostility to a vanguard of teachers (mostly female) seeking to reform practice to improve outcomes for everyone ultimately led to the resignation of the principal who had supported the vanguard teachers.[11]

This observation illustrates two important points. First, existing hierarchies of taken-for-granted privilege, such as gender, can provide resources the advantaged can use to resist the policy. Second, advantaged parents can use their connections with well-placed teachers or other key actors to agitate against the policy. Such resources of the advantaged must be considered as reformers draft the language, content, and strategy for implementing reform.

Stopping the analysis with resources of the advantaged would be a mistake. EMI processes may not be confined to situations where the wealthy and the poor compete for goods. Reforms can also exacerbate inequality amongst the disadvantaged. Even though the inequality might appear small compared to the difference between the advantaged and disadvantaged, EMI suggests that small differences can be consequential. Thus, not only can egalitarian proposals be undermined if elements pit the poor against the poorer, but also the result could be a pyrrhic egalitarian victory that advantages one sector of the socioeconomically disadvantaged at the expense of another (e.g., race/ethnicity, neighborhood, or language groups). Only by being sensitive to these dynamics might one be able to reduce this possibility.

Inventorying various actors' resources is only the first part of the answer; reformers must also consider whether the resource is costly to deploy (in terms of time, reputation, money, or some other good) and what other dis-incentives to use of the resource may exist. Answering these questions will not ensure success but will make it possible to anticipate the response of the various sectors of society and the effect their response will likely have. Such foreknowledge can help reformers devise proposals that decrease the effectiveness of resources employed to undermine them.

What Exit Options Do Various Actors Have, and How Effective Might They Be in Undermining Reform?

Long ago, Hirschman pointed to exit and voice (speaking up in the effort to make changes) as two options that unhappy institutional participants have available to them.[12] His first option—exit—is so important that it forms the basis of the final question of our triumvirate: What kind of exit options do members have, and how effective might they be?

The resource par excellence of the advantaged is exit, which they can exercise to obtain several advantages. They may be able to render any reform ineffective, either by threatening or actually taking a viable exit option, or both. If their threat is plausible, they may be able to force alterations in the reform that gut its egalitarian thrust. If they leave, their departure may simultaneously withdraw both material and symbolic resources necessary not only to implement the reform, but even to continue pre-reform operating procedures. Thus, actual exercise of the exit option may so weaken the institution(s) left behind that even if the egalitarian reform is adopted, it may fail to undermine the larger societal patterns of inequality that are the ultimate target of the reform.

At the same time, exiting allows the advantaged to insulate themselves from the difficult interactional challenges that would come with being visibly or publicly at fault for the failure. As a result, even though the cause of the reform's failure may be the drastic and perhaps unexpected change in the composition of the people involved, the failure may be seen as showing that good-faith efforts to implement reform are simply misplaced, that such reform could never succeed. Thus, when the advantaged exercise the exit option, they threaten to taint not only the particular reform to which they are responding, but also the very idea that egalitarian reform is possible. In this way, they may solidify the advantage they are able to live with and, perhaps, pass on to their children, even as they may be raising the costs of failing to have those advantages.

The most damaging exit pattern, however, entails threats of exit that coerce changes in the reform, only to be followed by large-scale exit anyway. In such a situation, administrators and policymakers may bargain away key aspects of the reform that are needed to allow the egalitarian reform to have any chance to succeed under the best of circumstances. The later exit by advantaged actors may leave in place a limping reform that could never succeed, implemented under conditions that would have challenged the previously developed, coherent reform had it been fully implemented. Given that the ultimate aim of reform transcends the particular sphere in which it occurs (i.e., school reform is about more than just schools), patterns of interaction that gut reform must be understood as damaging more than just the particular arena directly involved. When advantaged actors bargain and then exit anyway, they may severely challenge the reform effort where it is most important: in its implications for the success and ultimate life chances of those left behind.

Although the exit options of the advantaged may be most important to consider, the exit options of the disadvantaged should not escape attention. Rather than leaving themselves at the mercy of an institution configured against their perceived interests, the disadvantaged may also exit. However, their options may be less viable, such as dropping out of school altogether. They may exit by continuing to attend but disengage, thus further eroding the likelihood of any egalitarian reform's success. In any given case, one group may be more likely to exit than the other, but the exit option must be considered for both.

Seen in this way, debates about school reform become debates about how the next generation is to live. Accordingly, any reform that is not premised on a robust answer to this final key question—what kind of exit options do members have and how effective might they be?—is a reform that has not yet been responsibly evaluated as to its likely effects were it to be adopted. Again, detracking provides a useful illustration. Wells and Serna show that advantaged parents often agitated, using the threat of exit, to preserve some advantage for their children within the detracked school.[13] Of course, if some children win advantageous positions, then the logic of the entire detracking policy is undermined and the reform crippled.

Studies of detracking in the United States have not assessed the long-term implications of exit. But some research in Japan suggests that detracking can trigger the exit response, ultimately leading to less opportunity than existed previously. Kariya and Rosenbaum describe a detracking reform in Japan that over two decades inadvertently undermined school quality in the public sector.[14] Historically, private schools had been of lower quality than public schools, but detracking led to a slow exodus of the better and wealthier students from the public schools. Ultimately, the changing composition of the public high schools made rigorous education more difficult to sustain in that environment. Thus, poor children formerly had access to the same curriculum their wealthier peers had, were they able to do the work. After detracking, and after what Kariya and Rosenbaum call bright flight, students who remain in public schools have less access to demanding curricula.[15]

Taken together, these questions suggest the usefulness of EMI in shedding light on key actors' responses to reform. The illustration provided by the study of detracking initiatives suggests we may learn a great deal by considering such questions. The challenge, however, is to anticipate the response to a proposal before implementation, to increase the chance that the rhetoric, the policy, and the implementation will be crafted in ways that reduce opposition and still accomplish the egalitarian aims. The proposal to construct Multiple Pathways to college and career offers just such an opportunity.

CONSTRUCTING MULTIPLE PATHWAYS IN AN EFFECTIVELY MAINTAINED INEQUALITY SOCIETY

Theories of stratification and inequality such as EMI can help us anticipate the course of a proposed Multiple Pathways reform and, in the best case, devise ways to increase the likelihood of its success in reducing inequality. In California and elsewhere, connecting career and technical education and academic courses in Multiple Pathways programs often occurs through career academies or through programs that offer an integrated curriculum. However, pathways can be organized and offered not only through career academies, but also through industry/career majors, magnet schools, small learning communities, and other strategies that explicitly consider needs for program coherence and high standards.

Some of these proposals call for whole school programs, while others open programs to a subset of students at a school. Both scenarios raise contentious EMI-related questions about which students may participate, what resources will be used to support them, and whether the program will siphon off resources from elsewhere. The strategy reformers use in implementation will affect how any given Multiple Pathways proposal might fare.

Implementing Multiple Pathways schoolwide, and thus possibly benefiting the largest segment of students, requires reallocating resources such as prepared teachers from other programs, and seeking to persuade the advantaged parents that their children will benefit from the change. This is a confrontational strategy, for it directly confronts advantaged actors with the prospect that their advantages may be unfair. Persuasion is an admirable hope, signaling a faith in the value of rational discourse; persuasion can, in principle, follow from confrontation. Such confrontation has been a common approach to egalitarian reform, and it has tended to fail, perhaps owing to the emotion-laden nature of decisions concerning one's children. By failing, it has taken down what could have been effective programs.

Alternatively, stealth implementation (i.e., developing a partial-school program within the constraints of the existing flow of school resources to advantaged and disadvantaged students) is worthy of consideration. A stealth approach avoids altering resource allocation or attempting to convince advantaged actors of the value of the program for their children. School personnel work to ensure that implementation is arranged so as to have as small an impact on the experience of currently advantaged students as possible.

Two advantages may follow such an approach. First, it may provide space to construct successful programs for the disadvantaged. Rather than having to have all the answers, a stealth approach may allow a proposal to be fine-tuned over time so as to better match the particular students who form its target clientele. Second, a stealth approach may allow the program to develop a record of cognitive and post-school success that will strengthen the ability of the program to withstand initially negative attitudes of advantaged actors if and when it becomes necessary to alter the patterns of resource flows to continue or extend the program.

A stealth approach also has costs. It may require outside funding in the form of foundation grants to implement the program, particularly if existing funding for programs for the disadvantaged are insufficient or their use is inflexibly specified in law or bureaucratic regulation. Further, if foundation support is contingent on demonstrating success, the constraints of funding and personnel allocation that a stealth approach necessitates might make it very difficult to demonstrate success, even for programs headed toward success. Thus, a stealth approach may hobble the reform at the outset in ways that ultimately prevent its success.

Thus, from the perspective of obtaining resources for implementation, it is unclear which implementation strategy is better: confrontation or stealth.

Multiple Pathways: Attitudinal Insights from Effectively Maintained Inequality

EMI suggests that reformers consider what attitudes advantaged and disadvantaged persons might harbor toward the proposal. Perhaps the most important observation to make in this connection is that regardless of the content of the proposal, the initial attitudes will likely be driven by the label of the proposal. Indeed, policymakers may focus on the nuances of delivery systems and allocation plans, as well they might to make progress in their effort to devise successful policy. But public attitudes will be largely determined by whether the label does or does not resonate with cherished, perhaps unexamined values.

To the extent that Multiple Pathways reform connects with national ideals of opportunity, it may resonate with the views of the advantaged. If alternative pathways to success are acceptable, the proposal will nicely align with existing ideologies. However, if a more rigid view of what paths "make sense" prevails, then the very term "Multiple Pathways" may create discomfort and unease. This is a question with no ready-made answer, which reformers should address.

Attitudes will also likely differ, or have a differential impact, depending on the form of implementation adopted. Under a stealth implementation, the most obvious observation is that, unlike detracking, which changes the experience of the students who occupy advantaged locations in the school, Multiple Pathways does not do so in principle. Indeed, it would be possible for parents and students in advantaged locations in a school to be totally unaware of the installation of the Multiple Pathways curriculum. Hence, it is unlikely that it would provoke visceral, hostile attitudes on the part of the advantaged.

However, if a confrontational implementation is pursued, it will likely entail the reassignment of teachers and other resources. If this means that recognized teachers reduce their time with advantaged students, the attitudes of socioeconomically advantaged parents may turn hostile. This prediction is a specific manifestation of a general observation: that Multiple Pathways has the least chance of inspiring negative attitudes if it has no impact on the experience of currently advantaged children and families. If it does alter the experience of currently advantaged children and their families, the burden of proof will be on the reformers to demonstrate that Multiple Pathways not only fails to harm the currently advantaged but actually improves conditions for them. Although it might be possible to marshal that proof, making the case will siphon effort away from the focal aim: to improve possibilities for the currently disadvantaged.

The attitudes of the disadvantaged are another matter. The disadvantaged have been the focus of so many well-meaning reforms that one might be wise to expect at least some apathy, or even some hostility, toward the Multiple Pathways proposal. One cannot blame the socioeconomically disadvantaged for skepticism. Thus, Multiple Pathways reform would likely fare better if it is implemented in a noncoercive manner, voluntarily adopted by schools and students, and given time to demonstrate its efficacy in its target population. Any other approach may fail to take time to defuse the understandable skepticism, apathy, or hostility.

These observations about the likely attitudes of disadvantaged persons provide yet another reason why stealth may be a more appropriate approach, but it does not decide the matter. Stealth could also allow the program to become tailored to the perceived needs of the disadvantaged without being distracted by the highly contested process that would be needed to persuade advantaged persons to forego their advantages. Hence, stealth may offer possibilities of particularly noteworthy relevance with respect to the advantaged as well as the disadvantaged.

Multiple Pathways: Resource Insights from Effectively Maintained Inequality

The socioeconomically advantaged have all the resources we have seen them use in other school-focused conflicts about desegregation and detracking, among other controversial efforts. These include, but are likely not limited to, greater financial resources; connections with administrators and other powerful actors in the environment; greater control over their time; shared middle-class status with teachers; greater comfort with the institution of school[16]; their client status vis-à-vis professionals[17]; as well as easy access to potential advocates such as lawyers, legislators, and executive officials. Some of these resources may entail time or financial cost, but in the EMI context, the reputations of those who use them are not jeopardized. Consequently, any and all of these resources and more can be deployed should socioeconomically advantaged persons see their interests as threatened.

One means of responding to this state of affairs is to avoid threatening the perceived interests of the advantaged. Again, at least initially, stealth might be the best way to proceed. For example, implementation might be easiest if the school offered only nineteen AP classes instead of twenty and re-assigned a teacher to the Multiple Pathways curriculum, or hired different personnel. However, the terrain constructed by the resources of the advantaged may make this approach difficult. The advantaged have vast resources, often a feeling of entitlement, and a record of success in undermining proposals that may lead them to be trigger-happy. Also, the area under discussion is one of intense emotion: the opportunities and experiences of one's children. Therefore, a more strategic response may be to avoid the confrontation by continuing to offer the twenty AP classes. Only after the Multiple Pathways curriculum has a demonstrated record of success may one want consider the more confrontational implementation or adjustment that might entail some redirection of taken-for-granted resource flows, such as teacher allocations, room allocations, and number of sections.

One danger of stealth, however, is that a program developed in this manner may become stigmatized in much the same way that stigma has been a problem for students in lower tracks.[18] If the stigma is strong, even a developing record of success may not be compelling enough to eradicate it. Stigma is not an idle concern. It may place a limit on the full extension of the program or inhibit students from enrolling in the program. Thus, it will be important to consider ways to avoid stigmatizing a program, especially if one adopts a stealth orientation to implementation.

With a confrontational implementation approach, however, one must be aware of the danger that negotiation with the advantaged may entail. Past reform efforts have been gutted through this process. By the end of the negotiation, precious implementation time may have been lost, and major changes in the proposal made in an effort to satisfy dominant actors may have rendered it incoherent and even doomed to fail.[19] Consequently, if one pursues implementation directly, with an effort to obtain resources from currently advantaged sectors, one must be highly sensitized to what are and what are not negotiable aspects of the proposal. Only in this way will the proposal have any chance of being implemented without being transformed into just another tracking program.

The major way the Multiple Pathways proposal must respond to the resources of the disadvantaged is by avoiding the exacerbation of existing inequalities in disadvantaged groups, and by seriously thinking through the implications of those resources for what the Multiple Pathways proposal can and cannot do. For example, Multiple Pathways cannot require parents of students in the program to make major outlays for course materials. Because the target population will include many students who are living in poverty, requiring even modest expenses for course materials may pose a serious impediment to participation. Because ownership of the course materials, such as books and tools, and any items created in the process of completing the course, may encourage students to have ownership of their education, it would be ideal to arrange some creative financing to meet student need in this context. For example, perhaps students could borrow the course materials and work off their "debt" by completing assignments, such that by some time during the school year they own the books and tools for the course.

This kind of approach has the added advantage of ensuring that the students in each entering class obtain the latest text materials. This example, of course, suggests that creatively considering how one might navigate the terrain that is warped and formed by unequal resources of advantaged and disadvantaged actors can actually point the way toward greater opportunities for meeting student need.

Multiple Pathways: Exit Insights from Effectively Maintained Inequality

The advantaged and the disadvantaged have exit options. If a stealth strategy is followed, at least initially, the advantaged will not exit. Once the Multiple Pathways proposal has been implemented and has demonstrated some success over several years, exit of the advantaged will be decidedly less relevant. Indeed, were they to leave after the program has become institutionalized, their exit may simply produce additional opportunities for expanding the Multiple Pathways implementation.

Of course, to the extent that Multiple Pathways actually deepens students' knowledge and prepares students for college and career, the problem may not be the exit of the advantaged. On the contrary, the challenge may be an increasingly aggressive effort of the advantaged to take over the program and perhaps crowd out disadvantaged students. This new problem, if it occurs, will require strong norms of access in order for those aggressive moves to be resisted. For example, Multiple Pathways program admission criteria could favor those with a history of low grades, those who are likely to enter the labor market immediately, or even those with a history of having worked substantial hours in the paid labor force in the past. Such criteria might ensure that the program continues to serve disadvantaged students, at least unless and until the entire school is transformed to a Multiple Pathways curriculum. Even if the entire school implements a Multiple Pathways curriculum, in order to derail the emergence of de facto tracking, [20] possible stigmatization of certain curricula, and other problems, one would need to ensure that disadvantaged students have access to all curricula.

At the same time, exit of the disadvantaged is an issue of concern. Preventing exit requires a two-pronged strategy. One prong is to establish the trust necessary to reduce exit. A second prong is to make sure that material requirements for participation are minimized, as discussed above. At the same time, the cognitive demands of Multiple Pathways cannot be reduced, even if they can be fulfilled in increasingly flexible ways. With such an approach, exit of the disadvantaged may be minimized.

CONCLUDING REMARKS

The foregoing has likely fallen short in fully describing all the challenges that confront the egalitarian reformer. But the lens of EMI allows reformers to observe that advantaged actors will likely use any and all means at their disposal to resist reforms they perceive as threatening to their interests. Hence, the egalitarian reformer must find ways of rendering their efforts impotent.

EMI suggests that reformers need to ask essential questions to ascertain the likely attitudes, material capabilities, and exit options of the advantaged and disadvantaged. They also need to consider whether confrontation or stealth is the most promising orientation to adopt. Using this information, the reformer can craft a strategic articulation of the proposal and devise an implementation approach most likely to lead to program success.

Of course, and somewhat troublingly, hidden in that counsel is a great deal of work, dialogue, and planning. Most frustrating, perhaps, is the need for the egalitarian reformer to accept the limits of what may be possible at the moment. Much of the task may be unpleasant or even disheartening. However, if over time and through a series of reform efforts more space is pried open by strategic consideration of the possibilities realizable in the present, it is both hoped and expected that the possibilities of tomorrow cannot fail to be more conducive to the egalitarian dreams of the present night.

CHAPTER 13

Beyond Tracking?

Multiple Pathways of Possibility
and Challenge

Jeannie Oakes and Marisa Saunders

*Jeannie Oakes is director of Education and Scholarship at the Ford
Foundation. Until fall 2008, she was Presidential Professor in Educational
Equity and codirector of the Institute for Democracy, Education, and
Access at the University of California–Los Angeles, and director of the
University of California's All Campus Consortium on Research for
Diversity. She is the author of numerous articles and books that focus
on schooling inequalities, including* Keeping Track: How Schools
Structure Inequality *and, most recently,* Learning Power: Organizing
for Education and Justice *(coauthored with John Rogers). Oakes is a
current member of the University of California's Board of Admissions and
Relations with Schools. Marisa Saunders is a senior research associate at
the Institute for Democracy, Education, and Access at the University of
California–Los Angeles. Her research focuses on K–12 to postsecondary
transitions, and the postsecondary trajectories of underrepresented youth.*

*Oakes and Saunders look to this volume's authors to ascertain and
explore the potential of Multiple Pathways reform. They are mindful
of the difficulties involved in bringing Multiple Pathways to scale, and
the particular resistance of the American high school to fundamental
change. Confronting the resistance, schools must account for predictable
technical, normative, and political challenges that will require reformers
to frame proposals, rhetoric, and implementation strategies to minimize
these obstacles. Oakes and Saunders caution that these strategies must*

not undermine or compromise the potential of the reform or its essential
components. Ultimately, the authors conclude, success will depend on
a willingness to defy and change a long-standing social hierarchy that
determines academic and career success and opportunity.

The economy changes, the population diversifies, social and economic inequality grows, and gaps in educational attainment widen among racial groups. Education payoffs increase and so do the costs of dropping out. Most students are not served well enough by today's public schools, and low-income and minority students are least well served. Schools are not the exclusive cause of these social cleavages, but they are a part. School reform by itself won't solve the problems, but it must be a part of any solution.

The essays in this book examine Multiple Pathways, a strategy that promises to prepare all young people for college, career, and responsible civic participation. They consider the potential educational and economic benefits of Multiple Pathways for society at large and for individual students. They conclude that, under the right conditions, Multiple Pathways can greatly enhance access to school achievement, college preparation, career readiness, and groundwork for civic participation. However, the essays also point to the great challenges facing Multiple Pathways reforms.

In this concluding chapter, we survey the authors' perspectives and reflect on the potential of Multiple Pathways to bring fundamental reform to the comprehensive American high school. We do so with considerable humility. As David Tyack and Larry Cuban have argued elsewhere, the deep structure of schooling reflects the larger culture and politics, and that structure has proven extraordinarily robust. Most aspects of today's high school, including course schedules, basic subjects, lecture-based instruction, tests, grades, and extracurricular activities, have been in place for nearly a century. New things have been added, of course, but the most basic features have withstood many cycles of reform.[1] Why would a Multiple Pathways approach to high school reform fare differently?

Multiple Pathways has reform potential, in part because it promises what the comprehensive high school did early in the twentieth century. That is, it promises to reinvent the institution most responsible for young people's transition into the adult world so that it matches the needs and opportunities of that world. Changes in the economy and the nature of work call for significant alterations in workforce preparation: Some college (at least) and the academic readiness it requires has become the common path to middle-class jobs, rather than an exclusive route to elite professions. Dramatic demographic shifts, based in large part on waves of immigration, call for new versions of educational opportunity. In a diverse society, high schools stratified by race and social class violate our national commitments to equality and democracy.

This chapter focuses on themes in this collection of essays that address fundamental high school reform. We begin by tracing the history of Multiple Pathways reform to show how it departs from traditional schooling. Then we turn to the hopeful findings about the Multiple Pathways concept and trace the migration of Multiple Pathways into policy and practice. Finally, we look at the obstacles to bringing Multiple Pathways to scale. These challenges reside in the culture and politics of high school education that Multiple Pathways seeks to alter, as well as in the structural changes that such reform demands.

TRACING THE ROOTS OF MULTIPLE PATHWAYS[2]

Multiple Pathways challenges a century-old tradition that continues to make sense to most people. For almost a hundred years, high schools have offered college-bound and non-college-bound students different college and workforce preparation and provided separate courses for the two groups. These tracking practices have made hands-on, real-world education a terminal experience for students who were not believed to have the capacity for symbolic thought, and reformers reserved text-based, literacy-based education for students who are aiming for college. These practices have carried a racial, ethnic, gender, and social class bias from their inception.[3] As such, they have been central to the educational stratification and inequality that reinforces and contributes to larger economic and social disparities.

In the early 1900s, remarkable economic and demographic shifts posed significant social concerns that schools were expected to address. New restrictions on child labor and compulsory schooling laws responded to the growth of urban industrialization, in part to protect children from dangerous factory work. For the first time, high schools were expected to educate the masses, as well as a small fraction of elite young people. High schools also faced considerable pressure to "Americanize" children of southern and Eastern European immigrants, who sought economic opportunity and political refuge in American cities.

Much like today, these economic and demographic changes triggered a great school reform debate. Then, as now, race and cultural differences permeated these debates, shaped in large part by the widespread belief (bolstered by the emerging science of IQ) that non-English-speaking immigrant and black children were less intelligent than those of northern European stock. Convinced that a curriculum for elite groups could not be appropriate for those deemed less capable, vocational training seemed like a reasonable alternative. Intelligence-testing pioneer Lewis Terman wrote that "dullness" in immigrants, Mexicans, and blacks seems to be racial: "They cannot master abstractions, but they can often be made efficient workers."[4]

Terman's "science" was persuasive, partly because it coincided with the preferences of employers for hiring immigrants who had technical skills and were socialized with the work habits and attitudes required of factory workers (i.e., proper deportment, punctuality, and willingness to be supervised and managed). The newly emerging unions, too, preferred that schools do the training rather than employers, whose self-interest might not serve workers well.

Another link in the chain of influence was a new conception of democratic education in modern life. With increased diversity, different programs tailored to the students' diverse needs became a new standard for equitable schooling. As the superintendent of Boston schools wrote in 1908,

> Until very recently the schools have offered equal opportunity for all to receive one kind of education, but what will make them democratic is to provide opportunity for all to receive education as will fit them equally well for their particular life work.[5]

Manufacturers, unions, educators, and social reformers accepted this new definition of equitable schooling, believing that a differentiated curriculum would be relevant to students and would reduce the number of students leaving high school early.[6] It was embedded in the Smith-Hughes Act of 1917, the first federal funding of education, which provided new resources for high school vocational education programs.

By 1918, these ideas and proposals coalesced as a new American institution, the comprehensive American high school. Unlike the elite high schools of the past, it would enroll students of all backgrounds, providing separate curricula for working-class youth headed for industrial jobs and for advantaged students destined for college, leadership, and white-collar or other intellectually demanding work. From the beginning, however, vocational education had its critics as well as supporters. One of the earliest was John Dewey, whose sharp criticism identified vocational education as a form of class division.[7] The historic record suggests that Dewey's concerns were well-founded.[8]

In the mid-1980s, the debate about the value of vocational education was reopened, but social stratification was only one of many worries. High school vocational courses seemed out of sync with postindustrial workforce needs. Experts predicted that jobs in the new economy would require general cognitive abilities as well as occupationally specific skills. *A Nation at Risk* argued for increases in academic requirements for high school graduation as the way to ensure a more productive and competitive workforce.[9] Advocates for retaining traditional vocational programs had little evidence that the programs were effective in countering these pressures.[10]

Rather than abandoning vocational programs altogether, some reformers sought ways to integrate vocational and academic curricula, a direction that gained momentum with the passage of the 1990 and 1998 reauthorizations of the federal Carl D. Perkins Act (successor to Smith-Hughes). In 1998, 45 percent of public high schools reported integrating their curricula, including many schools experimenting with career academies and "tech-prep" programs that connected high school vocational education with community college coursework.[11] However, the quality and forms of these efforts are difficult to discern.

Also during this time, some vocational education programs expanded to include careers that might eventually require a baccalaureate degree, such as engineering and the health professions. Some programs prepared students for several options after graduation: two- or four-year college, the labor force, or both options simultaneously. Analysts examining the national data in 2000 noted, "The traditional focus of vocational education is giving way to a broader purpose—one that includes greater emphasis on academic preparation and provides a wider range of career choices."[12]

Vocational education also changed its name. In December of 1998, the American Vocational Association became the Association for Career and Technical Education, and members encouraged organizations and agencies to remove the term "vocational education" from documents and legislation and replace it with "career and technical education." In fall of 2000, The Journal of Vocational and Technical Education began to publish under the name The Journal of Career and Technical Education. The reauthorization of the Carl D. Perkins Vocational and Technical Act of 2006 used "career and technical education" (CTE) instead of "vocational education" throughout.

Despite these changes over the past 20 years, much of vocational education has remained the same, and there is little evidence that these reforms have affected the well-established consequences of tracked curriculum. For example, the college-going and labor-market experiences of the high school graduating classes of 1982 and 1992 were similar. Two years after graduation, vocational "concentrators"[13] were more likely than their college-prep peers to be in the labor force and less likely to have enrolled in a postsecondary institution. Moreover, rates of postsecondary completion were lower for vocational concentrators. In the labor market, a vocational concentration did not improve graduates' experiences or outcomes. The number of months employed and unemployed were similar, regardless of the student's course of study, although college-prep students enjoyed higher earnings in 1991 than their peers.[14]

In contrast, vocational concentrators who also completed college-preparatory academic courses had experiences much like those of their college-prep peers. They were as likely to enroll in a postsecondary institution during the ten-year period following graduation, and they were as likely to earn a postsecondary degree or certificate during this period.[15] Overall, two basic academic indicators—levels of educational attainment and academic achievement—predict students' abilities to earn a good living and sustain a career.[16] There appear to be no documented advantages for students taking today's vocational programs unless they also take challenging academics.

CURRENT MULTIPLE PATHWAYS POLICIES

This history, together with current shifts in the labor market, have led more and more education reformers and policymakers to argue that high schools should blur the distinction between college preparation and workforce preparation and prepare all students for both college and career. In light of the disappointing academic outcomes of high schools, combined with the sorry record of traditional vocational education, many have begun to advocate for an approach that combines rigorous academic preparation with career readiness. On the academic side, such an approach is likely to increase both the challenge and relevance of the high school curriculum, and, as a consequence, boost academic achievement and motivate students to stay in school. On the career-preparation side, such an approach fits with analysts' claims that jobs in the future will require high-level cognitive skills as well as specific technical competencies. Thus, a combined approach could also improve students' workforce outcomes and benefit the economy itself. The evidence suggests that these hopes are well placed.

Although Multiple Pathways is not the only strategy for integrating academic and career education, as the brief history above makes clear, several states and school districts have introduced reform policies that incorporate elements of the Multiple Pathways approach. For example, Pennsylvania's Education Project 720 is a voluntary program aimed at raising high school graduation and college-going rates. It provides grants (ranging from $30,000 to $175,000 in 2005–06) and technical assistance to school districts to help them develop rigorous college- and career-prep "core curriculum" and create "student-centered, results-focused, data-informed, and personalized" high school environments.[17] Participating districts commit to requiring all their students to complete a combined college- and career-prep program. Multiple Pathways is a key strategy, in that districts are encouraged to provide a variety of ways to prepare students for both postsecondary education and careers, including (1) work-based programs that help students understand available career options and develop the skills needed for those jobs, (2) dual-enrollment programs to earn college credit while still in high school, and (3) programs designed to reconnect out-of-school youth.[18]

The Texas High School Project is a $261 million public-private initiative with the following goal: "All Texas students will graduate high school ready for college and career success and be prepared to be contributing members of the community." Like other Multiple Pathways policies, its premise is that large, inflexible, and impersonal high schools fail many students, particularly low-income, Latino, and African American students. Consequently, the project seeks to meet the individual needs of a diverse student population with "variations in institutional arrangements, personalized learning environments, improved linkages to postsecondary institutions, and online instruction and assessments." To accomplish this, Texas has brought together several of its state initiatives under a single umbrella. Included are the state's early- and middle-college programs, dropout prevention programs, and schoolwide reform activities.[19]

California and about two dozen other states provide support for career academies that blend academic and technical coursework. As Stern and Stearns explain in their essay, career academies offer small classes, expect teachers to collaborate, seek to create a close-knit school community, and establish partnerships with employers and community organizations. In many places, career academies also allow students to take courses on community college campuses.[20]

In Massachusetts, the Department of Education partners with the Commonwealth Corporation (a state-level workforce development agency) in a program called Another Route to College. The program gives students who are struggling to pass the state's high school exit exam the opportunity to complete their senior year on a community college campus. The students study intensively for the exam while beginning college coursework that can be applied to a technical certificate, apprenticeship program, or associate's or bachelor's degree.[21]

Maine, Nevada, Connecticut, Virginia, New York, and other states provide support for "early-college high school" programs that combine high school and college programs. Other states, including Massachusetts, South Carolina, Illinois, Indiana, Pennsylvania, and West Virginia, support the High Schools That Work approach, which uses applied pedagogical strategies to blend college-preparatory mathematics, science, language arts, and social studies courses with modern career or technical studies in grades 9 through 12.[22] Nearly all states use their federal Perkins funding to support tech-prep programs linking the last two years of high school with two years of postsecondary education.[23] More than 737,600 students in the United States were involved in tech prep in 1995, and their numbers increase every year.[24]

Some school districts have also adopted Multiple Pathways-like policies. In Boston, the city's High School Renewal initiative supports a growing network of small high schools, including pilot schools, Horace Mann charter schools and the newer "small schools." Each small school has a unifying theme, many of which focus on careers, but others have what the city calls "teaching and learning" themes such as "project-based learning, college preparatory curriculum or leadership development."[25] Similarly, in the Los Angeles Unified School District, large comprehensive high schools are being reconfigured into small, theme-based learning communities in conjunction with making college preparation the default curriculum for all students.

The movement for Multiple Pathways has become strong enough that professional education organizations have begun to provide policy guidance. Groups range from mainstream organizations such as the National Association of Secondary School Principals[26] to those with a more specific focus, such as the Association for Career and Technical Education.[27]

MULTIPLE POSSIBILITIES AND CHALLENGES: WHAT'S THE EVIDENCE?

Viewing Multiple Pathways through different disciplinary lenses, each author in this volume looked beyond the historic split between academic and vocational curricula and rejected tracking systems that prepare students for work or college when they graduate high school. Each author sees in Multiple Pathways a third alternative that draws from the essential educative merits of the old academic and vocational dichotomy.

The themes that emerge from these essays are hopeful and cautious. The hopeful themes suggest that, done right, Multiple Pathways can meet students' needs and serve the collective good. We turn first to the hopeful themes.

- *Increase student engagement.* All students are likely to find the Multiple Pathways approach to academics more engaging than either the typical abstract, classroom-bound college-prep curriculum or the equally abstract, lower-level courses aimed at teaching basic skills.
- *Deepen learning.* Multiple Pathways can deepen students' understanding and retention of academic concepts required for college and can teach competencies that are similar to the broad skills that experts predict are essential to obtaining secure jobs in the future. [28]
- *Promote graduation and college readiness.* When struggling students take a well-defined sequence of college-preparatory and career and technical courses, they are less likely to fall into an unproductive course-taking pattern associated with dropping out of high school.[29] Moreover, learning opportunities that show how academic knowledge and skills relate to work may motivate students to stick with academic courses that prepare them for college.[30]
- *Keep college options open.* The alignment of college preparation with workforce readiness keeps college an option without sacrificing workforce preparation.[31] This is particularly important given that high school students are at a time in their lives when they are not well prepared to make irrevocable decisions.
- *Address the special needs of immigrants and English learners.* Multiple Pathways' integration of real-world contexts with academic skills gives English learners and immigrant students authentic opportunities, more time to practice the English they are learning, and more time to engage in project-based learning, where limited English poses fewer constraints on learning other subject matter.[32]
- *Link young people with meaningful, well-paying jobs.* The exposure to mentors, including well-employed adults, can inform career choices, improve college opportunity, and lead to greater success, particularly for young people without social networks or other connections to good jobs.

- *Prepare a skilled and nimble workforce.* Multiple Pathways can ready young people to move nimbly between work, on-the-job training, and higher education (two-year or four-year) as the changing economy and shifts in job requirements make retooling necessary.[33]
- *Promote a healthy economy in the context of changing demographics.* To the extent that Multiple Pathways can improve minority students' educational success at a number of points (i.e., public K–12, transitions to postsecondary, and lifelong education), there will be a significant return to the economy as a whole through higher wages and lower demand for government-subsidized services.[34]
- *Promote civic engagement.* The Multiple Pathways approach is well suited to engage young people in civic learning that includes the facts, skills, and values required for community participation and leadership. The approach creates contexts to study the relationship between democracy and the economy, and it extends the civic lessons into the workplace.[35]

Alongside these impressive possibilities, however, stand equally impressive obstacles. The essays identify many of these hurdles, and we review them below. We also describe some current policies that illustrate the consequences of not addressing these challenges adequately. As daunting as they may be, these obstacles do not condemn Multiple Pathways to failure. Rather, the success of the reform for deepening students' knowledge and preparing them for college and career will depend on how policymakers and educators regard the perceptions of diverse populations and divergent interest groups as they craft implementation strategies.[36] Ultimately, success will be determined by whether we, as a society, are willing to defy and seek to change a long-standing social hierarchy that provides different opportunities for different students.

- *School reform is extraordinarily difficult, and the scaling up of successful reform models has proven especially so.* We begin with the obvious. Countless studies point to generic implementation obstacles to Multiple Pathways, including the needs to reorganize time and space, establish collaborative relationships among teachers, alter curriculum and instruction, provide personalized learning environments, offer new and more flexible forms of academic support, address inadequate resources, adapt to local contexts while remaining faithful to the reform, ensure necessary technical assistance and professional development, and attain parents' support.[37]

The history of school reform is littered with innovations that have failed to outlast the tenure of even a single high school graduating class.[38] Even when reforms appear to stick, schools may make only superficial changes that actually perpetuate the status quo of school cultures and outcomes.[39] One of the most damaging results is that the failure to fully implement a reform is often mischaracterized as evidence that the reform doesn't "work," particularly for vulnerable students. Many potentially beneficial innovations have been discarded on just such grounds.

- *Multiple Pathways require ambitious structural changes.* The structural changes sought by Multiple Pathways are great: Divide large schools into small ones; design new schedules; develop and train teachers to use integrated, theme-based curriculum and project-based pedagogy; establish dual-enrollment programs; and extend learning and its evaluation beyond the school campus. These measures entail the bridging of current divides among program standards; funding streams and accountability requirements; and teachers with different professional backgrounds, capacities, and certifications. Compounding the difficulty of these changes is uncertainty about whether current educational funding can be reconfigured to cover the costs associated with these structural changes and about what new funding is needed.[40]

An example of how failure to make adequate structural changes can limit the effectiveness of Multiple Pathways approaches can be seen in Pennsylvania's ambitious Education Project 720. Although framed as a college- and career-prep core curriculum, the project stops short of integrating the two. However, a sequence of academic classes is required of all high school students: four years of traditional college-preparatory English and math, three years of science (biology, chemistry, and physics or physical science), three years of social studies (including U.S. and world history), and two years of foreign language (strongly recommended).[41] Although participating districts are advised to cooperate with local career and technical centers and embed career-preparation activities within core curricular offerings, requiring this traditional sequence of academic courses clearly limits the development of Multiple Pathways as we've defined it here.

- *Structural changes are necessary but insufficient.* Structural change is attractive because it provides what may look like a fundamental change. However, there are also normative and political considerations in establishing new ways of thinking about how education is delivered within the new structures. These include relationships and interactions in classrooms, which courses should count for university admission, which types of academic and social supports schools should provide, and parents' roles in holding schools accountable.[42] Finally, Multiple Pathways reform demands that schools avoid the current sharp distinctions between college and career preparation while presenting to parents, educators, and the public new possibilities and images for what high schools are "supposed" to give different groups of students.[43]

- *Collaboration between K–12 and postsecondary education cannot be assumed.* A Multiple Pathways approach requires permeable boundaries between high schools and postsecondary institutions; more flexible programs, such as dual enrollment; clear signals about what success in postsecondary institutions requires; and smoother transitions for students. Without these changes, Multiple Pathways reform is at risk for becoming a new form of vocational education for those who won't attend four-year colleges. Collaborative plans, strategies, and timetables for the transition between high school and postsecondary education must be coordinated by historically uncollaborative segments of public education: high schools, community colleges, and four-year institutions [44]

- *Partnerships with business and public entities may be difficult to establish.* With business and public partnerships, high schools can increase the probability that students have access to rigorous academic training complemented by real work experience. However, a major challenge will be to ensure that all students—not just the most advantaged—have equal access to work-based learning opportunities that provide exposure to potential careers. Placing high school students at worksites is one strategy for addressing racial and economic inequality in employment opportunities. Schools should aim to place students in growing or stable industries that can provide promising future careers rather than in worksites that lead to dead-end occupations. Such exposure to the labor market must go hand in hand with access to college-preparatory courses so that students can graduate with the training and information to pursue a variety of postsecondary education and career paths.

  However, these programs will require strategies to remove, overcome, or "work around" the spatial inequalities that limit success and participation.[45] Racial and class segregation in the housing market, along with unequal economic development across neighborhoods, can limit partnership opportunities. Schools can do very little to alter the inequalities embedded in local communities and economies, but districts and schools can allocate resources to equalize opportunities.

- *An explicit focus on college and career must maintain and improve education's democratic purposes.* A robust understanding and system of common public education must guide schools' attention to individual preparation.[46] A system of vocationally identified themed schools must not devolve into training with narrow, instrumental, economic tools.[47] Multiple Pathways must also prepare students to graduate from high school ready to participate in electoral politics, public institutions, and civic organizations and to act as change agents in the workplace.[48]

- *Policies and additional resources are especially contentious when they are directed to impoverished communities and English learners.* To provide the full range of college- and career-preparation opportunities to students of color, English learners, and low-income students, Multiple Pathways policies must address directly the unique problems associated with these communities: resource inadequacies in schools where these students are concentrated, spatial (geographic) mismatches between young people and meaningful work, and persistent discrimination by employers.[49] Furthermore, high-quality college and career preparation costs more when communities already have many problems and few resources. Because many states already spend too little on education, and schools in well-off communities also need help, targeting resources to poor communities may be seen as unwarranted preferential treatment.

  Moreover, even with targeted resources and policies, Multiple Pathways cannot address fully the educational, social, and economic constraints on students. Also needed are strong economic and employment conditions as well as public policies that focus on the unique labor force problems associated with low-income communities of color, such as spatial and skill barriers to employment, discrimination by employers, and access to good jobs. Ultimately, a Multiple Pathways approach to high school education, like any other educational reform strategy, will work best in the context of a social safety net that includes labor standards, health, housing, and other measures that address the negative effects of residential segregation, income inequality, and concentrated poverty.[50]

- *Multiple Pathways defies deep-seated cultural norms.* Many people find it normal and logical that schools would guide or determine adolescents' choices between two destinations: college (which is better than work) and work (for those who cannot succeed in college). Multiple Pathways reform discards the view that hands-on, real-world education is a terminal experience for those who are not considered to have the capacity for symbolic thought that text-based, literacy-based college preparation requires.

In addition, it rejects a tracking system that directs students into different curricula based on their expected post-high school destinations.

Multiple Pathways takes the socially jarring position that, given the right environment, all students can master complex academic and technical concepts, and that differentiated school practices do a disservice to all. The fundamental premise is that students who are academically adept and those who struggle academically (at some point in time) benefit from multidimensional learning experiences, problem-solving focus, and academics presented in the context of real-world experience. This premise does not comport with discredited, but still active, views about intelligence that continue to influence public perceptions and education policy. Some scholars continue to argue at prominent forums that education reformers must recognize the limiting and fixed influence of IQ on what schooling can accomplish: "Accept that some children will be left behind other children because of intellectual limitations, and think about what kind of education will give them the greatest chance for a fulfilling life nonetheless. Stop telling children that they need to go to college to be successful."[51] To the extent that the public or policymakers hang on to such beliefs, the basic premises of Multiple Pathways will simply not make sense.

Finally, Multiple Pathways also contests the racial, ethnic, gender, and social class biases inherent in traditional conceptions of intellectual potential. Unless these biases are accounted for in the course of implementation, they can undermine change in powerful ways.[52]

- *Powerful resistance to change may come from many sources.* On one hand, socioeconomically advantaged parents, whose children are currently in the college-prep track, may want to preserve status and resource advantages for their children. For example, better-prepared academic teachers would have to be shared among all students and possibly across communities. Parents may worry that CTE would diminish the status of college preparation and the quality of the college track.

  On the other hand, many strong equity advocates won't be easily convinced that Multiple Pathways can break high school tracking patterns that inevitably disadvantage groups that are already underserved.[53] Advocates are cognizant of the historic associations between tracking, race and ethnicity, vocational education, and educational opportunity; they will be skeptical of reforms that appear to offer low-level preparation to a targeted group.

  Some academic teachers will anticipate the loss of professional standing and devaluing of liberal arts education; and some CTE teachers will worry about resources for their occupationally specific training programs. Those in postsecondary institutions may fear compromising their standards for college eligibility.[54]

In sum, reformers will need to frame Multiple Pathways proposals, rhetoric, and implementation strategies so as to minimize these multiple forms of resistance without undermining the potential power of the reform.[55]

MULTIPLE PATHWAYS TO GRADUATION: INCREMENTAL BUT WITH NO COMPROMISE

On one hand, as Samuel Lucas argues in his essay, all-or-nothing confrontational approaches are unlikely to win needed converts or resources for the deep structural changes that Multiple Pathways reform requires. Also, there is no template for Multiple Pathways, no "correct" version to stamp into place—even supposing that the public will and resources exist. On the other hand, the many failed school reforms of the past teach us that Multiple Pathways cannot compromise on its key points. Such compromise simply wastes time and gives the illusion that progress is being made.

Accordingly, all pathways programs must provide the essential components we described in our introduction; here, we restate them briefly as "points of no compromise." Pathways programs must provide all students with both the challenging academic curriculum that prepares them for college and a core of technical knowledge; most schools will offer these as an integrated or hybrid curriculum that combines the best elements of academic instruction and CTE. Pathways must also provide all students with off-campus, "work-based" learning opportunities. Pathways must offer additional, flexible support to enable all students to achieve well in each of these demanding learning contexts. Perhaps most important is that these programs are understood to be just as enriching for high-achieving students as they are for struggling students.

Over the last few years, a more limited (we might even say compromised) version of Multiple Pathways has caught the attention of policymakers, funders, and school reformers. This version, most often framed as "multiple pathways to graduation," is designed for only a subset of American students: those who are struggling through high school or who have already left. Rather than challenging the irrelevance and limitations of the comprehensive high school itself, it presumes that this twentieth-century institution works well enough for most students, including those who are college bound. As such, it does not advance an intellectually rigorous, contextualized approach to academic learning for all students. Neither does it squarely address the needs of future workplaces or help build a wise and adept citizenry that can respond to future challenges to democracy.

New York City, for example, has established the Office of Multiple Pathways to Graduation, which is in the process of creating 67 new schools "designed specifically for older students who may be truant, thinking about dropping out, or are looking for another educational option."[56] This is a safety-net program that will help "over-age" and "under-credited" high school students meet graduation standards and prepare for postsecondary opportunities.[57] Although its aim is laudable, it leaves untouched the fundamental structure and culture of the comprehensive high school, thereby guaranteeing a steady supply of new students who likely have to become older, disaffected, and school failures before they enter a program that—with luck—will address their needs.

In a similar "safety-net" vein, the U.S. Department of Labor Employment and Training Administration (ETA) issued a notice in the 2007 Federal Register that approximately $3 million in grant funds would be available to develop "blueprints" for systems of "multiple education pathways" that will support young people at risk for dropping out of school or who have dropped out already. These plans seek partnerships among the various educational assets in a community and "leverage them to support multiple education pathways that move students to postsecondary education and career pathways and integrate education strategies that may cut across multiple schools and community colleges."[58] Notably, the blueprints were expected to "identify a wide range of innovative and academically rigorous learning environments" that address the needs of this group of vulnerable young people.[59] Seven cities were selected to participate: Mobile, Alabama; Gary, Indiana; Metairie, Louisiana; Pittsburgh, Pennsylvania; Brockton, Massachusetts; Fall River, Massachusetts; and Des Moines, Iowa.

Philanthropic organizations support this limited approach to Multiple Pathways to Graduation. New York City's Fund for Public Schools, for example, secured large grants from the Bill & Melinda Gates Foundation to help launch New York's Office of Multiple Pathways and to provide leadership training and support for principals committed to leading small, academically rigorous schools specifically designed for students at risk of dropping out of high school. A major collaborative of philanthropic funders has also taken up this cause.

Similar Multiple Pathways to Graduation proposals have appeared on the education agendas of 2008 presidential candidates John Edwards and Hillary Clinton.[60] More are sure to come. We are not surprised (or daunted) that adding a "special" program to the twentieth-century education system (a system that doesn't seem to have many fans) is more palatable than the prospect of joining diverse interests and communities to design a system for the twenty-first century. To the extent that Multiple Pathways becomes just another new wrinkle in the country's economic, social, and political fabric, we are all education failures. To the degree that a more comprehensive formulation of Multiple Pathways guides us to a smarter, more productive, and more just citizenry and workforce, we and future generations will rise to meet unforeseen challenges and opportunities.

Notes

INTRODUCTION

1. More information about the Stanley E. Foster Construction Technology Academy is available at http://kearnykomets.sandi.net.
2. Stanley E. Foster Construction Technology Academy School Accountability Report Card (2007) (available at http://studata.sandi.net/research/sarcs/2006-07/SARC736.pdf).
3. M. Magee, "Success in Small Doses: Optimism, Concern Greet Shift of 3 High Schools into 14 Academies," *San Diego Tribune*, April 25, 2004.
4. Magee, "Success in Small Doses."
5. For a more complete description of the Stanley E. Foster Construction Technology Academy, see D. Friedlaender and L. Darling-Hammond, *High Schools for Equity: Policy Supports for Student Learning in Communities of Color* (Stanford, CA: School Redesign Network, 2007).
6. D. Friedlaender and L. Darling-Hammond, *High Schools for Equity*, reporting analyses by the California State Department of Education.
7. Throughout this chapter we use the terms "career and technical education" and "vocational education" to refer to occupationally specific curriculum and courses. Although "vocational education" may be a familiar term, we respect the fact that the reauthorization of the Carl D. Perkins Vocational and Technical Act of 2006 replaced it with "career and technical education."
8. Russlyn Ali, as quoted in L. Rosenhall, "Hands-On Education," *Sacramento Bee*, January 10, 2007.
9. M. Lazerson and W. N. Grubb, *American Education and Vocationalism: A Documentary History, 1870–1970* (New York: Teachers College Press, 1974); H. Kliebard, *Schooled to Work: Vocationalism and the American Curriculum, 1876–1946* (New York: Teachers College Press, 1974).
10. G. Hoachlander, "Ready for College and Career," *The School Administrator*, January 2006; see also ConnectEd: The California Center for College and Career (available at http://www.connectedcalifornia.org).
11. R. Lynch, "High School Career and Technical Education for the First Decade of the 21st Century," *Journal of Vocational Education Research* 25, no. 2 (2000) (available at http://scholar.lib.vt.edu/ejournals/JVER/v25n2/lynch.html).
12. D. Parnell, "Cerebral Context," *Vocational Education Journal* 71, no. 3 (March 1996): 19–21.
13. Notably, integrated academic and vocational learning is not a new idea. Late-nineteenth-century advocates claimed that manual training would complement academic studies in a balanced education. They argued that students should learn mechanical processes rather than prepare for particular trades, and that they should master general

269

principles rather than specific skills. They argued that processes requiring skill with the hands would simultaneously present problems for the mind. In the twentieth century, John Dewey and other progressive reformers made a similar claim: If students worked with wood, metal, paper, and soil, they could achieve alternate and important "ways of knowing." These arguments hold today. Specific job skills that vocational students learn can become obsolete with a changing economy, but understandings based on physics, mathematics, or technological processes cannot. Students who understand these concepts have constructed a conceptual framework on which to erect new skills to assist them in an evolving workplace (W. Grubb, G. Davis, J. Lum, J. Plihal, & C. Morgaine, *The Cunning Hand, the Cultured Mind: Models for Integrating Vocational and Academic Education* (Berkeley, CA: National Center for Research in Vocational Education, 1991).

14. For a review, see J. Oakes, *Keeping Track: How Schools Structure Inequality* (New Haven, CT: Yale University Press, 1985/2005).

15. For example, students enrolled in challenging academic classes score higher on achievement tests than students in less challenging classes. They feel more challenged, have higher aspirations, do more homework, and go on to take more advanced courses later on in high school. While this may seem obvious if the students in the challenging classes are higher achieving to begin with, students in challenging classes show these academic gains even when we compare their achievements to students with equivalent levels of achievement who were not in challenging classes. In addition, students who take challenging academic courses have better prospects for high school completion (in other words, they drop out less frequently). They are more likely to attend college, they get better grades in college, and they are more likely to graduate than comparable students who don't take these courses (see Oakes, *Keeping Track*, for a review).

16. R. J. Monson, "Redefining the Comprehensive High School: The Multiple Pathways Model," *NASSP Bulletin* 81, no. 19 (1997): 19–27.

17. National Governors Association, *Ready for Tomorrow: Helping All Students Achieve Secondary and Postsecondary Success. A Guide for Governors* (2003), 4 (available at http://www.nga.org/cda/files/0310READY.pdf).

18. National Governors Association, *Ready for Tomorrow*, 7.

19. P. M. Callan and J. E. Finney, "Multiple Pathways and State Policy: Toward Education and Training Beyond High School," paper commissioned for the project *Redesigning High Schools: The Unfinished Agenda in State Education Reform* (Boston: Jobs for the Future, 2003), 2.

20. Callan and Finney, "Multiple Pathways," 2.

21. B. Brand, "Rigor and Relevance: A New Vision for Career and Technical Education," a white paper (Washington, DC: American Youth Policy Forum, 2003) (available at http://www.aypf.org/publications/aypf_rigor_0004v.3.pdf).

22. R. Schwartz, "Multiple Pathways—And How to Get There," in *Double the Numbers: Increasing Postsecondary Credentials for Underrepresented Youth*, ed. R. Kazis, J. Vargas, and N. Hoffman (Cambridge, MA: Harvard Education Press, 2004).

23. R. Kazis, *Remaking Career and Technical Education for the 21st Century: What Role for High School Programs?* (Boston: Jobs for the Future and the Aspen Institute, 2005), 2; (available at http://www.aspeninstitute.org/atf/cf/%7BDEB6F227-659B-4EC8-8F84-8DF23CA704F5%7D/ed_kazis-RemakingCTE.pdf).

24. Kazis, *Remaking,* 3.
25. "Creating a Portfolio of Great High Schools," Bill & Melinda Gates Foundation (2004) (available at http://www.gatesfoundation.org/nr/downloads/ed/GreatHighSchools.pdf).
26. The James Irvine Foundation (available at http://www.irvine.org/grants_program/ youth/youth.shtml).

CHAPTER 1

1. N. Maxwell and V. Rubin, *High School Career Academies: A Pathway to Educational Reform in Urban School Districts* (Kalamazoo, MI: W. E. Upjohn Institute, 2000); D. Stern, M. Raby, and C. Dayton, *Career Academies: Partnerships for Reconstructing American High Schools* (San Francisco: Jossey-Bass, 1992).
2. M. Silverberg, E. Warner, M. Fong, and D. Goodwin, *National Assessment of Vocational Education: Final Report to Congress* (2004) (available at www.ed.gov/rschstat/eval/sectech/ nave/reports.html).
3. M. Rose, *The Mind at Work: Valuing the Intelligence of the American Worker* (New York: Viking Penguin, 2004).
4. F. Levy and R. J. Murnane, *The New Division of Labor: How Computers Are Creating the Next Job Market* (Princeton, NJ: Princeton University Press, 2004).
5. R. L. Custer, *Performance-Based Education Implementation Handbook* (Columbia: University of Missouri, Instructional Materials Lab, 1994); D. D. Holt, *Alternative Approaches to Assessment and Evaluation in Family English Literacy Programs* (Sacramento: California Department of Education, 1992).
6. W. N. Grubb, *Education through Occupations in American High Schools* (New York: Teachers College Press, 1995).
7. Quoted in W. Greider, *One World, Ready or Not: The Manic Logic of Global Capitalism* (New York: Touchstone, 1997), 84.
8. R. P. Moses, M. Kamii, S. M. Swap, and J. Howard, "The Algebra Project: Organizing in the Spirit of Ella," *Harvard Educational Review* 59, no. 4 (1989): 423–43.

CHAPTER 2

1. See, for example, S. DeLuca, S. Plank, and A. Estacion, *Does Career and Technical Education Affect College Enrollment?* (St. Paul, MN: National Research Center for Career and Technical Education, 2006) (available from National Dissemination Center for Career and Technical Education, The Ohio State University, 1900 Kenny Road, Columbus, OH 43210-1016; http://www.nccte.org).
2. Statistical Abstract of the United States 2006, Table 216.
3. R. B. Freeman, *The Overeducated American* (New York: Academic Press, 1976); F. Levy and R. J. Murnane, "U.S. Earnings Levels and Earnings Inequality: A Review of the Recent Trends and Proposed Explanations," *Journal of Economic Literature* 30 (1992): 1333–81.
4. N. M. Fortin, "Higher-education Policies and the College Wage Premium: Cross-State Evidence from the 1990s," *American Economic Review* 96, no. 4 (2006): 959–87.

5. J. E. Rosenbaum, *Making Inequality: The Hidden Curriculum of High School Tracking* (New York: Wiley, 1976); J. Oakes, *Keeping Track: How Schools Structure Inequality* (New Haven, CT: Yale University Press, 1985/2005).

6. S. R. Lucas, *Tracking Inequality: Stratification and Mobility in American High Schools* (New York: Teachers College Press, 1999). See also Oakes, *Keeping Track.*

7. National Academy of Sciences, Panel on Secondary School Education and the Changing Workplace, *High Schools and the Changing Workplace, the Employers' View* (Washington, DC: National Academies Press, 1984); Committee for Economic Development, *Investing in Our Children* (New York: Committee for Economic Development, 1985); D. T. Kearns and D. P. Doyle, *Winning the Brain Race: A Bold Plan to Make Our Schools Competitive* (San Francisco: Institute for Contemporary Studies, ICS Press, 1988).

8. See, for example, W. N. Grubb, "The Cunning Hand, the Cultured Mind," in *Education through Occupations* (Vol. 1), ed. W. N. Grubb (New York: Teachers College Press, 1995).

9. S. Kang and J. Bishop, "Vocational and Academic Education in High School: Complements or Substitutes?" *Economics of Education Review* 8, no. 2 (1989): 133–48.

10. R. Arum and Y. Shavit, "Secondary Vocational Education and the Transition from School to Work," *Sociology of Education* 68 (1995): 187–204.

11. K. Levesque, D. Lauen, P. Teitelbaum, M. Alt, and S. Librera, *Vocational Education in the United States: Toward the Year 2000* (Washington, DC: U.S. Department of Education, National Center for Education Statistics, 2000).

12. S. B. Plank, "A Question of Balance: CTE, Academic Courses, High School Persistence, and Student Achievement," *Journal of Vocational Education Research* 26, no. 3 (2001): 279–327.

13. Plank, "A Question of Balance."

14. J. H. Bishop and F. Mane, "The Impacts of Career-Technical Education on High School Labor Market Outcomes," *Economics of Education Review* 23, no. 4 (2004): 381–402.

15. G. Bottoms and A. Presson, "Improving High Schools for Career-Bound Youth," in *Education through Occupations* (Vol. 2), ed. W. N. Grubb (New York: Teachers College Press, 1995), 35–54.

16. See www.sreb.org/Programs/hstw/hstwindex.asp.

17. D. Stern, M. Raby, and C. Dayton, *Career Academies: Partnerships for Reconstructing American High Schools* (San Francisco: Jossey-Bass/Wiley, 1992). Networks of career academies are sponsored or supported by organizations described at http://www.naf.org/cps/rde/xchg, http://www.academiesinc.org/, http://casn.berkeley.edu, http://www.ncacinc.org/ncacinc/site/default.asp, and http://www.cde.ca.gov/ci/gs/hs/cpagen.asp.

18. J. J. Kemple and J. L. Rock, *Career Academies: Early Implementation Lessons from a 10-Site Evaluation* (New York: MDRC, 1996).

19. For more detail on these studies, see D. Stern, "Career Academies and High School Reform before, during, and after the School-to-Work Movement," in *The School-to-Work Movement: Origins and Destinations*, ed. W. J. Stull and N. M. Sanders (Westport, CT: Praeger, 2003), 239–62. More recent non-experimental evidence is in D. Stern, C. Wu, C. Dayton, and A. Maul, "Learning by Doing Career Academies," in *Improving School-to-Work Transitions*, ed. D. Neumark (New York: Russell Sage, 2007).

20. For a fuller discussion, see D. Stern and J. Y. Wing, "Is There Solid Evidence of Positive Effects for High School Students?" in *High School Reform: Using Evidence to Improve Policy*

and Practice (New York: Manpower Development Research Corporation [MDRC], 2004) (available at http://www.mdrc.org/publications/391/conf_report.pdf).

21. J. J. Kemple, *Career Academies: Communities of Support for Students and Teachers, Emerging Findings from a 10-Site Evaluation* (New York: MDRC, 1997).

22. J. J. Kemple, S. M. Poglinco, and J. C. Snipes, *Career Academies: Building Career Awareness and Work-Based Learning Activities through Employer Partnerships* (New York: MDRC, 1999).

23. J. J. Kemple and J. C. Snipes, *Career Academies: Impacts on Students' Engagement and Performance in High School* (New York: MDRC, 2000).

24. Kemple and Snipes, *Career Academies.*

25. J. J. Kemple, *Career Academies: Impacts on Students' Initial Transitions to Post-Secondary Education and Employment* (New York: MDRC, 2001).

26. J. J. Kemple with J. Scott-Clayton, *Career Academies: Impacts on Labor Market Outcomes and Educational Attainment* (New York: MDRC, 2004).

27. J. R. Stone III, C. Alfeld, D. Pearson, M. V. Lewis, and S. Jensen, *Building Academic Skills in Context: Testing the Value of Enhanced Math Learning in CTE* (St. Paul, MN: National Research Center for Career and Technical Education, 2005) (available from National Dissemination Center for Career and Technical Education, The Ohio State University, 1900 Kenny Road, Columbus, OH 43210-1016; http://www.nccte.org).

28. Eligibility for UC and CSU also requires minimum GPA and test scores. The CSU Eligibility Index is accessible at http://www.csumentor.edu/planning/high_school/cal_residents.asp. The UC Eligibility Index is accessible at http://www.universityofcalifornia.edu/admissions/undergrad_adm/paths_to_adm/freshman/scholarship_reqs.html.

29. Viewable on the Doorways website, at www.ucop.edu/doorways/list.

30. Accessible at http://www.ucop.edu/a-gGuide/ag/content/CDE-UCApprovedCTECourses 2006-07_002.doc.

31. The project was funded initially by the California School-to-Career Interagency Partners (California Department of Education, Economic Development Department, California Community Colleges) and subsequently by the California Department of Education.

32. To receive a single subject teaching credential in an academic subject, a candidate must earn a baccalaureate degree, complete a graduate-level teacher-preparation program approved by the California Commission on Teacher Credentialing, pass the California Basic Education Skills Test (CBEST), and fulfill other requirements (see www.ctc.ca.gov/credentials/leaflets/cl560c.html). In contrast, to receive a vocational education designated subjects teaching credential, a candidate must demonstrate evidence of 5 years of work experience (or equivalent) directly related to the vocational subject to be named on the credential, hold a high school diploma (or equivalent), along with other requirements (see www.ctc.ca.gov/credentials/leaflets/cl698a.html).

33. CBEDS School Information Form, Item 30.

34. In this report, a course is classified as CTE if it "could be" taught by a credentialed CTE teacher, whether or not it actually is. For instance, the report lists more than 800 photography courses, of which only a small fraction are actually taught by credentialed CTE teachers.

35. Available at www.ConnectEdCalifornia.org

36. The James Irvine Foundation also sponsored the writing of this paper.

37. For instance, John Dewey, in *Democracy and Education* (1916), argues for this kind of integration.

CHAPTER 3

1. We would like to thank Charlie Mojkowski, David Bromley, Marisa Saunders, Jeannie Oakes, and Martin Lipton for their helpful comments on earlier versions of this paper.
2. The purpose of this essay is to examine in broad terms the tension between the individual and collective aims of schooling. To do this, we use several terms, such as "civic virtue," "common good," "individuate," and "social order," having specialized meanings within academic disciplines.
3. "Public virtue is the only foundation of republics. There must be a positive passion for the public good, the public interest, honour, power and glory, established in the minds of the people, or there can be no republican government, nor any real liberty." John Adams, as quoted in M. J. Sandel, *Democracy's Discontents: America in Search of a Public Philosophy* (Cambridge, MA: Harvard University Press, 1996), 126.
4. A. de Tocqueville, *Democracy in America*, ed. J. P. Mayer (New York: Doubleday, Anchor Books, 1835/1969); see also R. Bellah, R. Madsen, W. W. Sullivan, A. Swidler, and S. Tipton, *Habits of the Heart: Individualism and Commitment in American Life* (New York: Harper and Row, 1985).
5. J. Rawls, *A Theory of Justice* (Cambridge, MA: Harvard University Press, 1971).
6. A. Gutmann, *Democratic Education* (Princeton, NJ: Princeton University Press, 1987), 14.
7. Coalition of Essential Schools National Website available at www.essentialschools.org.
8. Student comment from Bronx New Century High Schools Youth Summit, May 2, 2003 (available at http://www.whatkidscando.org/intheirownwords/Perspectives.html#worth going, retrieved 8/5/06).
9. Student comment from Bronx New Century High Schools Youth Summit, May 2, 2003; Juan is a pseudonym.
10. Laura, a high school senior at The Met describes her own learning in L. Hughes, "Individualizing My Own Learning," *Horace* 19, no. 1 (Fall 2002) (available at http://www.essentialschools.org/pub/ces_docs/resources/horace/19_1/19_1_toc.html).
11. N. Noddings, *The Challenge to Care in Schools* (New York: Teachers College Press, 1992).
12. J. Oakes and M. Lipton, *Teaching to Change the World* (Boston: McGraw-Hill, 1999), 252.
13. William is a pseudonym. For an extensive bibliography of commentary and research on the Big Picture Company schools, see www.bigpicture.org.
14. Bill & Melinda Gates Foundation, *Creating a Portfolio of Great High Schools* (available at www.gatesfoundation.org/nr/downloads/ed/GreatHighSchools.pdf http://www.standup .org/pdf/GreatHighSchools.pdf).
15. Available at http://www.standup.org/pdf/GreatHighSchools.pdf, retrieved 8/2/06.
16. J. Oakes, *Keeping Track: How Schools Structure Inequality* (New Haven, CT: Yale University Press, 1985); S. Lucas, *Tracking Inequality: Stratification and Mobility in American High Schools* (New York: Teachers College Press, 1999).
17. Student comment from Bronx New Century High Schools Youth Summit, May 2, 2003.

18. A. S. Wells, A. Lopez, J. Scott, and J. J. Holme, "Charter Schools as Postmodern Paradox: Rethinking Social Stratification in an Age of Deregulated School Choice," *Harvard Educational Review* 69, no. 2 (1999): 172–204.

19. C. W. Cooper, "School Choice and the Standpoint of African American Mothers: Considering the Power of Positionality," *Journal of Negro Education* 74, no. 2 (2005): 174–89.

20. D. Stern, M. Raby, and C. Dayton, *Career Academies: Building Blocks for Reconstructing American High Schools* (Berkeley: Career Academy Support Network, University of California–Berkeley, 2000) (available at casn.berkeley.edu/resources/bldgblocks.html).

21. National Career Academy Coalition (available at www.ncacinc.org: http://www.ncacinc.org/3758%5F90430215819/site/default.asp).

22. J. Dewey, *Democracy and Education* (New York: Macmillan Company, 1916), as cited in E. J. Hyslop-Margison, "An Assessment of the Historical Arguments in Vocational Education Reform," *Journal of Career and Technical Education* 17, no. 1 (2001): 318.

23. A. G. Powell, E. Farrar, and D. K. Cohen, *The Shopping Mall High School: Winners and Losers in the Educational Marketplace* (Boston: Houghton Mifflin, 1985).

24. E. G. Hoachlander, P. Kaufman, K. Levesque, and J. Houser, *Vocational Education in the United States: 1969–1990* (Washington, DC: National Center for Educational Statistics, 1992), xxi.

25. Hoachlander et al., *Vocational Education in the United States*.

26. K. Levesque, D. Lauen, P. Teitelbaum, M. Alt, and S. Librera, *Vocational Education in the United States: Toward the Year 2000* (Washington, DC: U.S. Department of Education, National Center for Education Statistics, 2000).

27. J. J. Kemple and J. L. Rock, *Career Academies: Early Implementation Lessons from a 10-Site Evaluation* (New York: Manpower Demonstration Research Corporation [MDRC], 1996) (available at www.mdrc.org/publications/162/execsum.html).

28. D. Stern and R. Stearns, "Evidence and Challenges: Will Multiple Pathways Improve Students' Outcomes?" in this volume. One exception is an ongoing random-assignment evaluation of career academies, most recently reported in J. J. Kemple, with J. Scott-Clayton, *Career Academies: Impacts on Labor Market Outcomes and Educational Attainment* (New York: MDRC, 2004).

29. Available at http://schools.nyc.gov/NR/rdonlyres/F053E196-E2FE-4A46-9D47-7AA4D-2BB779E/314 42/2007MakingChoices_HSAdminPrep.pdf.

30. D. Tyack, *Seeking Common Ground: Public Schools in a Diverse Society* (Cambridge, MA: Harvard University Press, 2003), 70.

31. As quoted in G. Robinson, "Making High Schools Smaller," *Gotham Gazette* (November 15, 2004) (available at http://www.gothamgazette.com/article//20041115/200/1178, retrieved 9/2/06).

32. Stern et al., *Career Academies: Building Blocks*.

33. M. Sherif, O. J. Harvey, B. J. White, W. R. Hood, and C. W. Sherif, *Intergroup Conflict and Cooperation: The Robbers Cave Experiment (1954/1961)* (available at psychclassics.yorku.ca/Sherif/preface1954.htm).

34. J. Ancess and D. Allen, "Implementing Small Theme High Schools in New York City: Great Intentions and Great Tensions," *Harvard Educational Review* 76, no. 3 (2006): 401–16.

35. Small Schools Workshop (available at http://www.smallschoolsworkshop.org/research.html).

36. T. Sizer, *Horace's Hope: What Works for the American High School* (Boston: Houghton Mifflin, 1996), 154.

37. M. Rose, *The Mind at Work: Valuing the Intelligence of the American Worker* (New York: Viking, 2004), 216.

38. Ancess and Allen, "Implementing Small Theme High Schools."

39. S. M. Poglinco, *Career Academies as a Support for Students' College Goals: Perceptions of Students, Teachers, and Administrators in Three Academies*, as cited in Stern et al., *Career Academies: Building Blocks*.

40. F. Levy and R. Murnane, *The New Division of Labor: How Computers Are Creating the Next Job Market* (Princeton, NJ: Princeton University Press, 2004).

41. A–G refers to the sequence of courses high school students must complete for admission to public universities in California.

42. J. Oakes, K. H. Quartz, S. Ryan, and M. Lipton, *Becoming Good American Schools: The Struggle for Civic Virtue in Education Reform* (San Francisco: Jossey-Bass Education Series, 2000); J. Oakes, K. H. Quartz, S. Ryan, and M. Lipton, "Civic Virtue, School Reform and Character Education," in *Character Psychology and Character Education*, eds. D. Lapsey and C. Power (Notre Dame, IN: University of Notre Dame Press, 2005).

43. D. Meier, *In Schools We Trust* (Boston: Beacon Press, 2002).

44. E. J. Hyslop-Margison, *Liberalizing Vocational Study: Democratic Approaches to Career Education* (Lanham, MD: University Press of America, 2005).

45. Correspondence with Elliot Washor (undated).

46. M. Fine, "Not in Our Name: Reclaiming the Democratic Vision of Small School Reform," *Rethinking Schools* 19, no. 4 (2005).

CHAPTER 4

1. S. A. Camarota, *Immigrants in the United States—2000: A Snapshot of America's Foreign-Born Population* (Washington, DC: Center for Immigration Studies, 2001).

2. A. Kindler, *Survey of States' Limited English Proficient Students and Available Educational Programs and Services: 2000–2001*, Summary Report (Washington, DC: National Clearinghouse for English Language Acquisition, 2002).

3. Although data are not available on the college completion rates of immigrants, children of immigrants, and English learners, data on college completion by ethnicity provide a clue to these numbers.

4. W. N. Grubb, "The Cunning Hand, the Cultured Mind," in *Education through Occupations in American High Schools* (Vol. 1), ed. W. N. Grubb (New York: Teachers College Press, 1995), 11–25; J. Goodlad, *A Place Called School* (New York: McGraw-Hill, 1984).

5. S. Heaviside, N. Carey, and E. Farris, *Public Secondary School Teacher Survey on Vocational Education* (Washington, DC: National Center for Education Statistics, 1994).

6. ACT, Inc. (founded as American College Testing), *Ready for College and Ready for Work: Same or Different?* (Iowa City, IA: ACT, 2006) (available at www.act.org/path/policy/reports/workready.html).

7. California Performance Review (CPR) Commission, *Balance Career Technical Education and College Preparation in High Schools*, Report to the Governor (Sacramento, CA: CPR Commission, 2004).

8. M. Pastor, "United or Divided: Can Multiple Pathways Bring Together Multiple Communities?" in this volume.

9. D. Myers, *Immigrants and Boomers: Forging a New Social Contract for the Future of America* (New York: Russell Sage, 2007).

10. CPR Commission, *Balance Career Technical Education*.

11. P. Gándara, R. Rumberger, J. Maxwell-Jolly, and R. Callahan, "English Learners in California Schools: Unequal Resources; Unequal Outcomes," *Educational Policy Analysis Archives* 11, no. 6 (2003) (available at epaa.asu.edu/epaa/v11n36); R. Rumberger, P. Gándara, and B. Merino, "Where California's English Learners Attend School and Why It Matters," *UC LMRI Newsletter*, 15 (2006): 1–3.

12. California Department of Finance, *Current Population Survey* (2003) (available at www.dof.ca.gov/HTML/DEMOGRAP/SDC/DOCUMENTS/SF4.pdf); P. Gándara and R. Rumberger, "Immigration, Language, and Education: How Does Language Policy Structure Opportunity?" *Teachers College Record* (forthcoming).

13. California Department of Education, *Factbook* (Sacramento, CA: CDE, 2005) (available at www.cde.ca.gov/re/pn/fb/yr05ftepss.asp).

14. A. Gershberg, A. Danenberg, and P. Sánchez, *Beyond "Bilingual" Education: New Immigrants and Public School Policies in California* (Washington, DC: The Urban Institute, 2004).

15. R. Ream, *Uprooting Children: Mobility, Social Capital, and Mexican American Underachievement* (New York: LFB Scholarly Press, 2005).

16. National Center for Education Statistics, *The Condition of Education* (Washington, DC: NCES, 2003) (available at nces.ed.gov/programs/coe/).

17. G. Orfield and C. Lee, *Racial Transformation and the Changing Nature of Segregation* (Cambridge, MA: Civil Rights Project, Harvard University, 2006); J. Oakes et al., *California Educational Opportunity Report* (Los Angeles: Institute for Democracy, Education and Access [IDEA], University of California–Los Angeles, 2007).

18. A. Portes and R. G. Rumbaut, *Immigrant America: A Portrait* (Berkeley: University of California Press, 1996).

19. S. J. Lee, *Unraveling the Model Minority Stereotype: Listening to Asian American Youth* (New York: Teachers College Press, 1996); R. Callahan and P. Gándara, "On Nobody's Agenda: Improving English Language Learners' Access to Higher Education," in *Teaching Immigrant and Second Language Students*, ed. M. Sadowski (Cambridge, MA: Harvard Education Press, 2004).

20. Reliable data on dropouts are notoriously difficult to come by and there is no consensus in the field about dropout rates for any group of students. However, a recent analysis of Los Angeles Unified School District data for the graduating class of 2005 showed that only 27 percent of English learner students who were in the district in ninth grade were in the graduating class four years later.

21. R. Rumberger and G. Rodriguez, "Chicano Dropouts: An Update of Research and Policy Issues," in *Chicano School Failure and Success*, ed. R. Valencia (New York: Teachers College Press, 2002).

22. D. Hayes-Bautista, *La Nueva California: Latinos in the Golden State* (Berkeley: University of California Press, 2004); E. López, E. Ramirez, and R. Rochin, *Latinos and Economic Development in California* (Sacramento: California Research Bureau, 1999).

23. http://star.cde.ca.gov/star2007/Viewreport.asp

24. http://cahsee.cde.ca.gov/reports.asp

25. P. Gándara et al., "English Learners in California Schools."

26. L. Wong-Fillmore and C. E. Snow, *What Teachers Need to Know about Language* (Washington, DC: Center for Applied Linguistics, 2000) (available at: faculty.tamu-commerce. edu/jthompson/Resources/FillmoreSnow2000.pdf). A good discussion of the role of academic English in the achievement of English learners can be found in C. Connell, "English Language Learners: Boosting Academic Achievement," *AERA Research Points* 2, no. 1 (Winter 2004).

27. P. Gándara et al., "English Learners in California Schools"; A. M. Zehler, H. L. Fleischman, P. J. Hopstock, T. G. Stephenson, M. L Pendzick, and S. Sapru, *Descriptive Study of Services to Limited English Proficient Students* (Washington, DC: Development Associates, 2003); P. Gándara, J. Maxwell-Jolly, and A. Driscoll, *Listening to Teachers of English Learners* (Santa Cruz, CA: Center for the Future of Teaching and Learning, 2004).

28. G. Kao and M. Tienda, "Educational Aspirations of Minority Youth," *American Journal of Education* 106 (1998): 349–62; P. Gándara, D. Gutiérrez, and S. O'Hara, "Planning for the Future in Rural and Urban High Schools, *Journal of Education for Students Placed at Risk* 6 (2001): 73–93; R. Fry, *Latino Youth Finishing College: The Role of Selective Pathways* (Washington, DC: Pew Hispanic Center, 2004).

29. C. Brittain, *Transnational Messages: Experiences of Chinese and Mexican Americans in American Schools* (New York: LFB Scholarly Publishing, 2002).

30. E. Zarate and H. Pachón, *Perceptions of College Financial Aid among California Latino Youth* (Los Angeles: Tomás Rivera Policy Institute, University of Southern California, 2006).

31. Latino Eligibility Study, *Ya Basta* (Santa Cruz: Latino Eligibility Task Force, University of California–Santa Cruz, 1994); P. Gándara, "High School Puente: What We Have Learned about Preparing Latino Youth for Higher Education," *Educational Policy* 16, no. 4 (2002): 474–95; P. McDonough, *Choosing Colleges: How Social Class and Schools Structure Opportunity* (Albany: State University of New York Press, 1997).

32. Orfield and Lee, *Racial Transformation*.

33. P. Gándara, D. Gutiérrez, L. William-White, and S. O'Hara, "The Changing Shape of Aspirations: Peer Influence and Achievement Behavior," in *School Connections: U.S. Mexican Youth, Peers, and School Achievement,* eds. M. Gibson, P. Gándara, and J. Koyama (New York: Teachers College Press, 2004), 39–62.

34. Rumberger, Gándara, and Merino, "Where California's English Learners Attend School."

35. Gándara et al., "The Changing Shape of Aspirations."

36. G. Bottoms, *Making High Schools Work through Integration of Academic and Vocational Education* (Atlanta: Southern Regional Educational Board, 1992); D. Bragg, *Emerging Tech Prep Models: Promising Approaches to Educational Reform* (Berkeley, CA: National Center for Research in Vocational Education, 1994).

37. S. Bowles and H. Gintis, *Schooling in Capitalist America* (New York: Basic Books, 1976).

38. W. N. Grubb, "The Cunning Hand, the Cultured Mind," 11–25.

39. Bottoms, *Making High Schools Work*.

40. Bragg, *Emerging Tech Prep Models*.

41. Goodlad, *A Place Called School*.

42. J. Dewey, *Democracy and Education* (New York: Macmillan, 1916).

43. L. Darling-Hammond, *Testimony on Alternatives to the CAHSEE* (2006) (available at www.cde.ca.gov/nr/re/et/cahseealtmtg.asp).

44. W. N. Grubb, "A Continuum of Approaches to Curriculum Integration," in *Education through Occupations in American High Schools* (Vol. 1), ed. W. N. Grubb (New York: Teachers College Press, 1995), 59–81.

45. M. Raby, "Career Academies," in *Education through Occupations in American High Schools* (Vol. 1), ed. W. N. Grubb (New York: Teachers College Press, 1995), 82–96; G. Conchas, *The Color of Success: Race and High-Achieving Urban Youth* (Albany: State University of New York Press, 2005); see also W. N. Grubb, "Challenging the Deep Structure of High School: Weak and Strong Versions of Multiple Pathways," in this volume.

46. Callahan and Gándara, "On Nobody's Agenda."

47. N. Gonzalez, R. Andrade, M. Civil, and L. Moll, "Bridging Funds of Distributed Knowledge: Creating Zones of Practices in Mathematics," *Journal of Education for Students Placed at Risk* 6 (2001): 115–32.

48. J. Bransford, A. Brown, and R. Cocking, eds., *How People Learn: Brain, Mind, Experience, and School* (Washington, DC: National Academies Press, 1999); Goodlad, *A Place Called School.*

49. Grubb, "A Continuum of Approaches."

50. H. Wechsler and W. Reese, *Access to Success in the Urban High School: The Middle College Movement* (New York: Teachers College Press, 2001).

51. For example, H. Gardner, *The Arts and Human Development* (New York: Basic Books, 1994); R. Deasy, *Critical Links: Learning in the Arts and Student Academic and Social Development* (Washington, DC: Arts Education Partnership, National Endowment for the Arts, 2002); E. Eisner, *The Arts and the Creation of Mind* (New Haven, CT: Yale University Press, 2002).

52. L. Steinberg, *Beyond the Classroom* (New York: Simon & Schuster, 1996).

53. P. Gándara and F. Contreras, *The Latino Education Crisis: The Consequences of Failed Social Policies* (Cambridge, MA: Harvard University Press, forthcoming).

54. P. Ong and V. Terriquez, "Can Multiple Pathways Offset Inequalities in the Urban Spatial Structure?" in this volume.

55. L. Shepard and M. Smith, *Flunking Grades: Research and Policies on Retention* (New York: Falmer Press, 1989).

56. See, for example, D. Neumark, *The Effects of School-to-Career Programs on Postsecondary Enrollment and Employment* (San Francisco: Public Policy Institute of California, 2004).

57. California Department of Education, *California Basic Educational Data System* (Sacramento, CA: California Department of Education, 2007) (available at www.cde.ca.gov/ds/sd/cb/).

58. Grubb, "What Educational Resources Do Students Need?"

59. Grubb, "What Educational Resources Do Students Need?"

60. A. S. Wells and J. Oakes, "Potential Pitfalls of Systemic Reform: Lessons from Research on Detracking," *Sociology of Education*, extra issue (1996): 135–43; A. Lareau, *Home Advantage* (Philadelphia: Temple University Press, 1987).

61. L. Margolin, *Goodness Personified: The Emergence of Gifted Children* (New York: Aldine de Gruyter, 1994).

62. Heaviside et al., *Public Secondary School Teacher Survey.*

63. Wong-Fillmore and Snow, *What Teachers Need to Know.*
64. Ong and Terriquez, "Can Multiple Pathways Offset Inequalities?"
65. P. Gándara and M. Mejorado, "Putting Your Money Where Your Mouth Is: Mentoring as a Strategy to Increase Access to Higher Education," in *Preparing for College: Nine Elements of Effective Outreach*, eds. W. Tierney, Z. Corwin, and J. Colyar (Albany: State University of New York Press, 2004).
66. Ong and Terriquez, "Can Multiple Pathways Offset Inequalities?"

PART II INTRODUCTION

1. M. Pastor, "United or Divided: Can Multiple Pathways Bring Together Multiple Communities?" in this volume.

CHAPTER 5

1. Thanks to Miranda Smith for able research assistance and to Justin Scoggins and Jack Turner for preparing the data used in the calculations indicated in the text.
2. M. Landsberg, "L.A. Mayor Sees Dropout Rate as 'Civil Rights Issue,'" *Los Angeles Times*, March 2, 2006 (available at www.latimes.com/news/local/la-me dropout-2mar02,1,5830485.story?ctrack=1&cset=true).
3. J. Bernstein, E. McNichol, and K. Lyons, *Pulling Apart: A State-by-State Analysis of Income Trends* (Washington, DC: Economic Policy Institute/Center on Budget and Policy Priorities, 2006) (available at www.epinet.org/studies/pulling06/pulling_apart_2006.pdf).
4. P. A. Jargowsky, *Stunning Progress, Hidden Problems: The Dramatic Decline in Concentrated Poverty in the 1990s* (Washington, DC: Brookings Institution, Living Cities Census Series, 2003), 6 (available at www.brookings.edu/es/urban/publications/jargowskypoverty.pdf).
5. The demographic data are taken from the U.S. Census, with projections (and the 1970s figures) taken from the California Department of Finance Demographic Research Unit (available at www.dof.ca.gov/HTML/DEMOGRAP/Druhpar.asp).
6. The current estimates of the ethnic composition by age are taken from runs on the 2000 Public Use Microdata Sample from the U.S. Census (5% sample).
7. M. Pastor and D. Reed, "Understanding Equitable Infrastructure for California," in *California 2025: Taking on the Future*, eds. E. Hanak and M. Baldassare (San Francisco: Public Policy Institute of California, 2005).
8. Data on capital spending are from the U.S. Census of Governments for 1999–2000 in order to match with demographic and income data from the 2000 Census. Capital spending is measured as the sum of state and local capital outlays.
9. This dynamic is covered masterfully in P. Schrag, *Paradise Lost: California's Experience, America's Future* (New York: W. W. Norton, 1998).
10. M. Baldassare, *PPIC Statewide Survey: Special Survey on Californians and the Future* (San Francisco: Public Policy Institute of California, 2004).
11. Bernstein et al., *Pulling Apart.*
12. Bernstein et al., *Pulling Apart.*
13. Bernstein et al., *Pulling Apart.*

14. The latest iteration of the CPS available at the time of writing was from 2005, so I could only utilize 2004 income data.

15. See the fine discussion of the consequences of even conservative adjustments for housing prices in D. Reed, "Poverty in California: Moving Beyond the Federal Measure," *California Counts* 7, vol. 4 (2006) (available at www.ppic.org/content/pubs/cacounts/ CC_506DRCC.pdf).

16. Poverty rates were calculated by pooling multiple years of the March Supplement of the Current Population Survey for California; I pool multiple years in order to increase accuracy of estimates in population subsamples.

17. M. Pastor, "Rising Tides and Sinking Boats: The Economic Challenge for California's Latinos," in *Latinos and Public Policy in California: An Agenda for Opportunity*, eds. D. Lopez and A. Jimenez (Berkeley, CA: Berkeley Public Policy Press, 2003).

18. D. Reed and J. Cheng, *Racial and Ethnic Wage Gaps in the California Labor Market* (San Francisco: Public Policy Institute of California, 2003) (available at www.ppic.org/content/pubs/report/R_503DRR.pdf). The authors based their estimates on the Census Bureau's Public Use Microdata Sample for 1979 and 1989, and obtain the 2000 numbers by pooling the 1999–2001 figures from the Outgoing Rotation Group data from the Current Population Survey.

19. Jargowsky, *Stunning Progress*.

20. A. Berube and B. Katz, *Katrina's Window: Confronting Concentrated Poverty across America* (Washington, DC: Brookings Institution, 2005) (available at www.brookings.edu/metro/pubs/20051012_concentratedpoverty.htm).

21. J. C. Booza, J. Cutsinger, and G. Galster, *Where Did They Go? The Decline of Middle-Income Neighborhoods in Metropolitan America* (Washington, DC: Brookings Institution, 2006) (available at www.brookings.edu/metro/pubs/20060622_middleclass.htm).

22. Booza et al., *Where Did They Go?*

23. W. H. Frey, *Diversity Spreads Out: Metropolitan Shifts in Hispanic, Asian, and Black Populations Since 2000* (Washington, DC: Brookings Institution, 2006), 6 (available at www.brookings.edu/metro/pubs/20060307_frey.htm).

24. M. Pastor, "¿Quién es Más Urbanista? Latinos and 'Smart Growth,'" in *Growing Smarter: Achieving Livable Communities, Environmental Justice, and Regional Equity*, ed. R. Bullard (Cambridge, MA: MIT Press, 2007).

25. P. J. Ethington, W. H. Frey, and D. Myers, *The Racial Resegregation of Los Angeles County, Public Research Report 2001–04* (Los Angeles: University of Southern California Race Contours Project, 2001), 12–13 (available at www.rcf.usc.edu/~philipje/CENSUS_MAPS/ Haynes_Reports/Contours_PRR_2001-04e.pdf).

26. Researchers looked at a measure of residential segregation called the entropy index. The advantage of this measure is that it controls for the existing diversity of the overall population and is therefore a better measure of the geographic evenness of the population than either the traditional dissimilarity measure used in most segregation studies or the exposure index used above. See the discussion in J. Iceland, *The Multigroup Entropy Index (also known as Theil's H or the Information Theory Index)* (College Park: University of Maryland, 2004). The superiority of the entropy measure is explored in S. F. Reardon and G. Firebaugh, "Measures of Multigroup Segregation," *Sociological Methodology*, 32, vol. 1 (2002): 33–67. The data are also available at www.census.gov. There are 325 metropolitan areas for which this measure is available for 1980 through 2000. I calculated

the change in the score and found that 23 of 25 of California's metro areas were in the top one-third of the national set in terms of changes in the entropy score for non-Latino whites; 18 of these areas actually saw an increase in segregation over the time, which works against the modest national trends toward residential integration.

27. Field Research Corporation, "A Digest Summarizing California's Vote in the 2004 Presidential Election," *California Opinion Index* 1 (2005): 2–4 (available at field.com/fieldpollonline/subscribers/COI-05-Jan-Demography.pdf).

28. Field Research Corporation, "A Digest Summarizing California's Vote."

29. Field Research Corporation, "A Digest Summarizing California's Vote."

30. Baldassare, *PPIC Statewide Survey.*

31. Researchers have also found that inequity can lead to more health problems in the general population, which can reduce workers' efficiency. Others have focused on how income inequality can breed corruption leading to inefficiencies in economic markets. See A. Bernasek, "Income Inequality and Its Cost," *New York Times*, June 25, 2006.

32. W. Barnes and L. C. Ledebur, *The New Regional Economies: The U.S. Common Market and the Global Economy* (Thousand Oaks, CA: Sage Publications, 1998); M. Pastor, P. Dreier, E. Grigsby, and M. López-Garza, *Regions That Work: How Cities and Suburbs Can Grow Together* (Minneapolis: University of Minnesota Press, 2000); R. Voith, "Do Suburbs Need Cities?" *Journal of Regional Science* 38, no. 3 (1998): 445–65. See also M. Pastor, "Cohesion and Competitiveness: Business Leadership for Regional Growth and Social Equity," in *OECD Territorial Reviews, Competitive Cities in the Global Economy* (Paris: Organization for Economic Co-Operation and Development, 2006). This study looked at 341 metropolitan areas in the United States and found that spatial segregation was associated with lower economic growth.

33. R. Eberts, G. Erickcek, and J. Kleinhenz, *Dashboard Indicators for the Northeast Ohio Economy: Prepared for the Fund for Our Economic Future* (Cleveland, OH: Federal Reserve Bank of Cleveland, 2006).

34. Data are derived from percentage estimates in H. Johnson, "Differences among California Regions," Presentation at the conference, "Census 2000: Growing Together or Apart? Population Trends and Their Implications for Cities and Metropolitan Areas," sponsored by the Berkeley Program on Housing and Urban Policy (University of California, Berkeley, 2002); and California and U.S. population data taken from www.census.gov/dmd/www/resapport/states/california.pdf and www.censusscope.org/us/chart_popl.html.

35. M. Pastor, "Poverty, Work, and Public Policy: Latinos in California's New Economy," in *Mexicanos in California: Transformations and Challenges*, eds. P. Zavella, R. Gutiérrez, D. Segura, D. Trevizo, and J. V. Palerme (Champaign: University of Illinois Press, 2008).

36. G. Borjas, *Heaven's Door: Immigration Policy and the American Economy* (Princeton, NJ: Princeton University Press, 2001).

37. D. Card, "Is the New Immigration Really So Bad?" (Working Paper no. 11547, Cambridge, MA: National Bureau of Economic Research, 2005).

38. L. Mishel, J. Bernstein, and S. Allegretto, *The State of Working America, 2004/2005* (Washington, DC: Economic Policy Institute, 2005).

39. I use the hourly wage variable, which is only available for a portion of those in the March CPS sample, because it is only collected for those who are in particular months of the rotating sample and are actually employed.

40. Note, however, that the wage penalty for being African American actually increased slightly, perhaps reflecting issues of displacement or increased employer discrimination. For more on persistent and growing discrimination against African Americans in the hiring process, including in California, see P. Moss and C. Tilly, *Stories Employers Tell: Race, Skill, and Hiring in America* (New York: Russell Sage Press, 2001). The regressions also include a dummy variable for each year so as to control for business cycle effects on the stability of the coefficients. The importance of education as an explanation for poor Latino outcomes is stressed in S. J. Trejo, "Why Do Mexican Americans Earn Low Wages?" *Journal of Political Economy* 105, no. 6 (1997): 1235–68.

41. For comparability, I do this by running a regression without the migrant variable (as in table 5.1) for the same periods (1994–96 and 2003–05).

42. California Employment Development Department, *The Top Fifty Occupations with the Largest Estimated Growth from 2002 to 2012* (Sacramento, CA: California Employment Development Department, 2006) (available at www.labormarketinfo.edd.ca.gov/cgi/).

43. These analyses were conducted by downloading the state's occupational projections from http://www.labormarketinfo.edd.ca.gov/ and then conducting breakdowns on the education requirements. The wage figures shown later were derived by utilizing the median wage provided for the occupation by the Employment Development Department (in some cases, no median was available, often because of the part-time nature of the job, and the top code was $70), and then utilizing the number of projected new jobs as the weight for calculating the average and median wage for future jobs in those education categories.

44. R. Murnane and F. Levy, *Teaching the New Basic Skills* (New York: The Free Press, 1996).

45. F. Levy and R. J. Murnane, *The New Division of Labor: How Computers Are Creating the Next Job Market* (Princeton, NJ: Princeton University Press, 2004).

46. D. Neumark, *California's Economic Future and Infrastructure Challenges* (San Francisco: Public Policy Institute of California, 2005) (available at www.ppic.org/content/pubs/op/OP_605DNOP.pdf).

47. I take the aggregate numbers reported here from Public Policy Institute of California, *Just the Facts: California's Future Economy* (September 2006), which is based on projections from the California Department of Transportation (2005) (available at www.ppic.org/content/pubs/jtf/JTF_FutureEconomyJTF.pdf).

48. "Inequality and the American Dream," *The Economist*, U.S. edition (2006, June 17) (available at www.economist.com/opinion/displaystory.cfm?story_id=E1_SDVJTVV).

49. Baldassare, *PPIC Statewide Survey*.

50. M. Pastor and C. Zabin, "Recession and Reaction: The Impact of the Downturn on California Labor," in *The State of California Labor 2002*, ed. R. Milkman (Berkeley: University of California Press, 2002).

51. P. J. Murphy, *Financing California's Community Colleges* (San Francisco: Public Policy Institute of California, 2004).

52. M. Pastor and E. Marcelli, "Men in the Hood: Spatial, Skill, and Social Mismatch for Male Workers in Los Angeles," *Urban Geography* 21, no. 6 (2000).

53. For a good review of innovations in job training, particularly in California, see M. Bernick, *Job Training That Gets Results: Ten Principles of Effective Employment Programs* (Kalamazoo, MI: W.E. Upjohn Institute for Employment Research, 2005).

CHAPTER 6

1. See M. A. Stoll, *African Americans and the Color Line* (New York: Russell Sage Foundation and Population Reference Bureau, 2004). The category "college and above" includes those who completed a bachelor's, master's, doctorate, or other professional degree.

2. Stoll, *African Americans and the Color Line.*

3. K. J. Bauman, "Schools, Markets and Family in the History of African American Schooling," *American Journal of Education* 106, no. 4 (1998): 500–31.

4. L. Mishel, J. Bernstein, and H. Boushey, *The State of Working America 2002–03* (Ithaca, NY: Cornell University Press, 2003).

5. M. K. Blackburn, D. E. Bloom, and R. B. Freeman, "The Declining Economic Position of Less Skilled American Men," in *A Future of Lousy Jobs? The Changing Structure of U.S. Wages,* ed. G. Burtless (Washington, DC: Brookings Institution, 1990).

6. J. Bound and R. B. Freeman, "What Went Wrong? The Erosion of the Relative Earnings and Employment among Young Black Men in the 1980s," *Quarterly Journal of Economics* 107, no. 1 (1992): 201–32.

7. G. D. Jaynes and R. M. Williams, Jr., eds., *A Common Destiny: Blacks and American Society* (Washington, DC: National Academy Press, 1989).

8. M. L. Blackburn et al., "Declining Economic Position of Less Skilled American Men."

9. Jaynes and Williams, *A Common Destiny.*

10. Bound and Freeman, "What Went Wrong?"

11. S. Danziger, R. Farley, and H. J. Holzer, *Detroit Divided* (New York: Russell Sage Foundation, 2000).

12. J. D. Kasarda, "Industrial Restructuring and the Changing Location of Jobs," in *State of the Union: American in the 1990s, Vol. 1: Economic Trends,* ed. Reynolds Farley (New York: Russell Sage, 1995), 215–68.

13. W. J. Wilson, *The Truly Disadvantaged: The Inner City, the Underclass, and Public Policy* (Chicago: University of Chicago Press, 1987).

14. Bound and Freeman, "What Went Wrong?"; L. Quillian, "The Decline of Male Employment in Low-Income Black Neighborhoods, 1950–1990," *Social Science Research* 32, no. 2 (2002): 220–50.

15. M. A. Stoll, H. J. Holzer, and K. R. Ihlanfeldt, "Within Cities and Suburbs: Racial Residential Concentration and the Distribution of Employment Opportunities Across Sub-Metropolitan Areas," *Journal of Policy Analysis and Management* 19, no. 2 (2000): 207–31; S. Raphael, "The Spatial Mismatch Hypothesis of Black Youth Unemployment: Evidence from the San Francisco Bay Area," *Journal of Urban Economics* 43 (1998): 79–111; also see P. Ong and V. Terriquez, "Can Multiple Pathways Offset Inequalities in the Urban Spatial Structure?" in this volume.

16. P. A. Jargowsky, "Stunning Progress, Hidden Problems: The Dramatic Decline of Concentrated Poverty in the 1990s," *The Living Cities Census Series* (Washington, DC: Brookings Institution, Center on Urban and Metropolitan Policy, 2003).

17. Wilson, *The Truly Disadvantaged.*

18. For more evidence, see H. J. Holzer and P. Offner, "Trends in Employment Outcomes of Young Black Men, 1979–2000," in *Black Males Left Behind,* ed. R. Mincy (Washington, DC: The Urban Institute, 2006).

19. D. H. Autor, L. F. Katz, and A. B. Krueger, "Computing Inequality: Have Computers

Changed the Labor Market?" *Quarterly Journal of Economics* 113, no. 4 (November 1998): 1169–1214; D. H. Autor, F. Levy, and R. J. Murnane, "The Skill Content of Recent Technological Change: An Empirical Exploration," *Quarterly Journal of Economics* 118, no. 4 (July 2003).

20. P. Cappelli, "Technology and Skill Requirements: Implications for Establishment Wage Structure," *New England Economic Review* (May/June, 1996): 139–56.

21. Autor et al., "The Skill Content of Recent Technological Change."

22. U.S. Department of Commerce, *The Digital Workforce: Building Infotech Skill at the Speed of Innovation* (Washington, DC: U.S. Department of Commerce, 1999). Information technology positions range from technical support, network administration, web page design, software development, 3D animation, digital video editing, and mapping to hardware repair and maintenance and database management and design.

23. Autor et al., "Computing Inequality."

24. Heldrich Center for Workforce Development at Rutgers University and Center for Survey Research and Analysis at the University of Connecticut, *Nothing but Net: American Workers and the Information Economy* (Newark, NJ: Rutgers University, 2000).

25. U.S. Department of Commerce, *Digital Economy 2000* (Washington, DC: U.S. Department of Commerce, 2000).

26. M. Pastor, "United or Divided: Can Multiple Pathways Bring Together Multiple Communities?" in this volume.

27. U.S. Department of Commerce, *The Digital Workforce*.

28. The basis of this discussion was developed in H. J. Holzer, S. Raphael, and M. A. Stoll, "Can Employers Play a More Positive Role in Prisoner Reentry?" working paper (Washington, DC: The Urban Institute Reentry Roundtable, 2002).

29. H. J. Holzer, *What Employers Want* (New York: Russell, 1996); P. Moss and C. Tilly, *Stories Employers Tell: Race, Skill and Hiring in America* (New York: Russell Sage, 2001).

30. F. Levy and R. Murnane, *Teaching the New Basic Skills* (New York: Free Press, 1996).

31. H. J. Holzer, "Employer Skill Demands and Labor Market Outcomes of Blacks and Women," *Industrial and Labor Relations Review* 52, no. 1 (1998): 82–98.

32. H. J. Holzer and K. R. Ihlanfeldt, "Customer Discrimination and Employment Outcomes for Minority Workers," *Quarterly Journal of Economics* 113 (1998): 835–67.

33. H. J. Holzer, S. Raphael, and M. A. Stoll, "Perceived Criminality, Background Checks, and the Racial Hiring Practices of Employers?" *Journal of Law and Economics* 49, no. 2 (2006): 451–80; J. Kirschenman and K. Neckerman, "We'd Love to Hire Them But . . ." in *The Urban Underclass*, eds. C. Jencks and P. Peterson (Washington, DC: The Brookings Institution, 1991).

34. H. J. Holzer and K.R. Ihlanfeldt, "Spatial Factors and the Employment of Blacks at the Firm Level," *New England Economic Review* May/June (1996): 65–86.

35. Holzer et al., "Perceived Criminality, Background Checks."

36. R. Freeman and W. M. Rodgers III, "Area Economic Conditions and the Labor Market Outcomes of Young Men in the 1990's Expansion," in *Prosperity for All? The Economic Boom and African Americans*, eds. R. Cherry and W. M. Rodgers III (New York: Russell Sage, 2000), 50–87.

37. Ong and Terriquez, "Can Multiple Pathways Offset Inequalities?" in this volume.

38. M. A. Stoll, "Geographic Skills Mismatch, Job Search, and Race," *Urban Studies* 42, no. 4 (2005): 695–717.

39. Kasarda, "Industrial Restructuring and the Changing Location of Jobs."

40. J. Grogger and S. J. Trejo, *Falling Behind or Moving Up? The Intergenerational Progress of Mexican Americans* (San Francisco: Public Policy Institute of California, 2002).

41. M. Rose, "Blending 'Hand Work' and 'Brain Work': Can Multiple Pathways Deepen Learning?" in this volume.

42. R. J. LaLonde, "The Promise of Public Sector-Sponsored Training Programs," *Journal of Economic Perspectives* 9 (1995): 149–68.

43. B. Harrison and M. Weiss, *Workforce Development Networks: Community-Based Organizations and Regional Alliances* (Thousands Oaks, CA: Sage Publications, 1998); R. M. Blank, *It Takes a Nation: A New Agenda for Fighting Poverty*, (New York and Princeton, NJ: Russell Sage Foundation and Princeton University Press, 1997); C. F. Manski and I. Garfinkel, eds., *Evaluating Welfare and Training Programs* (Cambridge, MA: Harvard University Press, 1992).

44. U.S. Department of Labor, *Involving Employers in Training: Best Practices* (Washington, DC: Department of Labor, 1996).

45. R. I. Lerman and H. Pouncy, "The Compelling Case for Youth Apprenticeships," *The Public Interest* Fall (1990): 62–77.

46. M. A. Stoll, "Teaching Trades: A Pending Plan to Train America's Youth," *Dollars & Sense* November/December (1993): 25–36.

47. Lerman and Pouncy, "The Compelling Case for Youth Apprenticeships."

48. C. S. Clark, "Youth Apprenticeships: Can They Improve the School-To-Work Transition?" *CQ Researcher* 2, no. 39 (1992): 905–28.

49. W. B. Johnstone and A. E. Pcker, *Workforce 2000: Work and Workers for the 21st Century* (Indianapolis: Hudson Institute, 1987).

50. See J. Oakes, *Keeping Track: How Schools Structure Inequality* (New Haven, CT: Yale University Press, 1985/2005); S. R. Lucas, *Tracking Inequality: Stratification and Mobility in American High Schools* (New York: Teachers College Press, 1999); J. Oakes, A. Gamoran, and R. Page, "Curriculum Differentiation: Opportunities, Consequences, and Meanings," in *Handbook of Research on Curriculum*, ed. P. A. Jackson (New York: Macmillan, 1992).

51. D. Stern and R. Stearns, "Evidence and Challenges: Will Multiple Pathways Improve Students' Outcomes?" in this volume.

52. D. J. Reller, *The Peninsula Academies: Final Technical Evaluation Report* (Palo Alto, CA: The American Institutes for Research in the Behavioral Sciences, 1984); C. Dayton, A. Weisberg, and D. Stern, *California Partnership Academies: 1987–88 Evaluation Report* (Berkeley: University of California, Policy Analysis for California Education, 1989); D. Stern, C. Dayton, I. W. Paik, and A. Weisberg, "Benefits and Costs of Dropout Prevention in a High School Program Combining Academic and Vocational Education: Third-Year Results from Replications of the California Partnership Academies, *Educational Evaluation and Policy Analysis* 11, no. 4 (1989): 405–16; additional citations in D. Stern, M. Raby, and C. Dayton, *Career Academies: Partnerships for Reconstructing American High Schools* (San Francisco: Jossey-Bass, 1992); and M. Raby, "The Career Academies," in *Education through Occupations in American High Schools* (Vol. 1), ed. W. N. Grubb (New York: Teachers College Press, 1995), 82–96.

53. C. Dayton, *California Partnership Academies: 1995–96 Evaluation Report* (Nevada City, CA: Foothill Associates, 1997).

54. Oakes, *Keeping Track*; F. Mosteller, R. J. Light, and J. A. Sachs, "Sustained Inquiry in Education: Lessons in Skill Grouping and Class Size," *Harvard Educational Review* 66, no. 4 (1996): 707–842.

55. N. L. Maxwell and V. Rubin, *The Relative Impact of a Career Academy on Post-Secondary Work and Education Skills in Urban, Public High Schools*, HIRE Discussion Paper #97-2 (Hayward: The Human Investment Research and Education Center, School of Business and Economics, California State University–Hayward, 1997).

56. N. L. Maxwell and V. Rubin, *High School Career Academies: A Pathway to Educational Reform in Urban Schools?* (Kalamazoo, MI: W. E. Upjohn Institute for Employment Research, 2000).

57. N. L. Maxwell, *Step to College: Moving from the High School Career Academy through the Four-Year University* (Berkeley: National Center for Research in Vocational Education, University of California–Berkeley, 1999).

58. Employers spend a nontrivial amount of money to keep any one low-skill job filled, particularly when one factors in the high turnover rates that are characteristic of these jobs. Research indicates that employers' search costs for low- to semi-skilled workers are on average between $300 and $1,500, depending on how difficult it is to find appropriate labor, and that training costs for these workers range from $700 to $3,000, depending on the type of training required (H. Frazis, M. Gittleman, M. Horrigan, and M. Jovce, "Results from the 1995 Survey of Employer-Provided Training," *Monthly Labor Review* 121 (1998): 3–13; J. Bishop, *The Incidence of and Payoff to Employer Training*, CAHRS working paper #94-17 (Ithaca, NY: Cornell University, School of Industrial and Labor Relations, Center for Advanced Human Resource Studies, 1994).

59. F. Levy and R. Murnane, *Teaching the New Basic Skills* (New York: The Free Press, 1996).

60. M. A. Stoll, S. Raphael, and H. J. Holzer, "Black Job Applicants and the Hiring Officer's Race," *Industrial and Labor Relations Review* 57, no. 2 (2004): 267–87.

61. Northwest Center for Emerging Technologies (NWCET), *Building a Foundation for Tomorrow: Skill Standards for Information Technology* (Bellevue, WA: NWCET, 1999).

62. S. Bliss, *San Francisco Works: Toward an Employer-Led Approach to Welfare Reform and Workforce Development* (New York: Manpower Demonstration Research Corporation, 2000).

63. Annie E. Casey Foundation, *Stronger Links: New Ways to Connect Low-Skill Workers to Better Jobs* (Baltimore: Annie E. Casey Foundation, 2000); J. Strawn, *Beyond Job Search or Basic Education: Rethinking the Role of Skills in Welfare Reform* (Washington, DC: Center for Law and Social Policy, 1998).

64. Pastor, "United or Divided."

65. Bliss, *San Francisco Works*.

CHAPTER 7

1. Neither the University of California nor its All Campus Consortium on Research for Diversity (ACCORD) support or disavow the findings in this paper. University affiliations are for identification only, and the authors are solely responsible for all interpretations and any errors. The authors are indebted for the partial funding provided by ACCORD and for the assistance provided by the Asian American Studies Center.

2. See, for example, P. Ong and J. Rickles, "The Continued Nexus Between School and Residential Segregation," *African-American Law and Policy Report* 6 (2004): 178–93; J. Rickles and P. Ong, "The Integrating (and Segregating) Effect of Charter, Magnet, and Traditional Elementary Schools: The Case of Five California Metropolitan Areas," *Journal of California Politics and Policy* 9, no. 1 (2005): 16–38.

3. For poll results, see http://www.connectedcalifornia.org/downloads/irvine_poll.pdf.

4. D. Rattray, "Making It Real: Implementing Multiple Pathways," in this volume.

5. U.S. Bureau of Labor Statistics, "Labor Force Statistics from the Current Population Survey," table A-1. Employment status of the civilian population by sex and age (http://www.bls.gov/webapps/legacy/cpsatab1.htm).

6. U.S. Bureau of Labor Statistics, "Labor Force Statistics."

7. U.S. Department of Labor, "Report on the Youth Labor Force" (2000) (available at http://www.bls.gov/opub/rylf2000.pdf).

8. W. Carr, J. D. Wright, and C. Brody, "Effects of High School Work Experience a Decade Later: Evidence from the National Longitudinal Survey," *Sociology of Education* 69, no. 1 (1996): 66–81; K. Singh, "Part-Time Employment in High School and Its Effects on Academic Achievement," *Journal of Educational Research* 91, no. 3 (1998): 131–39.

9. C. Ruhm, "Is High School Employment Consumption or Investment?" *Journal of Labor Economics* 15, no. 4 (1997): 735–77; G. Oettinger, "Does High School Employment Affect High School Academic Performance?" *Industrial and Labor Relations Review* 53, no. 1 (1999): 136–51; U.S. Department of Labor, "Report on the Youth Labor Force"; J. Payne, "The Impact of Part-Time Jobs in Year 12 and 13 on Qualification Achievement," *British Educational Research Journal* 29, no. 4 (2003): 559–611.

10. National Research Council, *Protecting Youth at Work* (Washington, DC: National Academies Press, 1998).

11. W. Carr et al., "Effects of High School Work Experience a Decade Later."

12. C. Ruhm, "Is High School Employment Consumption or Investment?" *Journal of Labor Economics* 15, no. 4 (1997): 735–77.

13. J. W. Ainsworth and V. Rosigno, "Stratification, School-Work Linkages and Vocational Educations," *Social Forces* 84, no. 1 (2005): 257–84; S. Bowles and H. Gintis, "Schooling in Capitalist America Revisited," *Sociology of Education* 75 (2002): 1–18; S. Lucas and M. Berends, "Sociodemographic Diversity, Correlated Achievement and De Facto Tracking," *Sociology of Education* 75 (2002): 328–48; J. Oakes, *Keeping Track: How Schools Structure Inequality* (2nd ed.) (New Haven, CT: Yale University Press, 2005).

14. F. Linnehan, "The Relation of a Work-Based Mentoring Program to the Academic Performance and Behavior of African-American Students," *Journal of Vocational Behavior* 59, no. 3 (2001): 310–25.

15. D. E. Mitchell, *California Regional Occupational Centers and Programs (ROCP) 2004 Longitudinal Study Technical Report* (Riverside: School Improvement Research Group, University of California–Riverside, 2004).

16. J. H. Kemple and J. Scott-Clayton, *Career Academies: Impacts on Labor Market Outcomes and Educational Attainment* (New York: Manpower Demonstration Research Corporation, 2004) (available at mdrc.org/publications/336/full.pdf).

17. A. Furco, "Service-learning and School-to-work: Making the Connections," *Journal of Cooperative Education* 32, no. 1 (1995): 7–14; A. Rogers, *Learning from Experience: A Cross*

Case Comparison of Schools to Work Transition Initiatives (Washington, DC: Academy for Educational Development, 2002).

18. J. F. Kain., "Housing Segregation, Negro Employment, and Metropolitan Decentralization," *Quarterly Journal of Economics* 82, no. 2 (1968): 175–97; J. F. Kain, "A Pioneer's Perspective on the Spatial Mismatch Literature," *Urban Studies* 41, no. 1 (2004): 7–32.

19. J. Kasarda, "Urban Industrial Transition and the Underclass," *Annals of the American Academy of Political and Social Science* 501 (1990): 26–47.

20. M. M. Zonta, "Employment Opportunities Beyond the 'Hood,'" in *Jobs and Economic Development in Minority Communities*, eds. P. Ong and A. Loukiatou-Sideris (Philadelphia: Temple University Press, 2006), 119–140.

21. W. J. Wilson, *The Truly Disadvantaged: The Inner City, the Underclass, and Public Policy* (Chicago: University of Chicago Press, 1987); W. J. Wilson, *When Work Disappears in the City: The World of the New Urban Poor* (New York: Knopf, 1996).

22. In this sense, "networks" refers to many of the nuances found in these simple dictionary definitions of the term: (a) a system of lines or channels that cross or interconnect: *a network of railroads:* (b) an extended group of people with similar interests or concerns who interact and remain in informal contact for mutual assistance or support.

23. B. D. Taylor and P. Ong, "Spatial Mismatch or Auto Mobile Mismatch: An Examination of Race, Residence and Commuting in U.S. Metropolitan Areas," *Urban Studies* 32, no. 9 (1996): 1453–73; P. Ong and D. Miller, "Spatial and Transportation Mismatch in Los Angeles," *Journal of Planning, Education and Research* 25, no. 1 (2004): 43–65; Zonta, "Employment Opportunities."

24. Taylor and Ong, "Spatial Mismatch or Auto Mobile Mismatch"; P. Ong, "Work and Automobile Ownership among Welfare Recipients," *Social Work Research* 30, no. 4 (1996): 255–62; S. Raphael and M. A. Stoll, "Can Boosting Minority Car Ownership Rates Narrow Inter-Racial Employment Gaps?" *Brookings-Wharton Papers on Urban Affairs* 2 (2001): 99–137; S. Raphael and L. Rice, "Car Ownership, Employment, and Earnings," *Journal of Urban Economics* 52, no. 1 (2002): 109–30; P. Ong, "Car Ownership and Welfare-to-Work," *Journal of Policy Analysis and Management* 21, no. 2 (2002): 255–68; Ong and Miller, "Spatial and Transportation Mismatch in Los Angeles."

25. J. Kirschenman and K. M. Neckerman, "We'd Love to Hire Them, But . . . : The Meaning of Race for Employers" in *The Urban Underclass*, eds. C. Jencks and P. E. Peterson (Washington, DC: The Brookings Institution, 1991), 203–32.

26. T. Mouw, "Are Black Workers Missing the Connection? The Effect of Spatial Distance and Employee Referrals on Interfirm Racial Segregation," *Demography* 39, no. 3 (2002): 507–28.

27. K. O'Regan and J. Quigley, "Teenage Employment and the Spatial Isolation of Minority and Poverty Households," *Journal of Human Resources* 31 (1996): 692–702.

28. S. Raphael, "The Spatial Mismatch Hypothesis and Black Youth Joblessness: Evidence from the San Francisco Bay Area," *Journal of Urban Economics* 43 (1998): 79–111.

29. K. R. Ihlanfeldt and D. C. Sjoquist, "Job Accessibility and Racial Differences in Youth Employment Rates," *American Economic Review* 80, no. 1 (1990): 267–76.

30. D. Ellwood, "The Spatial Mismatch Hypothesis: Are There Teenage Jobs Missing in the Ghetto?" in *The Black Youth Employment Crisis*, eds. R. B. Freeman and H. J. Holzer (Chicago: University of Chicago Press, 1986), 147–85.

31. PUMS contains socioeconomic and demographic information for 5% of the population. Our sample is restricted to youth in Los Angeles County between the ages of 16 and 18 who are enrolled in high school and not in the military. Employment status is determined from two variables. The first variable is based on whether the person was employed during the week prior to the census. The second is based on employment in the prior year (e.g., in 1999 for the 2000 census) or any time up to the time of the census (based on occupation of current or any previous job). This information is used to construct three employment indicators: (1) currently employed ("current week"), (2) employed either currently or any time last year ("one plus year"), and (3) employed any time. Each measure provides a different time span in determining work experience.

32. The first is the most restrictive definition and captures employment during the school year, given that the census is conducted in April. The second captures any employment for a period greater than a year (current week and prior year), including summers and winter vacations. Finally, the third indicator provides the least restrictive definition of work experience.

33. The race/ethnicity categories are created by combining information from the single-race and Hispanic variables. The non-Hispanic (NH) white category includes those who are white (single-race) and not Hispanic. The black category includes single-race blacks regardless of Hispanic origin; the Asian category includes single-race Asians regardless of Hispanic origin; and the Hispanic category includes those of Hispanic origin but not in one of the major minority groups (single-race blacks, Asians, American Indians, and Pacific Islanders).

34. Interestingly, very little difference exists between these two groups (with one or no vehicle). This may be due to the fact that adults, rather than the high school student, use the vehicle when one is present.

35. In LAUSD, more than half of students who enrolled as ninth graders in September of 2001 did not graduate four years later. California Department of Education, *California Basic Educational Data System (CBEDS)* (Sacramento: California Department of Education, 2006) (available at www.cde.ca.gov/ds/sd/cb/).

36. Los Angeles Unified School District (LAUSD), *Career Academies* (Los Angeles: Author, 2006) (available at http://notebook.lausd.net/portal/page?_pageid=33,153246&_dad=ptl&_schema=PTL_EP).

37. As new schools opened and others closed, the number of LAUSD high schools has changed within the past year.

38. LAUSD, *Career Academies*.

39. One way for schools to integrate students into the local economy is through the business community. Most LAUSD career academies are linked to a business partner that can potentially help schools overcome spatial and transportation mismatches. Schools may also benefit from the assistance of Unite-LA, a nonprofit organization affiliated with the Los Angeles Chamber of Commerce that facilitates partnerships between the career academies and businesses.

40. Analysis of California Department of Education data for the 2004–05 school year indicates that more work-experience courses were offered at schools without career academies than those with career academies. California Department of Education, *California Basic Educational Data Systems (CBEDS)*.

41. California DOE, *CBEDS*.

42. Our findings are based on regression analyses using California Department of Education data for 2005–06.

43. Adults comprise 30% of enrollments, according to California Department of Education (CDE), *Regional Occupational Centers and Programs (ROCP) Basics* (Sacramento: CDE, 2007) (available at www.cde.ca.gov/ci/ct/rp/basics.asp).

44. Mitchell, *California Regional Occupational Centers and Programs.*

45. See www.verbumdei.us/about.html for more information.

46. In 2001, Verbum Dei enrolled 100 ninth graders. According to California Postsecondary Education Commission, 43 Verbum Dei graduates enrolled as first-time freshmen in California's public colleges four years later. Meanwhile, approximately 26 out of every 100 ninth graders statewide enrolled as first-time freshmen in California's public colleges and universities four years later. J. Rogers, V. Terriquez, S. Valladeres, and J. Oakes, *California Educational Opportunity Report 2006: Roadblocks to College* (Los Angeles: Institute for Democracy Education and Access, University of California–Los Angeles, 2006) (available at www.idea.gseis.ucla.edu/publications/eor06/fullreport/pdf/EOR-2006.pdf).

CHAPTER 8

Note: Frequent reference is made to portions of the 37-volume compilation of John Dewey's complete writings, *The Collected Works of John Dewey, 1882–1953*, ed. J. Boydston (Carbondale: Southern Illinois University Press 1969–1991). The work was published in three series, referenced herein in shorthand by series and volume number, as follows: *EW, The Early Works, 1882–1898* (vols. 1–5); *MW, The Middle Works, 1899–1924* (vols. 1–15); and *LW, The Later Works, 1925–1953* (vols. 1–17).

1. J. Dewey, "Some Dangers in the Present Movement for Industrial Education," *MW* 7 (1913), 98–103.

2. J. Dewey, "The Need of an Industrial Education in an Industrial Democracy," *MW* 10 (1916b), 137–43.

3. M. Lazerson and W. N. Grubb, eds., "American Education and Vocationalism: A Documentary History, 1870–1970," *Report of the Commission on National Aid to Vocational Education* (New York: Teachers College Press, 1913), 116–32.

4. Lazerson and Grubb, "American Education and Vocationalism," 124.

5. Lazerson and Grubb, "American Education and Vocationalism," 125–6.

6. Lazerson and Grubb, "American Education and Vocationalism," 127.

7. Our discussion of advocates of Multiple Pathways refers to a set of reports and articles from experts in career and technical education. These reports generally make a case for integrating career and technical education with academic preparation.

8. Kliebard argues that this focus on the economic ends of schooling is a direct result of the campaign to expand vocational education in the early twentieth century. That is, the early advocates for vocational education succeeded not just in expanding vocational education opportunities, but also in framing the purposes of curriculum in economic terms. H. Kliebard, *Schooled to Work: Vocationalism and the American Curriculum* (New York: Teachers College Press, 1999).

9. H. Meeder, *Reinventing the American High School for the 21st Century* (Washington, DC: Association for Career and Technical Education, 2006), 5.

10. Meeder, *Reinventing the American High School*, 5.
11. R. Kazis et al., *Ready for Tomorrow: Helping All Students Achieve Secondary and Postsecondary Success* (Washington, DC: National Governors Association, 2003).
12. Meeder, *Reinventing the American High School*; B. Brand, *Rigor and Relevance: A New Vision for Career and Technical Education* (Washington, DC: American Youth Policy Forum, 2003).
13. Brand, *Rigor and Relevance*, 7.
14. Brand, *Rigor and Relevance*, 1.
15. Lazerson and Grubb, "American Education and Vocationalism," 124.
16. Brand, *Rigor and Relevance*; Kazis, *Ready for Tomorrow*; Meeder, *Reinventing the American High School*.
17. Brand, *Rigor and Relevance*, ii; Meeder, *Reinventing the American High School*, 24.
18. R. Niemi and J. Junn, *Civic Education: What Makes Students Learn?* (New Haven, CT: Yale University Press, 1998); M. Delli-Carpini and S. Keeter, *What Americans Know about Politics and Why It Matters* (New Haven, CT: Yale University Press, 1996); C. Gibson and P. Levine, *The Civic Mission of Schools* (New York and Washington, DC: The Carnegie Corporation of New York and the Center for Information and Research on Civic Learning, 2003).
19. Gibson and Levine, *The Civic Mission of Schools*.
20. R. Putnam, *Bowling Alone: The Collapse and Revival of American Community* (New York: Simon and Schuster, 2000); H. Sanford, *The NASS New Millennium Survey: American Youth Attitudes on Politics, Citizenship, Government and Voting* (Washington, DC: The National Association of Secretaries of State, 1999) (available at www.stateofthevote.org/survey/index.htm); W. Galston, "Political Knowledge, Political Engagement, and Civic Education," *Annual Review of Political Science* 4 (2001): 217–34; S. Macedo et al., *Democracy at Risk: How Political Choices Undermine Citizen Participation, and What We Can Do about It* (Washington, DC: Brookings Institution Press, 2005); Gibson and Levine, *The Civic Mission of Schools*.
21. Educating for Democracy, *The California Survey of Civic Education* (Los Angeles: The Constitutional Rights Foundation, 2005) (available at www.cms-ca.org/research.htm). Joseph Kahne was the lead investigator on this study.
22. Educating for Democracy, *The California Survey of Civic Education*.
23. Educating for Democracy, *The California Survey of Civic Education*.
24. Their analysis of these data also indicate that the declining impact of educational institutions on students' civic knowledge rather than selection bias (the fact that a much smaller percentage of students went to college in the 1940s and 1950s) accounts for this outcome. See Delli-Carpini and Keeter, *What Americans Know about Politics and Why It Matters*.
25. A. D. Lutkus and A. R. Weiss, *The Nation's Report Card: Civics 2006*, NCES Publication no. 2007476 (Washington, DC: U.S. Department of Education, National Center for Education Statistics, U.S. Government Printing Office, 2007).
26. J. Lee and A. R. Weiss, *The Nation's Report Card: U.S. History 2006*, NCES Publication no. 2007476 (Washington, DC: U.S. Department of Education, National Center for Education Statistics, U.S. Government Printing Office, 2007).
27. C. Cohen and M. Dawson, "Neighborhood Poverty and African American Politics," *American Political Science Review* 87, no. 2 (1993): 286–302.

28. S. Verba, K. Schlozman, and H. Brady, *Voice and Equality: Civic Voluntarism in American Politics* (Cambridge, MA: Harvard University Press, 1995).

29. American Political Science Association Task Force on Inequality and American Democracy, "American Democracy in an Age of Rising Inequality," *Perspectives on Politics* 2, no. 4 (2004): 651–66.

30. Gibson and Levine, *The Civic Mission of Schools*; J. Torney-Purta, "The School's Role in Developing Civic Engagement: A Study of Adolescents in Twenty-Eight Countries," *Applied Developmental Science* 6, no. 4 (2002): 203–12; E. C. Metz and J. Youniss, "Longitudinal Gains in Civic Development through School-Based Required Service," *Political Psychology* 26, no. 3 (2005): 413–38; M. McDevitt and S. Kiousis, *Education for Deliberative Democracy: The Long-Term Influence of Kids Voting*, working paper no. 22 (College Park: Center for Information and Research on Civic Engagement, University of Maryland, 2006); J. Kahne, B. Chi, and E. Middaugh, "Building Social Capital for Civic and Political Engagement: The Potential of High School Civics Courses," *Canadian Journal of Education* 29, no. 2 (2006): 387–409; J. Kahne and J. Westheimer, "Teaching Democracy: What Schools Need to Do," *Phi Delta Kappan* 85, no. 1 (2003): 34–40, 57–67.

31. W. Galston, "Civic Education and Political Participation," *PS Online* (April 2004): 263–66.

32. Gibson and Levine, *The Civic Mission of Schools*.

33. J. Kahne and S. Sporte, "Developing Citizens: A Longitudinal Study of the Impact of Classroom Practices, Extra-Curricular Activities, Parent Discussions, and Neighborhood Contexts on Students' Commitments to Civic Participation," manuscript submitted for publication, 2007; Gibson and Levine, *The Civic Mission of Schools*.

34. Educating for Democracy, *California Survey of Civic Education*.

35. Educating for Democracy, *California Survey of Civic Education*.

36. Educating for Democracy, *California Survey of Civic Education*.

37. S. Baldi et al., *What Democracy Means to Ninth-Graders: U.S. Results from the International IEA Civic Education Study* (Washington, DC: National Center for Education Statistics, 2001).

38. Kahne and Middaugh, "Building Social Capital for Civic and Political Engagement."

39. H. Kantor, "Work, Education, and Vocational Reform: The Ideological Origins of Vocational Education, 1890–1920," *American Journal of Education* 94, no. 4 (1986): 201–26.

40. Kliebard, *Schooled to Work*.

41. Dewey, "Some Dangers," 98–103.

42. J. Rogers, *Education as Politics, Politics as Education: John Dewey and Critical Intelligence* (unpublished doctoral thesis, Stanford University, 1994), 120.

43. J. Dewey, *Democracy and Education, MW* 9 (1916a), 326.

44. J. Dewey, "Learning to Earn," *MW* 10 (1917), 150.

45. Snedden's student, Charles Prosser, was the principal author of the 1913 report referred to above by the Commission on National Aid to Vocational Education. E. Hyslop-Margison, "Principles for Democratic Learning in Career Education," *Canadian Journal of Education* 26, no. 3 (2001): 341–61.

46. Quoted in A. Wirth, *Education in the Technological Society: The Vocational-Liberal Studies Controversy in the Early Twentieth Century* (Scranton, PA: Intext Educational Publishers, 1972).

47. D. Snedden, "Two Communications," reprinted from *The New Republic* 3 (1915) in *Curriculum Inquiry* 7, no. 1 (1977): 37.

48. Snedden, "Two Communications," 34.

49. D. Snedden, *The Problem of Vocational Education* (Boston: Houghton Mifflin, 1910), 36.

50. Kantor, "Work, Education, and Vocational Reform," 415.

51. J. Dewey, "Education vs. Trade-Training: Reply to David Snedden," *MW* 8 (1915): 412.

52. Dewey, "Education vs. Trade-Training," 411.

53. J. Dewey, "A Policy of Industrial Education," *MW* 7 (1914): 93–97.

54. Dewey, *Democracy and Education*, 318.

55. Dewey, "Education vs. Trade-Training," 411.

56. Dewey, *Democracy and Education*, 320.

57. Dewey, *Democracy and Education*, 328.

58. Dewey, "Education vs. Trade-Training," 412.

59. Dewey, *Democracy and Education*, 326.

60. Dewey, "Education vs. Trade-Training," 411.

61. Dewey, "Some Dangers," 101.

62. Dewey, *Democracy and Education*, 324.

63. Dewey, *Democracy and Education*, 328.

64. Dewey, "The Need of an Industrial Education," 142.

65. Dewey, "The Need of an Industrial Education," 141.

66. Dewey, "Education vs. Trade-Training," 411.

67. Dewey later developed these ideas into a model for participatory social inquiry. See, generally, J. Oakes and J. Rogers, *Learning Power: Organizing for Education and Justice* (New York: Teachers College Press, 2006).

68. Dewey, "The Need of an Industrial Education," 138.

69. Dewey, "The Need of an Industrial Education," 142.

70. Dewey, "The Need of an Industrial Education," 142.

71. Dewey, "The Need of an Industrial Education," 142.

72. Dewey, "The Need of an Industrial Education," 142.

73. Dewey, "The Need of an Industrial Education," 142.

74. Dewey, *Democracy and Education*, 324.

75. Dewey, "Education vs. Trade-Training," 411.

76. For further discussion, see K. H. Quartz and E. Washor, "Meeting the Individual and Collective Aims of Schooling: "Can Multiple Pathways as Small Schools Strike a Balance?" in this volume.

77. H. Boyte and N. Kari, *Building America: The Democratic Promise of Public Work* (Philadelphia: Temple University Press, 1996).

78. Boyte and Kari, *Building America*, 9.

79. T. Lewis, "Towards a Liberal Vocational Education," *Journal of Philosophy of Education* 31, no. 3 (1997): 477–89; Hyslop-Margison, "Principles for Democratic Learning in Career Education"; J. Gregson, "The School-to-Work Movement and Youth Apprenticeship in the U.S.: Educational Reform and Democratic Renewal?" *Journal of Industrial Teacher Education* 32, no. 3 (1995): 1–13.

80. Dewey, "The Need of an Industrial Education," 138.

81. E. Morrell, *Becoming Critical Researchers: Literacy and Empowerment for Urban Youth* (New York: P. Lang, 2004); Oakes and Rogers, *Learning Power*.

82. Kliebard, *Schooled to Work*.

83. H. Kantor and R. Lowe, "Vocationalism Reconsidered," *American Journal of Education* 109, no. 1 (2000): 125–42.

84. Oakes and Rogers, *Learning Power*; J. Anyon, *Radical Possibilities: Public Policy, Urban Education, and a New Social Movement* (New York: Routledge, 2005).

PART III INTRODUCTION

1. J. Oakes, "Can Tracking Research Inform Practice?" *Educational Researcher* 21, no. 4 (1992): 12–22.

CHAPTER 9

1. The author would like to thank Cynthia Ruiz for her thoughtful research and editorial assistance.

2. The following perspectives are presented from my position as the president of UNITE-LA, a nonprofit education intermediary, and vice president of education and workforce development for the Los Angeles Area Chamber of Commerce (LA Chamber), which supports the relevance and rigor of academic and career and technical education opportunities within the Los Angeles Unified School District (LAUSD). In this capacity, UNITE-LA and the LA Chamber staff function as practitioners, researchers, policymakers, and advocates for all K–16 students.

3. The terms "small learning community" and "small school" are used interchangeably throughout this paper, although these two reform strategies often exhibit significant differences in their autonomy, design elements, and implementation. Although not all small schools have been theme-based, the emphasis here will be on the power of themes to contextualize learning and to drive effective schoolwide reform.

4. See, for example, T. L. Friedman, *The World Is Flat: A Brief History of the Twenty-First Century* (New York: Farrar, Strauss & Giroux, 2005).

5. California Association of Regional Occupational Centers and Programs, *ROCP Facts at a Glance 2007–2008* (available at www.carocp.org/pdf/factsheet.pdf).

6. K. Cotton, *New Small Learning Communities: Findings from Recent Literature* (Portland, OR: Northwest Regional Educational Laboratory, 2001) (retrieved from http://www.nwrel.org/scpd/sirs/nslc.pdf); J. Quint, *Meeting Five Critical Challenges of High School Reform: Lessons from Research on Three Reform Models* (New York: Manpower Demonstration Research Corporation [MDRC], 2006) (available at http://www.mdrc.org/publications/428/full.pdf).

7. N. Fogg and P. Harrington, *One Out of Five: Out of School and Out of Work Youth in Los Angeles and Long Beach* (Boston: Center for Labor Market Studies, Northeastern University, 2004).

8. See, for example, J. D. Bransford, A. L. Brown, and R. R. Cocking, eds., *How People Learn: Brain, Mind, Experience, and School* (Washington, DC: National Academies Press, 1999); National Research Council, *Engaging Schools: Fostering High School Students' Motivation to Learn* (Washington, DC: National Academies Press, 2004); B. Rogoff, *Apprenticeship in Thinking: Cognitive Development in Social Context* (New York: Oxford University Press, 1990).

9. J. M. Bridgeland, J. J. Dilulio, Jr., and K. B. Morison, *The Silent Epidemic: Perspectives of High School Dropouts*, a report by Civic Enterprises in association with Peter D. Hart Research Associates for the Bill & Melinda Gates Foundation (Washington, DC: Civic Enterprises LLC, March 2006).

10. K. Haycock, "Closing the Achievement Gap," Educational Leadership 58, no. 6 (2001, March): 6–11.

11. R. J. Murnane and F. Levy, *Teaching the New Basic Skills: Principles for Educating Children to Thrive in a Changing Economy* (New York: The Free Press, 1996).

12. R. Stearns, unpublished report, Office of the President, University of California (undated).

13. The stories of stakeholders who are undertaking the transition of their schools to SLCs are derived from my experiences with high schools in Los Angeles and throughout the United States. Pseudonyms are used in this report for the high schools and neighborhoods described to respect the progress of their efforts.

14. Quite recently, some Los Angeles officials proposed that a new school include a state-of-the-art culinary arts academy. The campus was being built in a community with a high percentage of families living at or below the federal poverty levels, and the plan for the academy was abandoned after the local district superintendent objected. Anticipating that such an academy would be a traditional vocational school, he argued that it would perpetuate the stereotype of low-potential, inner-city children being best suited for low-wage, entry-level service industry jobs.

15. Project Lead the Way (PLTW) is a national school partnership program that aims to prepare an increasing and more diverse group of students to be successful in science, engineering, and engineering technology. PLTW has developed a four-year sequence of courses that, when combined with college-preparatory mathematics and science courses, introduces students to the scope, rigor, and discipline of engineering and engineering technology.

16. See, for example, R. J. Murnane and F. Levy, *The New Division of Labor: How Computers Are Creating the Next Job Market* (New York: Russell Sage Foundation, 2004).

17. J. Kemple and C. Herlihy, *The Talent Development High School Model: Context, Components, and Initial Impacts on Ninth-Grade Students' Engagement and Performance* (New York: MDRC, 2004) (retrieved from http://www.mdrc.org/publications/388/full.pdf); J. Kemple, C. Herlihy, and T. Smith, *Making Progress toward Graduation: Evidence from the Talent Development High School Model* (New York: MDRC, 2005) (retrieved from http://www.mdrc.org/publications/408/full.pdf).

18. J. Rogers, V. Terriquez, S. Valladares, and J. Oakes, *California Educational Opportunity Report: Roadblocks to College* (Los Angeles: Institute for Democracy, Education and Access, University of California–Los Angeles, 2006).

19. C. Miller Lieber and R. A. Poliner, *The Advisory Guide: Designing and Implementing Effective Advisory Programs in Secondary Schools* (Cambridge, MA: Educators for Social Responsibility, 2004).

20. Miller Lieber and Poliner, *The Advisory Guide*.

21. M. A. Raywid, "Themes That Serve High School Well," *Phi Delta Kappan* 87, no. 9 (2006): 654–56.

22. Friedman, *The World Is Flat*.

CHAPTER 10

1. See the analysis of a discourse of crisis, contrasted with a discourse of possibility that leads to more student-centered and community-centered approaches, in J. Harvey and N. Housman, *Crisis or Possibility: Conversations about the American High School* (Washington, DC: National High School Alliance, 2004).

2. L. Cuban, "Reforming Again, Again, and Again," *Educational Researcher* 19, no. 1 (1990): 3–13.

3. See especially J. B. Conant, *The American High School Today: A First Report to Interested Citizens* (New York: McGraw-Hill, 1959); President's Science Advisory Committee, *Youth, Transition to Adulthood: A Report of the President's Science Advisory Committee, Panel on Youth* (Chicago: University of Chicago Press, 1974); National Panel on High School and Adolescent Education, *The Education of Adolescents* (Washington, DC: U.S. Government Printing Office, 1976); P. M. Timpane, S. Abramowitz, S. B. Bobrow, and A. Pascal, *Youth Policy in Transition* (Santa Monica, CA: Rand Corporation, 1976); National Commission on Youth, *The Transition of Youth to Adulthood: A Bridge Too Long* (Boulder, CO: Westview, 1980); Carnegie Council on Policy Studies in Higher Education, *A Summary of Reports and Recommendations* (San Francisco: Jossey, 1980).

4. L. Olson, "Calls for Revamping High Schools Intensify," *Education Week* (Jan. 26, 2005).

5. See, for example, A. Hershey, M. Silverberg, J. Haimson, P. Hudis, and R. Jackson, *Expanding Options for Students: Report to Congress on the National Evaluation of School-to-Work Implementation* (Princeton, NJ: Mathematica Policy Research, 1998) and W. Stull, "School-to-Work in Schools: An Overview," in *The School-to-Work Movement: Origins and Destinations*, eds. W. Stull and N. Sanders (Westport, CT: Praeger, 2003), 3–25.

6. See L. Cremin, *The Transformation of the School* (New York: Knopf, 1961), ch. 1.

7. W. N. Grubb and M. Lazerson, *The Education Gospel: The Economic Value of Schooling* (Cambridge, MA: Harvard University Press, 2004).

8. I first codified these approaches in W. N. Grubb, G. Davis, J. Lum, J. Plihal, and C. Morgaine, *The Cunning Hand, the Cultured Mind: Models for Integrating Academic and Vocational Education* (Berkeley, CA: National Center for Research in Vocational Education, 1991); see also W. N. Grubb, "Coherence for All Students: High Schools with Career Clusters and Majors," in *Education through Occupations in American High Schools*, vol. I: *Approaches to Integrating Academic and Vocational Education*, ed. W. N. Grubb (New York: Teachers College Press, 1995), 97–113. The three approaches I present here correspond to Oakes' second and third conceptions: academically rigorous high school CTE programs, and multiple theme-based small high schools (or schools-within-schools) in J. Oakes, *Multiple Definitions of Multiple Pathways* (Los Angeles: University of California–Los Angeles, Institute for Democracy, Education, and Access, undated).

9. Grubb, "Coherence for All Students," 97–113.

10. For this review I have examined the reports cited in Olson, "Calls for Revamping," and in National Research Council, *Engaging Schools: Fostering High School Students' Motivation to Learn* (Washington, DC: National Academies Press, 2004) and the reports cited in endnote 8 above.

11. C. Power, "Democratic Moral Education in the Large Public High School," in *Moral Edu-*

cation: Theory and Application, eds. M. Barkowitz and F. Oser (Hillsdale NJ: Lawrence Erlbaum, 1985).

12. See also K. Cushman and students, *Fires in the Bathrooms: Advice for Teachers from High School Students* (New York: What Kids Can Do, 2003).

13. National Association of Secondary School Principals (NASSP), *Breaking Ranks: Changing an American Institution* (Reston, VA: Author, 1996); NASSP, *Breaking Ranks II: Strategies for Leading High School Reform* (Reston, VA: Author, 2004).

14. W. N. Grubb, H. Kinlaw, L. Posey, and K. Young, "Dynamic Inequality III: Exploring What Schools Do for Low-performing Students," unpublished paper (School of Education, University of California–Berkeley, 2006).

15. National Research Council, *Engaging Schools*.

16. J. Kemple and J. Snipes, *Career Academies: Impacts on Student' Engagement and Performance in High School* (New York: Manpower Demonstration Research Corporation, March, 2000).

17. J. Kemple, Career Academies: Impacts on Students' Initial Transitions to Post-Secondary Education and Employment (New York: Manpower Demonstration Research Corporation, 2001) (available at http://www.mdrc.org/publications/105/full.pdf).

18. Conant, *The American High School Today*.

19. American Youth Policy Forum, *High Schools of the Millennium* (Washington, DC: Author, 2000).

20. K. H. Quartz and E. Washor, "Meeting the Individual and Collective Aims of Schooling: Can Multiple Pathways as Small Schools Strike Balance?" in this volume.

21. A. E. Ryken, *Content, Pedagogy, Results: A Thrice-Told Tale of Integrating Work-Based and School-Based Learning*, doctoral dissertation (Berkeley: University of California–Berkeley, School of Education, Spring, 2001).

22. P. Ong and V. Terriquez, "Can Multiple Pathways Offset Inequalities in the Urban Spatial Structure?" in this volume.

23. J. Bishop, "Why the Apathy in American High Schools?" *Educational Researcher* 18, no. 1 (1989): 6–10.

24. M. Tucker, *High School and Beyond: The System Is the Problem—and the Solution* (Washington, DC: National Center on Education and the Economy, 2004).

25. National Center on Education and the Economy, *Tough Choices or Tough Times: The Report of the New Commission on the Skills of the American Workplace* (New York: Wiley, 2007).

26. W. N. Grubb and J. Oakes, *"Restoring Value" to the High School Diploma: The Rhetoric and Practice of Higher Standards* (Tempe: Arizona State University, Education Policy Research Unit, 2007) (available at epsl.asu.edu/epru/documents/EPSL-0710-242-EPRU-press.pdf).

27. M. Tsuzuki, "Senior Projects: Flexible Opportunities for Integration," in *Education through Occupations in American High Schools, Vol. I: Approaches to Integrating Academic and Vocational Education*, ed. W. N. Grubb (New York: Teachers College Press, 1995).

28. Grubb and Lazerson, *The Education Gospel*.

29. P. Goodman, *Growing Up Absurd: Problems of Youth in the Organized System* (New York: Random House, 1956), 41.

30. National Research Council, *Engaging Schools*.

31. R. Pedraza, E. Pauly, and H. Kopp, *Home-Grown Progress: The Evolution of School-to-Work*

Programs (New York: Manpower Demonstration Research Corporation, 1997); D. Stern, M. Raby and C. Dayton, *Career Academies: Partnerships for Reconstructing American High Schools*, (San Francisco: Jossey-Bass, 1992).

32. Hershey et al., *Expanding Options for Students*.
33. The pedagogy of vocational education (including what "hands on" might mean) is in many ways more complex than that of academic instruction, though it has received little attention in the English-language literature. These results are drawn from W. N. Grubb, H. Worthen, B. Byrd, E. Webb, N. Badway, C. Case, S. Goto, and J. C. Villeneuve, *Honored but Invisible: An Inside Look at Teaching in Community Colleges* (New York: Routledge, 1999), ch. 3, and from the review in F. Achtenhagen and W. N. Grubb, "Vocational and Occupational Education: Pedagogical Complexity, Institutional Indifference," in *Handbook of Research on Teaching* (4th ed.), ed. V. Richardson (Washington, DC: American Educational Research Association, 2001).
34. A. Powell, E. Farrar, and D. Cohen, *The Shopping Mall High School* (Boston: Houghton Mifflin, 1985).
35. Described in J. C. Villeneuve and W. N. Grubb, *Indigenous School-to-Work Programs: Lessons from Cincinnati's Co-op Education* (Berkeley, CA: National Center for Research in Vocational Education, 1996).
36. Ryken, *Content, Pedagogy, Results*.
37. B. Schneider and D. Stevenson, *The Ambitious Generation: America's Teenagers, Motivated but Directionless* (New Haven: Yale University Press, 1999).
38. R. Crain et al., *The Effects of Academic Career Magnet Education on High Schools and Their Graduates, MDS-779* (Berkeley, CA: National Center for Research in Vocational Education, 1999); Pedraza et al., *Home-Grown Progress*.
39. Ryken, *Content, Pedagogy, Results*.
40. Individuals working in such programs usually say that only 25% of students stay with their high school major after high school. This practice is not, therefore, the German or Swiss practice of forcing students to make irreversible career decisions in grade 9.
41. Hershey et al., *Expanding Options for Students*.
42. See the discussion in Villeneuve and Grubb, *Indigenous School-to-Work Programs*, on the differences in work placements between employers with a "grow-your-own" philosophy and those who view interns as low-cost labor.
43. Reformers should examine the stories of implementation successes and failures, including G. Lichtenstein, "What Went Wrong at Manual High?" *Education Week* (May 17, 2006) on Denver's Manual Education Complex; L. Siskin, "When an Irresistible Force Meets an Immovable Object: Core Lessons about High Schools and Accountability," in *The New Accountability: High Schools and High-Stakes Testing*, eds. M. Carnoy, R. Elmore, and L. Siskin (New York: Routledge/Falmer, 2004) on high schools in four states; L. Darling-Hammond, J. Ancess, and S. Ort, "Reinventing High Schools: Outcomes of the Coalition Campus Schools Project," *American Educational Research Journal* 39, no. 3 (2002): 639–73; B. Neufeld, A. Lervy, and S. Chrismer, *High School Renewal in the Boston Public Schools: Focus on Organization and Leadership* (Cambridge, MA: Education Matters Inc., 2005). See also J. Oakes, *Keeping Track: How Schools Structure Inequality* (New Haven, CT: Yale University Press, 2005) on high school detracking reforms to prepare all students for college.

44. This is a variant of the goal of preparing for "college and careers," a phrase first articulated by David Stern, in "Improving Pathways in the United States from High School to College and Career," in *Preparing Youth for the 21st Century: The Transition from Education to the Labour Market* (Paris: Organization for Economic and Cultural Development, 1999).

45. W. N. Grubb, "Multiple Resources, Multiple Outcomes: 'Testing' the Improved School Finance with NELS88," *American Educational Research Journal* 45, no. 1 (2008): 104–44.

46. See J. Kemple and J. Snipes, *Career Academies: Impacts on Students' Engagement and Performance in High School* (New York: Manpower Demonstration Research Corporation, 2000); J. Kemple, C. Herlihy, and T. Snipes, *Making Progress toward Graduation: Evidence from the Talent Development High School Model* (New York: Manpower Demonstration Research Corporation, 2005); National Research Council, *Engaging Schools*, ch. 7; and P. Gándara, M. Mejorado, D. Gutierrez, and M. Molina, *Final Report of the Evaluation of High School Puente, 1994–1998* (Oakland: Puente Project, University of California, Office of the President, 1998).

47. J. Quint, H. Bloom, A. R. Black, L. Stephens, and T. Akey, *The Challenge of Scaling Up Educational Reform: Findings and Lessons from First Things First* (New York: Manpower Demonstration Research Corporation, 2005).

48. National Research Council, *Engaging Schools*, ch. 3.

49. J. W. Little, *Professional Development and Professional Community in the Learning-Centered School* (Washington, DC: National Education Association, 2006).

50. R. Lemons, T. Luschei, and L. Siskin, "Leadership and the Demands of Standards-based Accountability," in *The New Accountability: High Schools and High-Stakes Testing*, eds. M. Carnoy, R. Elmore, and L. Siskin (New York: Routledge/Falmer, 2003), 99–128.

51. S. Lucas, *Tracking Inequality: Stratification and Mobility in American High Schools* (New York: Teachers College Press, 1999); Oakes, *Keeping Track*.

52. M. A. Raywid, "Themes That Serve High Schools Well," *Phi Delta Kappan* 87, no. 9 (2006): 654–56.

53. In his introduction to *Experience and Education* (1938), Dewey wrote: "Mankind likes to think in terms of extreme opposites. It is given to formulating its beliefs in terms of Either-Ors, between which it recognizes no intermediate possibilities" (p. 17). In discussing traditional and progressive pedagogies, he lamented that "the problems are not even recognized, to say nothing of being solved, when it is assumed that it suffices to reject the ideas and practices of the old education and then go to the opposite extreme" (p. 22). A Deweyan approach is a synthesis of opposites rather than adoption of an either-or.

54. R. Balfanz, *Closing the Achievement Gap: What Works in Secondary Schools*, paper presented at the Harvard Achievement Gap Conference, June 2006.

55. See, for example, J. Dryfoos, *Full-Service Schools: A Revolution in Health and Social Services for Children, Youth, and Families* (San Francisco: Jossey-Bass, 1994).

56. Grubb et al., "Dynamic Inequality III."

57. See Grubb and Lazerson, *The Education Gospel*, ch. 1.

58. National Research Council, *Engaging Schools*.

59. National Commission on Excellence in Education, *A Nation at Risk: The Imperative for Education Reform* (Washington, DC: U.S. Government Printing Office, 1983).

60. See Grubb and Lazerson, *The Education Gospel.*

61. J. Goodlad, *A Place Called School: Prospects for the Future* (New York: McGraw-Hill, 1984).

62. R. Cox, *Navigating Community College Demands: Contradictory Goals, Expectations, and Outcomes in Composition,* unpublished doctoral dissertation, School of Education, University of California–Berkeley, 2004; B. Henderson, *Teaching at the People's University* (Boston: Anker Publishing, 2006); Grubb et al., *Honored but Invisible.*

63. R. Cox, *Navigating Community College Demands.*

64. Grubb, "Multiple Resources, Multiple Outcomes."

65. M. Carnoy, R. Elmore, and L. Siskin, eds., *The New Accountability: High Schools and High-Stakes Testing* (New York: Routledge/Falmer, 2003).

66. J. Spillane, R. Halverson, and J. Diamond, "Towards a Theory of Leadership Practice: A Distributed Perspective," *Journal of Curriculum Studies* 35 (2002): 1–32.

67. B. Rowan, "Commitment and Control: Alternative Strategies for the Organization Design of Schools," in *Review of Research in Education* (Vol. 16), ed. C. Cazden (Washington, DC: American Educational Research Association, 1990), 353–89.

68. Little, *Professional Development.*

69. Lemons et al., "Leadership and the Demands."

70. I am the faculty coordinator of the Principal Leadership Institute (PLI) at University of California–Berkeley, which prepares 45–50 individuals a year to become principals and other school leaders. While the PLI has adopted numerous innovative practices, we have not yet found a way to introduce preparation specific to high schools in a crowded curriculum. The National Association of Secondary School Principals has created some training modules accompanying Breaking Ranks II, but most of the seven "cornerstone strategies" are generic (e.g., using time flexibly) rather than specific to high schools. Conventional education administration textbooks say nothing on the special conditions of high schools. I know of only one preparation program with any special emphasis on the high school, the Aspiring Principals Program of the NYC Leadership Academy.

71. W. N. Grubb and J. Flessa, "'A Job Too Big for One': Multiple Principals and Other Nontraditional Approaches to School Leadership," *Educational Administration Quarterly* 42 (2006): 518–50.

CHAPTER 11

1. W. M. Aikin, *The Eight-Year Study* (New York: Harper & Brothers, 1942) (also available at www.8yearstudy.org).

2. M. Kirst and A. Venezia, *From High School to College* (San Francisco: Jossey-Bass, 2004).

3. See, for example, D. Conley, *College Knowledge: What It Takes for Students to Succeed and What We Can Do to Get Them Ready* (San Francisco: Jossey-Bass, 2005); and D. Conley, "Proficiency-based Admissions," in *Choosing Students: Higher Education Admission Tools for the 21st Century,* eds. W. Camara and E. W. Kimmell (Mahwah, NJ: Lawrence Erlbaum, 2005).

4. For example, in 2004, education and health leaders were convened by the Centers for Disease Control and Prevention and issued a statement urging national reforms targeted

at fighting the "culture of detachment" in U.S. schools. The group cited research show-ing that 40–60% of the nation's students are "chronically disengaged" from school, not including students who drop out. Johns Hopkins Bloomberg School of Public Health, "Education and Public Health Leaders Urge Sweeping Action to Address 'Culture of Detachment' in U.S. Schools," *Johns Hopkins University Public Health News*, September 8, 2004; available at www.jhsph.edu/publichealthnews/press_releases/PR_2004/Blum_wingspread.html.

5. The Education Trust, "Ticket to Nowhere: The Gap Between Leaving High School and Entering College and High Performance Jobs," in *Thinking K–16* (Vol. 3) (Washington, DC: The Education Trust, 1999).

6. J. Rogers, V. Terriquez, S. Valladares, and J. Oakes, *California Educational Opportu-nity Report: Roadblocks to College* (Los Angeles: Institute for Democracy Education and Access, University of California–Los Angeles, 2006) (available at www.idea.gseis.ucla.edu/publications/eor06/fullreport/pdf/EOR-2006.pdf).

7. The National Center for Public Policy and Higher Education, "Policy Alert Supplement: California's Educational Pipeline," April 2004 (available at www.highereducation.org).

8. T. Yosso and D. Solorzano, "Leaks in the Chicana and Chicano Educational Pipeline," *Latino Policy and Issues Brief*, March 2006 (available at www.chicano.ucla.edu).

9. J. Oakes et al., *African American Educational Opportunity Report, 2007: California's African American Opportunity Gap* (Los Angeles: Institute for Democracy Education and Access, University of California–Los Angeles, 2006) (available at http://www.idea.gseis.ucla.edu/publications/eor07/african_american_report/pdf/AfricanAmericanEOR07.pdf).

10. "Some form of postsecondary education" means anything from completing courses for job-related reasons to earning a certificate or a degree at a two-year or four-year institution.

11. See ACT, Inc., "Ready for College and Ready for Work: Same or Different?" *College and Workforce Training Readiness* (Iowa City, IA: ACT, 2006).

12. A. Venezia, M. Kirst, and A. L. Antonio, *Betraying the College Dream* (Stanford, CA: Stan-ford Institute for Higher Education Research, 2003).

13. The California Education Code states, "The Governing Board shall adopt alternative means for pupils to complete the prescribed course of study, which may include practi-cal demonstration of skills and competencies, supervised work experience, high school CTE, ROCP courses, interdisciplinary study, independent study, and credit earned at a postsecondary institution" (Section 51225.3 b, 1985).

14. University of California, Office of the President, *Overlap between UC/CSU "A–G" Require-ments and Typical Career-Technical Education Sequence* (Berkeley: Author, 2006) (available at http://www.ucop.edu/a-gGuide/ag/).

15. UC Office of the President, *Overlap between UC/CSU.*

16. The breakdown by CTE area is as follows: 667 in agriculture education; 408 in business education; 575 in health careers; 120 in home economics careers and technology; 314 in industrial and technical education; 1,934 in art, media, and entertainment; and 3 in "other CTE."

17. University of California, Office of the President, *California High School Career-Technical Education Courses Meeting University of California A–G Admission Requirements for 2005–2006* (Berkeley: Author, 2006) (available at www.ucop.edu/a-gGuide/ag/faq.html).

18. A. L. Antonio and S. H. Bersola, "Toward K–16 Coherence in California," in *From High School to College*, eds. M. W. Kirst and A. Venezia (San Francisco: Jossey-Bass, 2004).

19. A. Venezia, M. W. Kirst, and A. L. Antonio, *Betraying the College Dream* (Stanford, CA: Stanford Institute for Higher Education Research, 2003).

20. Honors courses are college-prep courses that are geared toward entry into more competitive colleges. "College prep" is often a track designed to meet the A–G requirements, but those courses might not include the same expectations as honors or AP courses in terms of preparation for a more competitive postsecondary institution. Finally, CTE courses, with notable exception, are usually not considered college prep.

21. Antonio and Bersola, "Toward K–16 Coherence in California."

22. Aikin, *Eight-Year Study*.

23. D. Stern and R. Stearns, "Evidence and Challenges: Will Multiple Pathways Improve Students' Outcomes?" in this volume.

24. J. K. Kemple with J. Scott-Clayton, *Career Academies: Impacts on Labor Market Outcomes and Educational Attainment* (New York: Manpower Demonstration Research Corporation, 2004) cited in Stern and Stearns, "Evidence and Challenges," this volume.

25. See, for example, R. D. Kaye, J. Lord, and G. Bottoms, "Getting Students Ready for College and Careers," in *Challenge to Lead Series* (Atlanta: Southern Regional Education Board, 2006); The American Diploma Project, *Ready or Not: Creating a High School Diploma That Counts* (Washington, DC: Achieve, Inc. 2004); ACT, Inc. "Ready for College and Ready for Work."

26. ACT, Inc., "Ready for College and Ready for Work."

27. P. Barton, *High School Reform and Work: Facing Labor Market Realities* (Princeton, NJ: Educational Testing Service, 2006).

28. Barton, *High School Reform and Work*, 3.

29. Barton, *High School Reform and Work*.

30. J. Davis, *Career Pathways: Aligning Public Resources to Support Individual and Regional Economic Advancement in the Knowledge Economy* (Brooklyn, NY: Workforce Strategy Center, 2006).

31. Of all these efforts, only the ADP included workforce skill requirements in the postsecondary standards. Notably, none of the models included Multiple Pathways as defined in this chapter.

32. Information about PASS was taken from the Bridge Project's Oregon case study, conducted by Andrea Conklin Bueschel and Andrea Venezia. See "Oregon's K–16 Reforms" in *From High School to College*, eds. M. W. Kirst and A. Venezia (San Francisco: Jossey-Bass, 2004).

33. With the passage of HB 2263 by the 2007 Oregon Legislature, the CIM, CAM, and subject area endorsements will be phased out in July 2008. Though the certificates will no longer be required, the State Board of Education is committed to maintaining a standards-based system with statewide expectations for student skills and proficiencies evaluated with a combination of state and local assessments. Oregon's graduation requirements, adopted by the State Board in January 2007 incorporate CIM academic content standards and assessments and the four CAM requirements into the high school diploma. For more information about the CAM requirements, see http://www.ode.state.or.us/teachlearn/certificates/cam/pdfs/cam-at-a-glance.pdf.

34. Students demonstrate proficiency in each of the six subject areas through activities in class and test-taking. Students receive a summary judgment score for each of the PASS standards in a content area. There are five possible scores: exemplary (E), high-level mastery (H), meets the proficiency (M), working toward the proficiency (W), and not meeting the proficiency (N). The training of teachers and other educators to score student work is the responsibility of schools, districts, and Education Service Districts. PASS includes scores on the state's tenth-grade assessment; scores on national assessments (such as AP, SAT II, and IB); and teacher judgments.

35. Information on the Early Assessment Program was taken from P. Callan, J. Finney, M. Kirst, M. Usdan, and A. Venezia, *Claiming Common Ground* (San Jose, CA: National Center for Public Policy and Higher Education, 2006).

36. The Legislature passed a bill in August 2006 to develop an Early Assessment Pilot Project for the CCC.

37. Information for this section was provided by the American Diploma Project, *Ready or Not*.

38. American Diploma Project (available at www.achieve.org).

39. The ADP based the workforce knowledge and skills on jobs that pay enough to support a small family and provide potential for career advancement.

40. The ADP based the postsecondary education knowledge and skills on what is required for success in entry-level, credit-bearing courses in English, mathematics, the sciences, the social sciences, and the humanities.

41. The English benchmarks are organized into the following strands: language, communication, writing, research, logic, informational text, media, and literature. These areas cross over into other subject areas within the humanities, social sciences, and sciences. The mathematics benchmarks are organized into the following strands: number sense and numerical operations, algebra, geometry, data interpretation, statistics, and probability. As with the English benchmarks, the mathematics benchmarks connect with other subject areas within the social sciences and sciences.

42. D. Conley, *College Knowledge*.

43. The KSUS cover six disciplinary areas: English, mathematics, natural sciences, social sciences, second languages, and the arts. The general breakdown of areas within the standards follows.
    - The English KSUS include reading, comprehension, and literature; writing and editing; information gathering; analysis, critique, and connections; orientation toward learning (e.g., time management, participating in public discourse).
    - The Mathematics KSUS include understanding mathematics (e.g., investigation); problem solving, technology, and communication; and orientation toward learning.
    - The Natural Sciences KSUS include basic knowledge (e.g., the significance of time, velocity); thinking about science (e.g., understanding scientific processes); solving problems, asking questions; reading, writing, and communication; and orientation toward learning.
    - The Social Sciences KSUS include social sciences knowledge and skills foundations (e.g., thinking analytically); general sense of history and geography; reading, research, and analysis; and orientation toward learning.
    - The Second Languages KSUS include the basics (e.g., grammar, vocabulary); commu-

nication, culture, comparisons (e.g., viewing facts from multiple perspectives); learning strategies (e.g., mnemonic devices, inference); and orientation toward learning.
- The Arts KSUS include arts knowledge and skills foundations (e.g., independent
  thinking, logical thinking) and art content standards (broken out by art history,
  dance, music, theater, and visual arts).

44. See, for example, Aikin, *Eight-Year Study*; Kaye, Lord, and Bottoms, "Getting Students
    Ready for College and Careers"; ADP, *Ready or Not*; Conley, *College Knowledge*.
45. Kirst and Venezia, *From High School to College*.
46. Aikin, *Eight-Year Study*.

CHAPTER 12

1. I am indebted to Amy Stuart Wells for this observation.
2. S. R. Lucas, "Effectively Maintained Inequality: Education Transitions, Track Mobility,
   and Social Background Effects," *American Journal of Sociology* 106 (2001): 1642–90.
3. See, for example, W. H. Sewell, A. O. Haller, and A. Portes, "The Educational and Early
   Occupational Attainment Process," *American Sociological Review* 34 (1969): 82–92.
4. H. O. Duleep, "Measuring the Effect of Income on Adult Mortality Using Longitudinal
   Administrative Record Data," *Journal of Human Resources* 21 (1986): 238–51.
5. A. E. Raftery and M. Hout, "Maximally Maintained Inequality: Expansion, Reform, and
   Opportunity in Irish Education, 1921–75," *Sociology of Education* 66 (1993): 41–62.
6. In the United States, Lucas, "Effectively Maintained Inequality"; D. R. Entwisle, K. L.
   Alexander, and L. S. Olson, "First Grade and Educational Attainment by Age 22: A New
   Story," *American Journal of Sociology* 110 (2005): 1458–1502. In Israel, H. Ayalon and Y.
   Shavit, "Educational Reforms and Inequalities in Israel: The MMI Hypothesis Revisited,"
   Sociology of Education 77 (2004): 103–20; H. Ayalon and A. Yogev, "Field of Study and
   Students' Stratification in an Expanded System of Higher Education: The Case of Israel,"
   European Sociological Review 21 (2005): 227–41.
7. See, for example, L. C. Thurow, "Education and Economic Inequality," *Public Interest* 28,
   no. 3 (1972): 66–81.
8. See, for example, T. S. Kuhn, *The Structure of Scientific Revolutions* (2nd ed.) (Chicago:
   University of Chicago Press, 1962/1970); M. Foucault, *The Order of Things: An Archaeol-
   ogy of Human Sciences* (New York: Random House, 1970/1994).
9. T. Frank, *What's the Matter with Kansas? How Conservatives Won the Heart of America* (New
   York: Metropolitan Books, 2004).
10. A. S. Wells and I. Serna, "The Politics of Culture: Understanding Local Political Resis-
    tance to Detracking in Racially Mixed Schools," *Harvard Educational Review* 66 (1996):
    93–118; see also J. Oakes, *Keeping Track: How Schools Structure Inequality* (2nd ed.) (New
    Haven, CT: Yale University Press, 2005).
11. A. Datnow, "Using Gender to Preserve Tracking's Status Hierarchy: The Defensive Strat-
    egy of Entrenched Teachers," *Anthropology and Education Quarterly* 28 (1997): 204–28.
12. A. O. Hirschman, *Exit, Voice, and Loyalty: Responses to Decline in Firms, Organizations, and
    States* (Cambridge, MA: Harvard University Press, 1970).
13. Wells and Serna, "The Politics of Culture."

14. T. Kariya and J. E. Rosenbaum, "Bright Flight: Unintended Consequences of Detracking Policy in Japan," *American Journal of Education* 107 (1999): 210–30.

15. Kariya and Rosenbaum, "Bright Flight."

16. For example, A. Lareau, *Home Advantage: Social Class and Parental Involvement in Elementary Education* (New York: The Falmer Press, 1989); Oakes, *Keeping Track*, 2005.

17. For example, A. Lareau, *Unequal Childhoods: Class, Race, and Family Life* (Berkeley: University of California Press, 2003).

18. G. Q. Conchas, "Structuring Failure and Success: Understanding the Variability in Latino School Engagement," *Harvard Educational Review* 71 (2001): 475–504.

19. Oakes, *Keeping Track*.

20. S. R. Lucas, *Tracking Inequality: Stratification and Mobility in American High Schools* (New York: Teachers College Press, 1999).

CHAPTER 13

1. D. Tyack and L. Cuban, *Tinkering toward Utopia* (Cambridge, MA: Harvard University Press, 1995).

2. Some of the material in this section is drawn from an earlier book chapter by J. Oakes, "Beyond Tinkering: Reconstructing Vocational Education," in *Re-Visioning Vocational Education in the Secondary School*, ed. G. Copa, J. Plihal, and M. Johnson (St. Paul: University of Minnesota, 1986).

3. W. N. Grubb, "Challenging the Deep Structure of High School: Weak and Strong Versions of Multiple Pathways," in this volume.

4. L. Terman, *Intelligence Tests and School Reorganization* (New York: World Book, 1923), 28.

5. Boston Schools, *School documents* (1908), no. 7.

6. W. N. Grubb and M. Lazerson, *The Education Gospel: The Economic Power of Schooling* (Cambridge, MA: Harvard University Press, 2004).

7. See J. Rogers, J. Kahne, and E. Middaugh, "Multiple Pathways and the Future of Democracy," in this volume.

8. J. Oakes, *Keeping Track: How Schools Structure Inequality* (New Haven: Yale University Press, 1985/2005); R. I. Simon, D. Dippo, and A. Schenke, *Learning Work: A Critical Pedagogy of Work Education* (New York: Bergin & Garvey, 1991).

9. National Commission of Excellence in Education, *A Nation at Risk: The Imperative for Educational Reform* (Washington, DC: U.S. Government Printing Office, 1983).

10. Research had made clear that vocational students had limited opportunities to acquire academic competencies. Oakes, *Keeping Track*; J. Oakes, "Two Cities: Tracking and Within-School Segregation," *Teachers' College Record* 96 (1995): 681–90; J. Oakes, A. Gamoran, and R. Page, "Curriculum Differentiation: Opportunities, Consequences, and Meanings," in *Handbook of Research on Curriculum*, ed. P. A. Jackson (New York: Macmillan, 1992). Moreover, students' participation in vocational high school programs did not seem to increase their chances of employment related to training, reduced unemployment, or higher wages. I. Berg, *Education and Jobs: The Great Training* Robbery (Boston: Beacon, 1971); S. E. Berryman, *Vocational Education and the Work Establishment of the Youth: Equity and Effectiveness* Issues (Santa Monica, CA: Rand Corporation, 1980);

J. Grasso and J. Shea, *Vocational Education and Training: Impact on Youth* (Berkeley, CA: Carnegie Council on Policy Studies in Higher Education, 1979); B. Rubens, "Vocational Education for All in High School?" in *Work and the Quality of Life*, ed. J. O'Toole (Cambridge, MA: MIT Press, 1975); D. Stern, G. Hoachlander, S. Choy, and C. S. Benson, *One Million Hours a Day: Vocational Education in California Public Secondary Schools* (Report to the California Policy Seminar) (Berkeley: University of California, 1985). These patterns were distressing, given the disproportionate percentages of poor and minority students in the lowest-track classes.

11. K. Levesque, D. Lauen, P. Teitelbaum, M. Alt, and S. Librera, *Vocational Education in the United States: Toward the Year 2000* (Washington, DC: U.S. Department of Education, National Center for Education Statistics, 2000).

12. Levesque et al., *Vocational Education in the United States.*

13. "Concentrators" are students who take a series of courses in a particular CTE area.

14. Levesque et al., *Vocational Education in the United States.*

15. Levesque et al., *Vocational Education in the United States.*

16. The indicators correlate strongly with improved worker productivity, less unemployment, greater benefits, ability to learn new skills and workplace operations, exposure to and engagement with computers, and ability to negotiate the labor market. R. Lynch, "High School Career and Technical Education for the First Decade of the 21st Century," *Journal of Vocational Education Research* 25 (2000): 2.

17. Information about Pennsylvania Education Project 720 is available at www.project720.org.

18. Pennsylvania Education Project 720, available at www.project720.org.

19. Information about the Texas project is available at http://www.tea.state.tx.us/ed_init/thsp/progs_mult_path.html.

20. E. K. Bragg and M. Rubin, *Academic Pathways to College: Policies and Practices of the Fifty States to Reach Underserved Students,* paper presented at the meeting of the Association for the Study of Higher Education, Philadelphia, November 2005.

21. Another Route to College (available at http://www.commcorp.org/arc/about.html).

22. Information about High Schools That Work is available at http://www.sreb.org/programs/hstw.

23. A full list of states providing support for a variety of these pathways is available at http://www.apass.uiuc.edu/.

24. Information about tech-prep education is available at http://www.ed.gov/programs/techprep/index.html.

25. Available at http://www.highschoolrenewal.org/schools/intro.htm.

26. National Association of Secondary School Principals (NASSP), *Breaking Ranks II: Strategies for Leading High School Reform* (2004) (available at http://www.principals.org/s_nassp/store_interior.asp?CID=706&DID=20013).

27. Association for Career and Technical Education (ACTE), *Reinventing the American High School for the 21st Century: Strengthening a New Vision for the American High School through the Experiences and Resources of Career and Technical Education* (2006) (available at http://www.aacteonline.org/policy/legislative-issues/upload/ACTEHSReform-Full).

28. M. Rose, "Blending 'Hand Work' and 'Brain Work': Can Multiple Pathways Deepen Learning?" in this volume.

29. D. Stern and R. Stearns, "Evidence and Challenges: Will Multiple Pathways Improve Students' Outcomes?" in this volume.

30. Stern and Stearns, "Evidence and Challenges." Note, however, that the authors make clear in their extensive review of the research that there is not yet conclusive evidence that blending CTE with academic coursework actually increases college-going and degree completion. Unfortunately, getting clear-cut research results has been difficult because most studies have not been able to determine whether apparent effects are due to particular programs or to selection of particular kinds of students into those programs.

31. A. Venezia, "Between High School and College: Can Multiple Pathways Bridge the Divide?" in this volume; Stern and Stearns, "Evidence and Challenges."

32. P. Gándara, "Immigrant and English Learners: Can Multiple Pathways Smooth Their Paths?" in this volume.

33. M. Pastor, "United or Divided: Can Multiple Pathways Bring Together Multiple Communities?" in this volume.

34. Pastor, "United or Divided"; D. Rattray, "Making It Real: Implementing Multiple Pathways," in this volume.

35. Rogers, Kahne, and Middaugh, "Multiple Pathways and the Future of Democracy."

36. S. R. Lucas, "Constructing Equal Pathways in an Effectively Maintained Inequality Society," in this volume; Gándara, "Immigrant and English Learners."

37. A. Datnow and S. Stringfield, "Working Together for Reliable School Reform," *Journal of Education for Students Placed at Risk* 5, nos. 1 & 2 (2000): 183–204; A. Hargreaves, *The International Handbook of Educational Change* (New York: Springer, 1998). For syntheses of the research on school change, see A. Hargreaves, *International Handbook*.

38. Tyack and Cuban, *Tinkering*.

39. S. Sarason, *The Culture of Schools and the Problem of Change* (Boston: Allyn and Bacon, 1982).

40. Stern and Stearns, "Evidence and Challenges."

41. www.project720.org.

42. Grubb, "Challenging the Deep Structure"; K. H. Quartz and E. Washor, "Meeting the Individual and Collective Aims of Schooling: Can Multiple Pathways as Small Schools Strike a Balance?" in this volume.

43. Grubb, "Challenging Deep Structure"; Rattray, "Making It Real."

44. Venezia, "Between High School and College."

45. P. Ong and V. Terriquez, "Can Multiple Pathways Offset Inequalities in the Urban Spatial Structure?" in this volume.

46. Quartz and Washor, "Meeting Individual and Collective Aims."

47. Rogers et al., "Multiple Pathways and the Future of Democracy."

48. Rogers et al., "Multiple Pathways and the Future of Democracy."

49. Gándara, "Immigrants and English Learners"; M. A. Stoll, "Can Multiple Pathways Link Vulnerable Groups to Changing Labor Markets?" in this volume; Ong and Terriquez, "Can Multiple Pathways Offset Inequalities?"

50. Ong and Terriquez, "Can Multiple Pathways Offset Inequalities?"; Pastor, "United or Divided"; Stoll, "Can Multiple Pathways Link Vulnerable Groups?"

51. C. Murray, "Intelligence in the Classroom," *Wall Street Journal*, January 16, 2007; C. Murray, "What's Wrong with Vocational School," *Wall Street Journal*, January 17, 2007; C. Murray, "Aztecs vs. Greeks," *Wall Street Journal*, January 18, 2007.

52. J. Oakes, A. S. Wells, S. Yonezawa, and K. Ray, "Change Agentry and the Quest for Equity: Lessons from Detracking Schools," in *Rethinking Educational Change with Mind*

and Heart, Yearbook for the Association for Supervision and Curriculum Development, ed. A. Hargreaves (Arlington, VA: Association for Supervision and Curriculum Development, 1997); J. Oakes, K. H. Quartz, S. Ryan, and M. Lipton, *Becoming Good American Schools: The Struggle for Civic Virtue in School Reform* (San Francisco: Jossey-Bass, 2000).

53. One prominent champion of this approach has been the American Diploma Project (ADP), a collaboration among Achieve, Inc.; the Fordham Foundation; the Education Trust; Jobs for the Future; and the Charles Dana Center at the University of Texas–Austin. An advocate for standards- and accountability-based high school reform, the ADP presses for state policies specifying that all high schools take a sequence of standards-based courses aligned with the "real-world demands of postsecondary education and work." Such courses should include four years of grade-level English (including literature, writing, reasoning, logic and communications skills) and four years of math (including algebra I and II, geometry, data analysis, and statistics). Additionally, regular assessments should measure students' progress toward specified benchmarks, and these should become the basis of education accountability. The ADP is on line at http://www. achieve.org. In California, the Education Trust's campaign to make the state university entrance requirements the default high school curriculum for all students is based on the argument that these courses also provide the competencies that employers want. See, for example, "The A–G Curriculum: College-Prep? Work-Prep? Life-Prep" (available at http://www2.edtrust.org/EdTrust/ETW/ETWreports_pubs).

54. Rattray, "Making It Real"; Venezia, "Between High School and College."

55. Lucas, "Constructing Equal Pathways."

56. Office of Multiple Pathways of the New York Public Schools (available at http://schools. nyc.gov/Offices/OMPG/default.htm).

57. Available at http://www.nyc.gov/html/om/pdf/ceo_report2006.pdf.

58. Department of Labor Employment and Training Administration, "Notice of Availability of Funds and Solicitation for Grant Applications (SGA) for Multiple Education Pathways Blueprint Grants (MEPB)," *Federal Register* 72, no. 88 (May 8, 2007): 26162–70 (available at http://edocket.access.gpo.gov/2007/pdf/E7-8720.pdf).

59. Department of Labor Employment and Training Administration, 2007.

60. John Edwards campaign site (http://www.johnedwards.com/issues/education/helping-every-child-graduate); Hillary Clinton campaign site (http://www.hillaryclinton.com/issues/education).

About the Editors

Jeannie Oakes is director of Education and Scholarship at the Ford Foundation. Until fall 2008, she was Presidential Professor in Educational Equity and codirector of the Institute for Democracy, Education, and Access at the University of California–Los Angeles, and director of the University of California's All Campus Consortium on Research for Diversity. Oakes's research addresses the impact of education policies on the opportunities and outcomes of low-income students of color. She is the author of twenty scholarly books and monographs and more than 125 other publications. Her book *Keeping Track: How Schools Structure Inequality* was honored as one of the twentieth century's most influential books on education. Oakes has received three major awards from the American Educational Research Association, as well as the National Association for Multicultural Education's Multicultural Research Award, and the Distinguished Achievement Award from the Educational Press Association of America. She is also the recipient of the Southern Christian Leadership Conference's Ralph David Abernathy Award for Public Service and, most recently, the 2002 World Cultural Council's Jose Vasconcelos World Award in Education. Professor Oakes is a member of the National Academy of Education.

Marisa Saunders is a senior research associate at the Institute for Democracy, Education, and Access at the University of California, Los Angeles. Her research focuses on the K–12 and postsecondary transitions and trajectories of underrepresented youth. This research has been documented in numerous publications, including "Making College Happen: The College Experiences of First-Generation Latino Students" (with Irene Serna) in the *Journal of Hispanic Higher Education*. Saunders has also conducted research on the disparities in students' access to basic educational resources and its impact on student outcomes. She coauthored (with Jeannie Oakes) "Education's Most Basic Tools: Access to Textbooks and Instructional Materials in California's Public Schools" in *Teachers College Record*. She has researched the impact of *Williams v. California* on the state's lowest performing schools and acted as the principal investigator for the ACLU study, "*Williams v. California*: The Statewide Impact of Two Years of Implementation."

Index